THE WORLD AS SACRAMENT

SACRAMENTALITY OF CREATION FROM THE PERSPECTIVES OF LEONARDO BOFF, ALEXANDER SCHMEMANN AND SAINT EPHREM

TEXTES ET ÉTUDES LITURGIQUES
STUDIES IN LITURGY

XX

THE WORLD AS SACRAMENT

Sacramentality of Creation from the Perspectives of Leonardo Boff, Alexander Schmemann and Saint Ephrem

by

Mathai KADAVIL

ABDIJ KEIZERSBERG
FACULTEIT GODGELEERDHEID

PEETERS
LEUVEN
2005

A CIP record for this book is available from the Library of Congress.

ISBN 90-429-1636-2 (Peeters-Leuven)

D/2005/0602/71

FOREWORD

Among the different sections of the Theology of the Catholic Church, Sacramental Theology has adopted various trends, especially after the Vatican Council II. Understanding the mystery of Christ as the great Sacrament of God the Father and presenting the Church as the primordial sacrament of Christ have given new insights into the theology of sacraments, which was so far prevalent in the scholastic circles. Going beyond the concept of sacrament as means of sanctification in the Church, sacraments have assumed great theological significance as the physical presence of God and the saving actions of the Risen Lord. Delving deeper into the mystery of God's presence in the world and His immanence to His creatures, ancient spiritual Fathers like Ephraem, the Syrian, had tried to apply the principles of sacramentality to the creation itself. In recent years the trend has gained momentum by the theological reflections of modern writers like Leonardo Boff, Alexander Schmemann. Fr. Mathai Kadavil OIC has made an effort to make a deeper study of the subject by closely examining the writings of some of the Theologians, both ancient and modern. His book 'World as Sacrament: Sacramentality of Creation from the Perspectives of Leonardo Boff, Alexander Schmemann and Saint Ephrem,' is the result of his careful & meticulous research. The merit of his study is two fold. First of all, the newly proposed paradigm is relevant in the multi-religious context of modern society. Secondly, in his effort to make it relevant, he related his study to the authentic teachings of the Church. Moreover, this study has succeeded in placing God-World-Human relationship in its proper order. Thus, while underscoring God's sacramental presence in the world, this study has emphasised the human role in relation to God and world.

This study has progressed by delineating the theme in four chapters. The first chapter demonstrates the transitions in sacramentology in relation to liturgy, theology, symbol and salvation history. The panoramic view of sacrament in relation to the above four themes has underscored the doctrinal development of the sacraments in the Apostolic, Patristic and Scholastic periods, incorporating the liturgical and sacramental renewal beginning from the eighteenth century and its further development with the Second Vatican Council. The emphasis on returning to the early traditions is to be seen against the later aberrations of a mere juridical and ritual understanding of sacraments. In particular, Fr. Mathai Kadavil focuses on the importance of the sacramentality of Christ and Church in contemporary sacramentology.

Christ and the Church understood as sacraments deepened the understanding of sacramentality. This understanding of the sacramentality of Christ and Church, indicates its opening to the whole world, and the author argues that the sacramentality of the world as a new paradigm is capable of opening new vistas in contemporary sacramentology.

Significantly, Fr. Kadavil in his effort to rediscover the theology of the sacramentality of the world has examined all the three early Christian traditions: Latin, Greek and Syrian in three separate chapters. The study of the first two traditions is done through the prism of two contemporary authors, namely Leonardo Boff and Alexander Schmemann. However, in the case of Syrian tradition, this study uses saint Ephrem, the fourth century Syrian Father, and the Syrian tradition in general as the point of reference. It seems justifiable in the absence of any serious study by contemporary authors on this theme. At the same time, although the focus is primarily on Ephrem, this study has extensively made use of recent researches in the Syrian tradition related to the topic.

It is also important to note that Boff and Schmemann, while representing the western theology of Latin and eastern theology of Greek traditions respectively, also represent two theological trends as well, namely liberation theology and liturgical theology. Hence while studying the sacramentality of the world, this study also looked into liberation theologians' emphasis on ethical response and liturgical theologians' emphasis on liturgical response to the sacramentality of the world. Similarly, "the poor" as the *locus theologicus* in Boff and liturgy as the *locus theologicus* in Schmemann is also examined. It is against this background Fr. Mathai Kadavil has proposed a harmonious view of both based on the Syrian tradition, which has not undergone much change as the other two.

Unlike the Greek or Latin Christian traditions' rational approach in the pursuit of God rooted in the Greco-Roman culture, the Syrian tradition rooted in the Semitic culture developed a different epistemology in explaining the God-World-Human relationship. Thus Ephrem, the Syrian who followed neither apophatic nor cataphatic method, developed a middle way which could be termed 'sacramental'. Fr. Mathai Kadavil has seized this approach of the Syrians in promoting the paradigm 'world as sacrament' enriching the contemporary sacramentology.

A serious reflection on the sacramentality of the world has wider implications in contemporary sacramentology. It can effectively mediate between various Christian denominations, between various religions and even between various ideologies.

Furthermore, the sacramentality of the world broadens the conventional understanding of liturgical and sacramental gestures conferring grace to a graceful living. In other words, the world as sacrament emphasizes the dynamic dimension of life and living in the world. This view encompasses a mystical response of man of praising God and his/her ethical responsibility to Creation.

The sacramental view of the World is also significant in the midst of the widespread threat of ecological crisis. It also serves as a genuine answer to the accusation of some early ecologists regarding the Jewish-Christian responsibility in the exploitation of nature. In this sense, the emphasis on the sacramentality of the world positively appreciates the goodness of Creation and exhorts our responsibility to respect the wholeness of the Creation.

I am confident that the scholarly work of Fr. Mathai Kadavil will provoke and promote further theological reflections in sacramentology and would bring out good results in the ecclesial life of the believers. I take this opportunity to congratulate him for the successful completion of his Doctoral Thesis and for having published it as a book for the benefit of the public at large. I wish him all the best and God's blessings on his educational apostolate.

Archbishop Most Rev Cyril Mar Baselios
Metropolitan of the Malankara Catholic Church

Greek notion of *mustèrion*, it emphasizes the participation in the divine live of the Holy Trinity. Hence in this dissertation there is a bridge between the oriental approaches and the western classical theology of the sacraments. Furthermore, by the recognition of the sacramentality of the whole creation, the old dichotomy and contrast between the sacred and the profane is bridged and situated in a new dialectic of apophatic and cataphatic theology.

Another characteristic of this study is that, in the analysis of sacramentality, one can find the contemporary post-modern accentuation of the hidden, absent, invisible character in the dialectical relation to the visible, present and unveiled expression of the divine reality. The liturgical celebration as anticipation of the Kingdom of God and the value of ethical commitment are complementary features of the human response to God's gift in creation.

The emphasis, given to the transformative and liberative power of the symbol and the sacrament, specifically comes from the action of the Holy Spirit. The pneumatological dimension is treated at length on side with the christological and ecclesiological dimensions in the sacrament. The pneumatological dimension finds its place in a balanced structure of sacramentality, especially in the approach of Saint Ephrem.

As regards the cosmology, this dissertation offers innovative insights, transcending the duality of matter and spirit, body and soul. Not only on the basis of incarnation, but mostly from creation and the eschatological destination, the whole cosmos is a space of sacramentality where God's salvation is present as a free gift.

This doctoral dissertation is the continuation of Father Mathai Kadavil's project for the Master's dissertation on the sacramental views of the Orthodox theologian Alexander Schmemann entitled: "The World as Sacrament: A Critical Appraisal of Alexander Schmemann's Sacramentology." It dealt with the most specific features of the sacramentology and liturgical theology of this Eastern theologian, within the centre of the picture: the topic of the world as sacrament, the predominant characteristic in the approach of Alexander Schmemann. It won the recognition on the international level by the triennial award of the 'Cardinal Willebrandsprize 1998', launched by the "Instituut voor Oosters Christendom" of the Catholic University Nijmegen (the Netherlands).

Prof. Dr. Lambert Leijssen
Faculty of Theology
Catholic University of Leuven, Belgium

TABLE OF CONTENTS

Chapter Three
World as Sacrament in Alexander Schmemann
A Liturgical Response to the Sacramentality of Creation

Chapter Four
World as Sacrament in Saint Ephrem
A Combination of Ethical and Liturgical Response

GENERAL INTRODUCTION

Sacramentology is one of the few theological disciplines that have undergone tremendous changes in the past. Taking inspiration from the Enlightenment, early liturgists and theologians showed great interest in the historical study of liturgies and sacraments as from the eighteenth century, leading to the rise of various liturgical movements. The Biblical and Patristic researches of the eighteenth and nineteenth centuries further accelerated the renewal efforts. The Orthodox theologians who have migrated to different parts of Western Europe from countries like Russia, East Europe and the Middle East also contributed to this endeavor. Moreover, the Christological and ecclesial renewals in the Church enriched the study of the sacraments. For example, sacramentology took a new turn with Karl Rahner and Schillebeeckx. Along with many other theologians, they developed new paradigms in sacramentology. Thus, they spoke of Christ as the original sacrament and the Church as the basic sacrament. In short, even before the Vatican Council, influenced by the liturgical and ecumenical movements, liturgical theology and sacramentology received an important place in theology.

The post-Vatican II period witnessed a flood of literature in the study of the liturgy and the sacraments. During this period various other disciplines strengthened the study of sacraments. Inspired by the conciliar call for *aggiornamento*, liturgical and sacramental studies were engaged in adapting liturgy and sacraments to different contexts. Thus, the theologians from Latin America, Africa, and Asia gave sacramentology new flavor through cultural assimilation. In particular, liberation and feminist theologians took sacramentology into new heights.

Shifts of emphasis on the study of theology also contributed to broaden the study of the sacraments. For example, the discussions centered on various dogmatic issues such as Ecclesiology, Christology, Eschatology, Creation and Trinity had their impacts on the liturgical and sacramental theology of the Church. These efforts affirmed the relevance of the traditional adage *lex orandi est lex credendi*. Such studies, on the one hand, contributed to strengthening the discussions concerning various dogmatic issues, but, on the other hand, became occasions to emphasize their importance, even in the liturgical observance of the Church. The axiom *lex orandi est lex credendi* was broadened further by adding a third element: *lex agendi*. All these dimensions have contributed to making the sacraments a focal point at the dawn of the third millennium. Lately, it seems that "postmodern" trends in sacramentology have given way to postmodern sacramentology, taking the sacraments as a matrix from which it addresses Christian life and theology.

In the background of all these developments, this study aims to look for a paradigm, "the world as sacrament," that encompasses various trends and is relevant to the multi-religious context of contemporary society. At the very outset it is important to state that the paradigm proposed is not entirely new. The aim of this study is to rediscover this paradigm that existed from the beginning of Christianity. Its main concern is to see the different possibilities it offers for today, as well as observing the different concerns that are present in it. It is done from the perspectives of Latin, Greek and Syrian Christian traditions. Hence the title of the project: *The World as Sacrament: Sacramentality of Creation from the Perspectives of Leonardo Boff, Alexander Schmemann and Saint Ephrem*.

This study is divided into four chapters. The first chapter analyzes the new trends as well as the existing paradigms in search of a new one befitting our age. In this effort, the study will begin by surveying the new trends in sacramentology that have broadened the juridical and liturgical understanding of sacraments to the concept of sacramentality. Secondly, it makes an overview of two post-conciliar paradigms: Christ and Church as sacraments. The focus here will be to expose the exclusive character of those paradigms in sacramentology and to show the need for a new paradigm that encompasses all Creation.

Two prominent schools of thought that speak of the sacramentality of the world, liberation theology and liturgical theology, will be the focus of attention in the second and third chapters. These two schools are selected mainly due to their contrasting views on the sacramentality of the world. On the one hand, this study will underscore the liberation theologians' emphasis on constant ethical engagement with the world realities and, on the other hand, it will demonstrate the liturgical theologians' emphasis on the cosmic and eschatological dimensions of the ecclesial liturgy. For this two authors are selected, namely, Leonardo Boff who represents liberation theology and Alexander Schmemann, who represents liturgical theology. Both of these theologians argue for the anticipation of the Kingdom of God already in this world. At the same time, they differ in the way that it is realized. For example, liberation theologians emphasize constant ethical engagement with the realities of the world, while liturgical theologians claim that liturgy is the mode of such an experience.

Leonardo Boff was important for our study because of his particular contribution to sacramentology within the realm of liberation theology. Boff, continuing the Franciscan tradition, contributed in the development of the notion of a broader understanding of sacramentality. It is also important to note that Boff's theology is permeated by the sacramentality of Creation. Francis of Assisi's love for Creation and for animals helped Boff to turn his interest towards eco-theology. His later writings are dominated by ecology. Boff is insistent on human responsibility in preserving Creation. His interpretation of the human being is to be understood against the background of three major cosmological models of the West: theocentric, anthropocentric, and the new cosmologies. The theocentric cosmology places God at the top of the hierarchy as the Supreme Being and Creator of the entire universe. The modern cosmology developed on the basis of the Copernican Revolution, the physics of Galileo and Newton, as well as the Cartesian scientific method, considers the world in dualistic terms of matter and spirit. This particular 'anthropocentric cosmology' presented God as an architect. Finally, the new cosmology emerged with Einstein's theory of relativity, the quantum physics of Bohr, the indeterminacy principle of Heisenberg, the findings in theoretical physics of Prigogine and Stengers, the contributions of depth psychology (Freud and Jung), transpersonal psychology (Maslow, P. Weil), biogenetics, cybernetics, and deep ecology. These new perspectives brought about a transition from a materialist worldview to a post-materialist and spiritual world interested in the integration of everyday life with the mystical dimension of things. Boff opts for the third and goes further, arguing for an integral vision of Creation. This new cosmocentric worldview emphasizes the harmonious meeting of God, world and human.

Alexander Schmemann, liturgical theologian *par excellence*, was selected because of his outstanding contribution to Orthodox theology, liturgical theology, and sacramentology. He was a prominent Orthodox theologian who wrote extensively on sacramentology. His reflections on sacramentality are important because of their close affinity with the discussion on Creation theology in the Russian Orthodox tradition. Vladimir Soloviev (1853-1900) initiated the first discussions on Church, world and God relations and founded the 'sophiological' school. Influenced by Jacob Boehme, Spinoza, Schopenhauer, Fichte, as well as Hegel, Soloviev sought to combine pantheism with the Christian doctrine of Incarnation. He interpreted the Incarnation as the fulfillment of an ontological and preexisting "becoming of the world into the Absolute."

His theology is accused of admitting gnostic elements to his system and for holding the existence of a female principle: 'Sophia', or the world soul. Paul Florensky (1882-1943), Sergius Bulgakov (1871-1944) and Nicholas A. Berdyaev (1874-1948) continued this line of thought. The theology of the Sophiological School was criticized by the 'Neopatristic School' of Georges Florovsky and Vladimir Lossky. Schmemann upheld the neopatristic view of 'theocentric' anthropology and 'anthropocentric' cosmology in order to interpret the God-world-human relationship. His main contribution lies in the fact that he placed the whole discussions on the God-world-human relation in the liturgical and sacramental tradition of the Church. In this effort he emphasized the sacramentality of Creation.

Although Boff and Schmemann represent liberation theology and liturgical theology respectively, it is also important to note that both are coming from two Christian traditions: Latin and Greek. In this sense, this study also has the advantage of looking at the sacramentality of Creation from the perspectives of Latin and Greek tradition.

It is a fact that many of our theological discussions revolve around the Latin and Greek Christian traditions. For various reasons the Syrian Christian tradition was not in the scene. Although there were a few studies on sacraments from the Syrian perspective, they did not receive proper attention. However, there are some recent efforts to study the sacraments in the Syrian tradition. These studies are mainly organized from an ecumenical perspective, and its purpose is to reach a certain consensus in the liturgical and sacramental practices of the Syrian Churches. At this juncture, this study makes an effort to see how the sacramentality of Creation is understood in the Syrian tradition. Thus, the fourth chapter investigates the sacramentology of the Syrian tradition based on the Syriac notion *Raza*, rooted in the Hebrew word *sôd* and on the writings of Saint Ephrem.

Raza, although similar to the Greek *mysterion* in its understanding of the sacraments, goes beyond that. On the one hand, it is understood in the liturgical sacramental sense. But, on the other hand, it is used in the exegetical tradition as the source of revelation. The World has an important place in both perspectives. This broader meaning of *raza* is a clear indication for its effective use in the study of the sacramentality of Creation. One remarkable fact about *raza* is that, unlike in the Greek *mysterion*, it does not share the cultic understanding of sacraments. The main function of *raza* is the revelation of a relation between Creator and Creation. In the Syrian tradition, there is an acknowledgement of an ontological 'chasm' that exists between Creator and Creation. Nevertheless, Ephrem suggests three ways to help the human intellect to cross this ontological ‘chasm’. These are types and symbols; the names, or metaphors; and the Incarnation. *Raza* plays an important role in this mediation. Furthermore, the Syrian tradition sees Creation as the source of revelation together with Scripture, and it is often referred to as the book of nature. Hence these three ways are all grounded on the principles of nature. For example, types are to be found throughout all Creation because of their origin from God. They are invitations that offer the possibility of acquiring some knowledge of divine reality. *Raza* in the liturgical-sacramental sense refers primarily to the sacrament of initiation and to the Eucharist. Its plural *raze* is the standard Syriac term for the Eucharist, and is also used for various liturgical and sacramental celebrations. *Raza* as sacraments has an eschatological dimension and emphasizes the anticipation of the Kingdom of God already in this world. In short, the Syriac understanding of *raza* has the potential to be used in the ethical and in the sacramental sense.

Finally, the study delineates some of the implications of this renewed paradigm to theology in the third millennium. Its main contribution is nothing but in affirming an important place for the ‘world’ in Christian theology today.

Writing this dissertation has not always been an easy task for me. Nevertheless, this task was made more pleasant and lighter by the timely help and encouragement of many people. The Promoter Prof. Lambert Leijssen’s interest for innovative ideas, scholarly guidance, critical reading and above all his warmth of appreciation and encouragement had been a great source of inspiration. Moreover he blessed me with an appraisal to this book. Sincere thanks are also extended to John Berchmans oic, Jozef Lamberts and Peter De Mey for their attentive reading and for the critical observations of this dissertation. I remember with gratitude the Dean Mathijs Lamberigts and other members of the staff of the theological faculty of K.U.Leuven. Indebted I am to the scholarship committee of the faculty of theology for granting the necessary scholarship for my living in Leuven. Professor Kristiaan Depoortere and the staff of the Holy Spirit College made my life in Leuven homely and cheerful.

Frs. Jerome, the former Superior General, and George Thomas, the present Superior General of the Congregation of the Order of the Imitation of Christ, are remembered with gratitude for allowing me to pursue my studies at the K.U.Leuven. I also gratefully acknowledge the constant support of my provincial superior Fr. Chacko Aerath, Fr. Thomas Reji, the provincial superior of Navajeevan province, and all confreres of Bethany community.

Discussions with Prof. Sebastian Brock (Oxford) and Robert Murray (Heythrop) strengthened the dissertation with their valid observations. Prof Teule and the Institute of Oriental Studies at the Catholic University of Nijmegen challenged me to take up this study by selecting me as the winner for the Second Kaardinal Willbrands Prize 1998. Participation and presentation of papers in International conferences like LEST III and Pro-Oriente 7 really sharpened my thoughts. I acknowledge them all for their great service on my ways of doing theology.

My gratitude also extends to Melanie Hall for reading the manuscript and for her constructive suggestions. The services rendered by my Leuven friends and colleagues Josy Chirackal, Jose Palackeel, Thomas Padiyath, Thomas Varghese Tharakanveedu (Vijayanand oic), Lawrance Thaikattil, Sabu John Panachikal, Thomas Anatharackal, Scaria Kanniyakonil and James Cherian Mudakodil are acknowledged with gratitude.

I must also thank Most Rev Cyril Mar Baselios OIC, the Metropolitan of the Malankara Catholic Church, who always fostered the budding theologians and lay leaders of the Malankara Catholic Church, for writing a foreword to this work. The *Liturgisch Instituut Leuven* headed by Prof. Jozef Lamberts has always encouraged me and took the trouble in bringing this book to light. I extend my sincere thanks to them.

Leuven
1 May 2004
Mathai Kadavil, oic

Chapter One

CHANGING PARADIGMS IN SACRAMENTOLOGY

In the twentieth century, the traditional understanding of sacraments underwent tremendous changes. However, the eighteenth and nineteenth-century renewal movements in liturgy and sacraments had already paved the way. 'Going back to the traditions' became the rallying cry of the various renewal movements, helping liturgists and sacramentologists to focus on the root meaning of sacraments in the Biblical and Patristic sources. In this process they rediscovered the earlier understanding of sacraments as *mysterion*. Furthermore, the post-Vatican period witnessed another turn in this renewal by incorporating other disciplines such as phenomenology, anthropology, sociology, psychology etc. in the study of the sacraments.[1] The multifaceted approaches in sacramentology had a great impact in broadening our understanding of the sacraments. Besides this, the critical theories against the ontological approaches in theology, particularly in sacramentology, have impacted a great shift in the understanding of classical theories in sacramentology.[2] These critical, albeit

1. For an overview of different approaches such as, historical, biblical, juridical, phenomenological, ecclesiological and Christological in the study of sacraments see Paul J. Levesque, "A Symbolical Sacramental Methodology: An Application of the Thought of Louis Dupré," *QL* 76 (1995) 161-181, pp. 166-173. Various theological trends such as ecumenical theology, liberation theology, contextual theology, feminist theology etc., broadened sacramentology further. For a general overview of various such trends in sacramentology see David N. Power, et al., "Sacramental Theology: A Review of Literature," *TS* 55 (1994) 657-705; Kenan B. Osborne, *Christian Sacraments in a Postmodern World: A Theology for the Third Millennium* (New York/Mahwah, NJ: Paulist, 1999).

2. In this study a distinction is made between traditional and classical understanding of sacramentology in line with Irwin's distinction between 'traditional' and 'conventional'. Traditional understanding of sacramentology denotes the premedieval understanding based mainly on Biblical and Patristic sources. On the other hand, classical understanding means the sacramental theories that were developed under scholastic influence. See Kevin Irwin, "Liturgical Actio: Sacramentality, Eschatology and Ecology," *Contemporary Sacramental Contours of a God Incarnate*, ed. Lieven Boeve & Lambert Leijssen (Leuven: Peeters, 2001) 111-123, p. 111 (note 1).

constructive, approaches brought attention to the studies in liturgy and sacraments and have made sacramentology the focal point in theology at the wake of third millennium.[3]

At this juncture, the complexities of various theories in sacramentology do not prevent me from looking at new trends in sacramentology in view of assessing the existing paradigms and in order to look for a new one befitting our age. Since the works on sacraments are extensive, it is beyond the reach of this study to have more than a bird's eye view of all of them. Hence, this study is limited mainly to the methods in doing sacramentology and on general theory. Here again, the objective of this study is limited to discover a new paradigm. To serve this objective this chapter is divided into two parts. The first part delineates some of the main concerns that renewed sacramentology and the second part follows with an overview of two renewed paradigms: Christ and Church as sacraments. The chapter will be concluded with an evaluation of these existing paradigms and elucidate the efforts for a new one.

1. Sacramentology in Transition

The current literature on sacramentology deals with various aspects of Christian life. From them, four themes, namely, sacramento-liturgical theology, sacramentology and fundamental theology, sacramental symbolism and sacramental economy are selected. This will become the springboard for further inquiry. The selections of authors and titles could be enhanced; however, it seems that the four themes selected have had a great influence in broadening sacramentology. The study of these themes shall be examined from three phases.[4] The first phase comprises doctrinal

3. Lieven Boeve has already made such a claim. In his opinion, while theologians generally showed interest in eschatology and ecclesiology in the 1960s, in Christology in the 1970s, and in the doctrine of God and Trinity in the 1980s and the 1990s, their interest is centered around a sacramentological and liturgical angle in the years around the millennium. Lieven Boeve, "Thinking Sacramental Presence in a Postmodern Context: A Playground for Theological Renewal," *Sacramental Presence in a Postmodern Context*, ed. Lieven Boeve & Lambert Leijssen (Leuven: Peeters, 2001) 3-35, p. 3.

4. One could divide the study of sacraments differently. Vaillancourt gives three phases of sacramental expression: the first phase spread from early Christianity to the Middle Ages, the second from the Middle Ages to the time of Vatican II and the third is the Post-Vatican era. Raymond Vaillancourt, *Toward a Renewal of Sacramental Theology*, trans. Matthew O' Connell (Collegeville, MN: Liturgical Press, 1979) 11-27. The Leuven theologians generally follow the pattern of Pre-modernity, Modernity and Postmodernity. See for example, Georges De Schrijver, "Experiencing the Sacramental Character of Existence: Transition from Premodernity to Modernity, Postmodernity, and the

development of the sacraments in the Apostolic, Patristic and Scholastic periods. The second phase begins with the liturgical and sacramental renewal, beginning from the eighteenth century. The third phase begins with the Second Vatican Council. This does not mean, however that all the topics discussed can be situated in the same order.

1.1. Sacramento-Liturgical Theology

One of the important factors in the sacramental renewal was the understanding of liturgy as the source of sacramentology. This understanding belongs within the broader issue of the relation between liturgy and theology and was one of the focal points for theologians of the liturgical movement. This section demonstrates the interrelation of liturgy and sacraments as perceived from the early Christian period and its shifts during the scholastic period. The main focus will be on some of the contemporary sacramentologists and liturgists, who seem to agree that "liturgical celebration is foundational for sacramental theology,"[5] to develop the notion of 'Sacramento-liturgical theology'.[6]

1.1.1. Liturgy and Sacraments

It was an accepted reality that the early Christians and the Fathers always understood liturgy and sacraments as one and the same reality. They made no distinction between sacraments and liturgy. Instead, they considered that "the divine liturgy itself is the ultimate symbol or sacra-

Rediscovery of Cosmos," *QL* 75 (1994) 12-27; Lieven Boeve, "Postmodern Sacramento-Theology: Retelling the Christian Story," *ETL* 74 (1998) 326-343.

5. Albert Houssiau, "La liturgie, lieu privilégié de la théologie sacramentaire," *QL* 54 (1973) 7-12.

6. Paul J. Levesque in line with Irénée-Henri Dalmais makes a distinction between sacramental theology and liturgical theology. According to him, "Sacramental theology has been interpreted as investigating what God does in acts of salvation *for* the Church, contrasted to liturgical theology understood as concerning the action *of* the Church in its worship." Levesque, "A Symbolical Sacramental Methodology," 174. See also Irénée-Henri Dalmais, *Introduction to the Liturgy*, trans. Roger Capel (Baltimore, MD: Helicon, 1961) 66. Houssiau makes it clear as he notes: "Liturgy is not a discourse *about* God, Christ, the Church and the World; it is a symbolical and ritual action in words and gestures, a celebration in which our communion with God is joined." On the other hand, "Sacramental theology is talk *about* this celebration, and especially these liturgical actions which faith has discerned as playing a privileged part in our participation in salvation." Albert Houssiau, "The Rediscovery of the Liturgy by Sacramental Theology (1950-1980)," *SL* 15 (1982-83) 158-177, pp. 158-159. At the same time Irwin notes the collapse of such a distinction in most recent authors. See, Kevin W. Irwin, *Liturgical Theology: A Primer*, American Essays in Liturgy (Collegeville, MN: Liturgical Press, 1990) 19.

ment."[7] For example, Symeon of Thessalonika notes that the Divine Liturgy constitutes "the mystery of mysteries ... the holy of holies, the initiation of all initiations."[8] For Nicholas Cabasilas, liturgy is the final mystery. Beyond this it is not possible to go, nor can anything be added to it.[9] It is also important to note that the patristic era offers a model "to develop the theology of sacraments through commentaries on the liturgical rites."[10] Thus the Fathers have always explained sacraments in the context of actual liturgical celebrations.[11] For them, explanations of sacraments are "exegesis of the liturgy."[12]

This interrelatedness of liturgy and sacraments starts to slightly change with Augustine. He makes a distinction between liturgy and sacraments. For him, not every celebration is sacramental.[13] In his opinion a celebration becomes a sacrament "when the commemoration of a past event is made in such a way that it is understood also to signify something which is to be taken in a holy way." He illustrates with an example:

> The birthday of the Lord is not celebrated *in sacramento*, but is simply recalled to memory. The Pasch, on the contrary, is celebrated *in sacramento*: there is a *sacramentum* in its celebration. ... Because by a multiple symbolism we not only recall Christ's passage from death to life, but also signify

7. John Chryssavgis, "The World as Sacrament: Insights into an Orthodox Worldview," *Pacifica* 10 (1997) 1-24, p. 9.

8. Symeon of Thessalonika, *De Sacramentis*, 78, *PG* 155: 223.

9. Nicholas Cabasilas, *De Vita in Christo*, Book II, *PG* 150: 548. Cabasilas emphasized the life in Christ expressed in the Eucharist (liturgy) superior to rigorist monastic ideals proposed by Hesychasm. It does not mean that he is "belittling monasticism or ascetic endeavour. But the very labours of ascetics cannot be sustained without recourse to divine grace, the Eucharistic food and intimacy with Christ." Boris Bobrinskoy, "Introduction," in Nicholas Cabasilas, *The Life in Christ*, trans. Carmino J. de Catanzaro (Crestwood, NY: St. Vladimir's Seminary Press, 1974) 17-42, p. 22.

10. Irwin, *Liturgical Theology*, 12-13.

11. Georges Florovsky, "The Elements of Liturgy," *The Orthodox Church in the Ecumenical Movement. Documents and Statements 1902-1975*, ed. Constantin G. Patelos (Geneva: World Council of Churches, 1978) 172-182, p. 179.

12. Alexander Schmemann, "Sacrament and Symbol," *For the Life of the World* (Crestwood, NY: St. Vladimir's Seminary Press, 1973) 135-151, p. 137.

13. Influenced by Neoplatonism, Augustine defined *sacramentum* as a visible sign that represents an invisible reality. "A *sacramentum* is a *sacrum signum*, that is, a sign designated by God to point to a divine reality (*res divina*) and containing that reality within itself." Augustine, *Letters*, 138. He used the Scriptural and Patristic traditions of explaining ritual action that was coupled with a word or prayer in interpreting the sacraments. For him, "the ecclesial ritual consists of matter and spirit i.e., the phenomena observed (*elementum*) and the words (*verbum*) pronounced in using the *elementum*." George S. Worgul, *From Magic to Metaphor: A Validation of the Christian Sacraments* (New York/Ramsey, NJ: Paulist, 1980) 203.

our own passage from death to life. Our passage is effected now *by faith*, for the remissions of sins, *in hope* of eternal life, of future resurrection and glory.[14]

In the medieval period the discussion on sacramentology was mainly centered around two themes: the composition of sacraments and sacramental causality.[15] First of all, even though the liturgy continued to function as foundational for sacramentology, it was concerned about giving a rational explanation to the composition of sacraments. This development, which led to a material conception of grace, is rooted in the sixteenth century development of the changed use of the Augustinian notion of *materia* to *elementum* and *forma sacramenti*, or *forma verborum*, to *verbum*.[16] This led to the understanding that *materia* and *forma* are the *res*, and in the sacramental behavior this *res* is considered grace.[17]

Secondly, the discussions on sacramental causality have further led to the separation of sacraments from liturgy. Two things are to be noted here: "the sacraments 'work' *ex opere operato*" and "the sacraments signify what they effect and effect what they signify."[18] For the great scho-

14. William A. Van Roo, *The Christian Sacrament*, Analecta Gregoriana, 262 (Rome: Pontificia Università Gregoriana, 1992) 39. See Augustine, *Epistola* 55.1.2-2.3, *CSEL* 34: 170-173; *PL* 33: 204-206.

15. Worgul, *From Magic to Metaphor*, 203-205. For details see Damian Van den Eynde, "The Theory of the Composition of the Sacraments in Early Scholasticism," *FrS* 11/1 (1951) 1-20; *FrS* 11/2 (1951) 117-144; id., "Stephen Langton and Hugh of St. Cher on the Causality of Sacraments," *FrS* 11/3-4 (1951) 141-155.

16. Worgul, *From Magic to Metaphor*, 203. Worgul considers linguistic changes behind this substitution rather than philosophical orientation. Joseph Martos observes that the tendency to look at the matter and form for validity was not a new development. It started already with the collapse of Roman Empire. In the aftermath of Roman Empire, and the Germanic invasions that followed, there was a missionary expansion to the West. The majority of the missionaries, who were illiterate, started reducing the long liturgical services to simple rites that were valid. Joseph Martos, *Doors to the Sacred: A Historical Introduction to Sacraments in the Catholic Church* (London: SCM, 1981, expanded edition 1992) 66-67.

17. Worgul, *From Magic to Metaphor*, 203. The early Scholastics, and even Aquinas, were not yet employing *materia* and *forma* in terms of Aristotelian hylomorphism. Hugh of St. Cher appears to have been the first to employ *materia* and *forma* in a hylemorphic sense. Van den Eynde, "The Theory of the Composition of the Sacraments in Early Scholasticism," 20. After Thomas, however, hylemorphism dominated scholasticism and *materia* and *forma* assumed their new technical meanings. *Ibid.* Thomas Aquinas, the sacramentologist *par excellence* in the West, is often projected for his rational explanation given to sacramentology. But he never undermined the importance of worship. As Van Roo observes, "the sacraments are intimately related to his general theology of worship. This relationship is suggested only in passing allusions in the questions which deal directly with the sacraments." Van Roo, *The Christian Sacrament*, 58-59.

18. Worgul, *From Magic to Metaphor*, 204. Worgul notes: "Whether dispositive,

lastics of the twelfth century, "there is *only one* level within which the divine initiative in Christ, expressed in the 'opus operatum' meets dialectically with our total and free acception of it in faith, properly called the 'opus operantis'."[19] Sadly, this organic unity was collapsed by the nominalist theologians in the fourteenth century.[20]

Post-Tridentine sacramentology, using sacramental cause, explained how the Sacraments give 'created' grace through the *valid* administrations of a Sacrament. "The sacramental 'cause' efficaciously produces some divine grace in us. The rest of the ritual, commonly called by scholastic theologians and canonists 'ceremonial rites' (*ceremoniae*) do not possess in themselves a proper sacramental efficacy. It may foster and feed our personal devotion and faith, which the later scholastics wrongly called 'opus operantis'." It means that Grace is "granted on two separate levels, as it were, the strict sacramental level of the 'opus operatum', and the non-sacramental personal and devotional level of the 'opus operantis'."[21] As from the post-tridentine period, we see a clear separation between liturgy and sacraments. "In the wake of the Tridentine concern for rubrical precision in the doing of the liturgy ... liturgy became equated with the external performance of the Church's rites. Sacramental theology was incorporated into manuals of dogmatic theology."[22] The recipient participates passively in the sacramental celebrations. The

physical, moral, occasional, or intentional causality is examined, the absolute freedom and gratuity of God's self-gift is vigorously defended." At the same time, he criticises these Scholastic theories in that they failed to explain how the sacraments cause grace and tended to view the sacraments mechanistically as producers of grace. Furthermore, he notes that "the great Scholastics would never have accepted this interpretation. Thomas, Scotus and Bonaventure would have found it abhorrent. Yet, later authors, who claimed these 'greats' as the initiators of this vision, secured the mechanistic-physical model as the unconscious model for Christian sacramentology for over three centuries." This mechanistic-physical model resulted in the collapse of the 'sign/symbol character of sacraments' in the theological traditions. In the mechanistic-physical model symbolism or symbolic activity has no place. Instead the questions of 'validity of performance' and 'accumulation of graces' became the exclusive thrust of sacramental investigations and writings (pp. 204-205).

19. Piet F. Fransen, "Sacraments as Celebrations," *Irish Theological Quarterly* 43 (1976) 151-170, p. 155. Fransen compares this mutual relationship in grace between God's initiative and our answer in faith with Rahnerian grace theology: the 'offered' and 'accepted' grace.

20. Fransen, "Sacraments as Celebrations," 155.

21. *Ibid.* The model used in this theology is the model of a 'cause' (technically called 'physical' cause to oppose it in scholastic terminology to an 'intentional' cause, as was defended by Cardinal Billot).

22. Irwin, *Liturgical Theology*, 13. The main focus of such manuals was on the Reformation debates about causality, the number of sacraments, and their institution. *Ibid.*

priests neglected the celebration because of the use of Latin language, together with the nominalist notion of *opus operatum*.[23]

As a result, one observes that the actual rites of the liturgy played a less central role in the medieval sacramental synthesis. At this juncture, the emphasis was placed more on when and how sacraments were administered. In their effort to systematize the study of sacraments, they undermined the importance of the totality of the rites compared to the patristic era.[24] The medieval *De Sacramentis* tendency to isolate the sacrament from its liturgical context impeded the development of a genuine sacramentology. As a consequence, the precise sacramental sign alone is considered the proper object of theological attention.[25] Its basic defect was that, "in its treatment of the sacraments, it proceeds not from the concrete liturgical tradition ... but from its own a priori and abstract categories and definitions."[26]

In other words, the scholastics "seldom used the images and categories of the liturgy or its structures in order to understand the meaning of sacraments and interpret them in a coherent way."[27] That is to say, that they began with a general theory of sacraments and then, 'applied' to each particular sacrament.[28] Furthermore, the theological discussions centered around philosophical themes like: transubstantiation, consubstantiation, etc. This resulted in the loss of the importance of the liturgy as such. Liturgy then came to be considered as a non-essential, symbolical 'framework' for the minimum of action and words necessary for validity. The whole liturgical action ceased to be understood as *sacramen-*

23. Fransen, "Sacraments as Celebrations," 158. According to Fransen, this pragmatic or utilitarian approach, i.e., to expect something from a sacrament, is a typical Western approach. It is seen in the more primitive forms of sacramental theology in Early Scholasticism and it continued in the handbooks of the later period. *Ibid.*

24. Irwin, *Liturgical Theology*, 13.

25. Schmemann, "Sacrament and Symbol," 137.

26. Alexander Schmemann, *The Eucharist: Sacrament of the Kingdom*, trans. Paul Kachur (Crestwood, NY: St. Vladimir's Seminary Press, 1988) 13. From the general definition of sacraments as the 'visible means of the invisible grace', one proceeds to the distinction between 'form' and 'matter', institution by Christ, numbering and classification and, finally, the proper administration for the validity and efficacy. Schmemann, "Sacrament and Symbol," 135. It had its impact on theology. The very discipline called liturgics dealt mainly with a practical study of the Church services together with an explanation of liturgical symbolism and some introductory chapters dealing with the theological and historical aspects of worship. Its main concern was to perform services in conformity with the rubrics and canonical requirements. Alexander Schmemann, "Liturgical Theology: Its Task and Method," *SVSQ* 1 (1957) 16-27, p. 16.

27. Houssiau, "The Rediscovery of the Liturgy by Sacramental Theology (1950-1980)," 159-160.

28. Alexander Schmemann, "Theology and Eucharist," *SVSQ* 5 (1961) 10-23, p. 17.

tal.[29] In this context, it is very important to note that "no attempt was made, in the ... cloisters and cathedral schools, to fashion a definition of sacraments that located them within liturgy and prayer."[30]

The process of estrangement of liturgy and sacraments was deepened in the late scholastic period. As Kevin Irwin notes: "The divorce between the *lex orandi* and *lex credendi* was exemplified in the division of what had been a single area of study into two: liturgy and sacramental theology."[31] This does not mean, however, that the notion of *lex orandi* was absent in theological study or in the magisterial teachings. There were occasional magisterial references to *lex orandi, lex credendi*, yet, "they do not necessarily recognize the liturgy as a privileged source and foundation for sacramental theology in particular or systematic theology in general."[32]

Although the Reformers protested against the medieval theology of worship, they failed to return to the early tradition. They actually replaced the medieval doctrine of worship by another theology of worship. In Protestant Churches the *leitourgia* remained a function of its theological conception and interpretation. Schmemann adds, in the subsequent developments in the Catholic and Protestant theology, "intellectual or anti-intellectual, liberal or pietistic, theology not only remained internally independent of worship, but claimed the right to control it, and to form it according to the *lex credendi*."[33]

1.1.2. Rediscovery of Liturgy as the Source for Sacramentology

The situation changed with the efforts of the liturgical movement. They contributed a lot in rediscovering the importance of liturgy and sacraments in Christian life.[34] According to Albert Houssiau, although "the

29. Alexander Schmemann, "Theology and Liturgical Tradition," *Liturgy and Tradition: Theological Reflections of Alexander Schmemann*, ed. Thomas Fisch (Crestwood, NY: St. Vladimir's Seminary Press, 1990) 11-20; Id., "Liturgy and Eschatology," *Sobornost* 7/1 (1985) 6-14, p. 10; Id., *The Eucharist: Sacrament of the Kingdom*, 28.

30. Herbert Vorgrimler, *Sacramental Theology*, trans. Linda M. Maloney (Collegeville, MN: Liturgical Press, 1992) 45.

31. Irwin, *Liturgical Theology*, 13.

32. *Ibid.*, 14. For a study on the magisterial teachings references on *lex orandi lex credendi* see, Herman Schmidt, "Lex orandi, lex credendi in recentioribus documentis pontificiis," *Periodica* 40 (1951) 5-28.

33. Schmemann, "Theology and Liturgical Tradition," 14.

34. Albert Houssiau presents two merits of the liturgical movement in connection to the study of sacramental theology. First, it promoted the active participation in the sacramental ministry. In this sense it had returned to the idea of the patristic understanding that the liturgical context is very important in the celebration of the sacraments. Secondly, it helped in avoiding the distinction "within the sacramental rite with what is essential with

fear of modernism delayed the acknowledgement that liturgical life is epistemologically first, and thus reduced the influence of liturgical studies on sacramental theology," people like "Odo Casel, Bernard Botte, J. A. Jungmann, A. Chavasse have *re*discovered liturgy, by correctly underlining its epistemological priority, in order to understand sacraments."[35] Their contribution has made the 'turn to mystery' a common background in sacramentology.[36] They were influenced mainly by two factors: Biblical and Patristic studies as well as the phenomenological approach. Thus, both the Biblical and Patristic studies helped to rediscover the idea of *mysterion* in the place of *sacramentum*.[37] Moreover, the study of the history of the sacraments made a great impact in retrieving the importance of liturgy in the sacraments.[38]

Today the liturgists and sacramentologists seem to agree that "there is no easy distinction between liturgy and sacrament."[39] Irwin draws attention to the efforts of liturgists "to develop a theology of the sacraments that transcends the conventional post Tridentine Roman Catholic divorce between liturgy and sacramental theology" in the revised liturgical

what is invariable." Houssiau, "The Rediscovery of the Liturgy by Sacramental Theology (1950-1980)," 161. Osborne also praises the liturgical movement for the retrieval of the celebrational aspect of liturgy and for giving a social dimension to the liturgy in particular by the leaders of the liturgical movement in the United States. Osborne, *Christian Sacraments in a Postmodern World*, 12-13.

35. Houssiau, "The Rediscovery of the Liturgy by Sacramental Theology (1950-1980)," 160.

36. For example this is seen in Odo Casel's "retrieval of the nature of the liturgy as mystery, or in Henri de Lubac's contrast between the symbolic approach of the Church Fathers and the concern with rational explanation, in keeping with philosophical demands, of scholastic theology." Both of them viewed liturgy "as an act of the Church which offers participation in Christ's mystery, and the nature of the Church is considered as a communion whose symbolic expression is found in sacrament." Power, et al., "Sacramental Theology: A Review of Literature," 662.

37. For a recent study on the etymological meaning of *mysterion* and *sacramentum* with its origin, its use in the different traditions, its use in Bible and Fathers see Thomas Poovathanikunnel, *The Sacraments: The Mystery Revealed* (Kottayam: OIRSI, 1998).

38. Osborne, *Christian Sacraments in a Postmodern World*, 6-9.

39. Power, et al., "Sacramental Theology: A Review of Literature," 658. In this article the authors draw our attention to some of the recent studies on the interrelatedness of liturgy and sacraments. Kevin Irwin in another article gives a detailed survey of the efforts of theologians and liturgists works of retrieving the relationship between liturgy and sacramentology. Kevin W. Irwin, "Recent Sacramental Theology: A Review Discussion," *The Thomist* 47 (1983) 592-608, p. 600. Arno Schilson in his survey on recent studies in sacramentology also stressed the contribution of sacramentology for retrieving the importance of actual celebration rather than abstract concepts. Arno Schilson, "Erneuerung der Sakramententheologie im 20. Jahrhundert," *LJ* 37 (1987) 18-41.

rites.[40] Lambert Leijssen affirms the same as he notes: "Methodologically speaking, liturgical expressions must be taken into consideration in an authentic sacramental theology."[41] The liturgical character of sacraments has also received due emphasis in the *Catechism of the Church.*[42]

But there are differences of opinions with regard to the appropriation of liturgy in the study of the sacraments. Lambert Leijssen criticizes Rahner for not giving ample emphasis to liturgy in his sacramentology, but apparently approves the different strand of liturgy in him.

> Rahner attaches virtually no importance to the liturgy or liturgical studies. The basic insight which is important to liturgists, namely that the liturgy must be the primary source for sacramental doctrine, is not even mentioned by Rahner. He apparently paid little attention to the liturgy, and certainly not to the rubrical aspect of the liturgy. His focus was more on the authentic expression of the attitude of faith and prayer in the liturgical tradition.[43]

Albert Houssiau, though acknowledging Rahner's contribution in associating sacraments with the Church, he also criticizes him for neglecting liturgy as a primary referent for his theology.[44]

Herbert Vorgrimler underscores that "the *whole* liturgical symbolic action constitutes the fulfillment of the sacrament."[45] Although he considers the sacraments as the Church's liturgy, he warns against overemphasis on liturgy. He notes, "The Liturgy, of which the sacraments are an essential component, cannot be regarded from the outset as the highest form of Church's realization."[46] According to him, the Church seeks to follow Jesus through divine worship (*leitourgia*), proclamation (*martyria*) and service to others and to society (*diakonia*).[47]

In short, one could say with Albert Houssiau that the "*re*discovery of liturgy, as a privileged source of sacramental theology" has contributed a great deal for the later development of sacramentology.[48] It has also become very relevant in the ecumenical context. As Vorgrimler observes,

40. Kevin W. Irwin, *Context and Text: Method in Liturgical Theology* (Collegeville, MN: Liturgical Press, 1994) x.

41. Lambert Leijssen, "Rahner's Contribution to the Renewal of Sacramentology," *Philosophy and Theology* 9 (1995) 201-222, p. 206.

42. Lambert Leijssen, "The Sacramental Economy of Salvation in the Catechism of the Church," *QL* 77 (1996) 229-239, pp. 231-232 and 238-239.

43. Leijssen, "Rahner's Contribution to the Renewal of Sacramentology," 206.

44. Albert Houssiau, "La liturgie, lieu privilégié de la théologie sacramentaire," 11.

45. Vorgrimler, *Sacramental Theology*, 79.

46. *Ibid.*, 20-21.

47. *Ibid.*, 20.

48. Houssiau, "The Rediscovery of the Liturgy by Sacramental Theology (1950-1980)," 158.

the sacramental renewal as a liturgy of prayer is important "as regards to the Eastern Churches and the Churches of the Reformation, and even in relation to Judaism, from which the Church received the structure of its highest sacrament, the form of the Eucharistic prayer."[49]

1.1.3. Challenges of Sacramento-Liturgical Theology

As we have seen, the liturgical movement and various other studies have succeeded in retrieving the importance of liturgy in the sacramental celebration. Benefited from the historical study of liturgical and sacramental celebrations, the conciliar and post-conciliar theologians took it into new realms. Various disciplines have contributed to make the liturgical and sacramental celebrations meaningful. Among the various literatures on the methods of studying liturgy, we shall see some of the pertinent ones in developing an adequate method for the study of 'sacramento-liturgical theology'.

The study of liturgical texts draws attention to the importance of the liturgical contexts in which they were developed. Thus, the traditional method of studying liturgical texts was challenged by liturgical theology and suggested to go beyond the text. For example, Kevin W. Irwin draws our attention into the study of liturgy based on the context. His main argument is that 'the context is text and text shapes context'. His contention is that we have to go beyond sacraments and about what they do in order to analyze and understand them and their efficacy from within their own expression and framework. For Irwin, the liturgical act itself generates an understanding of sacrament and one's participation in it. He claims that studies of the imagination and of liturgical performance could add to the comprehension of sacrament from within the act itself.[50] Joyce Ann

49. Vorgrimler, *Sacramental Theology*, 80. One could observe a flood of literature on the study of liturgy and sacraments from an ecumenical perspective in the Post-Vatican era. The ecumenical discussions at various levels (for example, Catholics with various Orthodox and other ecclesial denominations, within various Orthodox traditions, between Orthodox Churches and other renewal Churches) were instrumental in bringing out concerns of this kind to be spread beyond the boundaries of independent Churches. Although it is an important concern, we shall not deal with this in detail in our discussions. Our main focus is confined to the renewals within the Catholic traditions. At the same time non-Catholic authors' contribution on particular themes are given due importance in our discussions.

50. Irwin's book *Context and Text* is a brilliant work that studies the importance of the relation between context and text. Context for him signifies (1) the historical evolution of the origin, component parts, and variations of a given rite, (2) the liturgical act as a whole as an interrelation of words, symbols, gestures, and its appropriation and understanding by the assembly through environment and actions, (3) the contemporary cultural and ecclesial setting of celebration. Irwin, *Context and Text*, 54-55.

Zimmermann, relying on Paul Ricœur, also proposes a 'text hermeneutics' approach to liturgical studies. She tries to comprehend liturgical celebration through its textual form showing the essential connection between text and celebration and between liturgy and life.[51]

Another dimension, which has received attention among the contemporary theologians, is the emphasis on the experiential aspect of the celebration. For example, Piet F. Fransen calls attention to the personal experience one is receiving at the sacramental celebration. For him, it is a unique moment of intense feeling of joy, or freedom, or fullness. He calls this a festive approach and for him in the liturgical experience, "we festively acknowledge in faith and hope God's ineffable inner Presence."[52] One encounters God in "the inner voice, the inner depth of ourselves."[53] In this approach, he acknowledges the importance of nature. Thus he suggests that the "spiritual attitude is not necessarily individualistic, for it recognizes God also in the inner sanctuary of the others, in every creation."[54] As noted already, the liturgical movement also contributed to asserting the celebrational aspect of the liturgical and sacramental celebration.[55] Chauvet also acknowledges that the emphasis on liturgical celebration is the result of the rediscovery of the priority of liturgical action in recent decades.[56] He even notes that, "sacramental theology can say nothing about the *res* the faith proclaims except on the basis of the act of celebration."[57] Similarly he notes that "we can say nothing about

51. Joyce Ann Zimmermann, *Liturgy as Language of Faith: A Liturgical Methodology in the Mode of Paul Ricœur's Textual Hermeneutics* (New York: University Press of America, 1988). Jan Michael Joncas, "Joyce Ann Zimmermann's 'Text Hermeneutics' Approach to Liturgical Studies: A Review and Some Methodological Reflections," *QL* 74 (1993) 208-220.

52. Fransen, "Sacraments as Celebrations," 167. In this sense he calls this as a *festive* approach.

53. *Ibid.*, 168. In this regard he draws our attention to the Indian tradition that "sees God as the inner presence in the world and men. ... The great mystics of the past, the Greek hesychasts of the East, the Western mystics from St Augustine to John Ruysbroeck and the Spanish mystics found God in the inner depths of their own being, at the very centre of themselves. A stronger pneumatic and charismatic form of piety, more open to the inner voice of the Spirit within the inner shrine of our heart may foster this symbolic approach to God's Presence in grace" (p. 166).

54. *Ibid.*, 167. He acknowledges such a view already present in Teilhard de Chardin and others. For them God is "the inner power of the Universe, He is through Jesus Christ the inner soul of the cosmos and its history." He traces its background further into the great Franciscan theologians of the Middle Ages.

55. Osborne, *Christian Sacraments in a Postmodern World*, 12.

56. Louis-Marie Chauvet, "Liturgy and the Body" (Editorial), *Concilium* (1995), n. 3, vii-x, viii.

57. Louis-Marie Chauvet, *Symbol and Sacrament: A Sacramental Reinterpretation of*

the reality of "sacramental grace" outside the liturgical expression (the *sacramentum*) the Church provides in its acts of celebration." Unlike the Scholastic way of treating sacraments in terms of specific concepts like grace, causality, reality etc., he argues that: "[B]efore treating of grace itself, we must go into the question of effective expression, since in celebrating the sacraments, the Church speaks according to the concrete modality."[58]

Furthermore, liberation theologians, in general, advocate a *praxis*-oriented approach to liturgy and sacraments.[59] Jozef Lamberts calls attention to various justice issues, such as gender, sufferings of the individuals, war and genocide, injustice done to nature.[60] David Power draws our attention to liturgical study that reflects the influence of liberation and *praxis* methodologies. In his opinion, "[t]he task of theology is to appropriate the symbols in which liturgy expresses God, and to discourse on their meaning and their pertinence to praxis."[61] He, himself, claims that his main concern for twenty years after Vatican II was "the way of relating liturgy to praxis.[62] In a certain sense, the praxis oriented liturgical celebration emphasizes the ethical dimension of Christian liturgy. Thus Chauvet is right to observe that the understanding of celebration and ethical dimensions are inseparable. As Depoortere notes, in Chauvet, "there is a necessary interdependency between the arches of belief and ethics in relation to their keystone, the liturgy."[63] Feminist theologians have broadened this to include the concerns of gender issues.[64]

Christian Existence, trans. Patrick Madigan & Madeleine Beaumont (Collegeville, MN: Liturgical Press, 1995) 437.

58. Chauvet, *Symbol and Sacrament*, 430.

59. For a general overview of them see Power, et al., "Sacramental Theology: A Review of Literature," 675-684. In this review article Kevin Irwin presents the contributions of Juan Luis Segundo, Leonardo Boff, Francisco Taborda & Antonio Gonzalez Dorado.

60. Jozef Lamberts, "Contemporary Feeling and Liturgy," trans. John Bowden, *Concilium* (1995), n. 3, 130-136, pp. 134-135. These issues were also addressed from particular contexts too. For example, Sandanam reflects on the social dimension of the Eucharist based on a particular experience from the Indian context. John Peter Sandanam, "Do This in Remembrance of Me: A Social Dimension of the Eucharist with Special Reference to the Indian Christian Communities," *QL* 82 (2001) 225-246.

61. David N. Power, "Cult to Culture: The Liturgical Foundation of Theology," *Worship* 54 (1980) 482-495, p. 482.

62. David N. Power, *Worship: Culture and Theology* (Washington, DC: Pastoral Press, 1990) xi.

63. Kristiaan Depoortere, "From Sacramentality to Sacraments and Vice-versa," *Contemporary Sacramental Contours of a God Incarnate*, 51-62, p. 57.

64. There are many feminist theologians who express feminist concerns in developing the theology of liturgy and sacraments. For example, Susan Roll asks for due importance for a gender-inclusive language in the liturgy. Susan Roll, "Language and Justice in the

The integration of liturgy into various cultures is another important phenomenon that attracted many contemporary theologians. After a few years of liturgical and sacramental renewal in the post-Vatican era, many theologians' interest turned to cultural adaptation.[65] David Power goes further beyond liberation and praxis methodologies and calls for its acculturation. He notes that even though the liturgy had already been subjected to external changes, he criticizes its failure to become integrated into various cultures.[66] At the same time one should note the efforts already made in various cultures,[67] especially in the areas of popular liturgy.[68] In this regard the study of the anthropological dimension of liturgy is also of particular importance.[69]

Our above discussion on sacramento-liturgical theology has underlined the inter-relatedness of liturgy and sacraments. The retrieval of the liturgical nature of the sacramental celebration points to the celebrational character that belongs to the very nature of human beings. As Schme-

Liturgy," *Liturgy and Language: A Tribute to Silveer De Smet*, ed. Lambert Leijssen, Textes et études liturgiques / Studies in Liturgy, 12 (Leuven: Abdij Keizersberg/Faculteit der Godgeleerdheid, 1992) 66-81.

65. In this regard it is good to note the distinction Anscar Chupungco has made between cultural adaptation or acculturation and inculturation. While the former is the incorporation of cultural elements that are compatible with the 'Roman rite', the latter is the meaning given to pre-Christian ritual with Christian meaning. Anscar Chupungco, *Cultural Adaptation of the Liturgy* (New York: Paulist, 1982) 81, 84. He is one of the pioneers who wrote extensively on this topic. Chupungco addressed the issue of cultural adaptations from various angles. For example, he applies it to sacraments, sacramentals, the divine office and the liturgical year in his *Liturgies of the Future: The Process and Methods of Inculturation* (Mahwah, NJ: Paulist, 1989). See also Anscar J. Chupungco, *Liturgical Inculturation: Sacramentals, Religiosity, and Catechesis* (Collegeville, MN: Liturgical Press, 1992). Jozef Lamberts (ed.), *Liturgy and Inculturation*, Textes et études liturgiques / Studies in Liturgy, 14 (Louvain: Peeters, 1996).

66. David N. Power, "People at Liturgy," *Worship: Culture and Theology*, 273-283. David Power, through the collection of 16 articles of this book offers insights into the relation of liturgy to culture.

67. For example, Anselme Sanon, "Cultural Rooting of the Liturgy in Africa Since Vatican II," *Concilium* 162 (1983) 61-70; Paul Puthanangady, "Inculturation of the Liturgy in India Since Vatican II," *Concilium* 162 (1983) 71-77.

68. For a concise study on various aspects of popular religiosity see Jozef Lamberts (ed.), *Popular Religion, Liturgy and Evangelization*, Textes et études liturgiques / Studies in Liturgy, 15 (Leuven: Peeters, 1998).

69. On the anthropological dimension of liturgy see, Crispino Valenziano, "Liturgy and Anthropology: The Meaning of the Question and the Method for Answering It," *Handbook for Liturgical Studies*. Vol. II: *Fundamental Liturgy*, ed. Anscar J. Chupungco (Collegeville, MN: Liturgical Press, 1998) 189-226; Paul Post, "De synthese in de huidige liturgiewetenschap: Proeve van positionering van *De weg van de liturgie*," *Jaarboek voor liturgie-onderzoek* 14 (1998) 141-172.

mann observes, the human being is *homo adorans.*[70] This rediscovery of the 'sacramental nature of reality' helps us to go beyond a sacramentology that was perceived in a reductionist manner as merely "seven sacraments." The retrieval of the importance of liturgy has to a certain extent contributed to the emergence of a new branch in theology generally known as 'liturgical theology'.[71] It does not look at liturgy either as a source of theology or as an object of theology.[72] On the other hand, it emphasizes liturgy as the necessary condition in doing theology.[73] Hence, in the next section we shall discuss this in detail.

1.2. Sacramentology and Fundamental Theology

Locus Theologicus is one of the dominant themes of theological discussions. But in the early Christian tradition it was never an important concern because it was always intertwined with liturgical celebrations. The

70. Alexander Schmemann, *Sacraments and Orthodoxy* (New York: Herder and Herder, 1965) 16.

71. The term "liturgical theology" was first used in Maieul Cappuyns' paper "Liturgie et théologie" presented at the liturgical week at Mont César, Belgium. Maieul Cappuyns, "Liturgie et théologie," *Le vrai visage de la liturgie*, Cours et conférences des semaines liturgiques (Louvain: Abbaye de Mont César, 1938) 175-209, p. 199. But the terms: "liturgical theology" and "theology of the liturgy" were used synonymously. We are indebted very much to Alexander Schmemann for the development of this notion. As Fisch pointed out it was developed into its final form during the years 1957-69. Thomas Fisch, "Schmemann's Theological Contribution to the Liturgical Renewal of the Churches," *Liturgy and Tradition: Theological Reflections of Alexander Schmemann*, ed. Thomas Fisch (Crestwood, NY: St. Vladimir's Seminary Press, 1990) 1-10, p. 6. But in Grisbrooke's opinion the difference and distinction took final shape in the last article of Schmemann specifically devoted to the issue, "Liturgical Theology: Remarks on Method," written in 1981; in *Liturgy and Tradition*, 137-144. W. Jardine Grisbrooke, "An Orthodox Approach to Liturgical Theology: The Work of Alexander Schmemann," *SL* 23 (1993) 140-157, p. 153.

72. Schmemann, "Theology and Liturgical Tradition," 11-12. The former can be termed as "Liturgy from Theology" and the latter could be named as "Theology of Liturgy." For detailed explanations of these theories, See David W. Fagerberg, *What is Liturgical Theology? A Study in Methodology* (Collegeville, MN: Liturgical Press, 1992).

73. Since it is related to sacraments, Schmemann argues that the study of the liturgy should begin first with the Eucharist, and it must be preceded by the sacraments of integration into that life: Baptism and Holy Chrism. Secondly that worship which is primarily determined by time, in its three cycles – the day, the week and the year and finally, those services and rites whose purpose is to be found in the needs and life of the individual members of the Church. The family (Holy Matrimony), the sacraments of *healing* (penance and Holy Oil), the numerous rites of blessing, the liturgy for the departed, etc. constitute the special object of this third part of liturgical theology. Schmemann, "Liturgical Theology: Its Task and Method," 22-24.

Fathers expressed this in the axiom of *lex orandi est lex credendi.*[74] But from the medieval period, theologians began to use a more rational approach that undermined this axiom, and had a great impact in all areas of Christian life. In contemporary discussions, though the speculative approach is still very much in use, there is a growing awareness to go back to the early Christian's theological method: *lex orandi est lex credendi.*

1.2.1. Lex Orandi est Lex Credendi

The axiom *lex orandi est lex credendi* is considered as the core value in the early development of theology. Irwin sketches out how, for the Fathers "the meaning of such central theological tenets of Christian belief as the mystery of the Trinity, the divinity of Jesus, original sin and the need for grace were very frequently derived from their articulation in the Church's liturgy."[75] To the Fathers *lex orandi est lex credendi* was a natural milieu for theology. In this sense liturgy is neither a reflection on liturgy nor "an *object* of theological inquiry and definition, but rather the living source and the ultimate criterion of all Christian thought."[76] The importance is not on the dogmatic or authoritative character of the liturgy, rather it is considered as a necessary condition. Hence it is the life in the Church. For them, the Church is not an institution that keeps divinely revealed doctrines and teachings about the events of the past, but it is the very *epiphany* of those events.[77] As Schmemann puts it:

> [T]he problem of the relationship between liturgy and theology is not for the Fathers a problem of priority or authority. Liturgical tradition is not an 'authority' or a *locus theologicus*, it is the ontological condition of theology, of the proper understanding of *kerygma*, of the Word of God, because it is in the Church, of which the *leitourgia* is the expression and the life, that the sources of theology are functioning as precisely 'sources'.[78]

74. The dictum *lex orandi est lex credendi* is a shortened form of *ut legem credendi statuat lex supplicandi*. For the genesis and development of the expression and its development see Irwin, *Context and Text*, 1-43. Today, it is even added with *lex agendi*. Kevin Irwin, "Liturgical Theology," *The New Dictionary of Sacramental Worship*, ed. Peter E. Fink (Collegeville, MN: Liturgical Press, 1990) 721-733, p. 725.

75. Irwin, *Context and Text*, 4.

76. Schmemann, "Theology and Liturgical Tradition," 12.

77. Alexander Schmemann, "Liturgy and Theology," *Liturgy and Tradition: Theological Reflections of Alexander Schmemann*, ed. Thomas Fisch (Crestwood, NY: St. Vladimir's Seminary Press, 1990) 49-68, p. 55.

78. Schmemann, "Theology and Liturgical Tradition," 18. It does not mean that liturgy was the only source of theology. Along with liturgy Irwin lists, the use of Scripture, the teaching of other Fathers and neo-Platonism, as *locus theologicus* of the Fathers. Irwin, *Context and Text*, 15. In the Septuagint, "the term leitourgia had taken on a technical

There is an organic connection between theological thought and the liturgical experience of the Fathers.[79] It is well expressed in the words of Irenaeus: "our opinion is in accordance with the Eucharist and the Eucharist in turn establishes our opinion."[80] For them, faith as experience constitutes the source and the context of theology. It is the "description" of their experience in the Church and search for words and concepts adequate to express this experience.[81] The Fathers considered Christianity as "totally unique and *sui generis* experience of the Church."[82] In this sense Schmemann is right to say that theology is the expression and "conscience of the Church."[83] Though, for the Fathers, 'liturgical symbolism' has the key to liturgical studies and to its entire epistemology,[84] they were reluctant in adopting a rational approach to it.

As already stated, the situation changed in the medieval period. Even the term *leiturgia* became foreign to theologians like Aquinas.[85] Even so,

sense indicating Levitical worship; thus the dichotomy between spiritual worship and ritual worship is underlined, differing from the original notion that the spiritual component was intrinsic to worship. The New Testament generally leaves out this technical term and recovers the understanding of worship along spiritual lines, the most genuine line of the prophetic tradition." Alceste Catella, "Theology of the Liturgy," *Handbook for Liturgical Studies.* Vol. II, 3-28, p. 4. Similarly Schmemann notes that the Greek word '*leitourgia*' originally had no cultic connotation. It meant a public office, a service performed on behalf of a community and for its benefit. It acquired a religious meaning in the Septuagint but not necessarily a 'liturgical' one. "It implied the same idea of service, applied now to the chosen people of God whose specific 'leitourgia' is to fulfil God's design in history, to prepare the 'way of the Lord'. The early Christian use reflected the same meaning of 'leitourgia'. The fact that the Church adopted it finally for her cult, and especially for the Eucharist, indicates her special understanding of worship which is indeed a revolutionary one. If Christian worship is 'leitourgia' it cannot be simply reduced to, or expressed in, terms of 'cult'." Schmemann, "Theology and Eucharist," 17.

79. Schmemann, "Theology and Liturgical Tradition," 12.

80. *Adversus Haereses* 4.18.5, *PG* 7.

81. Schmemann, "Liturgy and Theology," 54.

82. Alexander Schmemann, "The Underlying Question," *Church, World, Mission: Reflections on Orthodoxy in the West*, ed. Alexander Schmemann (Crestwood, NY: St. Vladimir's Seminary Press, 1979) 7-24, p. 20. For him, experience as unique and *sui generis* means that the experience cannot be reduced to thc categories of the "subjective" and "objective," "individual" and "corporate." It is the experience of the Church as a new reality in terms of "creation and life renewed and transformed in Christ, made into the knowledge of and communion with God and His eternal Kingdom." In this sense "the 'alienation' of theology from the *real* Church and her *real* life always begins with its divorce from the experience of the Church." Schmemann, "The Underlying Question," 20-21.

83. Schmemann, "Theology and Eucharist," 11.

84. Crispino Valenziano, "Liturgy and Symbolism," *Handbook for Liturgical Studies.* Vol. II, 29-44, p. 29.

85. It was absent mainly because of the fact that "this Greek-inspired term had

Aquinas considered liturgy "as one of the *auctoritates* for theology alongside Scripture and Aristotelian philosophy."[86] Although Aquinas regarded liturgy as one of the Church's *auctoritates*, he never considered it as a *locus theologicus*."[87] The patristic approach to theology, based on liturgy, was replaced with a rational approach in scholastic theology.

> [In scholasticism theology had] an independent, rational status; it is a search for a system of consistent categories and concepts: *intellectus fidei*. The position of worship in relation to theology is reversed: from a *source* it becomes an *object*, which has to be defined and evaluated within the accepted categories (e.g. definitions of sacraments). Liturgy supplies theology with 'data', but the method of dealing with these data is independent of any liturgical context.[88]

Scholastic theology made a distinction between liturgy and theology. For them, the sources of theology – Scripture, Fathers, Councils – as *loci theologici*, were to supply the subject matter and criteria for theological speculation. In their effort to construct an objective, or scientific theology, they looked for an objective and clearly defined foundation. Hence, they identified faith in theological terms, with propositions; by doing this, they rejected any reference to the human dependence upon experience.[89] It was mainly because of the strange 'indifference' of scholastic theology that it failed to grasp the "Church as the Body of Christ, the idea of theandric nature and life." Instead, the Church came to be considered as the society of believers.[90]

This "scholastic form of theology" still continues in the West and, in a certain sense, also in the East.[91] In the Catholic Church, this state of af-

dropped out of common usage and was only reappropriated in the second half of the sixteenth century." Irwin, *Context and Text*, 11. At the same time he notes that although medieval theologians gave lesser importance to the sacramental rites as they were preoccupied with a systematization of sacraments compared to the patristic era, "the sacramental practices of the day continued to play an important role in the medieval understanding of the sacraments. The *lex orandi* was not absent; it was understood in a different way." Irwin, *Context and Text*, 14. See also Liam G. Walsh, "Liturgy in the Theology of St. Thomas," *The Thomist* 38 (1974) 557-583.

86. Irwin, *Context and Text*, 15.

87. *Ibid.*, 11.

88. Schmemann, "Theology and Liturgical Tradition," 13.

89. Schmemann, "Liturgy and Theology," 53-54.

90. Schmemann, "Liturgical Theology: Its Task and Method," 18.

91. According to Schmemann "in the East the Byzantine theology (with the possible exception of the 'hesychast' movement), the school of Kiev in the sixteenth-seventeenth centuries, Russian 'academic' theology, contemporary Greece, etc. – has been almost totally ignored, the liturgical tradition even as *locus theologicus.* Liturgy and theology have peacefully co-existed – the former in its traditional form, the latter as a sacred sci-

fairs continued until the nineteenth century. It was, however, the liturgical movement that made the "first attempt to break the scholastic monopoly, to restore to liturgical tradition its own theological status."[92]

1.2.2. Liturgical and Sacramental Celebrations as Locus Theologicus

The retrieval of the Patristic tradition of expressing theology through the liturgical and sacramental celebrations was one of the main concerns of the renewal theologians. The historical study of worship, the revival of ecclesiology and the liturgical movement have made liturgical theology a vital source for both liturgics and theology.[93]

The historical interest of the pioneer liturgical movements was the first step towards the rediscovery of liturgy's theological importance. It began with the awakening of historico-archaeological interest in worship that already began in the seventeenth century. Isaac Hubert and Jacques Goar were the pioneers who established a basis for historical leiturgiology, upon which it was further developed.[94] Later the neo-Gallican liturgy which arose in France in the spirit of enlightenment and against the baroque, created interest to return to the original status of liturgical pluralism.[95] Liturgical renewal of this period was mainly interested in the historical study of the growth of 'liturgics'. Later as the study progressed it has turned to be a true theological discipline.[96] As Schmemann clarifies:

ence – with no attempt made to correlate their respective languages." However in the West though it was not a peaceful co-existence, there was a direct impact of theological speculation (medieval, post-tridentine) on the very forms of liturgical life. See Schmemann, "Theology and Liturgical Tradition," 13.

92. Schmemann, "Liturgical Theology: Its Task and Method," 19.

93. *Ibid.*, 19.

94. *Ibid.*, 17. With the emergence of the liturgical movement historical interest in liturgy took new shapes. Especially the writings of theologians like Guéranger are very important in this regard. Schmemann also notes a similar trend of historical interest in the liturgical studies in Russian theology too.

95. For a concise history of the historical development of the various efforts for liturgical renewal beginning from the Council of Trent to the Second Vatican Council see Jozef Lamberts, "Active Participation as the Gateway towards an Ecclesial Liturgy," *Omnes Circumadstantes*, ed. C. Caspers & M. Schneiders (Kampen: Kok, 1990) 234-261, pp. 234-251.

96. Schmemann, "Liturgical Theology: Its Task and Method," 17. According to him:, "[T]he liturgical movement, whose 'golden age' occurred from 1920 to 1950, conferred upon the study of the liturgy (liturgical studies) a theological status which it had never commanded previously within the system of the sacred sciences, as this system developed and crystallised after the end of the patristic age, first in the West and then – under western influence – in the East." Schmemann, "Liturgical Theology: Remarks on Method," 137.

> [I]t was the *historical* rediscovery of the liturgy ... which made possible the liturgy's *theological* rediscovery. In truth, it is the historians of the liturgy who ... have helped us to discover this *specificity* of the liturgy which makes it the source of a *sui generis* theology, a theology of which the liturgy is both the unique source and the unique revelation.[97]

Secondly, the ecclesial revival also contributed to the theological rediscovery of liturgical experience. The ecclesial revival helped many Christians to realize their responsibility to the Church and to the world. In other words, it helped them to rediscover the true significance of *ecclesia.* Influenced by the ecclesial revival the liturgical movement focused on the rediscovery of *leiturgia* in its relation to the Church. Thus the liturgical movement tried to emphasize liturgy as "the *expression* of the Church, as the act which actualizes and fulfils the Church – 'makes her what she is'." In Schmemann's words:

> [The achievement of the liturgical movement] was a return from the pietistic and individualistic conception of worship to its understanding as the self-revelation of the Church. It was a return – through the 'leitourgia' – to the Church, and through the Church to the 'leitourgia'. Once again the truly Catholic experience of the 'leitourgia' as being the fulfilment of the 'laos' of God, the fulfilment of the Church as the Body of Christ, became central and gave the liturgical movement its dynamism and its 'philosophy'.[98]

The understanding of liturgical theology as the expression of the Church in the experience of the *leitourgia*, opened a new mode of doing theology. It is the study of the theological meaning of divine worship.[99]

Since the origin of the liturgical movement by Beauduin, the main objective of the liturgical movement was the theological renewal of the Church.[100] He continued the liturgical revival of Guéranger and contributed to the theological rediscovery of the sacramental nature of the Church.[101] For Lambert Beauduin ecclesiology is "the essential foundation for the theology of liturgy."[102] Guardini besides continuing the ecclesial perspective of the liturgy of Beauduin added a Christological perspective to it.[103]

The theological rediscovery of liturgy has made strong impact on the whole of theology. As Levesque notes "the liturgical shaping of theology

97. Schmemann, "Liturgical Theology: Remarks on Method," 142.
98. Schmemann, "Liturgical Theology: Its Task and Method," 18-19.
99. *Ibid.*, 20.
100. Fisch, "Schmemann's Theological Contribution," 2.
101. Lamberts, "Active Participation," 242.
102. Irwin, *Context and Text*, 20.
103. *Ibid.*, 20-21.

and the theological shaping of liturgy raise fundamental methodological issues."[104] For example, a theologian like Schmemann argued that the liturgical movement's "fundamental presupposition is that the liturgy not only has a theological meaning and is declarative of faith, but that it is the living norm of theology; it is in the liturgy that the sources of faith – the Bible and tradition – become a living reality."[105] For him, "theology, indeed, ought to be 'liturgical', yet not in the sense of having liturgy as its unique 'object' of study, but in that of having its ultimate term of reference in the faith of the Church as manifested and communicated in the liturgy."[106] Schmemann is critical about the use of liturgy merely as the source, or as the object, of liturgy. This only reduces theology to liturgy, which again results in the alienation of theology from liturgy. By using *leitourgia* as the *locus theologicus*, Schmemann means that liturgical experience is the first *datum* for theology.[107] For Aidan Kavanagh, "What emerges most directly from an assembly's liturgical act is not a new species of theology among others. It is *theologia* itself."[108] He calls this "primary theology."[109]

1.2.3. Sacramentology and Fundamental Theology

The sacraments as fundamental theology have found expression in many theologians of the post-Vatican period. It is generally accepted that liturgy as a source for sacramental theology belongs within the broader issue of the relationship between liturgy and theology. Liturgy "is often overlooked as a significant source of data in such areas of theology as the doctrine of God, Christology, ecclesiology, and Christian anthropology. Although one would expect to find it playing a prominent role in sacramental theology, this has often not been the case and theologians have had to argue for its inclusion as a source."[110] For example, "Karl Rahner wanted to give sacramentology a place of its own within theology as a

104. Levesque, "A Symbolical Sacramental Methodology," 174.

105. Schmemann, "Theology and Liturgical Tradition," 14.

106. Schmemann, "Liturgy and Theology," 61.

107. *Ibid.*, 63.

108. Aidan Kavanagh, *On Liturgical Theology* (New York: Pueblo, 1984) 75.

109. *Ibid.*, 89.

110. Margaret Mary Kelleher, "Liturgy as a Source for Sacramental Theology," *QL* 72 (1991) 25-42, p. 26. In her opinion this topic has received some attention in recent years. See for example, Teresa Berger, "Liturgy – a Forgotten Subject-matter of Theology?," *SL* 17 (1987) 10-18; Kavanagh, *On Liturgical Theology*; Geoffrey Wainwright, *Doxology: The Praise of God in Worship, Doctrine and Life* (New York: Oxford University Press, 1980).

whole."[111] Lambert Leijssen has well brought out Rahner's treatment of sacramentology at the crossroads of differing theological disciplines.[112]

David Power expresses the need for accepting liturgy as the foundation of Christology, ecclesiology and God-talk.[113] Power proposes that critical reflection in liturgical theology should include three elements: "(1) the development of a critical theory that would enable us to see the cultural and ideological factors that have influenced the shape of worship but which are not identifiable with its core, (2) attention to the connection that liturgy has with experience and praxis, and (3) the need to address issues raised by the liturgical acculturation called for at Vatican II."[114] According to Mary Collins, liturgical theology "is an integrative activity." In her opinion, "Liturgy has Trinitarian and Christological, Pneumatological and anthropological, ecclesiological and eschatological components."[115] Paul J. Levesque gives an excellent survey of some of the contemporary theologians' efforts for a comprehensive approach to theology based on the liturgical theology.[116]

Jeremy Driscoll presents a possible dialogue between liturgical theology and fundamental theology. Examining various themes in the thought of S. Marsili, R. Fisichella, G. Lafont, and H. U. von Balthasar, Driscoll argues that fundamental theology could profit from more systematic attention to the liturgy. In the same vein he notes that the work of fundamental theology could sharpen and deepen the theological dimensions of the work of liturgical scholars.[117] He demonstrates this point further by focussing on the Eucharist and seeing what is offered therein for advancing the work of fundamental theology. At the same time, he also notes that categories and themes from fundamental theology can help to deepen a theological grasp of the eucharistic ministry.[118] In another study, he focuses on two particular dimensions of a liturgical celebration; anamne-

111. Leijssen, "Rahner's Contribution to the Renewal of Sacramentology," 203.

112. Leijssen has demonstrated seven fundamental theological disciplines to which Rahner's sacramental theology is connected. See "Rahner's Contribution," 203-207.

113. Power, "Cult to Culture," 482-495.

114. Power, *Worship: Culture and Theology*, 10-11.

115. Mary Collins, "Critical Questions for Liturgical Theology," *Worship* 53 (1979) 302-317, p. 302.

116. Levesque, "A Symbolical Sacramental Methodology," 173-177.

117. Jeremy Driscoll, "Liturgy and Fundamental Theology: Frameworks for a Dialogue," *EO* 11 (1994) 69-99.

118. Jeremy Driscoll, "The Eucharist and Fundamental Theology," *EO* 13 (1996) 407-437.

sis and epiclesis. He tries to see their specific contribution for fundamental theology.[119]

Finally, we see the post-modern sacramentologists' stress on the need to look at the sacraments as fundamental theology. For example, Chauvet "intends his work to be not only a theology of sacraments in the traditional sense, but a symbolic theology of the whole order of salvation, looked at from within sacramental practice."[120] According to Jozef Lamberts, Chauvet presents "'the symbolic structure' of Christian belief with its three elements of word, sacraments and ethics."[121]

Albert Houssiau notes that even though the "liturgical Tradition had the status of a *locus theologicus* but, just like Scripture and Patristic writings, its only use was to determine the *an sit*, and not the *quid sit* of the various truths one had to believe."[122] On the other hand, today, there are a number of theologians who offer an integral approach to theology. For example, Gordon W. Lathrop points to three specific areas of theology: primary theology, secondary theology and pastoral theology.[123] Any study on sacraments needs to consider these three dimensions of liturgical theology. Aidan Kavanagh calls the first *theologia prima* and the second *theologia secunda* and argues for a synthesis in pastoral theology[124] Kevin Irwin also notes the efforts of contemporary liturgical theologians "to expand the *lex orandi*, *lex credendi* equation to include a third, viz., *lex agendi*."[125] For Irwin the "*lex credendi* does not mean repetition of what was done or said in the past; it means the true *reappropriation* in order that their core meaning be expressed and developed to suit contemporary needs."[126] Above all, these dimensions open the possibility for an ecumenical liturgical theology.[127]

119. Jeremy Driscoll, "Anamnesis, Epiclesis and Fundamental Theology," *EO* 15 (1998) 211-238.

120. Power, et al., "Sacramental Theology: A Review of Literature," 684-685.

121. Lamberts, "Contemporary Fccling and Liturgy," 133. Scc also Dcpoortcrc, "From Sacramentality to Sacraments and Vice-versa," 57-58.

122. Houssiau, "The Rediscovery of the Liturgy by Sacramental Theology (1950-1980)," 159. See also Id., "La liturgie, lieu privilégié de la théologie sacramentaire," 7-12.

123. Gordon W. Lathrop defines primary theology as "the communal meaning of the liturgy exercised by the gathering itself." For him secondary liturgical theology "is written and spoken discourse that attempts to find words for the experience of the liturgy and to illuminate its structures, intending to enable a more profound participation of those structures by the members of the assembly." And he calls its "reflections on the specific problems of our time," pastoral liturgical theology. See Gordon W. Lathrop, *Holy Things: A Liturgical Theology* (Minneapolis, MN: Fortress, 1993) 4-8.

124. Kavanagh, *On Liturgical Theology*, 74-77.

125. Irwin, "Liturgical Theology," 725.

126. Irwin, "Liturgical Actio: Sacramentality, Eschatology and Ecology," 112.

127. Lathrop, *Holy Things*, 4; Kavanagh, *On Liturgical Theology*, 78.

In short, sacramento-liturgical theology opens a new hermeneutical awareness for doing theology, combining both the experiential and rational dimensions. Though liturgical approaches were often criticized as mystical and outdated, we see that today the trend is to be engaged in a critical dialogue, while considering the needs of the time and changing cultures. The symbolic nature of liturgy was rediscovered behind the retrieval of the interrelation between liturgy and theology. Liturgy itself is acknowledged as a symbol, where the divine-human encounter is taking place. Keeping this renewed understanding of liturgy itself as symbol; we shall look for the meaning of symbol and sacrament.

1.3. Symbol and Sacrament

The symbolic character of sacrament is another important theme that has received attention in the contemporary study of sacraments. It has been subjected to manifold changes. This does not mean however, that the symbolic interpretation of liturgy and sacraments was previously absent in the theological discourse, only that the meaning it had acquired was changing. Unlike other areas under discussion, one can observe the changing views of symbolism already in the Patristic corpus.

1.3.1. Sacramental Symbolism

Symbol was understood as the essential dimension of the sacrament from the very beginning of early Christian worship. It was understood as a "means of knowledge of that which cannot be known otherwise," and this knowledge results from participation. It is "the living encounter with and entrance to that 'epiphany' of reality which the symbol is."[128] This encounter takes place within liturgy. As Schmemann observes:

> the entire liturgy is the symbol of the mystery of Christ's ascension and glorification, as well as of the mystery of the Kingdom of God, 'the world to come'. Through its symbols the liturgy gives us the *theoria*: the knowledge and the contemplation of these saving mysteries, just as, on another level of the same symbolism, the liturgy represents, makes present and active, the ascension of the human soul to God and communion with Him.[129]

128. Schmemann, "Sacrament and Symbol," 141. Elsewhere he notes, "It is impossible to explain and define the symbol. It is realized or 'actualized' in its *own* reality through its transformation into that to which it points and witnesses, of which it is a symbol." Schmemann, *The Eucharist*, 222.

129. Alexander Schmemann, "Symbols and Symbolism in the Byzantine Liturgy: Liturgical Symbols and Their Theological Interpretation," *Liturgy and Tradition: Theological Reflections of Alexander Schmemann*, ed. Thomas Fisch (Crestwood, NY: St. Vladimir's Seminary Press, 1990) 115-128, p. 123.

Sacrament is a means for the Fathers to understand God by a synthesis of holding together, on the one hand, the absolute 'otherness' of God, i.e., knowledge of God, and, on the other hand, the reality of man's communion with God, i.e., *theosis*. This synthesis is possible only through the "idea or rather intuition of the 'mysterion' and of its mode of presence and operation – the symbol."[130] Sacramental symbolism reveals the transcendence and immanence of God alike. This more dynamic understanding of sacrament, however, slowly disintegrated with the changing notions of symbolism. Schmemann convincingly presents this change in the patristic period through a threefold form of symbolism: eschatological, mystagogical and illustrative.[131]

The disintegration of symbol and reality goes back to the changes that already took place in Augustine. He used *sacramentum* and *mysterium* without a proper distinction. Unlike the Greek patristic term, *mysterion*, which depends upon a play of *hidden* and *manifest*, albeit emphasizing the *hidden*, Augustine's *sacramentum*, *mysterium*, *figura*, and other related words have an *obscure meaning*. That is for him sacraments are signs, and his emphasis is on understanding them. Thus, under the influence of Platonic and neo-Platonic philosophy, he taught that the sacrament is a visible sign of a sacred thing, or a visible form of an invisible grace.[132]

This shift was deepened with Isidore. He used both the Greek patristic *mysterion* and the Augustinian *sacramentum*. For example, in his treatment of the Paschal cycle he follows Augustine's argument "of both *recalling to memory* the death and resurrection of Christ, and *considering the meaning of "sacraments"* (the multiple symbolism). Yet in one of his formulae, which was destined to survive from the same context, he gives a definition which does not contain the notion of sign, which gives a bewildering example of a sacrament, and which shifts the emphasis to hidden." Isidore made a significant change in the use of Augustine's formulae: *rei gestae commemoratio* (the commemoration of an event) to *res gesta* (an event). According to Van Roo, in the Isidorean formulae: "One suspects that the *res gesta* is not the past event, but the action of the liturgical celebration. In any case, the explicit mention of commemoration is gone."[133]

The disintegration of symbol and reality reached its culmination with the eucharistic controversy that happened in the ninth and eleventh centu-

130. Schmemann, "Sacrament and Symbol," 141.

131. Since our third chapter is devoted to the writings of Schmemann, we shall deal with this in detail there.

132. Van Roo, *The Christian Sacrament*, 39.

133. *Ibid.*, 43-44.

ries.[134] Following the Isidorean conception, Paschasius Radbertus and Ratramnus upheld the connection between sign and reality. The main concern of Radbertus was to maintain the identity between the eucharistic body and the historical body of Jesus Christ, which was born from the Virgin Mary, as well as the identity of the blood in the Eucharist with the blood that flowed from the Cross. Ratramnus, on the other hand, distinguished between "the glorified state of Christ's body, which made it different from the way in which he had lived and suffered on earth, and of the figural or sacramental manner of his presence in the sacrament."[135]

The controversy took a new turn in the eleventh century with Berengar and Lanfranc who maintained a basic distinction between sign and reality.[136] Berengar used the Augustinean formulae, which was contrary to the Isidorean conception that had been popular during the previous four centuries. Berengar taught that because the presence of Christ in the eucharistic element is "mystical" or "symbolic," it is not *real.* The Lateran Council condemned him and proclaimed that since Christ's presence in the Eucharist is *real*, it is not "mystical."[137] What is truly important here is precisely the disconnection, and the opposition between the two terms *verum* and *mystice.* Furthermore there is an acceptance, on both sides, that they are mutually exclusive. This declaration became decisive and meant that that which is mystical, or symbolic, is not real, whereas that which is real is not symbolic. The latter on declaration, in fact, signaled the collapse of the fundamental Christian *Mysterion*, the

134. It was mainly due to the empirical outlook prevalent in that period. Thus Frank Senn notes, "The Gothic Age operated with an empirical outlook on the world that was interested in seeing reality. There is a correlation between the desire to see the sacrament of the altar, which led to practices of eucharistic reservation and exposition and the retrieval of Aristotle and the development of natural sciences at the same time in Western society. This empirical approach to reality had a profound affect on the theology of as well as practices associated with the doctrine of the real presence of Christ in the Eucharist ... in the world of late antiquity and in the early Middle Ages, people lived 'not in a world of visible facts but rather in a world of symbols'. The symbolic pointed to and participated in the unseen spiritual reality, but in the world-view of the Western Middle Ages, there was a desire to see reality." Frank C. Senn, *Christian Liturgy: Catholic and Evangelical* (Minneapolis, MN: Fortress, 1997) 240-241.

135. David N. Power, *The Eucharistic Mystery: Revitalizing the Tradition* (New York: Crossroad, 1992) 210. Though Ratramnus wanted to hold together the unity of "the historical body of Christ in heaven and the 'figurative' body of Christ in the sacrament, ... the world-view of his time saw a difference between *figura* and *veritas* ... The unseen spiritual reality was precisely what the medieval world-view increasingly resisted." Senn, *Christian Liturgy*, 249.

136. See Patricia McCormik Zirkel, "The Ninth-Century Eucharistic Context for the Beginnings of Eucharistic Doctrine in the West," *Worship* 68 (1994) 2-23.

137. Lanfrancus, *De Corpore et Sanguine Domini*, *PL* 150, 410 D.

antinomical holding together of the reality of the symbol, and of the symbolism of reality.[138] In other words, following their arguments, later theologians accepted sacraments in terms of either *signum* or *res*, instead of both *signum* and *res*.

In short, the question raised regarding the reality of sacramental symbols was started from the very beginning of the patristic period. These questions were broadened under various philosophical influences and the rational approach that was prevalent in the medieval period. The retrieval of precisely the reality of sacramental symbolism was one of the main concerns of renewal movements of the later period.

1.3.2. Sacrament as Mysterion

The liturgical movement has contributed a great deal in the rediscovery of sacramental symbolism. Influenced by phenomenology, the comparative school in the history of religions argued that Christianity was from the very outset born as a mysteriological religion. For them, the parallel between Christianity and pagan religions indicates the origin of Christianity as a mystery cult. But Biblical researchers, with their scientific study of the Jewish roots of the Christian cult and exegetical study of the New Testament, especially the Pauline use of the term 'mystery', denied any genetic connection between the Christian cult and the pagan mysteries.[139] The patristic studies of the period also contributed to this rebuttal.[140]

In this context, Dom Odo Casel came out with a synthesis between these two opposing views that demonstrated the connection between Christianity and the mystery religions.[141] Casel reversed the arguments

138. Alexander Schmemann, "Worship In a Secular Age," *SVTQ* 16 (1972) 3-16, pp. 11-12. Id., "Sacrament and Symbol," 143.

139. Gunthcr Bornkamm, "μυστήριον, μυέω," *Theological Dictionary of the New Testament*, ed. Gerhard Kittel, trans. & ed. Geoffrey W. Bromiley, vol. IV (Grand Rapids, MI: Eerdmans, 1967) 802-828, pp. 820-824; Raymond E. Brown, "The Semitic Background of the New Testament Mysterion," *Biblica* 39 (1958) 426-448; 40 (1958) 70-87; Id.., "The Pre-Christian Semitic Concept of 'Mystery'," *CBQ* 20 (1958) 417-443.

140. H. G. Marsh, "The Use of *mysterion* in the Writings of Clement of Alexandria with Special Reference to His Sacramental Doctrine," *JTS* 37 (1936) 64-80, pp. 75-80. Hans Urs von Balthasar, "Le mystère d'Origène," *Recherches de science religieuse* 26 (1937) 38-64. Gerard Fittkau, *Der Begriff des Mysteriums bei Johannes Chrysostomus* (Bonn: Hanstein, 1953).

141. See L. M. McMahon, "Towards a Theology of the Liturgy: Dom Odo Casel and the 'Mysterientheorie'," *SL* 3 (1964) 129-154, pp. 146-147. Burkhard Neunheuser, "Mystery Theology," *Sacramentum Mundi*, ed. Karl Rahner, gen. ed. Adolf Darlap (New York: Herder and Herder, 1970) 385-387, p. 385; See also: Id., "Odo Casel in Retrospect and Prospect," *Worship* 50 (1976) 489-504, p. 490; Id., "The Mystery Presence: Dom Odo

from the school of comparative religion and met their challenges, by appropriating their arguments to show that pagan antiquity was a preparation for the Gospel, the *Vorschule Christi*. He defined mystery as, "a sacred ritual action in which a saving deed is made present through the rite; the congregation, by performing the rite, takes part in the saving act, and thereby wins salvation."[142] In this sense he argued that, "Christianity is of its very essence a mystery religion."[143]

In the mystery approach, liturgy is considered as "*the* way to actively participate in the sacramental mystery." In the opinion of Casel, "one has to reintegrate the essential rite within the celebration as a whole, not only in the practice but also in the theoretical reflection."[144] The main contribution of Casel was that he moved "the focus in eucharistic theology away from the presence of Jesus' body and blood to the presence of the redemptive action itself."[145] It means that the "historical events can only be rendered present again through the sacramental mode of existence which can only be understood in faith."[146] The mystery theologians use mystery to consider that which "refers first of all to God himself as he exists in himself and in the things that he has made. Secondly, it refers to Christ, not just the person of Christ but Christ performing his salvific actions, especially his death, resurrection and ascension. Thirdly, mystery means the saving activity of Christ in the Church and in the sacra-

Casel and the Latest Research," *The Downside Review* 76 (1958) 266-273, p. 267; Id., "Masters in Israel: V. Odo Casel," *The Clergy Review* 55 (1970) 194-212, p. 199; Arno Schilson, *Theologie als Sakramententheologie: Die Mysterientheologie Odo Casels* (Mainz: Matthias-Grünewald-Verlag, 1982).

142. "Das Mysterium ist eine heilige kultische Handlung, in der eine Heilstatsache unter dem Ritus Gegenwart wird; indem die Kultgemeinde diesen Ritus vollzieht, nimmt sie an der Hellstat teil und erwirbt sich dadurch das Heil." Odo Casel, *Das christliche Kultmysterium* (Regensburg, Pustet, 1960) 79.

143. Odo Casel writes, "Das Christusmysterium, das sich an unserm Herrn in voller, geschichtlicher und wesenhafter Wahrheit vollzug, wird also an uns zunächst in bildlichen, symbolischen Formen vollzogen, die aber nicht rein äussere Bilder sind, sondern von der wirklichkeit des neuen, durch Christus uns vermittelten Lebens erfüllt sind. Diese eigentümliche Teilnahme am Leben Christi, die einesteils symbolisch anderenteils wirklich ist, nennen die Alten 'Mystisch'." Casel, *Das christliche Kultmysterium*, 34.

144. Houssiau, "The Rediscovery of the Liturgy by Sacramental Theology (1950-1980)," 161. Odo Casel, *The Mystery of Christian Worship and Other Writings*, ed. Burkhard Neunheuser (Westminster, MD: Newman, 1962) 38-49.

145. James L. Empereur, "Models for a Liturgical Theology," *The Sacraments: Readings in Contemporary Sacramental Theology*, ed. Michael J. Taylor (New York: Alba House, 1981) 53-70, p. 59.

146. Empereur, "Models for a Liturgical Theology," 60. Empereur criticizes Odo Casel for not explaining metaphysically how the mystery of Christ is sacramentally present in the liturgy.

ments."[147] Caselian retrieval of mystery theology played an important role in the later development of sacramentology.

The existentialists and phenomenologists broadened the understanding of symbols. Along with Odo Casel, theologians like Edward Schillebeeckx, Karl Rahner, Bernard Bro, Louis Bouyer, etc., stressed the importance of the sign-activity of Christian worship. Their main task was "to explain how the sign activity and the efficacious causality of the sacraments are to be theoretically coordinated."[148] At the same time, David Power notes: "No liturgist who has in any way been subject to the influence of Casel's theology of *Mysteriengegenwart* could be fully satisfied with this common explanation." For example, among others Anscar Vonier and Canon Eugène Masure "applied the sacramental principle, *sacramenta causant quod significant*, to the presence of Christ's mysteries, and so opted for a sacramental or symbolic mode of presence which is more than that of mere figure or representation."[149]

1.3.3. Widening Views on Sacramental Symbolism

In the aftermath of Second Vatican Council, one can observe an important turning point in the study of sacramental symbols. The theologians started using interdisciplinary methods to broaden the understanding of symbols. For example, Power underscores the need of sociology, anthropology and psychology in interpreting the meaning of symbols in worship.[150]

The question of presence and causality is also influenced by language studies. Jean Ladrière uses the distinction between constative and performative language to explain the action of the sacraments.[151] Appleyard

147. Empereur, "Models for a Liturgical Theology," 59.

148. David N. Power, "Theological Trends: Symbolism in Worship: A Survey, I, II, III, IV," *The Way* 13 (1973) 310-313; 14 (1974) 57-66; 56-64; 15 (1975) 137-146, esp. I, 311-312. See Karl Rahner, *The Church and the Sacraments* (London: Burns & Oates, 1957); Edward Schillebeeckx, *Christ the Sacrament of Encounter with God* (London: Sheed and Ward, 1963).

149. Power, "Theological Trends: Symbolism in Worship," I, 311-312. See Anscar Vonier, *A Key to the Doctrine of the Eucharist* (London: Burns & Oates, 1952); Canon Eugène Masure, *The Sacrifice of the Mystical Body* (London: Burns & Oates, 1954). According to Power, this idea has been taken up chiefly in the discussion of memorial in eucharistic theology, yet it still remains to give a clear explanation of what constitutes a symbolic mode of presence." *Ibid.*

150. The methodological importance of symbol in liturgical theology reaches its pinnacle for him in his book *Unsearchable Riches: The Symbolic Nature of Liturgy* (New York: Pueblo, 1984). See also Power, *The Eucharistic Mystery*, 320-324. Id., "Theological Trends: Symbolism in Worship."

151. Jean Ladrière, "The Language of Worship: The Performative of Liturgical Lan-

criticizes the classical theories of sacramental causality seen in Augustine and in Aquinas. In particular he criticized them for removing sacraments as the central expression of the community's life and to explain it as a means for individuals to acquire grace.[152] Instead, based on Susan Langer's symbol theory, J. L. Austin's performatives and Karl Rahner, he explains the operation of sacraments in terms of signification.[153] Along with Suzanne Langer, Mary Collins suggests the works of Clifford Geertz and Gregory Bateson, for the application of cultural anthropological and philosophical studies of ritual to liturgical theology.[154] Paul J. Levesque also notes that "Liturgical theology interacts with the general discipline of theology as well as receiving inspiration from the social sciences."[155]

Recently there has been a growing effort to study the 'symbolic non-verbal and non-literary elements of liturgy'.[156] For example, Gerard Lukken, criticizes the liturgical studies that focus on literary sources and discarding non-verbal dimensions such as art, architecture, arrangement of people in a space, music etc.[157] He even argues that the actual celebration of a liturgical event is the primary source for liturgical theology. He also calls our attention to other disciplines to explore the multifaceted reality of liturgy. In particular, he employs semiotics for the study of verbal, literary and non-verbal sources.[158]

guage," *Concilium* 9/2 (1973) 50-62; Id., *Language and Belief* (Dublin: Gill & Macmillan, 1972).

152. J. A. Appleyard, "How Does a Sacrament Cause by Signifying?," *Science et Esprit* 23 (1971) 167-200, pp. 167-168.

153. *Ibid.*, 191-200.

154. Mary Collins, "Liturgical Methodology and the Cultural Evolution of Worship in the United States," *Worship* 49 (1975) 85-102.

155. Levesque, "A Symbolical Sacramental Methodology," 175.

156. Gerard Lukken, "Plaidoyer pour une approche intégrale de la liturgie comme lieu théologique: un défi à toute la théologie," *QL* 68 (1987) 242-255; see *Per visibilia ad invisibilia: Anthropological, Theological, and Semiotic Studies on the Liturgy and Sacraments*, Liturgia Condenda, 2, ed. Louis van Tongeren & Charles Caspers (Kampen: Kok Pharos, 1994). For a concise study of Gerard Lukken see Irwin, *Liturgical Theology*, 29-31.

157. See Lukken, "Plaidoyer," 245-246. See also Id., "La liturgie comme lieu théologique irremplaçable," *QL* 56 (1975) 97-112.

158. Lukken, "Plaidoyer," 247-254; see also "Semiotics and the Study of Liturgy," *SL* 17 (1987) 108-117; "Die Architektonischen Dimensionen des Rituals," *LJ* 39 (1989) 19-36; "Liturgy and Language: An Approach from Semiotics," *Liturgy and Language: A Tribute to Silveer De Smet*, ed. Lambert Leijssen, Textes et études liturgiques / Studies in Liturgy, 12 (Leuven: Abdij Keizersberg/Faculteit der Godgeleerdheid, 1992) 36-52. He develops this mainly using the semiotic theory of A. J. Greimas. In recent years there is a growing interest in the use of semiotics in sacraments. For a concise view on the use of semiotics in the study of sacraments see, Michael Amaladoss, "Semiotics and Sacraments," *ITS* 16/17 (1979) 32-54. Gerard Lukken, "Semiotics of the Ritual: Signification

Garth Gillan uses the philosophy of language in order to understand the symbolic meaning of language in the celebration of sacraments.[159] For him the idea of the symbol is a word for the other.[160] He explains the word and gesture in the liturgy as expressions of intersubjectivity. For him, to speak and to act in the liturgy is 'celebrations of our co-humanity'.[161] In his opinion, in order to make liturgy "the expression of living symbols it is necessary to create a space of co-existence and a time of a common present which are dimensions of a festival of our co-humanity."[162] Timothy Crutcher goes further and notes the importance of 'relational thinking' arising from one's experience of God in Christ and the 'relational vectors' of theological and sacramental language in Christian theology. He underscores the importance of religious language in building up relationships both with God and with fellow human beings. He develops this 'relational view of language' in sacramentology based on Catholic theologians like Colman O'Neil, Edward Schillebeeckx, Louis-Marie Chauvet, Orthodox theologian Alexander Schmemann and Protestant theologian Jean Calvin.[163]

There were also some efforts to the psychological realm of symbols. For example, Louis Beirnaert uses psychology (some application of Jungian psychology) to explain sacramental rites and the use of symbolism in literature and arts.[164] Anton Vergote calls attention to the deep psychological feelings of the faithful participating in liturgical and sacramental celebrations.[165] He goes further to underscore the interaction

in Rituals as a Specific Mediation of Meaning," & "Zur theologischen Rezeption der Semiotik von Greimas: Widerstände und Mißverständnisse," *Per visibilia ad invisibilia*, 269-298.

159. In particular he reviews the contributions of Edmund Husserl, Maurice Merleau-Ponty, Martin Heidegger, Emmanuel Levinas, and Paul Ricœur. Garth Gillan, "Expression, Discourse and Symbol," *Worship* 41 (1967) 16-31. The impact of philosophy in giving a new turn for sacramentology is of particular importance. For example, the philosophical trends like existentialism, phenomenology, process thought, Marxism, linguistics, semiotics, and postmodern philosophy contributed in developing various aspects of sacramentology. Kenan B. Osborne, *Christian Sacraments in a Postmodern World*, 15-16.

160. Garth Gillan, "Symbol: Word for the Other," *Worship* 41 (1967) 275-283.

161. *Ibid.*, 279.

162. *Ibid.*, 283.

163. Timothy James Crutcher, "Personally Speaking: Reflections on Relational Thinking for the Ecumenical Sacramentological Dialogue," *Contemporary Sacramental Contours of a God Incarnate*, 154-165.

164. Louis Beirnaert, *Expérience chrétienne et psychologie* (Paris: Éditions de L'EPI, 1964). See also Rollo May, *Symbolism in Religion and Literature* (New York: Braziller, 1960).

165. Anton Vergote, "Regard du psychologue sur le symbolisme liturgique," *La Maison-Dieu* 91 (1967) 129-151; Id., "The Vertical and Horizontal Dimensions in Symbolic Language about God," *Lumen Vitae* 25 (1970) 185-208.

between the symbolic gestures with "the real space-time of the concrete human environment."[166] In particular, he argues that "the liturgical gesture is the point of union between man, the world and God."[167] Among other things Eugene S. Kennedy focuses on the impact of symbolic rituals in human beings' self experience, their relations with God and with others.[168]

Louis Marie-Chauvet goes beyond the traditional understanding of sacraments to a symbolic theology of the whole order of salvation, looked at from within sacramental practice. He develops his position in opposition to scholastic theology with its categories informed by classical metaphysics, which were mainly based on Plato and Aristotle.[169] As Depoortere suggests in Chauvet "the symbolic has replaced the scholastic metaphysical approach characterized as onto-theological and employing the *causa-signum* theory."[170] Chauvet's criticism of classical metaphysics follows Heidegger's writings on metaphysics. Using a Heideggerian critique, Chauvet criticizes in particular the use of the notion of causality. According to Miller Chauvet's position "is not merely an alternative to scholastic metaphysics but an alternative to any closed, metaphysical system."[171] As an alternative to metaphysical explanations, Chauvet appeals to studies of language and ritual.[172]

Finally, having seen the inter-relation between liturgy and theology, sacramento-liturgical theology and fundamental theology and the symbolic dimension of sacramento-liturgical theology, we shall come to one of the main concerns of the very purpose of liturgical and sacramental celebrations, namely, the participation in the salvific will of God. Hence, we treat the importance of sacramental economy in the study of sacraments in the next section.

1.4. Sacramental Economy

The sacrament of salvation history, or sacramental economy, is one of the most important themes that were subjected to change in the history of the doctrinal development of sacramentology. As we shall see, various un-

166. Anton Vergote, "Symbolic Gestures and Actions in the Liturgy," *Concilium* 7/2 (1971) 40-52, p. 52.

167. *Ibid.*, 40.

168. Eugene C. Kennedy, "The Contribution of Religious Ritual to Psychological Balance," *Concilium* 7/2 (1971) 53-58.

169. Chauvet, *Symbol and Sacrament*, 22-29.

170. Depoortere, "From Sacramentality to Sacraments and Vice-versa," 55.

171. Vincent J. Miller, "An Abyss at the Heart of Mediation: Louis-Marie Chauvet's Fundamental Theology of Sacramentality," *Horizons* 24 (1997) 230-247, p. 233.

172. Power, et al., "Sacramental Theology: A Review of Literature," 685.

derstandings in sacramentology belong to the domain of the salvific will of God. Nevertheless, for various reasons, theologians emphasized certain aspects such as Christ and Church as *the* sacrament. God's salvific plan revealed from eternity is manifested in its fullness in Jesus and is continued in the Church. The sacramental liturgy is a celebration of this salvific plan of God. Our participation in it enables us to enter into communion with God, which the Eastern Fathers term as deification or *theosis*. This is possible only through a proper understanding of God's revelation and a genuine human response to it.

The 'economy', refers to "God's salvific relationship with creation and humanity, especially insofar as the persons of the Trinity act for salvation and are thus revealed or identified by their individual activities."[173] 'Economy' underscores the trinitarian basis of salvation and the universality of God's salvific will. The trinitarian foundation is so basic to the economy of salvation, that it is even called the 'mystery of the Trinity'. In the strict sense, 'sacramental economy' means the ways in which liturgical and sacramental life help us to enter into God's plan.[174] It is described in the *Catechism of the Catholic Church* as "the communication (or 'dispensation') of the fruits of Christ's paschal mystery in the celebration of Church's 'sacramental' liturgy."[175] In short, the theological term 'economy' "refers to the redemptive mysteries enacted in sacrament."[176]

1.4.1. Oikonomia*: Trinitarian, Christological, Pneumatological and Ecclesial*

Contemporary understanding of trinitarian theology centers around two themes: immanent and economic Trinity. The distinction between immanent and economic Trinity is very important to understand the being of God and God's communication to us.[177] The immanent Trinity denotes

173. Michael R. Barnes, "Oeconomia," *Encyclopaedia of Early Christianity*, ed. Everett Ferguson (New York/London: Garland Publishing, 1997) 825-826, p. 825.

174. Regis A. Duffy, "The Sacramental Economy: (Paragraphs 1066-1209)," *Commentary on the Catechism of the Catholic Church*, ed. Michael J. Walsh (London: Geoffrey Chapman, 1994) 225-241, p. 225.

175. *Catechism of the Catholic Church*, revised edition (London: Geoffrey Chapman, 1999) no. 1076.

176. David N. Power, "Sacrament: An Economy of Gift," *LS* 23 (1998) 143-158, p. 146.

177. Though these terms, immanent and economic trinity, are often in use by contemporary theologians, it was formerly understood as *theologia* and *oikonomia* respectively. For a detailed study on the development of both immanent Trinity and economic Trinity see Catherine Mowry LaCugna, *God for Us: The Trinity and Christian Life* (San Francisco, CA: Harper, 1991).

'being as communion', whilst economic Trinity denotes 'God's salvific plan with humankind'. The latter deals with God's communication of His salvific plan to humanity. This communication is made possible through symbols and shows how even God Himself was compelled to use a symbolic sacramental language to reveal to human beings.[178] This revelation took place in history in three phases: Creation, Incarnation and Church and her sacraments.[179] As Gerard Lukken puts it, the sacramental sacred history "begins with the history of Israel in the Old Testament, and reaches its high point in the New Testament in Jesus of Nazareth, and is continued in and through the sacramental form of the church, and particularly in a concentrated way in the liturgy."[180] In short, all the three: Creation, Christ and the Church and sacraments are revelations of God.[181] In various capacities these three are considered as *the* sacraments. Since we shall consider each of these themes in detail in the second part of this chapter, we shall limit our study in this section to the trinitarian foundation of the sacrament of salvation history. The divine economy, whose aim is "the salvation of humanity and the world, involves each person of the Holy Trinity."[182] It means God's salvific mission, which was communicated to us in Christ and culminated in the Holy Spirit, gives a strong trinitarian basis for Christian faith and its celebration. According to Gregory of Nyssa: "All activities which extend from God to creation are described by different names, in accordance with the different ways in which they are presented to our thought: but every such activity originates from the Father, proceeds from the Son, and is brought to fulfillment in the Holy Spirit."[183]

178. Vorgrimler makes this clear when he says: "God as 'Logos' needed a created form, a human expression, in order to be recognizable to human beings." Vorgrimler, *Sacramental Theology*, 17.

179. Based on the theology of the sacramental economy of salvation Vorgrimler gives a fourfold division of sacraments: creation and election as sacrament, Jesus Christ as primordial sacrament, Church as the fundamental sacrament and the individual sacraments as actualizing fulfillments of the fundamental sacrament. Vorgrimler, *Sacramental Theology*, 28.

180. Gerard Lukken, "Church and Liturgy as Dynamic Sacrament of the Spirit," *Per visibilia ad invisibilia*, 140-157, p. 140.

181. This is the pivotal point of our dissertation. In the post-Vatican era though Christ and the Church were acknowledged as sacraments, the sacramental nature of creation has not received proper attention. Gradually we shall bring this theme in focus.

182. Thomas FitzGerald, "The Holy Eucharist as Theophany," *GOTR* 28 (1983) 27-38, p. 28.

183. Gregory of Nyssa, "An Answer to Ablabios: That We Should Not Think of Saying Three are Three Gods," *PG* 45. 126.

God's self-communication began with Creation reached its climax in the incarnation of Jesus. It is in this sense that the theological term *oikonomia* becomes important. The New Testament employs the term *oikonomia* mainly to mean "God's arrangement of salvation through Jesus Christ."[184] It is "the self-communication of God in the person of Christ and the activity of the Holy Spirit."[185] The economy of Christ and the economy of Spirit are rooted in the triune nature of God and are clearly expressed in the liturgical and sacramental celebrations of the early Church.

The Arian controversies and other debates, which were focused on the nature of Jesus Christ, brought about a serious theological shift in the history of Christian doctrines. The most significant change could be seen in the separation of the intertwined reality of the immanent and economic Trinity as two separate doctrinal themes. This transition of immanent Trinity to economic Trinity was even seen in the official liturgical celebrations. Catherine Mowry LaCugna demonstrates this transition from immanent Trinity to economic Trinity in the early Christian liturgy. For example, she notes how "The doxologies that arose naturally out of the Christian experience of being saved by God through Jesus Christ, such as 'Glory to the Father through the Son in the Holy Spirit', were replaced by *homoousios*-structured doxologies, for example; 'Glory to the Father and the Son and the Holy Spirit'.[186]

It was a split between economy (*lex orandi*) and theology (*lex credendi*). During this period, and later with the Calcedonian formulation of Christology, 'economic Trinity' became the focal point in theological discussions.[187] In other words, while, the relation within Godhead in the

184. John Reumann, "The 'Righteousness of God' and the 'Economy of God': Two Great Doctrinal Themes Historically Compared," *Aksum Thyateria: A Festschrift for Archbishop Methodios of Thyateira and Great Britain,* ed. George Dion. Dragas (London: Thyateira House, 1985) 615-637, p. 632. Paul uses the term *mysterion* in the sense of "God's saving intent as revealed and realized in the course of divine *oikonomia.* Its complete revelation and first realization of God's saving intent happened in Jesus Christ (Eph 1:9-10; 2:11–3:13; Col 1:20, 26-27; 2:2; cf. also Rom 16:25-26)." Vorgrimler, *Sacramental Theology*, 31. At the same time we do not ignore the observation of some exegetes that "there is room for doubt whether *oikonomia* denotes office or the divine plan of salvation." Michel Otto, "οἰκονομία," *Theological Dictionary of the New Testament*, vol. V, trans Geoffrey W. Bromiley, ed. Gerhard Friedrich (Grand Rapids, MI: Eerdmans, 1968) 119-159, p. 152. But Meyendorff seems to be right to say that in the New Testament, the term *oikonomia* designates the divine *plan of salvation.* John Meyendorff, *Byzantine Theology: Historical Trends and Doctrinal Themes* (New York: Fordham University Press, 1983) 88.

185. Mowry LaCugna, *God for Us*, 2.

186. *Ibid.*, 111-135.

187. The early Church never considered the interrelationship of the triune God from

immanent Trinity became a matter for speculative theology, the concerns of the economic Trinity became part of salvation history.[188] Even more, in the post-Nicene era, we saw an emphasis on the doctrine of the Incarnation in contrast to the doctrine of the Trinity. It is this 'overemphasis' on the Incarnation that made George L. Prestige say that the concept of 'economy' has a more fundamental connection with the doctrine of the Incarnation than with the doctrine of the Trinity.[189]

Jesus' Incarnation and redemptive ministry became the central theme in this context. The Incarnation and the work of redemption are understood as a continuous process of the recapitulation of all in Christ.[190] *Oikonomia* means "God's Dispensation or loving care and plan of salvation and 'recapitulation in Christ'."[191] It denotes the sacramental character of Jesus.[192]

The economy of Christ continues through the economy of the Spirit. Through the economy of the Spirit, the divine mission of recapitulating Creation into God is continued.

> The Holy Spirit's power of sanctification was the hinge on which turned God's loving communion with the first man and the first woman. When original sin destroyed this relationship, the Holy Spirit continued its work,

an ontological perspective using philosophical categories. Their main concern was on the scriptural revelation of the one God (Father) in the incarnation of Son and the sending of the Holy Spirit. It was against the subordinationist Christology of the pre-Nicene Fathers that Christian theologians went beyond the salvation historical or narrative categories of the economy to the metaphysical ground of the economy in 'theology'. Mowry LaCugna, *God for Us*, 22-24. For a detailed study of the development of the Trinitarian theology in the pre-Nicene period see: *Ibid.*, 21-52.

188. Christoph Schwöbel, "Introduction: The Renaissance of Trinitarian Theology: Reasons, Problems and Tasks," *Trinitarian Theology Today: Essays on Divine Being and Act*, ed. Christoph Schwöbel (Edinburgh: T & T Clark, 1995) 1-30, p. 6.

189. George L. Prestige, *God in Patristic Thought* (London: SPCK, 1952) 57. Prestige elaborates two usages of *oikonomia* in his work *God in Patristic Thought*. First, he explains the primary aspect of *oikonomia* as God's management of the world and his salvific works through the dispensation of grace. Secondly, he speaks of the "economical Trinity." *Ibid.*, 55-75, 97-111.

190. Dumitru Staniloae, "The Economy of Salvation and Ecclesiastical 'Economy'," *Diakonia* 5 (1970) 218-231, p. 221.

191. Constantine N. Tsirpanlis, *Introduction to Eastern Patristic Thought and Orthodox Theology* (Collegeville, MN: Liturgical Press, 1991) 11.

192. Rahner used the term *Ursakrament* to Christ as the historical self-communication of God. Though Jesus is the high point in a sacramental sacred history that begins with Israel and all the sacraments come together in him, with his ascension we lost his visibility and that opened us to "the sacramentality of sacred history." Lukken, "Church and Liturgy as Dynamic Sacrament of the Spirit," 140-141. We shall come to the sacramentality of Christ in detail in the second part of this chapter.

preparing for the reconciliation of humankind to God through shadowy figures in the Old Testament and pre-Christian world, and through an authentic 'indwelling' in the faithful of Christ's Church.[193]

It does not mean that the Holy Spirit is subordinated to Christ, but rather, that the relationship between the Son and the Spirit are complementary and reciprocal in God's salvific plan.[194] Irenaeus clearly expresses it when he notes that the Son and the Spirit are the 'two hands' of God the Father.[195] Through the Spirit, man ascends to the Son, and through the Son to the Father.[196] In this sense the role of the Holy Spirit is determined under the domain of God's economy as the continuation of the trinitarian life of God.[197] Thomas FitzGerald makes it clear: "The economy of the Holy Spirit is concerned with our personal participation in the act of God. It is the will of God as revealed to us through the Incarnation that we should personally enter into communion with the life and glory which by nature belong to the Holy Trinity."[198] Furthermore, Marta Ryk notes:

> The source and the giver of deifying energies of the Holy Trinity is the Holy Spirit. He communicates divine energies to us makes us open to receive them. Dealing with this question on a deeper level, Eastern theologians assert, according to the Trinitarian character of activity of God, that every energy comes *from* the Father and is given *by* the Son *in* the Holy Spirit. This process or action is called the 'economy' of the Holy Trinity.[199]

193. Gennadios Limouris, "The Sanctifying Grace of the Holy Spirit," *ER* 42 (1990) 288-297, p. 288. The central role of the Holy Spirit is celebrated in the sacramental mysteries in high esteem. Its culmination is seen in the "epiklesial services" which are central to many of the important liturgical celebrations. Marta Ryk, "The Holy Spirit's Role in the Deification of Man according to Contemporary Orthodox Theology II," *Diakonia* 10 (1975) 109-131, pp. 114-115.

194. FitzGerald, "The Holy Eucharist as Theophany," 29.

195. Irenaeus, *Adversus Haereses* 5.1.3.

196. Irenaeus, *Adversus Haereses* 3.15.3.

197. Marta Ryk, "The Holy Spirit's Role in the Deification of Man according to Contemporary Orthodox Theology," *Diakonia* 10 (1975) 24-39, p. 26.

198. FitzGerald, "The Holy Eucharist as Theophany," 29. This means that we must affirm not only their hypostatic independence but also the advent of the Holy Spirit in the world is not subordinated to the Son, but another Paraclete, who fashions Christ within us. Georges Khodr, "Christianity in a Pluralistic World – the Economy of the Holy Spirit," *The Ecumenical Movement: An Anthology of Key Texts and Voices* (Geneva: World Council of Churches, 1997) 401-406, p. 404.

199. Ryk, "The Holy Spirit's Role," 29.

The divine *economy* that was revealed in Jesus and brought to fulfillment through the Holy Spirit is present today in the ecclesial *economy*.[200] Jesus' recapitulation of humanity, which is made possible through redemption, is continued through the sacraments of the Church. It means to say that God's relation with humanity has a "sacramental structure, in the sense that the movement proceeding from God and, through the whole course of human history, returning home to God, is continually taking on more precise sacramental characteristics."[201] John Meyendorff makes it clear when he says:

> The Kingdom of God, an anticipation of the eschatological fulfilment, is already accessible in the Body of Christ: this possibility of 'being in Christ', of participating in divine life – the 'natural' state of humanity – is, for the Byzantines, essentially manifested in the sacraments, or *mysteria*, of the Church.[202]

The dispensation of Christ is the source from which the sacraments derive their grace.[203] The redemption by Jesus is not something imposed on the human being, but it is a gift from God in His grace. Thus, "[t]he sacraments of the Church make it possible for man to enter freely and personally into communion with the divinizing grace which the Logos of God bestowed upon human nature in assuming it."[204]

The source and strength of the Church is its relation to the Trinity. The Church "is an integral part and expression of the divine plan of salvation. Being the called and sanctified people of God in communion with the Triune God, the Church was established by Christ with the call of the first disciples and was enlivened by the Holy Spirit on the day of Pentecost." The economic function of the Church makes it a theandric reality. In this sense we could say that "the Church is a mystery of humanity in communion with divinity which exists in history but transcends time and space. She has her beginning and her end in the actions of the Triune God who seeks the free and personal participation of human persons in the glory of the kingdom."[205] It means to say that

> The Church is an expression of both horizontal and vertical relationships of love which are not bound by space and time. Within the life of the Church the reality of the Triune God and his mighty works of love are revealed and

200. Staniloae, "The Economy of Salvation and Ecclesiastical 'Economy'," 123.

201. Vorgrimler, *Sacramental Theology*, 27.

202. John Meyendorff, *Byzantine Theology*, 191.

203. Georgios I. Mantzaridis, *The Deification of Man* (Crestwood, NY: St. Vladimir's Seminary Press, 1984) 42.

204. *Ibid.*, 42.

205. FitzGerald, "The Holy Eucharist as Theophany," 30.

> experienced. The Church is the locus of divine life and activity through which human persons, with the aid of each other, pass from one degree of glory to another (2 Cor 3.18). The holiness of the Trinity becomes accessible to us through the life of the Church.[206]

It is "a community of human persons in communion with the three divine persons." Hence, every sacramental mystery "has a bearing upon the bond of unity which exists among the believers, as well as between the believers and the persons of the Trinity."[207] Thus, the ecclesial *economy* can be described as "the exchange between the divine and the human that takes place in the Word made flesh and is celebrated in the sacraments, to the benefit of humanity and in the liturgy of those who participate therein."[208] In this sense, one could say that the ultimate aim of liturgy and sacraments is to establish and to perpetuate an intimate communion with God. This takes place in Christ and in His Church. Our participation in the liturgy and sacraments are means to participate in the kingdom of God.

The distortion in the trinitarian approach was primarily begun with Augustine. He is criticized for sacrificing the sense of 'economic' Trinity. As Schwöbel notes:

> Augustine's emphasis on the unity of the divine essence of God's triune being, his stress on the undivided mode of God's relating to what is not God and his attempt to trace the intelligibility of the doctrine of the Trinity through the *vestigia trinitatis* in human consciousness, mediating unity and differentiation, defined the parameters of Western trinitarian reflection.[209]

At the same time one could observe contrasting views on this.[210] Rahner, on the other hand, placed the blame on Thomas Aquinas for the separation and sequence of 'On the One God' (*De Deo uno*) and 'On the Triune God' (*De Deo trino*), which made Trinity a secondary differentiation in the nature of the one God.[211] However, he notes its possible origin in Augustine, albeit not fully developed.[212] Later Western theology continued a Christological approach. This is clear in Thomas Aquinas who de-

206. *Ibid.*, 31.
207. *Ibid.*, 32.
208. Power, "Sacrament: An Economy of Gift," 146.
209. Schwöbel, "Introduction: The Renaissance of Trinitarian Theology," 5.
210. See Michel René Barnes, "Augustine in Contemporary Trinitarian Theology," *TS* 56 (1995) 237-250. Although René Barnes justifies Augustine, this study gives a good survey of some of the prominent studies on Augustine's theology of the Trinity.
211. Karl Rahner, *The Trinity*, trans. J. Donceel (New York: Seabury, 1974) 16.
212. *Ibid.*, 17.

fined the sacramental character as a sharing in the priesthood of Christ.[213] This he shows mainly by demonstrating "how the personal liturgy of Christ is the ground and prototype of the Christian liturgy."[214] Furthermore, Liam G. Walsh argues that the objective mystery of the liturgy is not limited to the human activity of Christ, rather it is a manifestation and realization of divine activity. In other words, "a christological definition of the liturgy supposes a theological one. Liturgy is the mystery of God before it is the mystery of Christ."[215] In his opinion, St. Thomas would "employ a strictly theological category to define the liturgy before specifying the christological property of it."[216] According to him, "The credibility of the trinitarian pattern of liturgy is supported by the establishment of basic trinitarian dogma, and the correlation of the visible mission of the Word with the invisible mission of the Holy Spirit shows how the pattern of visible shape and invisible grace found in the New Testament liturgy (law and grace in St. Thomas's terms) is grounded on the trinitarian economy of salvation."[217] It appears that during this period, the *economy* of the Spirit was not emphasised properly and there was little effort made to link the *economy* of Christ to the Trinity. This oversight unfortunately impacted the whole western medieval discussions on eucharistic realism, debates on validity, matter and form etc, whilst Eastern theology continued with its trinitarian foundation of liturgical and sacramental celebrations. The Orthodox doctrine of the Holy Trinity, as Vladimir Lossky says, is "the unshakeable foundation of all religious thought, of all piety, of all spiritual life and of all experience."[218]

1.4.2. Retrieval of Sacramental Economy

In the foregoing section, we discussed the Trinitarian foundation of sacramentology. However, entering into the retrieval efforts of the Trinitarian foundation of sacramentology, we will see how the ecclesial economy has acquired some specific meanings in contemporary discussions. The understanding of ecclesial economy took a new turn in the eighteenth century after the controversy in the Orthodox Churches on the validity of

213. Thomas Aquinas, *Summa Theologica*, III, q. 63, a. 3.

214. Thomas Aquinas, *Summa Theologica*, III, qq. 20-26.

215. Liam G. Walsh, "Liturgy in the Theology of St. Thomas," *The Thomist* 38 (1974) 557-583, p. 572.

216. *Ibid.*, 572. On the other hand he notes that, when liturgists "develop the trinitarian pattern of the liturgy they seldom go beyond an economic trinitarianism." For more details on the trinitarian foundation of liturgy and sacraments in Aquinas see *Ibid.*, 572-580.

217. Walsh, "Liturgy in the Theology of St. Thomas," 571.

218. FitzGerald, "The Holy Eucharist as Theophany," 27.

Baptism administered outside the Orthodox tradition.[219] In this context, they rediscovered the canonical principle of economy within the very order of sacramental economy.[220] This new trend has narrowed down the ecclesial economy to a restricted meaning of salvation through participation in sacramental celebrations, and is dependent on one's membership in the Church and on the merit of the celebrant.

Recent developments in ecclesial economy focused on two traditional debates on the salvific function of certain sacramental celebrations. On the one hand we see Cyprian's exhortation *extra ecclesiam nulla salus* that was used against the Novatianists.[221] This debate has become a crucial point in the discussions on the validity of the sacraments in the various Christian traditions. For Cyprian, "the sacraments are established in the church. That is to say, they are effected and can be effected only in the church, in communion and in community."[222] Based on this argument, Androutsos, Dyovouniotis, Metropolitan Anthony Khrapovitsky have emphasized the role of the Church as sole steward of divine grace, and which magnifies the power of economy accordingly. In their view, the sacraments of the heterodox "are not only legally irregular but also

219. John H. Erickson, "Sacramental 'Economy' in Recent Roman Catholic Thought," *The Jurist* 48 (1988) 653-667, p. 653. The very dispute regarding the use of the theology of *oikonomia* in deciding the validity of the sacrament created tensions between Russian and Greek Orthodox Churches. For details see, Francis J. Thomson, "Economy: An Examination of the Various Theories of Economy Held within the Orthodox Church, with Special Reference to the Economical Recognition of the Validity of Non-Orthodoxy Sacraments," *JTS* 16 (1965) 368-420.

220. Staniloae, "The Economy of Salvation," 115. According to Staniloae, *economy* is used in the Orthodox tradition as "a condescension on the part of the Church in view of human weakness by which the Church in some cases relaxes the strictness (*akrivia*) of its generally-enforced laws." He also examines the four areas in which this condescension is visible: Firstly, it "recognizes the Baptism of Christians residing outside of the Orthodox Church that has been performed in the name of the Holy Trinity." Secondly, it is "exercised when the Church recognizes couples as married without ever having been through the marriage ceremony." Thirdly, it is applied "when the Church accepts Orders without ordination of members of a hierarchy consecrated in a non-Orthodox community which has kept the apostolic succession." And finally, economy is used as a term to apply "to any procedure used by the Church on behalf of any of its members to permit them a dispensation from fulfilling certain laws or ceremonies such as fasting on certain fixed days, the obligation of the marriage service performed in the church or the forbidding of marriages performed during certain times."

221. Cyprian, *Epistolae* 73, *PL* 4, 413. The point of contention is the validity of sacraments administered outside the Church. Its origin goes back to the dispute between Cyprian of Carthage and Stephen of Rome over Novatianist Baptism.

222. George Florovsky, "The Limits of the Church," *CQR* 117 (1933-1934) 117-131, p. 117.

wholly invalid and worthless."[223] From this particular Orthodox perspective, in principle, the recipients of a heterodox baptism, who seek entrance into the Orthodox Church are no different from the unbaptized.[224] At the same time, though the unbaptized were banned from membership in the Church, they argued that "the Church, as holding the stewardship of divine grace, is able both to recognize the priesthood and the sacraments in general of schismatics and heretics among whom they are not accomplished canonically or the apostolic succession has been broken."[225]

At the other side of the spectrum, there is the theory of Peter Moghila (1596-1646) who developed a theology for the validity of sacraments based on Augustine's principle *ex opere operato*. Augustine employed this against the Donatists and argued that the sacraments are valid *ex opere operato*, even when administered "outside the Church," but when certain objective conditions are met, such as proper form, minister and intention.[226] Based on this Zernov, Florovsky, Alivizatos, Patriarch Sergius of Moscow, van der Mensbrugghe and Bria have argued that the economic approach would make the sacraments "merely unobligatory symbols of inward grace, which the Church administers so freely that it can dispense with them."[227] They also argued that when the sacraments are administered outside the canonical limits of the Orthodox Church, it is necessary to distinguish between those that are absolutely invalid, those that are valid and those which are existent, but in some way defective.[228] In their opinion, where certain formal elements are present, for example, apostolic succession in the case of orders, a special charisma is conferred which cannot be removed "precisely because the Church is not in that sense steward, but only the organ of the administration of divine grace."[229]

Here we do not intend to evaluate the arguments presented and defended by various schools within the Orthodox Church; even so, it is still important to note that these arguments are not contradictory, but complementary. Florovsky notes that "Augustine was not so very far from

223. John H. Erickson, "The Reception of Non-Orthodox into the Orthodox Church," *SVTQ* 41 (1997) 1-17, p. 3. See, Chrestos Androutsos, *The Validity of English Ordinations from an Orthodox Catholic Point of View* (London: Richards, 1909) 9-11.

224. Erickson, "Sacramental 'Economy'," 655.

225. K. I. Dyovouniotis, "The Principle of Economy," *CQR* 116 (1933) 93-101.

226. Erickson, "Sacramental 'Economy'," 653.

227. Erickson, "The Reception of Non-Orthodox into the Orthodox Church," 3. See also, Thomson, "Economy: An Examination," 389.

228. Erickson, "The Reception of Non-Orthodox into the Orthodox Church," 4.

229. Thomson, "Economy: An Examination," 382.

Cyprian. ... In his [Augustine's] reasoning about the unity of the church, about the unity of love, as the necessary and decisive condition of the saving power of the sacraments, Augustine really but repeats Cyprian in new words."[230] Both arguments underscore the importance of the sacramentality of the Church. According to Congar, the theology of economy leads us to a theology of the Church as primordial sacrament, or root-sacrament (*Ursakrament*), and this Church-sacrament continues as Christ-sacrament.[231] Killian McDonnell observes that the Church is related to order and ministry not merely in terms of what is properly and legitimately done, but that she is herself the original sacrament, the *Ursakrament*. Therefore, her presence and activity determines and establishes the validity.[232] What is important is that the ecclesial basis and its rootedness in Christ determine the validity of the sacrament.

The retrieval of the trinitarian foundation of sacramentology was a slow process compared to the renewal in other areas of sacramentology. This was mainly because of the ontological nature of the doctrine of Trinity.[233] Among the various efforts to renew trinitarian theology, one is able to observe two trends following the two traditional understandings that are based on the immanent and economic Trinity.[234] It is Rahner who made a first attempt to synthesize both immanent and economic Trinity. For him, "*The 'economic' trinity is the 'immanent' trinity and the 'immanent' Trinity is the 'economic' Trinity.*"[235] According to this theory, "who and how God is in the economy of salvation *is* (the same as) who and how God is eternally and transcendentally, and what one says or experiences of God's economic-historical activity is true as well of God's

230. Florovsky, "The Limits of the Church," 118.

231. Yves Congar, "Propos en vue d'une théologie de l'Économie dans la tradition latine," *Irénikon* 45 (1972) 205.

232. Killian McDonnell, "Ways of Validating Ministry," *JES* 7 (1970) 208-265, p. 257.

233. Even in systematic theology the renewal of the 'theology of Trinity' took place rather late compared to other theological disciplines.

234. See for a short description of the main figures and their trends of both traditions: Catherine Mowry LaCugna, "Problems with a Trinitarian Reformulation," *LS* 10 (1985) 324-340, p. 326.

235. Rahner, *The Trinity*, 22. The original published as Karl Rahner, "Der dreifaltige Gott als transzendenter Urgrund der Heilsgeschichte," *Mysterium Salutis: Grundriss heilsgeschichtlicher Dogmatik*, vol. 2, ed. Johannes Feiner & Magnus Löhrer (Einsiedeln: Benziger, 1967) 317-397 is to be credited as the ground breaking work in the revival of trinitarian theology in the Catholic Church. See also his other works: "Remarks on the Dogmatic Treatise 'de Trinitate'," *TI* 4, trans. Kevin Smyth (London: Darton, Longman & Todd, 1974) 77-102 and "The Mystery of the Trinity," *TI* 16, trans. David Morland (London: Darton, Longman & Todd, 1979) 255-259.

'inner' history of immanent life."[236] Based on this, Catherine Mowry LaCugna argues that "Rahner's *Grundaxiom* [immanent Trinity is the economic Trinity] is the precondition for re-conceiving the trinitarian doctrine *as* the mystery of salvation."[237]

Keeping the principle of the immanent Trinity is the economic Trinity, Rahner develops his theology of '*Real Symbol*' to realize what is essential in a being. It is grounded in his anthropological reflections and in the doctrine of Trinity.

> While Rahner draws his theology of the symbol from his anthropological understanding of how humans attempt to satisfy their restless drive for fulfillment, it is equally obvious that for him the symbolic nature of being human, being discursive, and being perfected imbibes its strength from the triune nature of God and the manner in which God has graced the world with God's spirit and word.[238]

This idea was further advanced by many other contemporary theologians. Hans Urs von Balthasar[239] and Edward Schillebeeckx[240] are some of the other important authors who have contributed in developing sacramentology from the trinitarian perspective.

1.4.3. Wider Use of Sacramental Economy

Sacramental economy has received wide acceptance in the Second Vatican Council and in the post-Conciliar period. Already in 1961, Taymans d'Eypernon underscored the importance of Trinity in the study of sacra-

236. Catherine Mowry LaCugna, "Re-conceiving the Trinity as the Mystery of Salvation," *Scot. Journ.* 38 (1985) 1-23, pp. 2-3.

237. *Ibid.*, 3.

238. *Karl Rahner: Theologian of the Graced Search for Meaning*, ed. Geffrey B. Kelly (Edinburgh: T&T Clark, 1993) 289. "The Logos, or Word of God, is the historical embodiment of God as triune. Through his enfleshment in a concrete human history, Christ becomes the revelatory symbol in which God, the Father of Jesus, reveals the true nature of their triune divinity. They send their Spirit of love to the church, which, in turn, becomes the symbol of Jesus' persistent presence in space and time, made visible and real in the sacraments in which the grace of God becomes historically manifest and God becomes approachable. It is because of Christ, finally, that one's relationship with the triune God will perdure through symbolization even when one has been brought by God to his or her salvific destiny."

239. For Balthasar, "The role of the esthetic in revelation and the Word's disclosure of the inner life and love of the Trinity are fundamental to a discussion of sacrament. The form or Gestalt of revelation is determined by the coming forth from the Trinity of the Word as manifestation of God's agape or love, that embraces humanity and the world." Power, et al., "Sacramental Theology: A Review of Literature," 664.

240. For Schillebeeckx sacrament is an encounter with God through Christ. See Schillebeeckx, *Christ, the Sacrament of Encounter with God.*

ments. Although theology generally maintains sacraments as the work of Christ, he focused on the presence of the Trinity in the works of Christ. According to him each sacrament aims "to bring man into greater conformity with the Son, and through Him to a close assimilation to the Blessed Trinity in Its inner life."[241] Furthermore, the "sacraments are a prolongation of the Life and action of the Saviour, and they in turn give us the Blessed Trinity."[242] In this sense d'Eypernon placed the sacraments within the wider spectrum of the salvific plan of God. For him "[S]alvation is in the strict sense an operation of the Blessed Trinity. The Three Divine Persons are together the author of salvation; the one act of redemption is realized by the Father, Son and Holy Ghost; salvation is a personal gift made by each of the Divine Persons."[243] Kevin W. Irwin argues that the notion of seven sacraments has been enhanced in the West by the restored notion of the sacramental economy.[244]

The Trinitarian grounding of sacrament has also been further advanced by some of the contemporary theologians.[245] Theodore Schneider underscores the Trinitarian foundation of sacraments, which lies behind their Christological and Ecclesiological dimensions.[246] His presentation of seven sacraments centres around this axiom. Another German author, Lothar Lies, criticizes the western approach that neglects the importance of Trinity and calls attention for the renewal of sacraments grounded on Trinitarian theology.[247] The importance of Trinitarian theology in liturgy also received attention in the current literature.[248]

241. Taymans d'Eypernon, *The Blessed Trinity and the Sacraments* (Dublin: Clonmore & Reynolds Ltd., 1961) 14.

242. *Ibid.*, 39.

243. *Ibid.*, 14.

244. Kevin W. Irwin, "Sacramentality and the Theology of Creation: A Recovered Paradigm for Sacramental Theology," *LS* 23 (1998) 159-179, p. 169.

245. For a brief overview: Power, et al., "Sacramental Theology: A Review of Literature," 665-667.

246. Theodore Schneider, *Zeichen der Nähe Gottes: Grundriss der Sakramententheologie* (Mainz: Matthias Grünewald, 1979) 45.

247. In his opinion, the neglect of trinitarian theology affected all areas of theology, in particular it was neglected fully in the sacramentology. Lothar Lies, "Trinitätsvergessenheit gegenwärtiger Sakramententheologie?" *ZKT* 105 (1983) 290-314; 415-429, p. 290. At the same time, in this article he reviews some efforts undertaken by some German theologians to this end. See also Lothar Lies, *Sakramententheologie: Eine personale Sicht* (Graz: Styria, 1990).

248. For a short survey of the importance of trinitarian doxology in some modern theological works see Christopher Cocksworth, "The Trinity Today: Opportunities and Challenges for Liturgical Study," *SL* 27 (1997) 61-78.

The Catechism of the Catholic Church has duly emphasized the aspect of sacramental economy.[249] In it we see positive affirmations of the immanent Trinity, economic Trinity and its continuation through the Church.

László Lukács, using the recent inquiries into the nature of communication and of symbols, "takes communication by symbols as a matrix for a fresh understanding of the sacramental nature of the history of salvation and the sacraments as real symbols."[250] In his opinion, "The church is sent by Christ to convert humankind into a communion of love, in communion with the Triune God and with one another" and this 'communio' achieved through 'communicatio'.[251] He underscores how Second Vatican Council's notion of revelation has opened awareness "to the realisation that revelation cannot be separated from salvation, and salvation is our loving communion with the Triune God."[252] Lukács affirms that this communication is realized in three ways: in the immanent Trinity, in the economical Trinity and in the Church and its sacraments.[253]

The foregoing discussion on the sacrament of salvation history has drawn our attention to the trinitarian foundation of sacramentology, and follows from this on the aspect of communion and its soteriological import. As stated, the character of sacramentology had undergone dramatic changes; this occurred already during the early Christian period by changing the focus from the Trinity to the Incarnation. The overemphasis led to a distortion and continued up until the twentieth century. It is also important to note that even though this "distortion" affected the Eastern

249. In this regard Lambert Leijssen's study is worth mentioning. See "The Sacramental Economy of Salvation in the Catechism of the Church." Regis A. Duffy's article, "The Sacramental Economy. (Paragraphs 1066-1209)" to which we have already referred also is of particular interest here.

250. László Lukács, "Communication – Symbols – Sacraments," *Contemporary Sacramental Contours of a God Incarnate*, 137-153, p. 138. The use of communication theories in the study of sacramentology is an important development in the post-conciliar sacramentology. Using the communication theory of Jürgen Habermas it was developed mainly among German theologians. For a brief survey of some such studies see Power, et al., "Sacramental Theology: A Review of Literature," 670-672. The liturgical studies organized by the Liturgical Institute of the Faculty of Theology of Leuven and the Abbey of Keizersberg also gave importance to the application of communication theories and linguistic analysis that it became the main agenda in the biannual liturgical colloquia of 1970's and 1980's. Lambert Leijssen, "Introduction: Liturgy and Language," *Liturgy and Language: A Tribute to Silveer De Smet*, ed. Lambert Leijssen, Textes et études liturgiques / Studies in Liturgy, 12 (Leuven: Abdij Keizersberg/Faculteit der Godgeleerdheid, 1992) 5-14, p. 5.

251. Lukács, "Communication – Symbols – Sacraments," 139.

252. *Ibid.*, 140.

253. *Ibid.*, 140-153.

Christian tradition, they balanced it through emphasising the economic Trinity, the Church and its sacramental celebrations within the Trinitarian context. The retrieval of the sacrament of salvation history helps us to view Creation, Christ and the Church as sacraments, and will be vital for our further discussions.

1.5. Sacraments and Sacramentality

In concluding our discussion on 'sacramentology in transition', we could say that the aforementioned factors contributed a great deal to the reaffirmation of the importance of liturgy and sacraments in Christian reflection today. It has also contributed to the broadening of the classical understanding of sacraments. The most important change lies in the retrieval of a broad and dynamic understanding of sacraments from a legalistic and reductionist one, and encourages one to see the sacraments from within the context of sacramentality.

From a historical perspective the distinction between sacraments and sacramentals are late in origin. This demarcation began sometime in the medieval period and became popular in the West. Accordingly, the sacraments were considered to be from Jesus Christ and confer grace by virtue of the work of redemption effected by Christ, whilst the sacramentals were instituted by the Church, and give grace based on the Church's intercession.[254] The Orthodox theologians, however, do not make a distinction between sacraments and sacramentals. For example, Timothy Ware notes that "when we talk of 'seven sacraments', we must never isolate these seven from the many other actions in the Church which also possess a sacramental character, and ... are termed *sacramentals*."[255] John Meyendorff also notes the same:

> Byzantine theology ignores the Western distinction between 'sacraments' and 'sacramentals', and never formally committed itself to any strict limitation of the number of sacraments. In the patristic period there was no technical term to designate 'sacraments' as a specific category of Church acts: the term *mysterion* was used primarily in the wider and general sense of 'mystery of salvation'.[256]

254. Thomas Lane, "The Sacramentals Revisited," *The Furrow* 33 (1982) 272-281, p. 272. Vorgrimler suggests that the word 'sacramental' is more appropriate than the word 'symbolic'. Because "everything sacramental is symbolic (in the sense of real symbols), but not everything symbolic is sacramental, since not every (real) symbol mediates the presence of God." Vorgrimler, *Sacramental Theology*, 27.

255. Timothy Ware, *The Orthodox Church* (Harmondsworth: Penguin Books, 1978) 282.

256. At the same time he notes that the term *mysterion* is used "in a subsidiary man-

Along these lines, William Van Roo suggests that "*Sacramentality* is a theological concept, elaborated first in a reflection on salvation history in the Old Testament, then extended to God's saving work in Christ, and finally to the continuation of that work in the Church. Beyond that development, one can recognize a universal sacramentality, coherent with the truths of the universality of both God's will to save, and the history of salvation."[257] Furthermore, "[t]he whole conception is based on belief of the truth revealed to Israel and then through Christ. Without such belief, the notion of the sacramentality of God's saving action is unintelligible."[258] Kristiaan Depoortere clarifies this by elucidating the shifts in the understanding of Greek *mysterion* and Latin *sacramentum*. While *mysterion* designates participation in the salvific plan of God, the inner reality of the sacraments, *sacramentum* is concerned with the administration, or the outer celebration, of the sacraments. According to him, "*mysterion* and *sacramentum*, emphasising respectively the invisible and visible part of God's hidden plan of salvation for the whole world, and the mysterious participation of God's people in this plan" as they are "the actualisations of the salvific *mysterion*, which is 'already' and 'not yet'."[259]

2. Changing Paradigms in Sacramentology

The liturgical and sacramental renewal which brought a significant shift from the understanding of sacramental rituals to sacramentality by placing them back into the 'mystery of salvation' was further deepened by renewed understandings in Christology and Ecclesiology. In this process theologians re-discovered the importance of Christ and the Church for a better understanding of sacramentology. Eventually, both came to be seen as *the* sacraments. The broader meaning of *mysterion* and *sacramentum* also helped theologians like Rahner and Schillebeeckx to develop the idea of Jesus as primordial sacrament and the Church as original sacrament.[260] As Osborne puts it:

ner to designate the particular *actions* which bestow salvation. In this second sense, it was used concurrently with such terms as "rites" or "sanctifications." Meyendorff, *Byzantine Theology*, 191. For the details on the number of sacraments differed from time to time see *Ibid*, 191-192.

257. Van Roo, *The Christian Sacrament*, 104.

258. *Ibid.*, 105.

259. Depoortere, "From Sacramentality to Sacraments and Vice-versa," 53.

260. See Schillebeeckx, *Christ the Sacrament of Encounter with God*; Rahner, *The Church and the Sacraments*. In this context it is also important to see the work of Otto Semmelroth, *Die Kirche als Ursakrament* (Frankfurt: Knecht, 1953).

Reaching beyond both scholasticism and neo-scholasticism to the patrisitc period of both East and West, these authors presented an approach to Christian sacramentality that was old and yet new. Sacramentality was seen by these authors as a more profound aspect of the Christian Church with a primordial base in the Incarnation itself and a foundational base in the church.[261]

In their approach, we see a shift from the traditional understanding of sacraments to a new theology of sacraments in terms of personalist and existential philosophies. This new understanding conceives Christ as the primary and fundamental sign (sacrament) of God's love as experienced in the life of the Church, and the Church itself is a sacrament of the presence of God. In this process, the language of ontology was changed to that of encounter and union.[262] In this new understanding, "sacrament" is used to refer primarily to Christ and the Church, and returns the meaning of sacrament to its more original one as *mysterion* and *sacramentum*.[263]

This understanding of Christ and the Church as sacraments has achieved prominence in the post-Vatican era. It seems that this new understanding had further broadened the notion of sacramentality. Hence, it is important to see the dynamic growth of the understanding of sacramentality based on Christ and the Church as sacraments. Since there are a number of studies both on Christ and the Church as sacraments, we shall avoid a detailed study of them. After seeing some of the pertinent issues involved, we shall then discuss the need for a new paradigm which includes the broader meaning of sacramentality, but also broadens our understanding of Christ and the Church as sacraments.

2.1. Christ as Sacrament

The notion of Jesus Christ as sacrament was developed based on the New Testament theology of *mysterion*.[264] The revelation of God's saving intent that was realized in Jesus Christ, is also seen behind the Church Fa-

261. Osborne, *Christian Sacraments in a Postmodern World*, 47.

262. Irwin, "Recent Sacramental Theology," 593; See also Matthew O'Connell, "New Perspectives in Sacramental Theology," *Worship* (1965) 196-206.

263. Isaac Padinjarekuttu, "Sacrament in Catholic History," *The World as Sacrament: Interdisciplinary Bridge-building of the Sacred and the Secular*, ed. Francis X. D'Sa, Isaac Padinjarekuttu & Jacob Parappally (Pune: Jnana-Deepa Vidyapeeth,1998) 17-37, p. 26.

264. For a short sketch on the 'notion of Christ as sacrament' in the biblical perspective, see Donald Senior, "God's Creative Word at Work in Our Midst," *The Sacraments: God's Love and Mercy Actualized* (Philadelphia, PA: Villanova University Press, 1979) 1-28.

thers' understanding of the sacramentality of Christ.[265] Accordingly Jesus is "the ultimate sign of God's salvation in the world."[266]

Later, with the emergence of a more juridical approach to the sacraments, the understanding of Jesus as sacrament faded. But its rediscovery started with the ecclesial revival. The ecclesial revival that created the awareness of the sacramentality of the Church also underscored the Church's relationship to the sacramentality of Jesus Christ. In this context, Jesus was first referred to as "the great sacrament."[267] The Christological renewal of sacramental theology helps us to see the sacraments in the perspective of the sacramental nature of Christ.[268] He is called the original sacrament because "Jesus Christ is the locus and the means of God's encounter with man."[269] This renewed understanding of "Jesus as primordial sacrament means that all other Christian sacraments have their meaning *only* in and through Jesus' sacramentality." In other words, "[i]f Jesus is the primordial, fundamental, basic, root sacrament, then it is only *because* he is sacrament that the others can be sacraments."[270] Jesus as the primordial sacrament neither denotes a sacrament along with the seven sacraments, nor is it used in an analogous sense. Moreover, it is to be noted that the very sacramentality of Jesus' humanity unifies the Christian sacraments. It is in this sense that Jesus becomes the primordial sacrament, the root-sacrament.[271]

2.1.1. Renewed Understanding of Christ as Sacrament

As noted already, it was Rahner and Schillebeeckx who popularized the notion of Jesus as sacrament. Although they agree on the sacramentality of Christ, they seem to differ in its explanation.

265. Augustine called him the *mysterium Dei*. Thomas Aquinas understood Jesus Christ to be "the fundamental sacrament, insofar as his human nature, as the instrument of divinity, effects salvation." *Summa Contra Gentiles* IV a. 41. Wolfgang Beinert, "Die Sakramentalität der Kirche im theologischen Gespräch," *Theologische Berichte* 9 (1980) 13-66, pp. 17-18.

266. Michael Schmaus, *The Church as Sacrament* (London: Sheed and Ward, 1975) 7.

267. Beinert, "Die Sakramentalität der Kirche im theologischen Gespräch," 22.

268. Vaillancourt, *Toward a Renewal of Sacramental Theology*, 36-41.

269. Schmaus, *The Church as Sacrament*, 7.

270. Kenan Osborne, *Sacramental Theology: A General Introduction* (Mahwah, NJ: Paulist, 1988) 76.

271. *Ibid.*, 77. As Vaillancourt notes the shift from the early Christological renewal rooted in the Alexandrian tradition of the divinity of Jesus to the Antiochene tradition of the humanity of Jesus contributed to the broadening of the sacramentality of Christ. Vaillancourt, *Toward a Renewal of Sacramental Theology*, 36.

The Rahnerian understanding of sacraments, based on transcendental anthropology, conceives Christ as the *Ursakrament*.[272] In Jesus, the self-communication of God is manifested in its entirety. Rahner explains Christ as the historical real presence of God. In Christ is "the real presence in history of the victorious eschatological mercy of God in the world," or as "the sacramental primordial Word of God in the history of one humanity."[273] According to Rahner "Christ in his historical existence is both reality and sign, *sacramentum* and *res sacramenti*, of the redemptive grace of God."[274]

Furthermore, Osborne contends that bodiliness is an important theme to understand Jesus as the primordial sacrament. In his opinion, Rahner uses of the "body-soul symbol to the sacramental causation,"[275] based on the "scholastic approach of body and soul to the humanness of Jesus as the primordial sacrament." From this Osborne concludes that for Rahner "the bodiliness of Jesus is the natural sign of his human soul. In other words Jesus' body is a sacrament of his human soul." Osborne's contention is that by emphasizing the 'intrinsic body-soul symbol' Rahner points to the fact that "Jesus' bodiliness is a sacrament of his soul, and Jesus' soul is the sacrament of God's presence." He further notes that while Rahner alone makes such distinctions, "[m]ost theologians claim that it is his total humanity, body and soul, that is primordially sacramental, not simply one part of his humanity that is primordially sacramental."[276]

Existentialist philosophy, as well as the developments in theology of the fifties, led to a new sacramental approach grounded in the human encounter with God in the sacraments. It is in this background that Edward Schillebeeckx described Jesus Christ as the sacrament of the encounter with God.[277] He elaborates the notion of the sacramental experience of

272. In his early writings on sacraments (Karl Rahner, "Sakramententheologie," *LTK* 9 [1964] 240-243) Rahner is not employing the notion *Ursakrament* to Christ. Leijssen explains the absence of the term 'sacrament' applicable to Jesus in his early writings because of "the fact that he did not consider mediation by a sign necessary, since Jesus made God immediately present in the revelation of his own person." Leijssen, "Rahner's Contribution to the Renewal of Sacramentology," 204.

273. Rahner, *The Church and the Sacraments*, 99.

274. *Ibid.*, 15-16.

275. See *Ibid*, 38.

276. Osborne, *Christian Sacraments in a Postmodern World*, 86.

277. Schillebeeckx, *Christ the Sacrament of the Encounter with God.* Prior to this work he published an edited version of his doctorate entitled: *De Sacramentele Heilseconomie: Theologische bezinning op S. Thomas' Sacramentenleer in het licht van de traditie en van de hedendaagse sacramentsproblematiek* (Antwerp/Bilthoven: 't Groeit/H. Nelis-

the divine as a meeting between God and humankind through the encounter with Christ in the sacraments. Schillebeeckx explains the humanity of Jesus Christ as the primordial sacrament in a "twofold movement consisting of the inbreaking of grace 'from above', and the cultus of love of God 'from below'."[278] According to him, "The man Jesus, as the personal visible realization of the divine grace of redemption, is *the* sacrament, the primordial sacrament, because this man, the Son of God himself, is intended by the Father to be in his humanity the only way to the actuality of redemption."[279] Thus, Schillebeeckx clearly underscores the humanness of Jesus at the root of the sacramentality of Jesus.

Kenan Osborne, using his phenomenological approach,[280] presents a good account of the place of the humanity of Christ in sacramental activity. In his opinion, the "'humanness'" of Jesus is *the* sign *the* symbol, *the* sacrament of God's self communication to us," and this is why Christ is called the *Ursakrament*, or the 'original sacrament'.[281] The thrust of the

sen, 1952). In this book he explained the traditional sacramental teaching using the historical sources in a Thomistic framework.

278. Schillebeeckx, *Christ the Sacrament of the Encounter with God*, 17-18.

279. *Ibid.*, 15. It is also important to note that Schillebeeckx's notion of 'Jesus as the primordial sacrament' is rooted in the Trinitarian God. He notes: "The dogmatic definition of Chalcedon, according to which Christ is 'one person in two natures', implies that one and the same person, the Son of God, also took on a visible human form. Even in his humanity Christ is the Son of God. The second person of the most Holy Trinity is personally man; and this man is personally God." *Ibid*, 13.

280. Phenomenology has done a great deal in developing the notion of 'Christ as sacrament'. G. van der Leeuw has noted that the sacraments in the Christian tradition had become a sort of "epiphenomenon" (a phenomenon on top of [*epi*] the human phenomenon) to human life. In his opinion sacraments are anchored deep in human structures and also concerning this relationship to the human structures of life is called a phenomenological approach. This is because sacraments respond to the phenomenon of being human. [G. van der Leeuw, *Sakramentstheologie* (G. F. Callenbach, 1949) 219]. But Osborne criticizes this approach and notes that "[t]he incarnation is based on the entry of the divine into the human, not on the divine as an epiphenomenon of the human. Consequently, we have today a sort of 'unpacking' of the human dimension to see how each sacrament helps perfect human life." Osborne, *Sacramental Theology: A General Introduction*, 38-39. The phenomenological approach generally stresses on "how the sacraments accompany human life from birth to death and take place at important moments in human life."

281. Kenan Osborne, "Methodology and the Christian Sacraments," *The Sacraments: Readings in Contemporary Sacramental Theology*, ed. Michael Taylor (New York: Alba House, 1981) 39-52, p. 41. For Osborne, the basis of a Christological approach is that, "only within the context of the humaneness of Jesus as the original sacrament does the sacramentality of the Church take on meaning and reality, and only within the context of the twofold sacramentality of the humaneness of Christ and the Church itself do the individual sacraments find their significance and function." Osborne, "Methodology and the Christian Sacraments," 46. He even categorically states that "Jesus in human nature *alone* is the original sacrament." *Ibid.*, 36. He also criticizes Karl Rahner and Schillebeeckx for

phenomenological approach is that it focuses "on a wider dimension of interpersonal activity than that circumscribed by a particular sacrament."[282] In this approach, sacramentality always involves a relational factor and means that "sacrament is always *of* something *for* someone. It is in this sense that Christ may be said to be the sacrament of God's active love for all people."[283] Osborne explains this relational character of sacraments using the traditional terms. He notes:

> [T]he very concept of *sacramentum tantum* is unintelligible, since to be a sacrament something or someone must be a sacrament *of* something and *for* someone. Otherwise, it is simply another entity among others. It is precisely this relationality to the *of* and to the *for* that is at the heart of sacramentality, so that there is always a relationship to the *res*.
>
> Similarly, the *res* alone has no sacramental meaning, since in the case of the Christian sacraments, the reality would remain unknown unless a revelation were made to us in word and sacrament (both signs) which adapted themselves to our intelligence. ... The reality of God's grace, forgiveness and presence comes to us in and through signs which we call word and sacrament.[284]

In the phenomenological approach of Osborne and later, in the writings of liberation theologians, we often see an overemphasis on Jesus' human nature. Still, it is not our concern to analyze the adequacy of emphasis on either Christ's divine or human nature. Our main concern is to see the significance of Christ as sacrament in the contemporary pluralistic setting.

2.1.2. Christ as Sacrament in a Pluralistic Society

'Christ as sacrament' gives the impression that this concerns exclusively Christians. In Christ, however, God's universal salvific will is extended to all humanity, and then immediately offers a wider spectrum for the understanding of Christ as sacrament. The sacramental nature of Christ Himself points to a movement of universal salvation, having a two-fold significance. It encompasses salvation to all humanity and to the whole cosmos.

not giving enough stress on the humanity of Jesus in their understanding of sacraments. *Ibid.*, 35.

282. Osborne, "Methodology and the Christian Sacraments," 48. Osborne specifies the interrelationships of the Christological and phenomenological aspects in sacramentology in his article, "Jesus as Human Expression of the Divine Presence: Toward a New Incarnation of the Sacraments." *The Sacraments: God's Love and Mercy Actualized*, ed. Francis A. Eigo (Philadelphia, PA: Villanova University Press, 1979) 29-58.

283. Irwin, "Recent Sacramental Theology," 594.

284. Osborne, *Sacramental Theology: A General Introduction*, 78-79.

God's universal salvific will means that the signs of the Spirit's action are present in all human beings. Furthermore, as with the seven sacraments, the sacred symbolisms of non-Christians are potential gateways for them to enter into the mystery of Christ. This understanding of Jesus as sacrament helps us to go beyond the understanding of sacraments as mere "Church practices" and from the notion of sacraments as signs of grace for its participants. In other words, Christ as the sacrament of God "transcends all exclusivism regarding sacraments and paves the way for assuming the sacred symbolism of the non-Christians into that of Christ."[285]

The new understanding of 'Jesus as sacrament' goes back to the promise of a Saviour who is already prefigured in Creation. With the Fall, the sacramental nature of Creation was lost. However, the redemption in Jesus gave Creation a new meaning. "God's grace has been made and remains available throughout all creation and history. But the mystery of God's love which inheres at the heart of all creation has become explicit in Jesus."[286] As Schmaus notes, the sacramental sign character of Jesus Christ's human nature enables the things of earth to receive a share in the sacramental significance of Jesus.[287] The Incarnation and redemption of Jesus is seen as the recognition of the sacramental nature of Creation. By redemption, the world is created anew. As Thomas Lane suggests "[f]rom incarnation to glorification he touched and ennobled everything in creation, ... In this context, all creation is sacramental creation; the exalted Christ has given a new significance to everything in the universe."[288]

Osborne applies Chauvet's criticism of scholastic theologians to Rahner and Schillebeeckx, who fall within the Thomistic tradition.[289] Speaking of the sacramentality of Christ, Louis-Marie Chauvet criticises the scholastic theologians for taking the hypostatic union as the point of departure in their understanding of liturgical sacraments. In contrast he suggests the Pasch of Christ as the point of departure.[290] It does not rule out the importance of the Incarnation. Although affirming its importance, Chauvet tries to go further to the salvific mission of God. "We believe

285. Padinjarekuttu, "Sacrament in Catholic History," 31. Padinjarekuttu cautions against "Christologizing the sacraments" and warns that it has serious consequences for theology in the multi-religious and multi-cultural contexts like that of India. *Ibid.*, 32.

286. Michael Downey, "Widening Contexts of Sacramental Worship," *Pastoral Science* 13 (1994) 139-156, p. 143.

287. Schmaus, *The Church as Sacrament*, 8.

288. Lane, "The Sacramentals Revisited," 272.

289. Osborne, *Christian Sacraments in a Postmodern World*, 90.

290. Chauvet, *Symbol and Sacrament*, 453.

that the dogmatic affirmation, according to which the sacraments are events of grace, is inseparable, on the theological plane, from the humanity of God and, on the economic plane, from the sacramentality of history and world."[291]

In short, the meaning of the incarnation and Jesus' redemptive mission has been aimed up with respect to Creation. From this perspective, we can now look at the sacramentality of the world prior to Jesus as sacrament. This will be of great significance, especially within the contemporary multi-pluralistic context. It will also help us to recognize the symbolic meanings present in other religions.

2.2. Church as Sacrament

The sacramental concept applied to the Church is also based on the theology of *mysterion* (Ephesians). The sacramentality of the Church was also an important theme since the time of the Fathers.[292] This theme received a prominent place in theological discourse until the twelfth century. Nevertheless, the narrow and technical concept of sacrament that developed from the middle of the twelfth century impacted the self-image of the Church. During this period, the external, institutional dimension of the Church was overemphasized. This persisted into the nineteenth century. As Peter De Mey notes, the medieval scholastic theology as well as Trent's critique of the Protestant distinction between the visible and invisible Church brought about a diminished understanding of the sacramental nature of the Church. In his opinion, this led to a "juridical approach to the Church as *societas perfecta*."[293]

The ecclesial revival, beginning from the nineteenth century, contributed to retrieving the notion of the sacramentality of the Church. In this period, the concept of "sacrament" as a designation for the Church in its deeper dimension was rediscovered, not only in the romanticism of the first half-century, but also among the neo-Scholastics of the second

291. *Ibid.*, 491.

292. In the East the first witness of this goes back to the *Didache* (Syro-Palestine, first half of the second century), which calls the Church a "cosmic mystery." In the West it goes back to Cyprian (d. 258), who referred to the Church as *sacramentum unitatis*. Church Fathers like Augustine, referred to the sacrament (or *mysterium*) of the Church in the context of a description of the entire economy of salvation. See Beinert, "Sakramentalität der Kirche," 15-17.

293. Peter De Mey, "Church as Sacrament: A Conciliar Concept and Its Reception in Contemporary Theology," *The Presence of Transcendence: Thinking 'Sacrament in a Postmodern Age'*, ed. Lieven Boeve & John C. Ries (Leuven: Peeters, 2001) 181-196, p. 182.

half.[294] Although they tried to retrieve the Church's sacramental nature in reaction to modernism, the Church re-emphasized its hierarchical nature. But as already mentioned, pre-conciliar theology, through the writings of Otto Semmelroth, Karl Rahner and Edward Schillebeeckx, was finally able to retrieve the sacramentality of the Church. The Second Vatican Council's new vision of 'the Church for the world' again opened up new meanings for understanding sacramentality.[295] Reviewing the council documents, Avery Dulles notes that "the theme of the Church as an organized society or institution is clearly subordinated to those of the Church as mystery, sacrament, and communion of grace."[296]

2.2.1. The Sacramentality of the Church

The sacramentality of the Church is an assertion of the historical continuation of the Christ-symbol.[297] The Church, as the extension of Christ, contributed to the conception of the Church as the *Grundsakrament*, or 'basic sacrament'.[298] This means to say that "anyone who seeks a continuation of sacramental sacred history after the departure of Jesus finds this first and foremost in the Church that began after Jesus' departure and continues to this very day."[299] In other words, although Christ is the sole mediator between God and human beings, "the mystery of the Church, founded and willed by Christ as his body, has provided the value of sacramental mediation over the ages."[300]

Rahner, who developed the sacramentality of the Church, based on his Christology,[301] conceived the Church as the historical perceptibility of

294. Vorgrimler, *Sacramental Theology*, 35. The contributions of Johann E. Kuhn (d.1887), Johann H. Oswald (d.1903) and Matthias J. Scheeben (d.1888) are of particular importance in this context.

295. The history of the teaching which describes the Church as *mysterium* (sacrament), and in particular its context in Vatican II, has been exhaustively explored by Leonardo Boff in his book: *Die Kirche als Sakrament im Horizont der Welterfahrung: Versuch einer Legitimation und einer struktur-funktionalistischen Grundlegung der Kirche im Anschluß an das II. Vatikanische Konzil* (Paderborn: Bonifacius, 1972).

296. Avery Dulles, "A Half Century of Ecclesiology," *TS* 50 (1989) 419-442, p. 429.

297. The Scholastic tradition in the West followed a tendency to depict the relationship of Christ to the Church in terms of principal and instrumental causality. On the other hand the Eastern patristic tradition, especially Cyril of Alexandria, stressed the physical and organic union between the head and the members. The Church according to this view is a prolongation of Christ, who acts upon it from within rather than as an external efficient cause. Dulles, "A Half Century of Ecclesiology," 423-424.

298. Osborne, "Methodology and Christian the Sacraments," 41.

299. Lukken, "Church and Liturgy as Dynamic Sacrament of the Spirit," 142.

300. Catella, "Theology of the Liturgy," 3.

301. On this point Dulles notes that Rahner's "basic understanding of the Church was closely correlated with his vision of salvation history, with Jesus Christ as the culmination

Christ in space and time. In his opinion, the permanent union with Christ makes the Church the sign of God. Thus Rahner defines the sacramentality of the Church as:

> [T]he abiding presence of the primal sacramental word of definitive grace, which Christ is in the world, effecting what is uttered by uttering it in sign. By the very fact of being in that way the enduring presence of Christ in the world, the Church is truly the fundamental sacrament, the well-spring of the sacraments in the strict sense. From Christ the Church has an intrinsically sacramental structure.[302]

The continuing presence of the mystery of the salvation in Christ and of his grace makes the Church the primordial sacrament. "The sacrament as the fulfillment of the essence of this primordial sacrament are intrinsically linked to Christ and his grace."[303]

There are also others who have developed a theology based on a pneumatological perspective. For example, Kilmartin argues that, "strictly speaking, the Church is not the continuation of the Incarnation as such. There is a world of difference between the personalization of the human reality by the Logos in the Incarnation and the gathering of a New people into Christ through the Spirit."[304] By emphasizing "the relationship between Logos and Spirit in the sacraments, as experienced in the Church through Christ" Kilmartin tried to unpack the Christocentrism of some contemporary writing on the sacraments.[305]

2.2.2. Church for the World

The sacramental nature of the Church, besides the dignity of the Church, points to the mystery of the kingdom.[306] The kingdom of God is the pres-

of that history." Dulles, "A Half Century of Ecclesiology," 431.

302. Rahner, *The Church and the Sacraments*, 18.

303. Leijssen, "Rahner's Contribution to the Renewal of Sacramentology," 205. See Karl Rahner, "Membership of the Church according to the Teaching of Pius XII's Encyclical 'Mystici Corporis Christi'," *TI* 2 (Baltimore, MD: Helicon, 1969) 253-269.

304. Edward Kilmartin, "A Modern Approach to the Word of God and Sacraments of Christ: Perspectives and Principles," *The Sacraments: God's Love and Mercy Actualized*, ed. Francis A. Eigo (Philadelphia, PA: Villanova University Press, 1979) 59-110, p. 68.

305. *Ibid.*, 63.

306. We do not ignore the twofold interpretation of the kingdom of God. On the one hand, the kingdom of God is interpreted from an eschatological perspective. Especially the images like 'pilgrim Church' refer to the kingdom's eschatological nature. From this perspective, Avery Dulles notes that there was a new development in the 1950s where eschatology was reintegrated into ecclesiology. Accordingly, some ecclesiologists, drawing on new biblical studies, came to look upon the Church as the pilgrim people of God. For them, "the biblical concept of the *basileia theou* was seen not as identical with the

ence of God in Jesus for all humanity and the world at large. In this sense, the Church can be seen as the sacrament of the kingdom.[307] This means that the Church must be involved in Jesus' work as bearers of hope and liberation for a better future. It also challenges "mere" sacramental celebrations and exhorts the Church to consider the living realities of everyday life. In an age where Church and social life are often separated, the sacraments need, all the more, a human-social context. The sacraments are not simply an inner-Church affair but go beyond it to the greater social, religious and political sphere. Because "sacrament" cannot be reduced to 'the seven sacraments', it includes the possibility of seeing God in the secular. Real worship is to be found in responsible and loving behavior with other human beings, and in our readiness to engage ourselves for a more humane world.[308]

The salvific role of the Church, and the sacramental character of the Church, makes every entry to the Church a means of salvation.[309] For the Council Fathers, the Church is "a universal sacrament and, more pointedly, a universal sacrament of salvation."[310] Furthermore, the question of the salvific mission of the Church and its relation to outside the Church received new attention in post-Vatican ecclesiology.[311] Many authors argued that "the fruitfulness of the Church as sacrament (its *res sacramenti*) did not necessarily depend upon actual membership in the Church as effective sign (*sacramentum*)."[312] According to Avery Dulles, the assumption of Vatican II "seems to be that the Church plays an instrumen-

Church but as God's sovereign lordship bringing the Church, and indeed all creation, to their eschatological goal." Dulles, "A Half Century of Ecclesiology," 427. On the other hand, there is another tendency especially from the perspective of secular and political theology as well as the liberation theology to look at the Church as a sign and sacrament of the coming reign of God. *Ibid.*, 437-439.

307. Osborne, *Sacramental Theology: A General Introduction*, 95-96.

308. Padinjarekuttu, "Sacrament in Catholic History," 33.

309. Rahner, *The Church and the Sacraments*, 21-22.

310. Osborne, *Christian Sacraments in a Postmodern World*, 21.

311. Prior to the Council, the salvific mission of the Church to nonmembers was in discussion. For example Avery Dulles notes this already in the *votum* doctrine of Pius XII, in *Mystici corporis* and the "anonymous Christian" theory of Rahner. In order to explain the salvific efficacy of the Church for nonmembers, Rahner made a distinction between the Church and the people of God. In his opinion, "All human beings ... are ontologically consecrated to God by reason of the incarnation of the divine Logos, and thus are members of the People of God, even though only a relatively small minority belong to the Church as sacrament." Dulles, "A Half Century of Ecclesiology," 432.

312. *Ibid.*, 428. He also notes that, "The ancient idea of justification by baptism *in voto*, which the Council of Trent had applied also to penance [DS 1524 (on *votum baptismi*) and 1677 (on *votum* for the sacrament of penance)] was applied to the Church itself." The Church has taken up this view in 1949. DS 3866-73.

tal role in the salvation of everyone who is saved."[313] It acknowledges "salvation in non-Christian religions and cultures, encourage respect for the world, and ask the disciples of Christ to humanize the world, which is an essential ingredient of the proclamation of the Kingdom of God."[314]

The concern of the Church is not limited to its adherents alone and to every human being but even to the whole cosmos. "The Church is a sacrament, in so far as she communicates divine salvation as it operates in human life and the cosmos. The Church does this in and through the mystery of Christ and effects it in so far as she effects the liberation and unity of all human beings and the cosmos."[315] Hence, the worship of the Church and her sacraments should integrate the whole reality of humankind as well as the cosmos. Gerard Lukken draws our attention to the universal role of the Church as sacrament. In his opinion, the Church as the people of God is the bearer of Christian sacred history. At the same time, he points out that Christian sacred history rises above a particular people of God. The Church has a universal history intended for all humanity and for the whole cosmos. He underscores its mission for all, as one of service to all and for all peoples. He also notes the Church's unmistakable mission with regard to the cosmos.[316]

Communion ecclesiology[317] extends salvation to the whole universe. The communion ecclesiology proposes "the Church as a tangible and normative manifestation of the trinitarian structure of reality." The Church, in the trinitarian sense, "is *sacramentum mundi*, the sacramental realisation of God's design for the universe. ... It is also the sacrament of the human community as it reflects the many-in-one-communion character of the Trinity." The trinitarian being as communion is not only applicable to the human being but is also "the ground, source and pattern of all

313. *Ibid.* 430. In his opinion, "Without denying the necessity of the Church as means of salvation, he [Rahner] preferred to describe it as a result of God's grace offered to, and received by, human beings as incarnate spirits. The Church, in this perspective, is regarded as a sign of grace rather than as a cause of grace, even an instrumental cause." *Ibid.*, 433.

314. Padinjarckuttu, "Sacrament in Catholic History," 32.

315. *Ibid.*, 32-33.

316. Lukken, "Church and Liturgy as Dynamic Sacrament of the Spirit," 146.

317. Though Ernest Skublics terms it as 'a *Lumen Gentium* kind of ecclesiology', he tries to encompass in *Gaudium et Spes* as well. Ernest Skublics, "Communion Ecclesiology and the World: the Church as *Sacramentum Mundi*," *One in Christ* 34 (1998) 125-135, p. 125. In his opinion, in communion ecclesiology, one could percieve "a certain tension between an 'Alexandrian' emphasis on divinisation and recapitulation ... echoed by *Lumen Gentium*, on the one hand, and an 'Antiochean' tendency on the part of various political and liberation theologies, perhaps even in *Gaudium et Spes*, on the other hand, stressing the autonomy of the secular." *Ibid.*, 126.

being."[318] To experience this *koinonia* character of communion ecclesiology within the Church and in relation to the whole created universe, Ernest Skublics suggests to understand the Church not only as "the sacrament of *created* reality – the world – bu t reality as encompassing all."[319]

The Orthodox theologian, John D. Zizioulas, has expressed this idea by explaining the mystery of the Church through four theological presuppositions. He begins by situating ecclesiology in a trinitarian context with a clear distinction of the three persons in the Trinity as did the Cappadocian Fathers. Secondly, he suggests that "Christology must be conditioned by pneumatology in a constitutive way." Beyond recognizing the importance in the Spirit, it is equally important to see how the Spirit is active in the economy of the Son. Thirdly, he emphasizes the eschatological aspect of ecclesiology, by underscoring that Eschaton as not "the *end* of Church's pilgrimage." Rather, he suggests that the *eschata* is to be seen at "the beginning of the Church's life, the *arche*." Finally, he focuses on the cosmic dimension of ecclesiology. In his opinion, "the sacraments involve *all* creation in the being of the Church – not only humans – and the Church becomes in this way the very core and nucleus of the destiny of the world."[320]

For Skublics, the sacramental action is cosmically consecratory and it is a movement towards the 'recapitulation of all things' into the final perfect communion.[321] Communion, in the theological sense, brings people into solidarity with one another by giving them a share in the life of the triune God. It is a common participation in the gifts of salvation gained by Jesus Christ and bestowed by the Holy Spirit.[322] The Bishop's synod of 1985 declares: "The Church as communion is a sacrament for the salvation of the world."[323]

To conclude our discussion on the post-conciliar paradigms – Christ and Church as sacraments – one could say that it was the result of the retrieval efforts of the classical understanding of liturgy and sacraments. In this sense Irwin has rightfully observed that while Schillebeeckx and Rahner have emphasized the supreme value of the seven sacraments as explicated in the Tridentine doctrine, they also demonstrated how these

318. Skublics, "Communion Ecclesiology and the World," 126.

319. *Ibid.*, 127.

320. John Zizioulas, "The Mystery of the Church in Orthodox Tradition," *One in Christ* 24 (1988) 294-303, pp. 295-296.

321. Skublics, "Communion Ecclesiology and the World," 127-128.

322. Dulles, "A Half Century of Ecclesiology," 436.

323. Xavier Rynne, *Pope John Paul's Extraordinary Synod* (Wilmington, DE: Michael Glazier, 1986) 112-132, p. 127.

can be at the same time an "engagement with Christ and the church." In other words, Irwin has shown how these theologians have respected the sacramentology of Catholics since the Middle Ages and "as *sign and instrument of salvation* can be applied to other realities –Christ and the church – which operate in the act of engaging in the seven sacraments (as well as other liturgy)."[324] From this we see that the post-conciliar paradigms are basically not contradictory to the classical understanding of sacraments. Moreover, as Osborne argues, it is "the primordial relationship between the ritual sacraments and the Incarnation and the foundational relationship between ritual sacraments and the church," which "must be continued and developed."[325]

Positively, both these dimensions have broadened the understanding of sacramental rites from an individual centered understanding to include everything that is related to the salvific will of God. For example, Christ as the primordial sacrament of God's revelation to human beings and our response to God should address the existential context of his living.[326] In the same way the sacramentality of the Church makes sense only in its pastoral contexts, and by this the "new" understanding moves towards the patristic understanding of sacrament "as an event for the community and not as an event for the individual."[327] This broader view of the sacramentality of Christ and the Church equally undergirds the importance of the signification of sacrament in the world. It shows that the human relationship to God and to the world is an important concern in the understanding of the sacraments. Negatively, these paradigms set certain limitations, and are confined to the boundaries of the adherents of the Christian faith. For this reason, we should look for a new paradigm which will be able to address the issue of the significance of sacraments in the world and the possibility of going beyond the confines of the Church.

2.3. In Search of a New Paradigm

Osborne suggests three presuppositions in the study of the sacraments: "First of all, there is an ecclesiology which undergirds any theology and practice of sacraments. Undergirding the theology, on the other hand, is a Christology which shapes one's understanding of Church. ... A third presupposition involves the way in which one interprets the Scriptures, particularly the New Testament."[328] It is the Christological and ecclesiologi-

324. Irwin, "Sacramentality and the Theology of Creation," 162.
325. Osborne, *Christian Sacraments in a Postmodern World*, 48.
326. Vaillancourt, *Toward a Renewal of Sacramental Theology*, 39.
327. *Ibid.*, 45.
328 Osborne, *Sacramental Theology: A General Introduction*, 2.

cal presuppositions that helped theologians to rediscover Christ and the Church as paradigms in sacramentology. But it seems to us that we need to go even deeper than this to the Biblical presuppositions that shape sacramentology in a fundamental way. As already noted in the sacrament of salvation history, God's presence was always seen as revealed through Creation and through the persons and events in the Bible. It seems to us that any study of sacramentology has to consider this reality. Hence we take the Bible as the point of departure for our search for a new paradigm.

The Bible and Revelation are the first source of God's revelation prior to the historical incarnation of Jesus. It leads us to Creation, which is the beginning of God's presence in the world. At the very outset it should be made clear that going back to the Creation is not something new, rather it is the result of our ongoing effort to rediscover the earlier understanding of sacraments. For example, classical theology classified God's encounter with humanity in terms of 'natural sacraments' or 'Old Testament sacraments'. In this sense they tried to identify institutionalized rites and objects as sacraments.[329] Nevertheless, the goodness of all created things, which served as the matrix for the sacramentality of creation, fell into disuse in the course of time.[330] In Thomas Lane's opinion, "As the theology of the sacraments became more systematized, many other aspects of the sacramentality of the whole of creation were given less than due attention." He laments that "[i]t was not always recognized that the Lord had instituted the sacraments in the very movement of bringing his Church into existence. It was sometimes forgotten that there is a close,

329. Vorgrimler, *Sacramental Theology*, 15. "Under the concept of 'natural sacraments', sacramental theology discusses the question whether there were and are (a) in human history *before* the Jewish-Christian revelation or (b) in non-Christian, non-Jewish humanity upto the present day symbols – primarily cultic ones – of divine presence an activity ("embodiments of the general saving will of God," as Otto Semmelroth wrote)." Vorgrimler, *Sacramental Theology*, 16. On the classical theology of the pre-Christian sacraments, see Josef Finkenzeller, *Die Lehre von den Sakramenten im allgemeinen. Von der Schrift bis zur Scholastik*, Handbuch der Dogmengeschichte, 4/1a (Freiburg: Herder, 1980) 66-68; Otto Semmelroth, "Natursakramente," *LTK* 7 (1962) 829-830; Karl Rahner, "Sakramente, alttestamentliche," *LTK* 9 (1964) 239-240.

330. "Tertullian for example will list sacred actions and objects that sanctify as *sacramenta* and Augustine names over three hundred realities as 'sacraments' or 'mysteries'. Undergirding this theology is the understanding that created reality is good, which teaching contrasts with the Gnostics and Manichees. That creation is good and that sacraments reflect the goodness of creation are corollaries from the first delineation of Christian beliefs. Unfortunately this assumption tended to be understated (if not ignored) in the debates that the Church engaged in over sacraments through the Middle Ages." Irwin, "Sacramentality and the Theology of Creation," 167-168.

indeed essential, link between our bodiliness and our myriad links with all the elements of the created universe, through them with Christ."[331]

Considering the pitfalls even of the recent contributions in sacramental theology from various aspects, many theologians have called attention to the need for a new paradigm. It is beyond the limits of this study and it will be a Herculean task even to sketch out some such studies. At the same time we indicate a few points to show how this shift has guided theologians in articulating their concern.

As in the case of the aforementioned renewals, Orthodox theologians have made vital contributions in stimulating Catholic theologians to find such an option. Among the Orthodox theologians, approval of the failure in maintaining the sacramentality of Creation is already echoed in Alexander Schmemann, who in 1964, presenting the theme "The World as Sacrament" said: "[O]ur subject here is one that is only now beginning to be studied."[332] Although in recent years, one could see a flood of literature on the sacramentality of Creation from an Orthodox perspective, people like John Chryssavgis observes that the subject is still in its ascent stage.[333] At the same time one could observe that Orthodox sacramentology, rooted in the Greek *mysterion*, is better equipped to explain the sacramentality of Creation than the Latin *sacramentum*. John Chryssavgis explains that through the Greek use of *mysterion*, the number of sacraments is limitless, including everything in the cosmos that reflects the divine and inspires human beings with awe.[334] Philip Sherrard holds the same when he notes that "everything is capable of serving as the object of the sacrament, for everything is intrinsically consecrated and divine; is in fact, intrinsically a 'mysterium'."[335] At the same time, while emphasizing the essential sacramental nature of everything, the particular hierarchy of mysteries was not excluded. These are not contradictory, but complementary. The particular mysteries are considered as a sacred hierarchy of mysteries established in view of the particular conditions of individual existence in the world. Hence, as from the very beginning, the Church has upheld particular '*mysteria*' of special significance in the mystagogic,

331. Lane, "The Sacramentals Revisited," 273.

332. Alexander Schmemann, "The World as Sacrament," *Church, World, Mission*, ed. Alexander Schmemann (Crestwood, NY: St. Vladimir's Seminary Press, 1979) 217-227, p. 217. We shall see Schmemann's view in detail in the third chapter of this book.

333. John Chryssavgis remarked that 'world understood as sacrament' is now at last beginning to be studied. See Chryssavgis, "The World as Sacrament," 1.

334. Chryssavgis, "The World as Sacrament," 6.

335. Philip Sherrard, "The Sacrament," *The Orthodox Ethos: Essays in Honour of the Centenary of the Greek Orthodox Archdiocese of North and South America*, ed. A. J. Philippou (Oxford: Holy Well Press, 1964) 133-139, pp. 133-134.

or liturgical, life of the Church such as the two evangelic 'mysteries' of Baptism and the Eucharist. Sherrard lists the advantages of such a view. First of all, the broader view of sacramentality helps us to overcome the sacred profane dichotomy. For him, the sacramental principle is first based upon the recognition that the created order is not something which is divided into the sacred and profane. Secondly, it brings about the recognition of the essential 'likeness' the sanctifying power, what is sanctified, between the uncreated and the created. Finally, it helps us to recognize that the sacrament has a cosmic significance and is intimately related to every single aspect of created existence.[336] In this sense Philip Sherrard says:

> [S]acrament is not something set over against, or existing outside, the rest of life, so that it is sacred while the rest of life and all other things are non-sacred or profane or non-sacramental; it is not something extrinsic and fixed in its extrinsicality, as if by some sort of magical operation or *Deus ex machina* the sacramental object is suddenly turned into something other than itself and different from all other created objects. On the contrary, what is indicated or revealed in the sacrament is something universal, the intrinsic sanctity and spirituality of all things, what one might call their real nature.[337]

As John Chryssavgis notes: "There is a need for us constantly to recall the sacramental principle, which ultimately demands from us the recognition that nothing whatsoever in life is profane or unsacred. There is a likeness-in-the-very-difference between that which sanctifies (God) and that which is sanctified (creation), between uncreated and created."[338]

Among the Catholic theologians, Kevin Irwin using the importance of 'sacramentality' as the basic principle of liturgical and sacramental theology suggests such a paradigm.[339] Irwin asks to reconsider the relevance of the paradigms of Christ and the Church as sacraments. He critically questions the effectiveness of these paradigms "in bridging the gap between what occurs in liturgy and sacraments and what humans are engaged in the whole of human life."[340] In his opinion:

> [C]alling Christ and church (and other realities) 'sacraments' is to place the cart before the horse. The better approach would be to revisit the classical emphasis on the goodness of creation from the early Christian apologists on in order to substantiate how many things were understood to be 'sacraments'

336. Sherrard, "The Sacrament," 133-134.
337. *Ibid.*, 134.
338. Chryssavgis, "The World as Sacrament," 1.
339. Irwin, "Sacramentality and the Theology of Creation," 164.
340. Irwin, "Liturgical Actio: Sacramentality, Eschatology and Ecology," 114.

before the number of seven was assumed by Peter Lombard. This would mean combining the study of sacraments with Catholic theology's emphasis on the goodness of creation through and in which we discover the handiwork and hand of God for our salvation.[341]

According to him, "a return to emphasizing a positive theology of creation and sacramentality, characteristic of the Catholic tradition, can offer a most helpful complementary and contemporary paradigm for sacramental theology."[342] Irwin proposes "a sacramental theology that discusses sacramentality and the theology of creation at the outset and as a framework continually referred to for the study of liturgy and sacraments."[343] In his opinion, "the earliest textual references to what we have come to call 'liturgy and sacraments' are articulated as evidences of the church's belief in the goodness of creation which the liturgy uses to praise God."[344] In this sense he suggests a vision of sacramentality to articulate the Catholic sacramental vision, and advocates us to focus on the meaning of 'liturgical blessing'.[345] According to Irwin, though "things from creation are used in the liturgy to praise God and to sanctify humans ... not all of them have been termed *sacraments*. Their very use helps to orchestrate a sense of the whole universe as praising God the creator and redeemer."[346] From this he concludes that, "the number 'seven' for sacraments did not limit other liturgical uses of things from creation."[347]

341. Irwin, "Sacramentality and the Theology of Creation," 65.

342. *Ibid.*, 159-179. In this context we do not ignore the contributions of theologians like Teilhard de Chardin and Karl Rahner who engaged in retrieving the sacramentality of the world. For a brief survey of their contributions see Leijssen, "Rahner's Contribution to the Renewal of Sacramentology," 213-218.

343. Irwin, "Sacramentality and the Theology of Creation," 173.

344. *Ibid.*, 168.

345. *Ibid.*, 173-174. Irwin elaborates this theology of 'blessing', which is pivotal in the theology of the 'sacramentality of creation' in the following pages: 174-179.

346. *Ibid.*, 163. For Aquinas, "The explanation of the purpose of creation as the communication of God's goodness provides the basic key for understanding how in promoting the glory of God liturgy is not benefitting God but perfecting his creatures." *Summa Theologica* I, q. 44, a. 4; cf. II-III, q. 81, a. 7. Walsh, "Liturgy in the Theology of St. Thomas," 582.

347. Irwin, "Sacramentality and the Theology of Creation," 164. In his opinion, "The church's practice here signals the wide lens which Catholic belief has placed on reality and the way the whole of creation is incorporated in its central acts of prayer." *Ibid.* He even proposes "to reflect on evidences of ways the present reformed liturgy of the Catholic Church reflects our belief in the God of creation." *Ibid.*, 168. See also Kevin W. Irwin, "The Sacramentality of Creation and the Role of Creation in Liturgy and Sacraments," *Preserving the Creation: Environmental Theology and Ethics*, ed. Kevin W. Irwin & Edmund D. Pellegrino (Washington, DC: Georgetown University Press, 1994) 67-111.

Taking advantage of the view of the sacramental nature of things of Creation Irwin reverses Schillebeeckx's paradigm from "God to Christ to Church" to "sacraments, to human life and (finally) creation." Using Creation as the ground of theology, both natural and revealed, he asks theologians to study sacraments based on how the God of Creation and redemption is incarnated in the world and, therefore, discovered in the world and in all of human life. In his opinion, it will help to restore the integral vision of Catholicism and will support the value of life in the world, not out of the world, as well as the credibility of the Catholic sacramental structure. This will enable us to celebrate liturgy based on how Christians have always experience God – in nature, creation and human life.[348] He further argues that this broader understanding of sacramentality will enable Christians to envision all reality from a sacramental perspective. Furthermore, the celebration of sacraments will help them to better appreciate things in the world, resulting in a sacramental theology that combines humans' redemption and freedom from sin with a deepened sense of seeing sacraments as the crucial means to experience reality and to more deeply revere the goodness of God's Creation. This will also help us to see how God is discovered in all of Creation and human life, underscoring that true Catholic spirituality does not take us "out of the world." Rather, a sacramental spirituality uses the world and the things from the world to articulate our belief in the God of both redemption and Creation.[349]

Philosophical-theology also made significant contributions in affirming the need for a new paradigm in theology, emphasizing 'the sacramental presence of God in the world'. Twentieth century affirmations of the value of the body and the cosmos helped these theologians to critically value the goodness of Creation. This affirmation of the goodness, or the sacramentality, of Creation is potential to reveal the Creator. It goes beyond the immanence of God in Creation and speaks of mediating grace. Thus, Chauvet speaks of it as the 'gift of God'.[350] To a certain extent, he has helped to lay a foundation for the discussions on the 'Sacramental Presence in a Postmodern Context'.[351]

348. Irwin, "Sacramentality and the Theology of Creation," 173.

349. *Ibid.*, 165-166.

350. Chauvet already indicated the need for a new paradigm affirming the 'sacramentality of the world'. Chauvet, *Symbol and Sacrament*, 548-555. Mary Catherine Hilkert, *Naming Grace: Preaching and the Sacramental Imagination* (New York: Continuum, 1997).

351. It was the theme of the international conference of LEST II (Leuven Encounters in Systematic Theology). The conference in general affirmed this changing shift of the 'presence of God in the world'. *Sacramental Presence in a Postmodern Context*, ed.

There are also numbers of voices from liberation theology and third world theologians, who also stress the need for a new paradigm centered on 'world'.[352]

3. Conclusion

Our discussions on sacramentology in transition and the changing paradigms in sacramentology have pointed towards a paradigm shift in sacramentology, affirming the sacramentality of Creation. We have also seen glimpses of such reflections already in some contemporary writers. Considering the acceptance of such a paradigm in sacramentology, we go further to see the human response to the sacramentality of Creation. We undertake this study through a close reading of Alexander Schmemann representing liturgical theology and Leonardo Boff representing liberation theology in the next two chapters. As we shall see, both of them argue for the anticipation of the kingdom of God already in this world. At the same time, they differ in the way it is realized. For liturgical theologians, liturgy is the mode of such an experience. On the other hand, liberation theologians emphasize the need for constant engagement with the realities of the world.[353] Hence, our main focus is to see how the sacramentality of the world is appropriated by Schmemann, who keeps liturgical life as the center, and Boff, who keeps social engagement as the center.

Lieven Boeve & Lambert Leijssen (Leuven: Peeters, 2001); *Contemporary Sacramental Contours of a God Incarnate*, ed. Lieven Boeve & Lambert Leijssen (Leuven: Peeters, 2001); *The Presence of Transcendence: Thinking 'Sacrament in a Postmodern Age*, ed. Lieven Boeve & John C. Ries (Leuven: Peeters, 2001).

352. Mary Catherine Hilkert makes scant reference to ecology, despite citing a number of ecofeminist contributions. See reference among the feminist theologians, liberation theologians and third world theologians.

353. Nicholas Wolterstorff explicates this dichotomy well. According to him: "There are some for whom participation in the liturgy of the church replaces the struggle for justice; there are others for whom engaging in the struggle for justice replaces participation in the liturgy." At the same it is not opposed, because "[w]hat grounds and shapes our participation in the liturgy and is at the same time evoked by our experience of injustice, is suffering." Nicholas Wolterstorff, "Liturgy, Justice, and Tears," *Worship* 62 (1988) 386-403, p. 386.

Chapter Two

WORLD AS SACRAMENT IN LEONARDO BOFF
AN ETHICAL RESPONSE TO
THE SACRAMENTALITY OF CREATION

In this chapter we focus on "World as Sacrament" from the matrix of liberation theology of Leonardo Boff.[1] Although Boff affirms the sacramentality of Creation, his understanding of it is colored by liberation theology, which addresses the relevance of Christian faith in the face of injustice, not only done to the poor but also to Creation at large. This is neither a study on liberation theology, nor on the theology of sacraments in the liberation theology school. Rather, this study aims at a liberationist response to the sacramentality of Creation from the perspective of Boff. The selection of Leonardo Boff from various authors among the liberation theologians seems justifiable because of his numerous writings on sacraments and ecology. He is one among the prominent liberation theologians who has written extensively on mediated grace in the world.

This chapter is basically divided into two parts. In the first part we deal with his theology of sacraments and world-view. It will be followed in the second part on the world as sacrament. But before entering into these discussions, this study begins by mapping out Boff's theological concerns.

1. Leonardo Boff, born in 1938, entered the minor seminary at the age of 10 and subsequently became a Franciscan. He studied theology and philosophy at Curitiba and Petrópolis in Brazil and later studied at Oxford, Louvain, Würzburg, and Munich. He received his doctorate in Munich in 1972. For a time he was a research assistant for Karl Rahner in Munich. He was ordained in 1964. In 1985 he was asked to observe an 'obedient silence' by Rome mainly for his critical approach towards the institutional Church. He left the Franciscans and the ministerial priesthood in 1992. Economic globalization, the spread of poverty and the ecological crisis are some of the important concerns that are expressed in Boff's recent writings.

1. Theological Horizons of Leonardo Boff

Harvey Cox places Boff in the Franciscan tradition of Francis and Bonaventure. However, he also notes that Boff's study originally begins with the Bible and the Fathers of the Church. German and French theologies, and various schools of social analysis gave a good flavor to it.[2] In an earlier stage, Boff himself acknowledged various strands of influences in his theology and noted: "On the strength of my spiritual formation and basic option alike, I follow the Franciscan school – the synoptic, Antiochene, and Scotist tradition."[3] Given Boff's new state of life, these observations were of earlier origin and addressed primarily to assess his contribution to liberation theology. Considering various strands in Boff's theology, this study delineates a fourfold influence or concern in Boff: Franciscan tradition, European theology, liberation theology and ecological concerns.

1.1. Franciscan Tradition

Having undergone a Franciscan formation, the Franciscan tradition laid the foundation not only for Boff's theological thinking, but also for his entire life. As a Franciscan friar he gave a Franciscan flavor to all his theological engagements. Richard L. Payne underscores this especially in the case of his approach to sacramental theology.[4]

Besides, the various references to Francis of Assisi and to theologians from the Franciscan tradition in his writings, his book *Saint Francis: A Model for Human Liberation* is a tribute to the influence of Francis on him.[5] It was so fundamental that when he left the Franciscan Order, he said: "I am giving up the Franciscan Order, but not the dream, tender and fraternal, of St Francis of Assisi."[6] It seems that Boff is indebted to Francis of Assisi and Franciscan tradition in developing his theological methodology, sacramentology and option for the poor.

2. Harvey Cox, *The Silencing of Leonardo Boff: The Vatican and the Future of World Christianity* (Oak Park: Meyer/Stone, 1988) 43.

3. Leonardo Boff, *Passion of Christ, Passion of the World: The Facts, Their Interpretation, and Their Meaning Yesterday and Today* (Maryknoll, NY: Orbis, 1987) xii.

4. Richard L. Payne, *Sacramentality in the Writings of Leonardo Boff: Its Franciscan Roots, Its Elaboration, and Its Role in the Process of Liberation*, Thesis submitted for the licentiate degree (M.A.) in Religious Studies at K.U.Leuven (Leuven, 1993) 35.

5. Leonardo Boff, *Saint Francis: A Model for Human Liberation* (New York: Crossroad, 1982).

6. Reported in "Le P. Leonardo Boff renonce au sacerdoce," *La Libre Belgique* (1.7.92) 20.

First, it seems that the early Franciscan paradigm of "act, reflect, act"[7] is central in Boff's thought. In a certain sense, one can see its parallel in his seeing, judging, acting and celebrating hermeneutics of liberation theology.[8] Francis, who was not educated in the scholastic tradition, developed his own hermeneutic of doing theology. This is clearly seen by the hermeneutical criteria that Francis adopted to interpret the Scriptures, against the method used by the medieval schools.[9] Francis' reading of the Scripture was to practice it. Regarding this approach to Scripture, Théophile Desbonnets notes: "Francis opens the book of the gospels at random, reads the first passage he sees and, immediately, puts into practice, to the letter and without a gloss!"[10] This kind of reading of Scripture was not the kind of the fundamentalism of nineteenth century American Protestantism. On the contrary, "Francis did not read the gospel 'to the letter' but 'beyond the letter', in other words, according to the spirit."[11] This hermeneutical approach is also seen behind his emphasis on the lay ministry in the Church.[12]

Secondly, as a Franciscan, Boff remained within the Franciscan sacramental tradition that was expounded by Bonaventure (1217-1274) and Duns Scotus (1365-1408). The re-reading of Franciscan tradition helped him to go beyond the traditional sense of sacramentology and to look at various aspects of life as sacramentals. His theology of "sacramentality" might be his contribution to the Franciscan theology of the sacraments, without losing its original spirit.[13] In this regard, Francis' relation to the universe is also of particular importance.[14] It seems that "the trinitarian

7. Thomas of Celano, "The First Life of St Francis," *Saint Francis of Assisi: Writings and Early Biographies: English Omnibus of the Sources for the Life of St Francis*, ed. Marion A. Habig (Chicago, IL: Franciscan Herald Press, 1979) 29-31.

8. Leonardo Boff, *Cry of the Earth, Cry of the Poor*, trans Philip Berryman (Maryknoll, NY: Orbis, 1997) 109-110. See also Leonardo Boff, "Liberation Theology and Ecology: Alternative, Confrontation or Complementarity?" *Concilium* (1995), n. 5, 67-77, pp. 72-73.

9. Payne, *Sacramentality in the Writings of Leonardo Boff*, 6. It is important to note that Francis had even discouraged his members from full time learning and advocated them to engage in the service of the people. *Ibid.* 36.

10. Théophile Desbonnets, "The Franciscan Reading of the Scriptures," *Concilium* 149 (1981) 37-45, p. 41.

11. Desbonnets, "The Franciscan Reading of the Scriptures," 43.

12. Harvey Cox delineates this influence of Boff from Francis who initiated to place laity in the heart of the Church. Cox, *The Silencing of Leonardo Boff*, 34-35. One could see such an influence in his notion of 'ecclesiogenesis' and his stress on the mission of the basic Christian communities.

13. Payne, *Sacramentality in the Writings of Leonardo Boff*, 4.

14. Donald St John, "The Symbolic Spirituality of St Francis," *FrS* 39 (1979) 192-205, p. 197.

roots of Francis's picture of harmony and fraternity" grounds the foundation of Boff's vision of all things sacramental."[15] Francis' respect for Creation, however, must be understood as part of the medieval trend of the "anti-sacrament" of Creation.[16] Harvey Cox is right to note that "[C]ontrary to many of the prevailing theologies of the day, Francis did not consider natural beauty a distraction from God. For him it was a luminous medium through which the divine and human could meet." Furthermore Cox considered him as "a forerunner of that affirmation of the terrestrial world that blossomed later in the Renaissance."[17]

Thirdly, along with other liberation theologians he emphasizes the "option for the poor." In his option for the poor, he presents Francis as a model for liberation. It is clear from the fact that his book on Francis Assisi bears the subtitle *Saint Francis: A Model for Human Liberation*. Taking inspiration from real life situations in Latin America, Boff interprets fundamental dogmatic issues into their context. One observes a twin attitude of Francis towards the poor: "One is at the level of justice, the other at that of charity in the highest sense: love."[18] This approach is clearly seen in Boff's attitude towards the poor. Francis' way of looking at life from the common man's viewpoint is one of the factors that had a major influence on him. He explains Francis' "option for the poor" as a message for contemporary society.[19]

1.2. European Theology

European trends in theology and theologians also influenced the writings of liberation theologians from Latin America. As Turner points: "This hermeneutical switch resulted from the training Latin American theologians gained in European and American universities where they were exposed to various branches of hermeneutics, Marxism, critical theory etc."[20] Further he notes:

15. Payne, *Sacramentality in the Writings of Leonardo Boff*, 11.

16. *Ibid.*, 25. Payne observes three trends in Francis. First, "There is no trace of the wary dualism found among the Cathari or the Albigensians of his time." Secondly he had gone beyond the conventional neoplatonic understanding of nature. Thirdly, he "uses allegory as well. He saw a lamb and reflects on the Lamb of God, or a tree which reminds him of the wood of the cross." *Ibid.*, 25-27.

17. Cox, *The Silencing of Leonardo Boff*, 34.

18. Michael Mollat, "The Poverty of Francis: A Christian and Social Option," *Concilium* 149 (1981) 23-29, p. 26.

19. Boff, *Saint Francis: A Model for Human Liberation*, 48-80.

20. J. David Turner, *An Introduction to Liberation Theology* (Lanham, MD/New York/London: University Press of America, 1994) 14.

Latin American theologian exposure to Marxism, Critical Theory, and other European influences, has profoundly changed their way of doing theology. This 'new hermeneutic' was arrived at by critical theory, and it has evolved into a full blown theology that constantly questions religious activity in light of Biblical themes. Critical theory is one of the European philosophical disciplines that has greatly influenced liberation theologians.[21]

Boff is not an exception to this. He spent quite a long period in various European universities. In his earlier writings, one sees the reflections of the European mindset, especially in the areas of Ecclesiology, Sacraments, Trinity, Christology etc. These were written again combining his experience with the people of Latin America and by addressing their concerns. This is clearly seen in his writings. For example his writings on all major topics like sacraments, christology, ecclesiology, trinity etc. had later additions.[22]

Boff also endorses the need for other disciplines in order to develop a genuine theology.[23] This is very clearly seen in Boff's later writings. Especially his recent writings contain studies done in the areas of science, culture, anthropology, sociology etc.,

1.3. Liberation Theology

The third major influence on Boff is grounded on the liberation theology movement in which he is a fellow traveler. It grew out of a dialogue between Church and society, between Christian faith and the liberation aspirations of people in the midst of all kinds of injustice.[24] For Boff, "liberation theology must not be a topic within theology, rather it must be a perspective from which other things are understood, analyzed and ex-

21. *Ibid.*, 16, see also 43-54. For a short sketch of the influence of European theology on Liberation theology see Rosino Gibellini, *The Liberation Theology Debate* (Maryknoll, NY: Orbis, 1987) 13-19.

22. A close reading of his bibliography will make this fact clear. His earlier writings on each topic bear a classical method of explaining the dogmatic issues scientifically based on biblical, patristic and scholarly works. But his later writings are based on his reflections of these themes based on his encounter with the living realities of the world.

23. See Leonardo Boff, *Faith on the Edge, Religion and Marginalized Existence*, trans. Robert R. Barr (Maryknoll, NY: Orbis, 1989) 61, 113; *Jesus Christ Liberator: A Critical Christology for our Time* (Maryknoll, NY: Orbis, 1978) 272; "Salvation in Liberation: The Theological Meaning of Socio-historical Liberation," *Salvation and Liberation: In Search of a Balance between Faith and Politics*, ed. Leonardo & Clodovis Boff (Maryknoll, NY: Orbis, 1984) 1-13, pp. 4-8; "Integral Liberation and Partial Liberation," *Ibid.*, 46-50.

24. Leonardo & Clodovis Boff, *Introducing Liberation Theology* (Maryknoll, NY: Orbis, 1987) 68-69.

plained."[25] As already indicated, his involvement with the movement significantly transformed his theological thinking. Along with other theologians from Latin America, Boff engaged himself with the struggles of the people for liberation from a twofold experience: political and theological.[26]

From the political perspective he looks at the poor as a social and epistemological *locus* for "a particular and specific reading of history and society."[27] For Boff "the poor occupy the central epistemological place in liberation theology."[28] From this perspective he argues that liberation theology is "a fact-finding exercise from the point of view of the oppressed people themselves."[29] He even argues that "to understand the theology of liberation, we must first understand and take an active part in the real and historical process of liberating the oppressed."[30] He looks into "the presence of God, and God's grace – or the presence of the evil one, and sin – within economic and social processes."[31] As Turner rightly observes, "Liberation theology resulted from a 'hermeneutic switch' in doing theology" by writing it from the perspective of the poor.[32]

Boff also uses theological experience in order to deepen political experience. From this perspective, he notes that basic Christian communi-

25. Leonardo Boff, "The Originality of the Theology of Liberation," *The Future of Liberation Theology: Essays in Honor of Gustavo Gutierrez*, ed. Marc Ellis & Otto Maduro (Maryknoll, NY: Orbis, 1989) 38-48, p. 38.

26. Leonardo Boff, *Ecology and Liberation: A New Paradigm*, trans. John Cumming (Maryknoll, NY: Orbis, 1995) 97.

27. *Ibid.*, 97. According to Boff, "[t]he main thrust of liberation theology, back in the 1960's, was ethical indignation ... in the face of the collective poverty and wretchedness of the masses." Furthermore, he contends that "[t]he option for the poor against their poverty and for their liberty constituted and still constitutes the central axis of liberation theology." Boff, "Liberation Theology and Ecology," 70. Gustavo Gutierrez says the same when he notes: "Our job today is to reveal history in terms of the poor." Gustavo Gutierrez, "Statement by Gustavo Gutierrez," *Theology in the Americas*, ed. Sergio Torres & John Eagleson (Maryknoll, NY: Orbis, 1976) 310. John Sobrino also speaks of the poor as *locus theologicus* by explaining how the poor are kept as a source of theological thinking in the Gospels. John Sobrino, *Jesus the Liberator*, trans. Paul Barns & Francis McDonagh (Maryknoll, NY: Orbis, 1993) 79-82.

28. Boff, "Liberation Theology and Ecology," 71. In this sense from the perspective of the poor they "try and define the concept of God, of Christ, of grace, of history, of churches' mission, the meaning of economics, politics and the future of societies and human beings."

29. Boff, "The Originality of the Theology of Liberation," 44.

30. L. & C. Boff, *Introducing Liberation Theology*, 9.

31. Leonardo Boff, "Integral Liberation and Partial Liberations," *Salvation and Liberation: In Search of a Balance between Faith and Politics*, ed. Leonardo & Clodovis Boff (Maryknoll, NY: Orbis, 1984) 46-47.

32. Turner, *An Introduction to Liberation Theology*, 14.

ties interpret Scripture with the pages of life. Thus, he attempts that it is God, "who hears the cry of the Hebrews in their servitude in Egypt and sets them free. This God hears the cry of Jesus on the cross and raises him up. Today this God legitimizes the liberation struggles of millions of human beings."[33]

In this sense, Boff argues that "[a]ll theology is built from a twin point of departure – a double locus ... from the locus of faith [The *Kairological* Today] and from the locus of the social reality [The Chronological Today] in which faith is lived." In other words, theology has two eyes: "'one before and one behind' (*theologia ante et retro oculata*). With the 'eye behind' theology looks to the past, where God's definitive salvific presence has burst in upon our universe." [This is drawn from the Scripture, conciliar texts, testimonials of saints, traditions of the people of God.] "With the 'eye before', theology looks to the present," and is correct only "when it succeeds in expressing the truth of faith (glimpsed by its backward-looking eye) in such a manner as to produce an existential, social meaning in the present (viewed by the forward-looking eye). Only then we are certain that we are not seeing double; we are seeing both the reality of faith and the reality of our present day in a correctly balanced binocular perspective."[34]

1.4. Ecology

In recent years, however, Boff's writings seem to have taken a different cause. After leaving the ministerial priesthood, he broadened his theological horizons and began to concentrate more on issues like ecology. Unlike his earlier writings, which were re-readings and reinterpretations of Christian tradition in favor of liberation process, his new writings look also into the non-Christian religious traditions and scientific theories.

He applies the logic of liberation theology to eco-theology. For him, "human catastrophe is liberation theology's starting point for considering

33. Boff, *Ecology and Liberation*, 97-98.

34. Boff, *Faith on the Edge*, 111. This idea is repeatedly present in his writings. For example, his *Way of Cross – Way of Justice* indicates the same. The 'way of cross' refers to the focus on the historical Jesus and the 'way of justice' refers to the focus on the Christ of Faith "who continues his passion today in his brothers and sisters who are being condemned, tortured and killed for the cause of justice." Leonardo Boff, *Way of Cross – Way of Justice* (Maryknoll, NY: Orbis, 1980) viii. Similarly in his book, *The Lord's Prayer: The Prayer of Integral Liberation* (Maryknoll, NY: Orbis, 1983), he examines the Lord's Prayer from theology's two eyes. Thus, prayer is always toward God and toward us. Robert McAfee Brown, "Leonardo Boff: Theologian for All Christians," *Christian Century* (July 2-9, 1986) 615.

ecology."[35] In his opinion: "The logic that exploits classes and subjects peoples to the interests of a few rich and powerful countries is the same as the logic that devastates the Earth and plunders its wealth."[36] Therefore, he argues that "[i]t is not only the poor and the oppressed that must be liberated; today all humans must be liberated." Therefore, he claims that he is "extending the intuitions of liberation theology and demonstrating their validity and applicability for the questions enveloping the earth."[37]

Furthermore, Boff is influenced by various ecological challenges from the world at large.[38] Along with many of the early ecologists he blames Christianity for the ecological crisis.[39] Accepting this reality, he tries to reinterpret Christian responsibility to work for the betterment of Creation. He underscores how the ecological question leads to a new level of global awareness emphasizing "the importance of the earth as a whole, the common good of nature and of humankind, the interdependence of all, and the apocalyptic dangers that threaten the creation."[40]

The worldwide ecological crisis forced him to devote his energies to the mystery of Creation itself. For him, "the true and really radical mystery is the mystery of the world."[41] In this sense, Boff links ecological discussions with theology by interpreting Creation as the sacrament of God. For him, Creation is a sacrament of God because his notion of sacraments expresses the interplay among human beings, the world and God. He explains the interplay between human beings and the world in three levels. The first level is the human experience of *awe and wonder*. Its *domestication* happens in the second level, where humans try to understand the reasons behind their awe and wonder. Finally, they become *habituated* to objects, and they become part of their landscape.[42] In this process or interplay, there is also a change taking place in human beings and the objects themselves. The domesticated objects begin to tell the

35. Boff, *Cry of the Earth, Cry of the Poor*, 112. In this sense, social ecology, or the way human beings relate to one another and to other beings in nature, becomes the starting point.

36. *Ibid.*, xi.

37. *Ibid.*, xii.

38. In his book *Cry of the Earth, Cry of the Poor* he has given a lot of statistics to show the damage of the earth through the exploitation of nature. For example see Boff, *Cry of the Earth*, 1-6, 86-104.

39. Boff, *Ecology and Liberation*, 43-45.

40. *Ibid.*, 15.

41. Leonardo Boff, *The Path to Hope: Fragments from a Theologian's Journey*, trans. Phillip Berryman (Maryknoll, NY: Orbis, 1993) 6.

42. Leonardo Boff, *Sacraments of Life, Life of the Sacraments: Story Theology*, trans. John Drury (Beltsville, MD: Pastoral Press, 1987) 2-3.

story of their interplay with humanity. Thus they are transformed into sacraments.[43] For him, "[t]hings are bearers of salvation and a Mystery. That is why they are sacramental."[44]

2. Sacrament and World in Boff

Before entering further into the discussions on the sacramentality of the world and human responsibility towards the sacramentality of the world, it is worth seeing how Boff understands sacramentology and world-view. In this regard this study is limited to some important notions that are specific to Boff and relevant to our topic.

2.1. Sacraments

Boff's theology of sacraments could be seen at the center of his theological odyssey. He holds a broader understanding that goes beyond the sevenfold ritual understanding. This broader notion of sacraments is an important tool to understand his theological concerns in general. Therefore, this section begins by clarifying some important notions pertinent to his sacramentology. It follows with his understanding of sacraments in terms of sacramental economy, Christ as sacrament and Church as sacrament.

2.1.1. Some Basic Notions on Sacraments in Boff

Some terminological clarifications are important, not only to understand Boff's theology of sacraments, but also to understand his theology in general. Although there are different notions that often occur in his writings, with their particular meanings, this study is limited to three notions: transparence, experience and theological language.

2.1.1.1. Transparence

The term 'transparence' is a key notion in Boff's sacramentology. He draws this from his own interpretation of Ephesians 4:6: "There is only one God and Father of all, who is over all (transcendence), works through all (transparence), and is in all (immanence)."[45] For him, transparence is a middle dimension between transcendence and immanence. Transcendence and transparence "are not two separate entities" rather "two dimen-

43. *Ibid.*, 3.

44. *Ibid.*, 4.

45. Leonardo Boff, *Die Kirche als Sakrament im Horizont der Welterfahrung: Versuch einer Legitimation und einer struktur-funktionalistischen Grundlegung der Kirche im Anschluß an das II. Vatikanische Konzil* (Paderborn: Bonifacius, 1972), 125-130; Id., *Sacraments of Life*, 24-25, p. 31.

sions of one and the same life. They come joined together in the historicity of human beings as two facets of their radical reality."[46] He believes that the term transparence not only helps to avoid the dualism between immanence and transcendence, but it explains the coexistence of both in the one and the same thing. Transparence "manifest the presence of transcendence within immanence, making each transparent to the other."[47] For him, transparence is symbolic. It "is neither transcendence nor immanence but rather 'one in the other' or 'the other in the one'."[48]

> No longer is the world divided between immanence and transcendence. There is another intermediary category, transparence, that embraces both immanence and transcendence. The latter two realities are not opposed to one another or mutually exclusive. They meet and communicate with each other. Here 'transparence' means that the transcendence is rendered present in the immanent so that the latter makes the reality of the former transparent. The transcendent breaks through into the immanent, transfigures it, and thus makes it transparent.[49]

The notion of transparence, which holds transcendence and immanence in tension, makes the sacrament unique. A sacrament becomes opaque when it becomes "wholly immanent and excludes the transcendent;" and it becomes abstract when it is "wholly transcendental and excludes the immanent."[50] The transparence of things in reference to God has a positive value that "enables us to understand sacramental structure and sacramental thinking."[51] Furthermore, an acceptance of this 'sacramental thinking' transforms us into a sacramental being. For him, sacramental thinking enables one to look at things of the earth that we come across in our life and the persons whom we encounter in a different way. They become unique and incomparable and become part of our lives. In this sense "they are no longer merely things. They are sacraments in our life, be it blessed or cursed."[52] The paradoxical nature of sacrament is made clear in that it "is part of the (immanent) world, but it holds within

46. Leonardo Boff, *Liberating Grace*, trans. John Drury (Maryknoll, NY: Orbis, 1990) 36.

47. Boff, *The Lord's Prayer: A Prayer of Integral Liberation*, 2.

48. Boff, *Die Kirche*, 126.

49. Boff, *Sacraments of Life*, 24-25.

50. *Ibid.*, 25.

51. *Ibid.*, 31.

52. *Ibid.*, 18. Using the narrative theology Boff expounded this theory throughout in his book: *Sacraments of Life, Life of the Sacraments*.

it another (transcendent) world: God. And insofar as it makes God present, it is part of that other world as well."[53]

The advantage of a sacramental thinking is that such a view does not make a distinction between the sacred and the profane. Therefore, sacred-profane dichotomy has no place in his thinking. In his opinion, "God's self-communication occurs in both the sacred and the profane. Both stand under God's loving activity and are forms of God's self-communication to creation and humankind." It means that both faith and religion can and must be worked out both in the sacred and profane world. This understanding helps him to justify secularization. For him, it is not opposed to religion and faith. At the same time, he cautions against sacralization. In his opinion "[s]ecularization is a different way of living out our faith and our relationship with God."[54]

2.1.1.2. Experience

The notion 'experience' is also very important in Boff's understanding of sacramentality. For Boff, "*[e]x-peri-ence* is the knowledge a person acquires when one goes forth from oneself (*ex*) and studies from every angle and perspective (*peri*) the world of things or realities (*ence*) around one."[55] In this sense it is an encounter between "a subjective element (existence) and an objective element (things)."[56] It is not a kind of knowledge, which is theoretical, but something that is acquired by working with realities.[57] Boff's understanding of 'experience' is centered on two areas of human 'experience'. Experience, on the one hand, "has to do with danger and trials (*periculum* and *periclitatio*). On the other hand it has to do with knowledge acquired (*peritia, scientia, notitia*)."[58] In this sense experience "is not just a *scientia*, a kind of knowledge," rather it denotes "an authentic *conscientia*, a kind of awareness."[59]

For Boff experience becomes sacramental as we experience God in it. Therefore, "Grace can be grace for us today only if it emerges from

53. *Ibid.*, 31.

54. Boff, *The Path to Hope*, 42.

55. Leonardo Boff, *God's Witness in the Heart of the World* (Chicago, IL: Claret Center for Resources in Spirituality, 1981) 32. Experience is "the way in which we relate ourselves to the world: the way in which we make the world present inside ourselves and the way in which we render ourselves present in the world. Experience is our particular way, within a given culture, of interpreting all the reality we find around us, e.g., the self, others, society, nature, God, the past, the present, and the future." Boff, *Liberating Grace*, 38.

56. Boff, *God's Witness in the Heart of the World*, 34.

57. *Ibid.*, 32-33.

58. Boff, *Liberating Grace*, 39.

59. *Ibid.*, 40.

within the world in which we ourselves are immersed." He even argues that "[o]nly by immersing ourselves in the reality around us can we experience its aspects of gratuitousness and grace."[60] In other words, grace is the result of an interiorization of a reality by situating "ourselves in the world and the world in us."[61] Therefore, he insists that instead of placing the traditional emphasis on the doctrinal aspect of grace, theology "must *ponder* and think about the experience of grace that is taking place today in the world and in the church." Based on this he prefers to allow "grace do the talking" instead of "talking *about* grace."[62] It is also important to note that Boff is not limiting grace to an experience in the personal level. For him, grace is also an experience of God reflected in all of Creation, especially in human beings and in their history. It "signifies the presence of God in the world and in human beings" and "the openness of human beings to God." It is an "encounter between a God who gives himself and a human being who does likewise." From this perspective, he argues that "grace signifies the reconciliation of heaven and earth, of God and humans, of time and eternity."[63]

For Boff, grace is an experience of God's kenotic love for us. For human beings, it is an experience of being loved by God.[64] Boff asserts that "grace is given not extrinsically by an ad hoc, extraneous gesture of God but intrinsically through the very experience itself."[65] Even a negative experience can be sacramental. In liberation Christology, "the real situation with all its contradictions is here perceived by an intuitive and sapiential process of cognition." It is considered 'sacramental' because in the facts of real life it symbolically intuits the presence of oppression and the urgent need for liberation.[66]

For him, "Grace and dis-grace are two possibilities of freedom." It belongs to "the mystery of creation, ... to which reason does not have access." In this sense he even notes the experience "of being simultaneously graced and dis-graced: '*Omnis homo Adam, omnis homo Christus*'."[67] He demonstrates this through two movements: one 'from above'

60. *Ibid.*, 40.

61. Boff, *God's Witness in the Heart of the World*, 35.

62. Boff, *Liberating Grace*, 5.

63. *Ibid.*, 3. For Boff, human beings become central in the sense that all known creation humans alone have a vocation, an invitation from God to dialogue with God in the building up of this world. Boff, *Faith on the Edge*, 98.

64. Boff, *Liberating Grace*, 3.

65. Thus, Boff joins Schillebeeckx in emphasizing the "this-worldliness" of grace. See Herman-Emiel Mertens, "Nature and Grace in Twentieth-Century Catholic Theology," *LS* 16/3 (1991) 224-262, p. 262.

66. Boff, *Jesus Christ Liberator*, 269.

67. Boff, *Liberating Grace*, 4-5.

and the other 'from below'. The first is a movement "running from God to the thing," which he calls the *indicatory* or sign function of a sacrament. The second is a movement "running from the thing to God" called *revelatory*, or expression of a sacrament.[68] In his opinion: "At the first stage of sacramental thinking, everything is seen *sub specie humanitatis*."[69] It means that "[v]iewed *sub specie humanitatis*, all things express and symbolize humanity. They are human sacraments."[70] In other words, "[s]acramental thinking views reality not as a thing but as a symbol."[71] All things can become sacraments for human beings, "so long as human beings open up to all things and welcome them into their human abode."[72]

Faith plays an important role in this regard.[73] From this perspective he

68. The *indicatory function* of a sacrament means: "a sacramental object points to God present within it. God is apprehended *in* the object, not *along* with the object." And it is our responsibility to "transcend the object and see the God communicated in the sacrament." The *revelatory function of a sacrament* is understood as that truly reveals, communicates, and expresses God, who is present in an object. Through this movement God who is invisible and intangible, becomes visible and tangible. "God's ineffable presence in the object means that the latter becomes transfigured and diaphanous. Without ceasing to belong to this world, it becomes an instrument and vehicle of communication with God's world, the place of God's transparence and diaphany." Boff, *Sacraments of Life*, 31-32.

69. Boff, *Sacraments of Life*, 17.

70. *Ibid.*, 29.

71. *Ibid.*, 17.

72. *Ibid.*, 19.

73. Boff delineates five aspects of faith to understand sacrament as a symbolic thrust or movement. "*First*, a sacrament presupposes faith. Without faith a sacrament says nothing about anything." "*Second*, a sacrament expresses faith." This does not mean adherence to any particular creed. Rather it "is an attitude whereby human beings open themselves up to welcoming a transcendent reality that is heralded in the world." ... "*Third*, a sacrament nurtures faith." "In expressing themselves, human beings change both themselves and the world. By ex-carnating and objectifying themselves, they elaborate the words and actions that help to nurture their faith and their religion." "*Fourth*, a sacrament concretizes the universal church for a specific crucial situation in life: birth, marriage, eating, sickness, and so forth. Hence ... To experience and live the reality of a specific sacrament, which concretizes the universal sacrament of the church, one must adequately live the experience of the universal sacrament (the church). Only then does a sacrament cease to be mere magic and assume its authentic symbolic function." "*Finally*, a sacrament embodies and displays a threefold symbolic dimension. It *remembers the past*, where the experience of grace and salvation burst into the world; it keeps alive the memory of the cause of all liberation, Jesus Christ and the history of his mystery. A sacrament also *celebrates a presence in the here and now faith*: that is, grace being made visible in the rite and being communicated to human life. Thirdly, a sacrament *anticipates the future* in the present: that is, eternal life, communion with God, and the shared banquet with all the just." Boff, *Sacraments of Life*, 83-85.

notes that sacraments "are deeply rooted in human life."[74] For him, sacramental moments occur wherever Christians celebrate the breakthrough of grace into their lives and communities. Hence, the family mug, a rock or a tree becomes sacrament as we experience God through these symbols. "If God is the unique Absolute, then everything in existence is a revelation of God. For those who experience God as alive in this way, the immanent world becomes transparent, allowing this divine, transcendent reality to shine through it. The world becomes diaphanous. As St. Irenaeus put it: "Nothing is a vacuum in the face of God. Everything is a sign of God. (*Adversus Haeresis* 4.21)."[75] In this sense those human beings who are able to see things from God's perspective, or to have a religious experience of it, then the whole world becomes a sacrament.[76]

2.1.1.3. Theological Language

Boff criticizes the traditional argumentative use of theological language. Its main concern was to convince human beings of the truth of religion, which in his opinion is an illusion. On the contrary, he argues that religious truth "is basically and primarily a vital experience, an encounter with ultimate meaning." This experience is later articulated rationally in different cultures.[77]

For him, the sacramental language and sacramental symbols that failed to relate to experience are behind the denial of the traditional understanding of symbols and sacraments by modern humanity. It does not mean, however, that they lost the sense of the symbolic and the sacramental. They are critical to sacramental symbols that had become now strict and anachronistic. Their reaction is precisely to the "ritual mummification of Christian sacraments."[78] Boff gives three reasons for the distortion of sacramental symbolism that give sacraments a diabolic thrust or movement. First, "[a] sacrament can be distorted into mere *sacramentalism*" in the sense of participating in sacraments without proper preparation and conversion. Secondly, there is "the *infiltration of a capitalistic spirit.*" This means that believers participate in the sacramental celebrations in view of "accumulating grace." Thirdly, there is the *spirit of magic* that becomes attached to sacramental celebrations.[79]

74. *Ibid.*, 4.

75. *Ibid.*, 30.

76. Boff, *Die Kirche*, 131. "Für die Menschen, die alles von Gott her sehen oder ein religiöses Erlebnis haben, wird der ganze Kosmos ein Sakrament, die ganze Natur eine grosse sakrale Hierophanie."

77. Boff, *Sacraments of Life*, 6.

78. *Ibid.*, 2.

79. *Ibid.*, 85-86.

Boff proposes a language for sacraments that 'is narrative and celebratory'. For him, it must enable humans to encounter God, which leads to involvement and conversion.[80] Accordingly, he explains three characteristics of sacramental language. First of all, there is an evocative nature that "narrates an event, relates a miracle, or describes a revelatory divine breakthrough in order to evoke in human beings God's reality, behavior, and promise of salvation." In this sense "[s]acraments are essentially evocations of a past and a future that are lived in the present." Secondly there is a call for self-involvement. Finally, he notes the performance-oriented nature of religious and sacramental language, which "tends to alter human praxis, to induce conversion."[81] In this way, narrative language helps him to call the family mug a sacrament. It belongs to the basic constituents of human life, present in the most elementary acts of life. It is faith that ritualizes them and elevates them to sacramental life.[82]

2.1.1.4. Number of Sacraments

Boff considers the sacraments as part of God's saving plan; derived from the eternal preexistent Word, along with the saving plan that is also derived from the eternal Word. Thus, he interprets the institution of Christian sacraments by Christ on four levels. First, through the eternal Word, God communicates himself in the rites that express the relationship of human beings with God. Secondly, the incarnate Word in history links everything to his Mystery, giving Christic depth to everything. Thirdly, the three sacraments – Baptism, the Eucharist and Penance – explicitly refer to Christ as their author. Fourthly, Christ instituted the sacraments in the sense that he instituted the Church as the universal sacrament.[83] Hence Grace is not limited to the seven signs of faith, rather "[e]verything the church does have a sacramental density because the church is fundamentally a sacrament."[84] In this sense "the Church as sacrament extends over all human life. The seven rites are not isolated events, but essential rites of a faith whose roots are christological and

80. *Ibid.*, 5.

81. *Ibid.*, 6-7.

82. *Ibid.*, 7. This is clear from the way that "Boff discloses how persons (his father and his school teacher), nature (light), and things (bread, house) can be sacramental, often linking these narratives with principles of sacramental theology (such as their symbolic substructure)." David N. Power, et al., "Sacramental Theology: A Review of Literature," *TS* 55 (1994) 657-705, p. 676.

83. Boff, *Sacraments of Life*, 67-68.

84. *Ibid.*, 5.

ecclesiological."[85] They "are acts of the church that touch human beings at the crucial moments in their lives."[86]

In the Church, the sacrament takes concrete shape in various situations of life through the seven fold sacramental structure.[87] Boff conceives two answers for the legitimacy of seven sacraments. First, at the level of conscious history, he considers the historical development of fixing the sacrament into seven. Second, at the unconscious or structural level, the seven sacraments are considered as unconscious expressions of the pivotal points of human life.[88]

Having seen some of the basic notions in understanding Boff's sacramentology, we shall now see how he underscores salvation history, Christ and Church as sacraments.

85. *Ibid.*, 56, 59, 73. "The church as sacrament extends its activity over the whole of life, but it does so in different ways. It presents itself at the key moments of existence, making explicit the presence of God who graciously accompanies us. These are the essential rites of the faith, which give reality and actuality to the very essence of the church as a sign of salvation in the world. Once the essence of the church is made real, theology can detect it and specify it. It can determine the essential sacraments of the faith are seven. The principal sacraments of the faith are made concrete in the principal and pivotal points of human life. Life is replete with grace." Boff, *Sacraments of Life*, 59.

86. *Ibid.*, 73.

87. *Ibid.* , 5.

88. According to Boff, from the historical perspective "there are seven sacraments because the church decided that and Jesus Christ wanted it!" In his opinion, the oldest tradition of the church considered everything as sacred. For example, he notes that Augustine had numbered 304 sacraments. From among the hundreds of sacraments, theologians of the twelfth century began to pinpoint seven primordial acts of the Church as sacraments. It began with such theologians as Rudulfus Ardens (d.1200), Otto of Bamberg (d.1139), and Hugh of Victor (d.1141). The Church officially adopted this at the Synod of Lyons in 1274 and at the Council of Florence in 1439 and finally at the Council of Trent in 1547. From the point of sacraments as pivotal points of human life he illustrates how each of these seven is crucial to our life. He also draws our attention to the symbolic meaning of seven. It comprises of 3 plus 4. Based on depth psychology, structuralism, the Bible and tradition, he argues that 7 is the specific symbol of the totality of an ordered plurality. "The number 4 is the symbol of the cosmos (with its four elements: earth, air, fire, and water), of movement, and immanence. The number 3 is the symbol of the Absolute (the Holy Trinity), of spirit, of rest, and of transcendence. The sum of both, the number 7, signifies the union of the immanent and the transcendent, the synthesis of movement and rest, and the meeting of God and humanity (that is, the incarnate Word of God, Jesus Christ). With the number 7, we are trying to express the fact that the totality of human existence, with its material and spiritual dimensions, is consecrated by the grace of God. Salvation is not restricted to seven channels of communication. The totality of salvation is communicated to the totality of human life, and it is manifested in a significantly tangible way in the pivotal points of life. This is the fundamental meaning of seven." Boff, *Sacraments of Life*, 56-60.

2.1.2. Sacramental Nature of History

Boff considers history as a sacrament because of the revelatory character of God's saving plan manifested in it.[89] In his opinion, the early Church considered human history as sacrament because it reveals God's salvation plan, by way of acceptance or rejection of God's grace by human beings. The events of the Old Testament on the one hand, "bore a transcendent meaning, fleshing out God's saving plan," and on the other hand it bore witness to a human 'no' to God's salvific plan through the actions against the will of God. In this sense human history is presented as the history of salvation or damnation. Their particular experience at a particular time becomes an occasion to look retrospectively and to see its implicit presence in the past events. This continual rereading of the history enabled them to look at the past as "sacrament of the present."[90] In this sense, he even notes that "history itself could be a sacrament."[91]

> [Grace is understood] in terms of history, e.g., the liberation from Egypt, the fact of creation, and the election of Israel. ... The theme of the covenant, in particular, expresses the experience of something *more* that is bound up with grace. Out of pure benevolence God chooses the lowliest people of all to proclaim and bear witness to the one God. Israel experiences the reality of its singular place in history as a grace that goes beyond the fact of creation common to all peoples. Grace is always lived as the merciful goodness of God, not in abstract but in historical terms.[92]

For Boff, historical liberations are not only historical, but are sacraments of a salvation. At the same time it is important to note that Boff does not identify salvation with "historical liberations, because the latter are always fragmentary, never full." Conversely, for him "salvation is

89. Boff's view of salvation history is directed against classical theology's "archeological concept of a revelation occuring in the past and closing with the death of the last apostle." On the other hand, he locates revelation or Christian Scriptures "within the vaster horizon of God's permanent, or ongoing revelation." Leonardo Boff, "Images of Jesus in Brazilian Liberal Christianity," *Faces of Jesus: Latin American christologies*, ed. José Miguez Bonino (Maryknoll, NY: Orbis, 1984) 9-29, pp. 11-12.

90. Boff, *Sacraments of Life*, 38-39. Boff illustrates this with the examples of the Yahwist and Elohist authors of the Old Testament. For example he notes how the Yahwist reader interpreted the glorious days of Israel under David and Solomon around 950 B.C.E. as the gradual preparation beginning from the very Creation and later manifested through Noah, Abraham, and Moses and so on. At the same time the Elohist reader seeing the decadence of Israel around the year 740 B.C.E. interpreted it as the gradual result of their infidelity to God beginning from the Fall. In this sense "[t]he events of the past are so many sacraments of Israel's present infidelity."*Ibid.*, 39-40.

91. Boff, *Sacraments of Life*, 46.

92. Boff, *Liberating Grace*, 8.

identifiable *in* historical liberations introduced by human beings. That is, salvation is concretized, manifested, and anticipated in these historical liberations."[93] For example, "the saving event of the Exodus becomes the paradigm of God's saving plan" for the Hebrews. It "recounts the epic of the politico-religious liberation of a mass of slaves who through the power of the covenant with God, became the people of God."[94]

This sacramental aspect can also be seen in the lives of the prophets and biblical authors, who are the 'sacraments' of the expression of God's designs. They look after the interests of the poor, the widow and the alien.[95] Particular persons or events emerge as grace-filled moments and situations can "serve as basic reference points for the historical memory" of the people. These are memories where we "recognize the concrete goodness of God." Thus for example, "the exodus from Egypt, the Babylonian exile, cultic worship, and the tranquility of a society at peace" are sacramental moments in the life of the Israelites.[96]

This sort of rereading of history as the history of salvation or damnation contributed in developing the emergence of a universal concept of God. With the emergence of such a universal concept the idea of salvation was projected back towards Creation and then presented as "the first event of salvation history."[97]

Salvation history started with the Old Testament is continued through the New Testament. Boff considers both the Old Testament history and the New Testament history "as one sacramental history (sign and instrument), the conscious reflection of salvation offered to all peoples."[98] As we shall see, Jesus became, in a certain sense, the culmination of Creation. Therefore, he argues that *mysterion* is at the same time God's salvific plan and the revelation given in Jesus.[99] *Mysterion* as God's salvific will is seen in manifold ways.

93. Boff, *The Path to Hope*, 43.

94. L. & C. Boff, *Introducing Liberation Theology*, 35.

95. Boff, *Die Kirche*, 133. In this sense he even points to Fathers who presented historical figures like Abraham, Noah, David, Sarah, Rebecca, Anna, Mary and the like sacraments. Boff, *Sacraments of Life*, 46.

96. Boff, *Liberating Grace*, 9.

97. Boff, *Die Kirche*, 133.

98. Leonardo Boff, *Church: Charism and Power: Liberation Theology and the Institutional Church*, trans. John W. Diercksmeier (New York: Crossroad, 1985) 16.

99. "Der Heilsplan und dessen Durchführung machen das eine mysterion aus. ... Deswegen kann mysterion zu gleicher Zeit Christus-mysterion und Heilsplan-mysterion besagen." Boff, *Die Kirche*, 56. For his discussion on the meaning of *mysterion* see, *Ibid*, 49-56.

> Die Sophia ist der Ursprung des mysterion (Röm 11, 33; Eph 3, 10) im vollzug des mysterion durch Christus ist sie dessen Inhalt (1 Kor 2, 7; Kol 2, 3) und im Hinblick auf die Anteilnahme seitens der Gläubigen erfüllt sie sich im Glauben an das mysterion (Eph 1, 7-9). Das nachziel besteht in der Konstituierung des neuen Menschen (anèr teleiós en Christó), das Mittelziel in der Unterwerfung aller unter Christus oder in der Zusammenfassung des Ganzen in ihm (1 Kor 15, 28; Eph 1, 10); das Fernziel besteht in der Doxa, in dem Lob Gottes (Eph 1, 6. 12) oder in dem Gott alles in allem (1 Kor 15, 28).[100]

In the New Testament grace is presented as "a saving way of acting in particular." Thus Jesus Christ became "the presence of God's salvation [grace] embodied in history."[101] Boff considers the New Testament as "the ultimate major rereading of all past history." From this perspective he argues that the apostles and evangelists are deciphering the hidden meaning of the past from the death and resurrection of Jesus. Therefore, as Boff rightly pointed out the salvific event of Jesus "was not an accident or miscarriage. It had been prepared in history, had been gestating within creation."[102] The same is continued in the Church. Hence the early Church had seen in history "the carrying out of God's salvation plan, the acceptance or rejection of God's grace by human beings. The meaning of events also bore a transcendent meaning, fleshing out God's saving plan."[103] For Boff, both Christ and Church are cosmic sacraments from the beginning.[104] Thus Christ and Church are two expressions of sacramental economy.

100. Boff, *Die Kirche*, 56. *Mysterium-sacramentum* contains different phases of sacramental economy (*Heilsökonomie*), in particular, the time before Jesus, the time of Jesus, the time of the Church and the time of the eschatological realization. "sacramentum bedeutet ferner die Beziehungen zwischen den Phasen." The time before Jesus contains the sacrament of "die praeparatio, figura, typus, symbolon, parabola, species, praeformatio." The time of Jesus means the fulfillment of promises and the incarnation of God in human form. The time after Jesus "besagt sacramentum Anteilnahme, sakramentaler Vollzug der Geheimnisse Jesu in der Liturgie." *Ibid.*, 64.

101. Boff, *Liberating Grace*, 9.

102. Boff, *Sacraments of Life*, 40.

103. *Ibid.*, 38.

104. "Christus und die Kirche wirken von Anbeginn der Welt, so dass beiden eine komische Grösse zugeschrieben worden war; Es ist dann von der Kirche 'ab Abel iusto' oder 'ab Adamo' die Rede, worauf wir später noch ausführlich eingehen müssen." Boff, *Die Kirche*, 66.

2.1.3. Jesus as Sacrament

In order to understand the sacramental character of Jesus, it is important to delve into Boff's Christology.[105] In line with many sacramentologists of his time Boff considers Jesus "the original and fontal sacrament of God and divine salvation."[106] One will find strong emphasis on the cosmic dimensions of Christology in his writings. Following the tenets of 'cosmic Christology', he notes that "[t]he whole of creation is already oriented toward him. Adam is the image and likeness of Christ. Christ was secretly present in Abraham, Moses, and Isaiah."[107] Elsewhere he observes that "Christ is first intended in God's plan and in him everything else was carried out."[108] Jesus of Nazareth is the culmination of the incarnation of the saving plan of God. There, we see "the complete and total union of the creature with the Creator, and shows us, by way of anticipation, the ultimate destiny of all redeemed human beings."[109]

For Boff sacrament is basically "a meeting between God, who descends to the human being, and the human being, who ascends to God."[110] In this sense he conceives Jesus Christ as the sacrament of the

105. Although Boff agrees with the discussions on Jesuology which means "how Jesus understood himself and allowed others to understand him by his words and attitudes" and Christology which is "the clarification done by the community afterwards," he surpasses such distinctions and attempts to bring them together to understand the meaning of Jesus in his particular Latin American context. His *Jesus Christ Liberator: A Critical Christology for Our Time*, which he published immediately after his return from Europe, serves as foundational to his Christology. However Segundo does not regard this work from the liberation Christology perspective. Rather he includes *Passion of Christ, Passion of the World* in this line. But one could find the liberationist perspective already in his first book. The five characteristics of his Christology are good examples of this. They are: 1) The primacy of the anthropological element over the ecclesiastical: human beings are focus of attention rather than ecclesiastical dogma and structure. 2) The primacy of the utopian element over the factual: its orientation will be toward the future, looking for what Christ can do for the oppressed. 3) The primacy of the critical element over the dogmatic: dialogue with the world rather than preserving the religious *status quo*. 4) The primacy of the social over the personal: the dimension of the message of Christ to liberate the oppressed. 5) The primacy of *orthopraxis* over orthodoxy. Boff, *Jesus Christ Liberator*, 43-47.

106. Boff, *Sacraments of Life*, 73. Elsewhere he notes that Jesus is 'the primary sacrament of God'. Boff, *Liberating Grace*, 121.

107. Boff, *Sacraments of Life*, 40-41. Boff's cosmic Christology seems to have two realms. One, it speaks of Jesus' saving intent present from the beginning of creation and its fulfilment in the eschaton. Two, he looks for revelations similar to Jesus present in other historic persons in various contexts.

108. Boff, *Die Kirche*, 178.

109. Boff, *Sacraments of Life*, 46.

110. *Ibid.*, 76.

encounter with God. In Jesus, both the divine and human meet together. "Through the human Jesus one goes to God, and through the God-Jesus one goes to human beings. ... In him the two movements of ascent and descent meet. On the one hand he is the palpable expression of God's love (descent); on the other hand he is the definitive form of human love (ascent). Whoever dialogued with Christ was having an encounter with God."[111] The sacramentality of Jesus is based on the divine-human encounter in him and it makes humans the sacrament of Christ and Christ the sacrament of humans. It is this divine and human dimension in Jesus that makes him "the greatest and highest sacrament and sign of God."[112] He goes further and notes that "Jesus Christ is the encounter between the human being seeking God and God seeking the human being. He is at the crossroads where God's descending road and humankind's ascending road meet."[113] It is not God who enters our world rather we enter his world.[114] Each human can therefore remind us of the human being, Jesus, and Jesus can remind us of what it means to be human.[115]

Although Boff equally emphasizes the divine and human elements in Jesus,[116] it seems that following the Franciscan tradition, Boff stresses Jesus' humanity against the traditional emphasis of his divinity.[117] He himself expresses this clearly by saying:

> In the New Testament, Saint John's Gospel underscores Jesus' divinity, whereas the synoptics stress his humanity. In the ancient world, the school of

111. Boff, *Sacraments of Life*, 47. He illustrates this notion of Christ as sacrament of the encounter with the image of a Schoolteacher. In this sense Boff considers his Schoolteacher Mansueto to the historical figures of the Bible like Abraham, Noah, Rebecca, Anna, Mary etc., whom the Fathers called sacraments. *Ibid.*, 46, 43-47. It echoes Schillebeeckx's notion of Christ the sacrament of encounter with God.

112. Boff, *Die Kirche*, 137.

113. Boff, *The Path to Hope*, 52.

114. Boff, *Liberating Grace*, 37, 17, 44.

115. Boff, *Jesus Christ Liberator*, 217-221. In this context he does not find any difficulty in accepting Christ present in all people devoid of their ideological and religious convictions.

116. He even notes that "One neither overstresses the human nor the divine, one neither diminishes the man nor diminishes God." Boff, *Jesus Christ Liberator*, 183.

117. Boff, *Passion of Christ*, 15. The "traditional approaches to Christology often begin with abstract analyses of humanity and divinity in order to illuminate the mystery of Jesus. Boff, on the other hand, guided by his anthropological vision, wishes to elaborate an understanding of the human and the divine with the historical Jesus as its starting point." David Carey Dixon, *A Critical Analysis of Liberationist Christology in the Writings of Gustavo Gutierrez, Leonardo Boff, and John Sobrino* (Fort Worth, TX, Southwestern Baptist Theological Seminary: A Dissertation presented to the Faculty of the School of Theology, 1988) 133-134.

> Alexandria represents the first tendency; Antioch stresses the second... In the medieval world the Thomistic school opted to reflect on Jesus from a point of departure in his divinity; the Franciscan school, from his humanity ... For my own part, on the strength of my spiritual formation and basic option alike, I follow the Franciscan school – the synoptic, Antiochene, and Scotist tradition. I find God precisely in Jesus' total, complete humanity.[118]

For Boff, Christ's human nature remains "the prototype and sacrament of all beings."[119] Therefore, for a meaningful understanding of sacraments, Boff suggests to encounter the poor and needy of our time. According to him, "[o]nly those who commune in his history with the poor and needy, who are Christ's sacraments, will commune definitively with Christ."[120] In this sense Boff suggests that "Jesus wants to be God's answer to the human condition."[121] Therefore along with a social-analytic articulation of liberation Christology, he presents a 'sacramental' articulation of liberation Christology.[122]

It does not mean that he ruled out the importance given to divinity. Conversely, while emphasizing the humanity of Jesus, he retains Jesus' divinity. Jesus of Nazareth is not an ordinary human being, rather, "[h]e is the Christ, the living sacrament of God incarnated in him."[123]

He also cautions against any possible misunderstanding of Jesus Christ based on the symbolic and diabolic movements. "It is essentially bound to be *symbolic* for those who understand it, and *diabolic* for those who do not understand it. This is the intrinsic risk in every sign, and it was true in the case of Jesus Christ, who was the ultimate, definitive sign of God."[124]

118. Boff, *Passion of Christ*, xi-xii. See also *Ibid*, 285-286. See also Boff, *Jesus Christ Liberator*, 189-194.

119. Boff, *Die Kirche*, 137.

120. L. & C. Boff, *Introducing Liberation Theology*, 45.

121. Boff, *Jesus Christ Liberator*, 50. In this sense Boff even says that the liberation from the oppressed system anticipates the Kingdom of God. For him, the sign of the Kingdom of God is identical with the theology of liberation. Leonardo Boff, "Salvation in Jesus Christ and the Process of Liberation," *Concilium* 10/6 (1974) 78-91, p. 80.

122. It is an effort to develop a Christology in so far as it can bring out the liberative dimensions present in the Jesus of history. It attempts to go beyond the popular piety centered on the suffering of Jesus or the image of Jesus as the glorious King in heaven. Boff, *Jesus Christ Liberator*, 269-272. See also Boff, "Salvation in Liberation."

123. Boff, *Sacraments of Life*, 30.

124. *Ibid.*, 83. "As the original Greek verb (*sym-ballo*) suggests," Jesus was understood by many as the one who "brings together, unites, and points toward God." He was understood and accepted by people as the source of salvation liberation from their present situation of decadence and despair. These people discovered who Jesus was and bore witness to their discovery: "You are the Messiah, the Son of the living God" (Mt 16:17)."

It is also important to note how Boff delineates the place of Christians and non-Christians in the sacramentality of Jesus.[125] As we have already indicated, "Boff's christology certainly asserts that all people, as linked with Christ, are included in the saving plan of God, whether they be aware of it or not." This helps him to justify the validity of "the sacramentalism of the pagans, Hebrews and Greeks." With regard to atheists, Boff makes no exception. For him, "[i]t is not those who are Christian who are good, true, and just. Rather the good, the true, and the just are Christians."[126]

In his opinion, "[t]he christic structure is anterior to the historical Jesus of Nazareth." He grounds the christic structure on certain values that are present when "a human being opens to God and the other, wherever true love exists and egoism is surpassed, when human beings seek justice, reconciliation and forgiveness, there we have true Christianity and the christic structure emerges within human history." Christic structure is also valid in the case of christic structure that exists outside Christian limits. It means that the christic structure "emerges wherever a human being says 'Yes' to goodness, truth, and love. Before Christ, Christianity was anonymous and latent. Though it existed and was lived by people, it did not yet have a name. With Jesus Christ Christianity received its

On the other hand there were also people who recognized him as the source of diabolic movement. For them, "[a]s the original Greek verb (*dia-ballo*) suggests, Jesus seemed to cause separation and division, to jeopardize the existing religion and state." But Jesus did not tolerate them, so they persecuted and crucified him. *Ibid*, 82.

125. As we have already seen Boff traces the origin of sacraments as part of God's saving plan, derives from the eternal preexistent Word. In the same vein, he argues that the sacraments of pagan religions are also rooted in the divine Word. According to him: "The Christian sacraments articulated in the world's religions pointed vertically to the eternal Word. They were sacraments of God." In this sense, he argues that "the sacraments we possess today in the church preexisted the church. Human beings of every age were sacramentaly related to the deity (the eternal Word)." "When the sacraments of God (the eternal Word), which point vertically upward, are related to and inserted in the history of Jesus Christ, which registers horizontally as does any other history, then these sacraments become specifically Christian sacraments." The particularity of the Christian sacrament is that "the Christian faith discovered the relationship of these sacraments to the incarnate God. The vertical dimension crossed paths with the horizontal dimension. The Christian sacrament is that encounter. On the one hand it presupposes and assumes the divine sacrament preexisting in human religions. On the other hand it discovers a reality that is present in the divine sacraments but hidden to the world's religions and now made manifest through the light of Christ's mystery: that is, the presence of the eternal Word who is acting through the divine sacraments. It also inserts these sacraments into the history of Jesus Christ in such a way that Christ assumes a specific authorship." *Ibid.*, 65-66.

126. Boff, *Jesus Christ Liberator*, 250.

name."[127] According to him, it "existed before Christ even though we could not name it, eventually achieving its highest revelation, explicitness, and patency in Jesus."[128] Christianity involves "concrete and consistent living in a christic structure, a living of that which Jesus of Nazareth lived: total openness to others and the Great other."[129]

2.1.4. The Church as Sacrament

One of Boff's major concerns in the study of the theology of sacraments lies in his theology of the Church.[130] The Church as sacrament has a cosmic dimension in Boff. Thus, the early Christians "saw the church being prepared with Adam and Eve at the start of creation. Adam and Eve had formed the first community of love."[131] In this sense the Church as the *Ursakrament* has been working since the beginning of Creation in different forms and in different living situations.[132] It was "gradually prepared for its full manifestation at Pentecost."[133] From Pentecost on the Church has become the continuation of Jesus in history.[134] Therefore Boff considers the Church as the radical sacrament of Christ.[135] The Church as the society of the baptized has an even deeper meaning in Boff, as "it is the sacrament of the resurrected Christ making himself present in history."[136] The Church "as the community of the faithful and of the history of their faith in the risen Jesus Christ ... has always been called the great sacrament of grace and salvation in the world."[137] In this sense Boff calls for a "wider understanding of sacraments as visible signs of a grace that is offered constantly and present to humanity, rather than as the instruments of preexisting grace."[138]

127. *Ibid.*, 248.

128. *Ibid.*, 249.

129. *Ibid.*, 250. "Anonymous Christians are those 'who in the vast ambit of history and life carry forward the cause' of the risen Christ who is present and active in them" (p. 219).

130. His theology of the Church as sacrament is well delineated in his doctoral dissertation. In his study he made a historical overview of 'Church as sacrament' as seen in the New Testament, Fathers, Scholastic period and finally in the post-Scholastic period till the time of ecclesial renewal of J. M. Scheeben. Boff, *Die Kirche*, 83-123.

131. Boff, *Sacraments of Life*, 41.

132. *Ibid.*, 383.

133. *Ibid.*, 41.

134. *Ibid.*, 52.

135. Boff, *Liberating Grace*, 121.

136. Boff, *Sacraments of Life*, 30.

137. *Ibid.*, 51.

138. Boff, *Church: Charism and Power*, 16.

Although there is no hypostatic union in the Church as in Christ, Boff perceives the divine and human character in the Church in an analogous way. For him, "the divine element is always incarnated in the human element, making the latter transparent" and "the human element is in the service of the divine element, making the latter historical." In this sense he considers the church as "a living organism than an organization, a community of salvation rather than an institution of salvation."[139] It seems that in Boff's understanding of the sacramentality of the Church he underscores its limitation compared to the sacramentality of Christ. Since "the Church is not hypostatically united to the Logos as was the humanity of Jesus," the Church has its limitation of being in a sinful situation that needs conversion and reform.[140] For him, "[t]he Church is Christ's sacrament, not Christ himself. The Church must itself be liberated, day after day. The Church is always a pilgrim Church, both holy and sinful."[141] It is in this sense only that he notes Christianity "as the prolongation of God's incarnational process."[142]

It is also important to note that the realities that transcend the Church, namely, the Kingdom and the world, are important to understand the real meaning of the Church in Boff. They are "the two pillars that support the entire edifice of the Church."[143] Hence he suggests that Kingdom, world and Church are to be spelled out in their proper order. For him, the Kingdom is the primary reality. The other two realities arise from this. The world, for him, is the reality where "the Kingdom is concretized and the Church is realized." The Church is the sign (explicit symbol) and instrument (mediation) of the Kingdom of God in the world. In other words the Church is "the anticipatory and sacramental realization of the Kingdom in the world, as well as the means whereby the Kingdom is anticipated most concretely in the world."[144] At the same time he cautions against a too close identification of the Church and Kingdom and Church and the world. The former "creates an abstract and idealistic image of the Church

139. Boff, *Sacraments of Life*, 53.

140. Boff, *Church: Charism and Power*, 144.

141. Boff, *Faith on the Edge*, 146.

142. Boff, *The Lord's Prayer*, 2.

143. Boff, *Church: Charism and Power*, 1. He considers the Kingdom as the one which defines the world and the Church. It is Jesus' unique intention (*ipsissima intentio*) and "the utopia that is realized in the world, the final good of the whole of Creation in God, completely liberated from all imperfection and penetrated by the Divine. The *world* is the arena for the historical realization of the Kingdom ... The *Church* is that part of the world that, in the strength of the Spirit, has accepted the Kingdom made explicit in the person of Jesus Christ, the Son of God incarnated in oppression. It preserves the constant memory and consciousness of the Kingdom." *Ibid*, 1-2.

144. Boff, *Church: Charism and Power*, 2.

that is spiritualized and wholly indifferent to the traumas of history." And the latter, leads to a secular image of the Church. He also cautions against distancing the Church both from the Kingdom and the world. Then "it becomes a self-sufficient, triumphal, and perfect society, many times duplicating the services normally found in civil society, failing to recognize the relative autonomy of the secular realm." Hence he argues for a healthy and "right relationship between Kingdom-world-Church, in such a way that the Church is always seen as a concrete and historical sign (of the Kingdom and of salvation) and as its instrument (mediation) in salvific service to the world."[145] Therefore, he notes that the Church "preserves and maintains the mystery of Christ in all its concrete explication."[146] It becomes sacrament only "insofar as it participates in, and daily actualizes, the sacrament of Christ."[147] In this sense Boff contends that the early Christian communities continued the rereading of God's presence through the Church.

For a deeper understanding of the sacramentality of the Church, he demonstrated the pitfalls of the existing models of the Church as the Church as "City of God," the Church as "*mater et magistra*" and the Church as "sacrament of Salvation."[148] Instead, he proposes a new model: a Church from the poor. He explores the existence of such a Church in the basic ecclesial communities. Their understanding of the Church first began by deepening "the faith of its member, to prepare the liturgy, the sacraments, and the life of prayer." In a later stage, it took a different turn. In the process of spiritual deepening, they realized the limits of the liberation from personal sins and the importance of "a liberation that has economic, political, and cultural dimensions."[149] Although the basic Christian community is not a political entity and remained "a place for the reflection and celebration of faith," it has also become the place "where human situations are judged ethically in the light of God." In this sense, Christian communities have two spheres: the Christian community and the political community. In this new model, the ecclesial community is not merely an instrument for the Church to reach the people, rather, it

145. *Ibid.* For him the real issue of theology is not the Church, but the humankind itself. "From the standpoint of grace and salvation history, it is not the church that stands at the center of God's endeavor, but humankind." Boff, *The Path to Hope*, 5.

146. Boff, *Sacraments of Life*, 73.

147. *Ibid.*, 52; Leonardo Boff, *Ecclesiogenesis: The Base Communities Reinvent the Church*, trans. Robert R. Barr (Maryknoll, NY: Orbis, 1986) 48-49.

148. Boff, *Church: Charism and Power*, 2-7.

149. *Ibid.*, 8.

is a new realm of living Christian faith. Hence, the unity of faith (Gospel) and life (liberation) gives rise to "a rich ecclesial sacramentality."[150]

Boff also strongly emphasizes the pneumatological dimension of the Church.[151] For him the Church is "of Christ and also that of the Holy Spirit."[152] Based on the pneumatological dimension of the Church he criticizes the comparative model of the Church as the mystical body of Christ.[153] In his opinion the latter "fail to take into account the decisive event of the resurrection." For him, through the resurrection, Jesus' body was transformed into a spiritual body (cf. 1 Cor 14:44ff), giving way to the pneumatological origin of the Church along with its christological origin.[154] In this sense, he argues that the Church is not only the sacrament of Christ but also the sacrament of the Holy Spirit. The pneumatological grounding of the Church is fundamental to his understanding of the sacramentality of the Church, and helps him to go beyond the institutional dimension. Thus, gifts and charisms (cf. 1 Cor 12; Rom 12) in the Church are important. He further advocates the need "of charismatic figures who shake the rigid body of the institution, who open new horizons to faith from their new experience of the divine mystery, who usher in new ways of attending to the historical needs of the community."[155]

He underscores the importance of faith for a better understanding of the sacramentality of the Church. In his opinion, the sacramentality of the Church is not based on its creeds, its liturgy, or its traditions, but on faith in the Lord and in the Spirit animating it.[156] This becomes important for Boff especially in the context of the contradictory appearance of the Church today. In such situations "faith discovers and recognizes an inner, divine secret: the presence of the risen Lord. That is why the Church Fa-

150. *Ibid.*, 9.

151. Boff has made a historical study on this already in his dissertation. Boff, *Die Kirche*, 161-175. In his emphasis on the Church as the sacrament of the Holy Spirit, he severely criticized the institutional nature of the Church. It was one of the central issues for which Boff was silenced from teaching.

152. Leonardo Boff, *Trinity and Society* (London: Burns & Oates, 1988) 209. At the same time with regard to the origin of the Church he places it with the time of the Spirit. For him, the Church "is not a creation of the time of Jesus, but a creation of the time of the Spirit." Boff, *Ecclesiogenesis*, 49.

153. Boff, *Church: Charism and Power*, 145. Boff cautions that the Church as the body of Christ is "well-defined and limited so that members are clearly defined (one is either a member or a nonmember) as are the institutions that must maintain the Church's unity and strength in the world."

154. *Ibid.*; Boff, *Liberating Grace*, 50.

155. Boff, *Trinity and Society*, 209.

156. Boff, *Sacraments of Life*, 52.

thers often called the church a wondrous and ineffable sacrament (*mirabile et ineffabile sacramentum*)."[157]

The Church has got a cosmic dimension in the sense that it embraces and penetrates everything. "All created things, sacraments and symbols of God and Christ, especially the Church, are united in Christ so that everything is full of Christ and full of the Church, the cosmic Mystery of the Church."[158] Boff also finds no difficulty in perceiving God's manifestation in communities other than the Church. According to him, "[a]ll authentic grace reveals an ecclesial character in the sense that it tends to manifest itself visibly and to form a community. God, Christ, and grace ... manifest themselves in the world through many mediations. The church is one such mediation."[159] He interprets the *Didache* use of the Church as "a cosmic mystery." The patristic notion of cosmic Church or Church as cosmic mystery points to the mystery that penetrates all those signs and all historical humanity can make its presence felt in all phases of the world. In this sense he justifies the patristic reference to the Church as "the church of natural law, the church of the world's religions, the church of Judaism, the church of Jesus Christ, the church of the apostles and the glorious church in heaven. (*Lumen gentium*, 2)."[160]

He applies the sacramentality of the Church to the non-Christians as well. He explains this from the perspective that "[t]o be a Christian is to live human life in that profoundity and radicality where it opens itself to and communicate the mystery of God."[161] According to him, "[t]he anonymous Church visibly touches all human beings, from the just Abel onwards."[162] In this sense "[t]he religions of the world, the people of Israel, and the apostolic community made up of Jesus and the Twelve were so many sacraments and symbols of Church."[163] Furthermore, "[w]here a person turns to goodness and truth he has already said 'yes' to the principle of the order of salvation and membership in the Church, and stands therefore within the ambit of the sacramental Church."[164] Thus he argues that the Church as sacrament is not limited to "the confines of the Roman Catholic Church."[165] It "is the sacrament of definitive salvation, already

157. *Ibid.*, 53.
158. Boff, *Die Kirche*, 180-181.
159. Boff, *Liberating Grace*, 6.
160. Boff, *Sacraments of Life*, 54.
161. Boff, *Jesus Christ Liberator*, 250.
162. Boff, *Die Kirche*, 403, 407, 401.
163. Boff, *Sacraments of Life*, 41.
164. Boff, *Die Kirche*, 409.
165. Boff, *Ecclesiogenesis*, 22.

achieved by Jesus Christ and being realized not only in the Church but in the vast field of the world."[166]

In concluding our discussion on the understanding of sacraments in Boff, we could summarize it in his request to "view everything in terms of the ultimate end and goal of history, in terms of heaven or hell. Then everything becomes a sacrament paving the way for the final end, including creation, all nations, all religions, all political communities, Jesus Christ, and the church."[167] From this we see that his understanding of sacraments is very broad and cuts across the conventional understanding.

2.2. Cosmology in Transition

Having seen the important notions of Boff's sacramentology, we shall now see his world-view.[168] Boff delineates three major cosmological models of the West: theocentric, anthropocentric and new cosmologies. In his opinion, these three cosmologies "represent God in its own particular way, as well as offering a globalizing, integrative, and sacramental understanding of the world."[169] For him, cosmology has an important role in the understanding of grace.[170] Therefore, the historical and cul-

166. Boff, *Faith on the Edge*, 178.

167. Boff, *Sacraments of Life*, 41.

168. Based on Durkheim, Boff delineates the importance of cosmology in religion. For him, religion is not confined to the forms of expression we know as ritual, worship, and doctrine. Rather it gives rise to a cosmology. By cosmology he means "a form of discourse about the world." Its concern is not a discourse in scientific terms but rather, to produce "a global image of the world to indicate its connection with the divine dimension." Boff, *Ecology and Liberation*, 62. Elsewhere, he notes cosmology as "the image of the world that a society fashions for itself by artfully combining widely varying types of knowledge, traditions, and institutions." Boff, *Cry of the Earth, Cry of the Poor*, 35.

169. Boff, *Ecology and Liberation*, 62.

170. The term grace is used to express the basic original experience of the whole Christian mystery, which was rare in the gospels. Mathew and Mark use it only once, John uses it three times in the prologue and Luke uses it eight times (1:28-30; 2:40-52; 4:22; 6:32-34) and seventeen times in the Acts. It was Paul who introduced it into the New Testament as "the chief expression of the new reality embodied in Christianity." For him, "Grace is the gift of the Father himself in Jesus Christ, the gratuitous and merciful love of the Father and Christ which penetrates human beings, liberating them, saving them from perdition, and turning them into new creatures (2 Cor 5:17; Gal 6:15)." "Paul's use of the word 'grace' embodies a concrete experience: God loved me first, despite my sins, because he is good, benevolent and merciful. Paul feels graced by a gift, the gift of God himself in Jesus Christ. Christ is grace: God present to us. This experience of being surprised by an unexpected gift is what Paul expresses with the word 'grace'." Boff, *Liberating Grace*, 48-49.

tural factors are also important to know more about the development of the theology of grace.[171]

2.2.1. Theocentric Cosmology

The theocentric cosmology, the typical cosmology of antiquity, considers the world as "a hierarchical, sacred, and unchangeable whole." God is envisioned at the top, as the Supreme Being and Creator of the entire universe.[172] Boff delineates how such a hierarchical order is seen both in Greek and Latin theology and is continued in the medieval and later periods in the West. The sacraments in terms of grace play an important role in this worldview. Liturgy and sacraments mediate between the Creator and Creation.

According to Boff there are various factors that led to the development of grace in Christian thinking, stemming first of all, from different cultural contexts.[173] For him, all theological discourses are cultural discourses.[174] In particular, Boff notes how Christianity speaks of grace from two cultural worlds: the world of Greek metaphysical thought and the world of Roman political and juridical experience. The Greek understanding of divinization denotes the elevation of human beings into the realm of the divine. It is not God entering human beings, rather "human beings are raised up by God; they give up their old situation and enter the divine realm through deification."[175]

Greek theology expressed grace as "the glory that radiates from the deity and transforms humanity. It comes to human beings ontologically through the sacraments, ethically through a life based on the divine virtues and the imitation of God and Christ, and mystically through ecstatic union with the deity."[176] The model of hypostatic union is central to them. In this view they emphasize the divinization of the human being in Jesus of Nazareth. Based on this theology they developed the theology of the "deification of human beings."

While Greek theology emphasized God and deification, Latin theology emphasized "the human experience of sinfulness and on grace as the

171. Regarding the influence of culture on religious and mystical phenomenon, he follows the study of the Dutch sociologist Geert Hofstede. Boff, *Ecology and Liberation*, 67. In his opinion, "In all cultures every major shift in the direction of history issues in a new world view or cosmology." Boff, *Cry of the Earth*, 35.

172. Boff, *Ecology and Liberation*, 62.

173. He underscores in many places the importance of culture in delineating religious experience. For example see Boff, *Ecology and Liberation*, 62, 66-68.

174. Boff, *Liberating Grace*, 20.

175. *Ibid*, 21.

176. *Ibid.*, 9.

justification of human beings."[177] They described grace present in Jesus Christ and the church "in terms of liberation from sin and the corruption of human nature." For them, grace is the "alteration of human beings (created grace) effected by the loving, purifying presence of God (uncreated grace)."[178] In the Latin tradition grace is expressed "as justification and human recuperation. Grace was seen as a process of making humanity human and then enabling it to reach total fulfillment."[179] Boff criticizes this theology of grace for clinging to the experiential world of the past.[180] Thus, he sums up the Western theological approach on grace that takes its starting points from four areas: psychological experience, classical metaphysics, personhood and dialogue as well as social and structural realities.[181]

In the pre-scholastic period, mainly under Augustinian influence theology, concentrated more on the ethical aspect of grace. For them, "grace is *illuminatio* and *delectatio* that are lived out in a virtuous life."[182] Boff also delineates how classical metaphysics hypostatized transcendence. In this view, "[t]ranscendence came to signify the realm of the supernatural, while immanence came to signify the natural realm."[183] He considers

177. *Ibid.*, 15.

178. *Ibid.*, 10.

179. *Ibid.*, 22. According to Boff, Latin theology reflects a lot of Roman culture that has got an affirmative nature. Boff, *Ecology and Liberation*, 67.

180. Boff, *Liberating Grace*, 20.

181. *Ibid.*, 13-15.

182. *Ibid.*, 10.

183. *Ibid.*, 36. Though the term supernatural became a technical theological term only in the thirteenth century with Thomas Aquinas, who used it in his *Quaestiones Disputatae de Veritate*, Boff traces its origin to the Greek fathers. Based on "a neoplatonic world view, which depicted reality as a series of hierarchical levels, they talked about a reality that was supercosmic (*hypercosmikos*), superphysical (*hyperfues*), and supercelestial (*hyperouranios*)." The Latin term *supernaturale* was first used in the sixth century. Slowly its use had grown with the translations of the works of Pseudo-Dionysius. Here one should note that the term was not in use in the Bible and in the early Christian literature. Instead "God's gratuitous, salvific love was expressed in terms of relationship, encounter, covenant, and so forth." But as the biblical experience was being translated into other cultural categories, grace was used "in terms of nature rather than in terms of itself. Hence grace could only be something supernatural, lying beyond the bounds of normal, natural human experience." During the Renaissance, nature and human beings became objects of science culminating its development in the Council of Trent, presented in terms of natural and supernatural as two complete realities. The Augustinian tradition "tended to reject it" on the pretext that "nature and grace were not separate from each other." But for the scholastics, "[a] nature which is complete in itself and has everything necessary for itself receives the supernatural as something added on to it." [F. Diekamp, *Katholische Dogmatik*, 2:47.] In the theoretical level "nature seems to enjoy independence and reason seems to enjoy autonomy. ... grace appears in what seems to be its own distinctive form." Thus

such notions as "objectifications of a human experience."[184] In the medieval period, theologians started to adopt metaphysical categories. Following Aristotle, Thomas Aquinas and Duns Scotus argued that action follows from being: *Agere sequitur esse*. In the case of grace as well, there are some prior principles that generate virtue. It "is a new ontological quality of the soul that originates action." This, however, cannot be a substance, because that presupposes the human subject; rather, "it must be an accident that affects human beings ontologically and produce virtues in them." It is this created grace in humans that "makes them pleasing to God and justifies them."[185] Later, under the Augustinian influence, the Franciscan school criticised the ontological interpretation of grace. Accordingly, they argued that created grace cannot "make us pleasing to God." For them, "[g]race basically is a new relationship between humanity and God, which was made feasible and real through Jesus Christ and his mediating efforts." The discussion on created grace was further deepened in the postscholastic period by the Thomist school of Benez and the Jesuit school of Molina with their debate on "predestination of glory and the problem of sufficient and efficacious grace." For the Protestant Reformers, "grace was basically the benevolent and merciful attitude of God."[186]

In the nineteenth century, 'a trinitarian view of grace' was introduced in the Catholic Church. For example Scheeben, under the influence of Romanticism, stressed "the experiential aspect of faith that had been neglected in the classic theology of grace." Based on the Greek fathers Scheeben rediscovered 'the mystical dimension and the inner life'. "Grace was seen as the symbol for the life of the triune God which is communicated to humans in their inner depths. Humans thereby share in

Natural is what belongs to nature by virtue of its constitution, its consequences, or its exigencies ('*Naturale est, quod vel constitutive, vel consecutive vel exegitive ad naturam pertinet*') and Supernatural is that which does not belong to nature by virtue of its constitution, its consequences, or its exigencies ("*Supernaturale est id, quod neque constitutive, neque consecutive, neque exegitive ad naturam pertinet*'). In this framework, "All possibility of experiencing grace is ruled out. ... For grace belongs to the supernatural realm, which infinitely exceeds the natural realm. Any possible human experience must fall within the horizon of nature; hence it cannot be an experience of grace." "This theological view of grace and human nature as two separate realms began to crumble [degenerate] in the twentieth century. Theologians came around to the view that, in the concrete, nature is ever suffused with the supernatural." Boff, *Liberating Grace*, 41-42. In his opinion, "More and more present-day theology is rejecting the contrast between a natural end and a supernatural end." Boff, *Liberating Grace*, 45.

184. *Ibid*, 36.

185. *Ibid* , 10.

186. *Ibid.*, 11.

the life of the Trinity." But, "Neo-scholastic theology maintained that created grace transforms humans from sinners into just people. It prepares human beings to share in the divine nature, in uncreated grace." On the other hand, Scheeben argued that "Instead God comes to human beings, and his entry into humanity produces an alteration in the latter. This alteration is what is known as created grace, and it is the result of uncreated grace. Uncreated grace comes first. Thus grace is an indwelling that leads to the adoption of human beings as the children of God."[187]

Along with historical and cultural conditioning, Boff draws attention to biographical conditionings. He demonstrates this through the personal examples of Paul, Augustine, and Martin Luther who encountered personal problems in their lives. They wrote extensively on the nature of grace. In their contexts, salvation was offered to people who lived a virtuous life and who tried "to ascend to perfection and God." At the same time, they find it difficult for human beings to reach holiness; hence, they solve this problem by presenting God's intervention to help humanity in their inability. Therefore, grace is "a gift from God that aids and sanctifies human beings and enables them to rediscover their lost identity." The same view of grace can be seen in the later theologians, who were primarily monks. In the contrast experience of having a high religious status, and yet experiencing frailty in life, they explain the gratuitous help extended to them in their life as grace.[188]

For Boff, a third conditioning came from societal and class factors. In his opinion, theologians belonging to the mainstream of society "did not experience social marginalization, nor did they live out their lives in close contact with groups of believers at the grass-root level. All this helped to narrow the horizons of their reflection on grace. Their talk is almost never about human beings; it is about the soul. It is the soul that is graced, justified, and inhabited by the holy Trinity. This led to a spiritualization of grace and a loss of historical substance." "Real-life situations are not seen as possible sacraments of the communication of divine grace or of human dis-grace."[189]

In short, in the theocentric cosmology of both the Greek and Latin tradition revolve around God, who provides grace (Latin), or elevates human beings to a graced world (Greek). Both versions basically continue the Platonic or neo-Platonic worldview that upheld a distinction between sacred and profane.

187. *Ibid.*, 11-12.
188. *Ibid.*, 23-24.
189. *Ibid.*, 24-25.

2.2.2. Anthropocentric Cosmology

The modern cosmology that was developed on the basis of Newtonian physics, the physics of Copernicus and Galileo, and the Cartesian scientific method continued the dualistic cosmology of the West that considers the world in terms of matter and spirit.[190] This cosmology presents God as an architect. It is the responsibility of humanity to elucidate and establish their function within the world. In this sense this cosmology is anthropocentric.[191] Boff even calls it "an arrogant anthropocentrism." In this vision human beings are seen as "being above other beings and lords over their life and death." In their effort to dominate the world, the world is even reduced "to 'natural resources', with no respect for their relative autonomy."[192] Later, Modernity reduced the world to an object for human experimentation and provided the reasons to dominate and to accumulate wealth.[193] Three characteristics are important in this 'modern anthropocentric cosmology'.

The first characteristic of this worldview is that of secularism. In this worldview, God is no longer "a universally accepted starting point in the tract of grace." It is our responsibility to "articulate the meaning of grace and see the experience of grace."[194] In the twentieth century, there was a great stress on the revitalized mediation of grace. Many factors like "the historico-cultural influence on personalism, existential categories, a higher regard for real life-experience, sounder views of humanity, and the renewed interest in biblical and patristic sources" contributed to this. It helped "to explore the ecclesial, christological, and eschatological implications of grace. Grace was integrated into an approach centered around salvation history."[195]

190. Boff, *Ecology and Liberation*, 62. For Boff, "the classical paradigm of science remains in place with its well-known dualisms, such as the division of the world into the material and the spiritual, the separation between nature and culture, human being and world, reason and emotion, female and male, God and world, and atomization of scientific knowledge." "Natural science analyzes the world of matter but leaves the world of spirit to philosophy and theology." Boff, *Cry of the Earth*, 11.

191. Boff, *Ecology and Liberation*, 63.

192. Boff, "Liberation Theology and Ecology," 68.

193. Boff, *Ecology and Liberation*, 78.

194. Boff, *Liberating Grace*, 26. For different traits of this world-view see pp. 26-31.

195. *Ibid.*, 12. In particular Boff focuses on the contributions of Henri de Lubac, Karl Rahner, and Romano Guardini in general and Juan Luis Segundo in the particular context of Latin America. For de Lubac grace is on the one hand a gratis from God and on the other hand it is human yearning for God. For Rahner, grace is something that exists in the human, *supernatural existential.* For Guardini, grace is the result of a dialogue between God and humans. Segundo, on the other hand, focuses more on the social dimension of God's grace. For him it is a force for social and personal liberation in history. *Ibid.*, 12-13.

Secondly, this cosmology has a critical attitude towards 'metaphysics'. This does not mean a denial or rejection of the classical metaphysics of the Greeks and the medieval age, rather it is a "stage in human thought, a stage when Being was conceived in terms of an entity (*ens*)."[196] Boff observes how modern thought considers history as the original reality and the means by which human beings fashion their identity through their encounter with others in society. For this, one has to "open out to the world and others, and commit themselves to the process of liberation." In his opinion, the experience of immanence and transcendence takes place in such encounters. For him, immanence and transcendence "are two dimensions of one and the same life. They come joined together in the history of human beings as two facets of their radical reality. Human beings appear as beings who are immanent and transcendent, already fashioned and still in the making, established in the present and open toward a yet unknown future."[197] Thus, he argues that "God possesses real meaning only if he emerges from within human history. In the real-life struggles, decisions, and yearnings of human beings, there appears something that always escapes them." It means a meaningful talk of God "emerges from within the experience of humans and their way of life with others and the world."[198]

196. *Ibid.*, 36. According to Boff, "[m]odern thought from Kant onward seeks to do its reflection from a more original starting point than that of classical metaphysics. It regards the latter as a mistake for neglecting being as being and identifying its representative images – e.g., transcendence and immanence as two opposite realities – with reality itself. But in language we always create two worlds, so modern thought is semantically as dualistic as was classical thought. Within the context of this semantic dualism, however, it attempts to ponder the original reality that is one and identical." *Ibid.*, 36.

197. *Ibid.*, 36. For him the experience of immanence means the experience of human beings in the world with others, who have the possibility of manipulating their world and their relationships. The experience of transcendence is that experience which allows people to rise infinitely above the situation in which they are confined. It allows them to accept, to reject, or to protest against the given situation, opening them up to a future that has not yet been experienced or defined. *Ibid.*, 36.

198. *Ibid.*, 37. According to him, modernity is seen in its two embodiments in history. First, "bourgeois modernity, which created industrial society, the market and consumption, as well as liberal-representative democracy." Secondly, "the proletarian modernity that introduced a new historical agent to the hegemony of society, the builders and agenda of socialism, now falling apart in its Marxist-Leninist version." He calls attention to the need for a convergence between these two and proposes an alternative called an "integral modernity." It conjoins the vast patrimony of science and technology (the fruit of bourgeois modernity) with social democracy, for the good of all humanity (the meaning of proletarian modernity) in an enhanced awareness of a common destiny." Although he speaks of the need for a revolution to this end, he finds it difficult to expect such a thing from the first world. Thus, he envisions the poor to be the bearers of a new hope. He even

Finally, there is a trend to recover the religious and mystical dimension.[199] For modernity religion is something "pre-modern."[200] Boff considers contemporary religious movements in two categories. Some of them are "pre-modern" in that they do not recognize the problem of science and technology. Others have already made the break with modernity and have included the problem of science and technology within their process of reflection. Although they do not stress the crisis of instrumental reason, the victory of scientific messianism (power of reason) is taken for granted in these movements. In this sense, they are new and alternative, and no longer modern.[201] There are two tendencies apparent in the

dreams that it is possible for the worldwide problem of the poor to become the centre of political gravity. This is due to the collapse of the East-West, capitalism-versus-socialism confrontation and the slow progress of North-South, rich industrialized nations versus poor nations. He is convinced of the strength of the poor and asserts "the poor will certainly become the world's point of balance, because they will be the major threat to any system that excludes them." Boff, *Ecology and Liberation*, 102-105.

199. Boff, *Ecology and Liberation*, 59. It is important to note that this recovery has not generally occurred through any religious institutions. They speak of God and of miracles but find it difficult to agree to experience God and to live God's breaking forth in life. They find it difficult to do what is needed: to seek personal and communitarian experience of a new immersion in the utterly absorbing mystery of God, present in history and in the transformation of life." *Ibid.*

200. *Ibid.*, 57. For example he notes how religion was criticized by various philosophers. For Comte, "religion reproduces a primitive form of knowledge that has to be replaced by critical and scientific thought." For Marx, it "is viewed as weak and opium, alienation and false consciousness of what has not yet been discovered, and of what has just been lost." For Freud, it is "the illusions of a neurotic mind trying to satisfy the desire for protection and to make fear tolerable." For Weber, "religion is seen as a reality that (in spite of its capacity to transform society) tends to ignore the process of rationalization, secularization, and disenchantment of the world." For Popper and Carnap of the the Vienna School, religion is "meaningless, because religious discourse has no verifiable object." *Ibid.*

201. *Ibid.*, 70-71. He notes two trends in the historical churches. One group upholds "loyalty to their own traditions, formulated in premodern terms." The other looks for the right response to modern problems that arise due to cultural change. For example he notes that the Roman Catholic Church, on the one hand, reconciled itself with modernity and recognized the autonomy of science. On the other hand, the hierarchy asserted "absolute priority of humankind over the logic of science and technology," using the ethics of natural law. There, the Church failed to give "enough room for the human freedom intended by God" under natural law. He considers this as part of a premodern cosmology. The claim to have monopoly of ethical truth is to be attributed more to the ideology of absolute power built up by pope and hierarchy. In this effort the submission of history to divine will, which is always directed to participation and to the promotion of freedom is lost. In his opinion, the Orthodox "do not interpret the testimony of the Christian scriptures in this imperial perspective." But the Reformation churches that came into existence along with modernity locate themselves within its perspective. They "looked on the scien-

scientific-technological process. The "first group tends to take to their ultimate consequences the possibilities of applying reason to nature."[202] "The second tendency considers that it has already entered the holistic, ecological, and spiritual phase."[203] "Religion helps culture to take up this second position," because "[w]e can no longer live under the threat of a modernity that conceives of, and wishes to use, science as a means of dominating nature as well as other peoples and cultures."[204] He also criticizes the Church for the present global crisis of the biosphere. In his opinion, the Church was not critical enough to create a relational mentality of respect and concern for Creation.[205]

tific-technological process as a positive reality directed to the acquisition of human autonomy in history and liberated by God within the framework of a logic of gratuitiousness. Consequently, they are very open to what is new." Their ethical basis is not based on natural law but on the Kingdom of justice, integrity of Creation, and of peace proclaimed by Jesus. *Ibid.*, 71-74.

202. Science and technology, in particular, nuclear research, avant-garde physics, cybernetics and biotechnology are capable of far-reaching interference with the genetic code as well as the transformation of nature to the extent of solving serious human infrastructural problems. Consequently, we now have a technocratic messianism that claims to satisfy basic human needs. "The churches and religions acknowledge the importance of science and technology for the satisfaction of human needs and the promotion of life. Nevertheless, they tend to distance themselves from the solution proposed by this kind of messianism, which guarantees survival though does not sufficiently promote life. Human beings are not only creatures with needs; humans are also beings endowed with freedom. Human beings feel human not only when they receive public benefactions or the kindness of others. They wish to participate and cooperate, as subjects, in a collective and personal history; that is, they wish to bring about, by means of science and technology, forms of human participation at all levels. This is the process that humanizes us." *Ibid.*, 75.

203. This trend subjects instrumental reason to relentless criticism. It has now become a veritable "earthly demon," because it threatens to destroy nature. The *hybris* ("arrogance") of its logic has to be restricted so that it can be included in a greater whole, where it can recognize various forms of access to awareness that are not only scientific but holistic and symbolic. By sharing in these various forms of knowledge and self-fulfillment, human beings become integrated in the whole. They are harmonized and effectively transformed until they become cultivators of the garden of creation as well as its high-priests." *Ibid.*, 76.

204. *Ibid.* Thus the final declaration of the 1990 Canberra meeting of the Assembly of the World Council of Churches on the theme of ecology and the increased marginalization of the Third World notes that "technology should work *with* nature and its mysteries and not to seek to dominate it. (Final Declaration of the Assembly, 1:12.) It also remarked, the more theology has insisted on God's transcendence and distance from the material world, the more the earth has come to be seen as a mere object of human exploitation and as a 'non-spiritual' reality (Final Declaration 1:13)." *Ibid.*, 76-77.

205. *Ibid.*, 76.

2.2.3. New Cosmology

Besides the aforementioned two cosmologies Boff delineates a new cosmology that developed as the outcome of the relativity theory of Einstein, the quantum physics of Bohr, the indeterminacy principle of Heisenberg, the theoretical physics of Prigogine and Stengers, the depth psychology of Freud and Jung, the transpersonal psychology of Maslow P Weil, as well as biogenetics, cybernetics, and deep ecology. It shows the "transition from the industrial age to the era of communication and the rule of complexity." To be precise, it is a transition from a materialist world to a post-materialist and spiritual one that integrates the everyday with the mystical dimension of things.[206] This new worldview has integrated a lot from the mystical tradition of religions.

The new cosmology attempts to make a holistic approach to reality. It "is marked by a perception of the whole as differentiated, organic, masculine/feminine, and spiritual."[207] It proposes a unified vision "that is organic, holistic, feminine/masculine, and spiritual." Accordingly, living beings are not juxtaposed but rather interrelated. "Everything that exists is a complex bundle of energy in perpetual interrelativity."[208] Compared to the dualistic vision of body and soul, matter and spirit, this new vision speaks of energy and of life. Instead of the dominating character of the human being in modernity, it is proposed that humans "be seen as a part of reality, ... who has to preserve and respect the complexity and variety of that whole." The spirit or soul is to be seen "as the totality of human being in the sense of a living spring of vital energy. ... There is no discontinuity between matter and spirit, between body and soul, but one between life (spirit) and death (the denial of life)." But the new cosmology is "an integrative form of cosmology."[209] Furthermore, he believes that eastern and western mystics see this mystery "as an energy system that is always relational and interactive referring us to the supreme Spirit who penetrates and enlivens everything and renders it transparent."[210]

Boff also calls attention to the emergence of a new religious dimension grounded on this new cosmology. It is the experience of the divine as a globalizing phenomenon. An important characteristic of this experience of globality is that it can discern the presence of God both in the

206. *Ibid.*, 63.

207. *Ibid.*, 78. It is important to note the significant feminine elements present in the new cosmology.

208. *Ibid.*, 63-64. This is especially convincing from the viewpoint of quantum physics and the later version of the theory of relativity.

209. *Ibid.*, 64.

210. *Ibid.*, 78.

secular and in the sacred. Moreover it contains an integrative tendency present in all dimensions. This religious experience makes everything sacramental because of the presence of the divine in every thing. The divine is not something added to human experience from outside, rather it is transparent in the world process and manifested through all experience. "Everything has a depth that constitutes its other aspect and that mystery which refers to Mystery."[211]

For him, religion and religious experience "is not pathological but salvific. It is a basic anthropological patrimony and is not reducible to another more primordial experience. It always exists in humankind in the most varied forms."[212] It is also important to note that this religious experience is not accessible to reason.[213] On the contrary, it is distinct from reason and locates it in the realms of imagination, feeling and desire.[214] This makes mystics to "speak of God as a presence: the presence of the sublime, of the luminous, of ultimate receptivity, of the sacred, and of ultimate meaning."[215] For Boff, the new cosmology envisions "an era of integration of all aspects of the human and cosmic dimension. ... God does not appear as the antagonist of humankind. Instead, we and God cooperate in a reciprocal accession to and appearance of one another." It bears witness to the presence of the divine in Creation and in nature.[216]

While emphasizing mystical tradition, Boff notes that new religious movements can not neglect the question of social justice. He cautions the mystical dimension that "can degenerate into mystification, and the religious dimension [that] can become escape to a private world or group life without enough interest in the socially responsible construction of justice or an appropriate ecological relationship."[217]

He also requires us to look at human problems from a global perspective and even calls attention to its cosmic dimensions as "to live with stones, plants, animals, and the stars as new citizens of the human

211. *Ibid.*, 61.

212. *Ibid.*, 62.

213. *Ibid.*, 61.

214. *Ibid.*, 57. For example, he notes how Ludwig Wittgenstein remarked the limitations of "the rational and scientific attitude that is always concerned to investigate how things are and to seek an answer to everything." On the other hand, he also notes that "[t]here is also the human capability of rapture and wonder" and "[t]he limits of the scientific spirit are to be found where there is that which we must pass over in silence." *Ibid.* Blaise Pascal notes that the "religious experience is derived from instinct and feeling." For him "it is the heart that sees God and not the reason." *Ibid.*, 59.

215. *Ibid.*, 58.

216. *Ibid.*, 79.

217. *Ibid.*, 69-70.

city."[218] At the same time, he is critical of the current process of globalization, in particular for undermining the importance of religion, ethics or even ideology, because of its overemphasis on the global market.[219] Hence, he argues that "[t]echnological globalization should be directed toward a worldwide political agenda (a new political economy), including a minimum of humanization, citizenship, equity, human, and ecological welfare, and respect for cultural differences and openness to cultural reciprocity and complementarity."[220] Further, he notes that instead of globalizing the market economy, "we need to globalize other cultural values, such as solidarity, collective compassion for victims, respect for cultures, sharing of goods, effective integration with nature, and feelings of humanity and mercy for the humiliated and offended."[221]

"The globalization of human destiny shows the urgent need to deal with a question still more basic than that of socialism." For this, he suggests democracy, but not "as a system of government, but as a universal spirit and value."[222] He also considers the importance of religions in this regard and suggests that it is a grace of the Spirit if Christian churches and other world religions make connections with socialist movements and discover a cohesion between religious propositions and socialist dreams.[223]

Boff posits ecology as a force dealing with the relations, interaction, and dialogue of all creatures. It means that "everything that exists, co-exists. Everything that co-exists and pre-exists subsists by means of an infinitive web of all-inclusive relations." In other words "ecology reaf-

218. *Ibid.*, 100.

219. Boff, *Ecology and Liberation*, 127. For example he notes how "in the name of modernity, Latin American Governments are bringing the logic of domination up to date through the grandiose schemes of multinational corporations from Japan, Germany, Italy, and the United States." *Ibid.*, 102.

220. *Ibid.*, 128. Boff is concerned how science and technology are used for the good of the poor. From a liberation theology perspective, he asks that these are used for "the satisfaction of basic needs, justice for society, and power." From the viewpoint of the poor science and technology are viewed as "the main weapons for upholding political dependence and ensuring economic dominance over nations and their populations." In this sense "liberation theology is opposed to the technological messianism (the gospel of technocracy) of the ruling system." It seeks to make "intensive use of science and technology to produce food and everything else necessary for human sustenance, and by distributing them to those who are without them." *Ibid.*, 125-126.

221. *Ibid.*, 105.

222. *Ibid.*, 106. "Democracy, as envisaged now by so many groups in Latin America, is based on the co-existence and articulation of five founding forces: participation, solidarity, equality, difference, and communion."

223. *Ibid.*, 114.

firms the interdependence of beings."[224] It not only deals with relationships among persons but also "their relationship with their environment."[225] For him the "notion of ecology is always holistic and maintains an alliance of solidarity with nature."[226] Thus, "ecology is defined only within the framework of the relations that it connects in all directions and with every type of knowledge about the way in which all beings are dependent upon one another, constituting the vast fabric of their interdependencies."[227] Moreover, he defines "ecology as the science and art of relations and of related beings. The home/habitat/oikos, in fact, is made up of living beings, matter, energy, bodies, and forces in permanent relation to one another." From this perspective, he notes "that ecology is eminently theological by nature."[228] For him, Creation is an affirmation that we are coming from God and "bear in ourselves the marks of God, and that we are travelling toward God."[229]

In short, through the aforementioned transition towards cosmology, Boff has brilliantly delineated how this evolution in thinking broadened the cosmologies of the respective times. The transition from theocentrism to anthropocentrism and finally to the integral and holistic worldview of new cosmology, defined by philosophical and scientific thinking, contributed to a better understanding of grace in the world. The holistic approach in the new cosmology helps us to understand the world from a sacramental perspective. Therefore, in the following section we continue our search from this perspective.

224. *Ibid.*, 7. see also pp. 9-11. The term ecology was coined in 1866 by a German biologist Haeckel. "It derives from two Greek words, *oikos*, which means 'house' or 'home', and *logos*, meaning 'reflection' or 'study'. Therefore *ecology* means the study of the conditions and relations that make up the habitat (the house) of each and every person and, indeed, organism in nature." According to Haeckel's definition, "Ecology is the study of the interdependence and interaction of living organisms (animals and plants) and their environment (inanimate nature)." *Ibid.*, 9; Boff, *Cry of the Earth*, 3.

225. Boff, *Ecology and Liberation*, 84. It "includes not only nature (natural ecology) but culture and society (human ecology, social ecology). *Ibid.*, 7.

226. *Ibid.*, 14.

227. Boff, *Cry of the Earth*, 3.

228. Boff, *Ecology and Liberation*, 11. Formerly ecology was understood as a branch of biology, a subsection in natural science. As a subsystem its concern was "the inter-retro-relationships of living bodies one with another and with their environment." Boff, "Liberation Theology and Ecology," 67-68. But today it has a wider spectrum comprising all of our life, planetary system. At the same time it does not replace particular bodies of knowledge, rather it is a holistic approach. Boff, *Ecology and Liberation*, 11-12; Boff, *Cry of the Earth*, 3-4.

229. Boff, *Ecology and Liberation*, 45. From the Christian perspective one could say that "it comes from God and returns to God." *Ibid.*, 7.

3. The World as Sacrament

Having seen Boff's basic notions of sacramentology and worldview, we shall now focus on the sacramentality of the world and our response to it. In this section, we delineate the sacramentality of the world relevant mainly to the new cosmology. In the first part we shall see how God's sacramental presence is perceived under the new cosmology, and in the second, we shall concentrate more on the human response to it.

3.1. Mystery of Creation

Following a Trinitarian framework, Boff delineates God's presence from three perspectives: from God, Spirit and Christ respectively. He even tries to see "the origin and destiny of all things" as seen in the Trinity.[230] In this sense, he even notes that "all beings are image and likeness of the Trinity." The Father "fashions creation, with the Intelligence that is his Son, and with Love, which is the Holy Spirit."[231] Besides the Christian tradition, he uses other disciplines such as philosophy, science, culture, anthropology etc., and similar teachings in other religions to delineate God's presence in the world.

3.1.1. The Theosphere

First of all, Boff understands God as the "mystery enveloping us on all sides and flowing over us in all realms."[232] As earlier indicated, this mystery is articulated differently in different cosmologies. The new cosmology does not rule out the realm of reason, rather, it goes deeper into its limits. It is a contrasting experience of being known and remains to be unknown. It "challenges knowledge to delve more deeply."[233]

In the new cosmology, God is perceived as a 'feeling' within us, who first belonged to the universe and then became conscious in the human being. Its "primordial subject is the universe and the immediate subject expressing it is the human being." Although it existed for billions of years, its latent manifestation emerged only with the emergence of human

230. Boff, *Cry of the Earth*, 184. The Trinity is communion of all life among the Divine Persons and an interplay of perichoretic relations of love grounding the unity and unicity of God." Like in the Platonic dialogues and as taught in Christian theology, it is the nature of love to be *diffusivum sui*, that is, to communicate and spread in all directions." *Ibid.*

231. Leonardo Boff, *Holy Trinity: Perfect Community* (Maryknoll, NY: Orbis, 1988) 105.

232. Boff, *Cry of the Earth*, 140.

233. *Ibid.*, 141.

beings. "The species *Homo* is the organ that the entire universe employs to reveal what it holds from its beginning, the mystery of God acting within it." He explains that this "feeling of God" emerges in human consciousness in various ways such as: "quantum reality, the cosmic evolutionary process, the process and eschatological character of nature, the sacramentality of all things, and panentheism."[234]

Boff further tries to demonstrate how scientists explain the 'unexplainable' realities they confront in terms of "God-Mystery."[235] For example, Arno Penzias, one of the discoverers of the 'big bang', explains that one cannot rule out that there was nothing before the 'big bang'. Since "nothing is the negation of being," he presumes that there was something, which he calls the Unknowable. The origin of things from nothing is a sign that 'Someone' created them from nothing and he calls this nothing (Unknowable) God. From a scientific perspective what is perceivable is the presence of the 'Unknowable'. However, where science and discursive reason fail to comprehend this Unknowable, many pursue it "from mysticism, spirituality, religions and the realm of symbol." This way of knowing becomes "a way of loving, sharing, and communing. It is the discovery of the whole above and beyond the parts, of synthesis above and beyond analysis, of the other side of each question or each being. Knowing means discovering oneself within the whole, internalizing it, and plunging into it."[236] Thus Boff argues that both science and mysticism wonder at the Creation alike.

> Science arose out of wonder in an effort to decipher the hidden code of all phenomena. Reverence leads to mysticism and the ethic of responsibility. Science seeks to explain the how of things. Mysticism surrenders to ecstasy over the fact that things exist, and it shows reverence to the One revealed in them and veiled behind them. It seeks to experience that fact and establish communion with it. What mathematics is for the scientists, the spiritual laboratory is for the mystic.[237]

It is the sense of wonder that unites science and mysticism. As he notes, "scientists, sages, and mystics are coming together around wonder and reverence toward the universe." They share "the same root experience: the *mirandum*, fascination over beauty, harmony, and the mystery of reality."[238]

234. *Ibid.*, 141-142.

235. *Ibid.*, 57-59. In his opinion, the religious and sapiential tradition name this principle that creates, sets in motion and orders everything God. *Ibid.*, 142.

236. *Ibid.*, 143.

237. *Ibid.*, 144.

238. *Ibid.*, 144. From the perspective of science, the Big Bang is a "point of instability

Boff also uses the theories of cosmic evolution to explain the mystic presence of God in the universe.[239] Accordingly he argues that "the universe is not blind but filled with purpose and intentionality." The famous atheistic astrophyscist Fred Hoyle considers "a supremely intelligent agent" behind such principle. For him, it "is the initial mover, the power accompanying and continually energizing all, and the supreme attracting magnet of the entire universe." Boff tries to explain it further by using testimonies from scientists like Einstein, Bohm, Prigogine, Hawking, Swimme, Berry and others who noted the presence of "an order implicit in all things that subsists beyond the dimension of chaos." For them "[t]his implicit order points toward a supreme Order; consciousness and spirit point toward a Supreme Consciousness and toward an unsurpassably intelligent Spirit." According to Boff the aforementioned arguments clearly indicate that "the world is seen to be a system inherently open to God and in all its stages and developments transparent to God."[240]

Furthermore, Boff notes how process philosophers and theologians made use of this evolutionary understanding of the new cosmology. They look into the evolutionary processes both from the perspective of God and of the world. They have set God "within the process of the world and the world is regarded as within God's process. They are perichoretically involved in one another; everything that happens in the world somehow affects God, and everything that happens in God somehow affects the world." It is correlative, at the same distinctive. In this sense "God is not identified *with* the cosmic process (one is not simply the other; otherness remains in relationship), but God is identified *in* the cosmic process (is embodied, is unveiled and makes known God's otherness in relation)." Similarly he argues that "the universe is not identified *with* God (one is

(chaos) that through relations and interactions (consciousness) makes possible the emergence of ever more interconnected holistic units and orders (cosmos). This is the expanding universe, a metaphor of God and image of God's exuberance in being, living, and celebrating." In his opinion, the mystical intuitions and spiritual traditions also hold the same. Thus, for the Jewish and Christian traditions God is in communion with Creation and in covenant with all beings, especially with human beings. *Ibid.*, 145.

239. It speaks primarily of the evolution of the cosmos. For example he explains how "[t]he theory of the flaming explosion (the "Flaming Forth" of Swimme and Berry, or Lemaître's big bang)" explains the movement of the universe "in a direction set by the arrow of time." It is different from "Einstein's cosmological principle, which is static and established in a uniform manner on all sides," it is a cosmogenic principle ... that provides an account of the permanent genesis of the universe at all moments and everywhere." He also notes the harmonious vibration of the most elementary article, the top quark to the complex life makes a unity. Furthermore, he cites the example of how the anthropic principle is helpful to perceive the mystery of life. *Ibid.*, 146.

240. *Ibid.*, 147.

not the other) but is identified *in* God (in God it gains its true being and meaning)."[241]

Hence, evolution does not happen within the "same circle." But God and world "are related like an oval with two centers – God and World – but related and mutually implicated in one another because of the mystery character of God." This very fact makes the world sacrament.

> God is immanent in the world, shares in its open process, reveals God's self in it and is enriched with it. God is also transparent in the world and through the world, and hence the world in its totality and its details constitutes a boundless divine sacrament. God is also transcendent vis-à-vis the world in God's character as absolute mystery beyond any imagination and cosmic grandeur. God is in the world and beyond it, continually creating it, permeating it, and drawing it toward ever more complex, participatory and commuting forms.[242]

Having presented the mystery of God in nature and the universe as created, Boff queried the intention of the Creator behind the world order. He explores how some contemporary thinkers in cosmology present this intention as order, harmony, and the arrow of time. They "are revealed through the four basic interactions that govern the entire process of evolution and cosmogenesis: gravity, electromagnetism, and the strong and weak nuclear forces."[243] Based on this, Boff argues that creation is not something mechanical. The world is an organism that is always open to things around in ongoing interplay in which potentialities not yet embodied are being realized. It is a true *creatio continua* seen in the Christian tradition.[244] Boff characterizes this ongoing operation of Creation as a process in terms of its "complexity, interiority, and connectedness."[245] For him, "creation is a vast book written internally and externally that bears God's signature: '*Deo creato, made by God, egressus de coelis*'." Boff notes that the reading of the book of Creation makes one "to be joyful and celebrate, to thank and praise the Creator. It contains God's ongo-

241. *Ibid.*

242. *Ibid.*, 147-148.

243. *Ibid.*, 148. These forces are not something that point beyond anything. They are the universe themselves and work in union. "They constitute a perfect perichoresis – mutual and inter(retro)relationship. The universe as an active organism is the subject of everything that happens in the cosmos." *Ibid.*, 148-149.

244. *Ibid.*, 149. Here he makes particular reference to Orthodoxy and the article of Evdokimov on Nature. In his opinion, God is also involved in this cosmic dance. "My Father works until today and I also work" (Jn 5:17). *Ibid.* See Paul Evdokimov, "Nature," *Scot. Jour.* 18 (1965) 1-22.

245. Boff, *Cry of the Earth*, 150.

ing revelation and is the most deep-rooted and continuous manifestation of the sacred."[246] In his opinion, a Creation-centered theology must be at the service of the cosmic revelation that applies to all. Hence he asks us to "recover original grace above and beyond original sin." Moreover, he argues to "extend to the cosmos theological claims that have been applied only to human beings (theological anthropocentrism) but that are valid for the entire universe, such as grace, final destiny, divinization, resurrection, eternal life, and the reign of the Trinity." He positively admires the creation-centered spirituality because it helps to overcome "the dualism of God and world, person and nature, matter and spirit and fashions an overall experience of being in the world as in our own house, and in the social and cosmic body that are the temple of the Divinity."[247]

The aforementioned discussions concern the immanence of God in the world. God is involved in all the processes of the world, however, not absorbed into it. In this process, God is acting as Spirit of the world, who shares the feeling of pain in suffering and rejoices in its growth towards the "Omega Point."[248] Boff employs the term *panentheism* to explain the idea of mutual interpenetration of God's presence in the cosmos and the cosmos in God, which is traditionally explained through the concept of *perichoresis*. *Panentheism* denotes "God in all and all in God" and is based on God's assurance of His permanent presence in the creature from Creation itself. It views the transcendence and immanence of God "through the intermediate category, transparency, which is precisely the presence of transcendence within immanence."[249]

246. *Ibid.*, 151. He even says that "[t]he sacred texts and traditions that attest to revelations are only possible because the sacred and the revelations are first in the world." In his opinion, many religions are hostages to their founding texts. At the same time, he acknowledges the few who have tried to connect the book of Creation to the book of scriptures. For example: Origen, Augustine, Bonaventure and the representatives of eco-theology. *Ibid.*

247. *Ibid.*, 151. As we shall see, Boff even considers Christ and Spirit as cosmic realities in this sense.

248. *Ibid.*, 152-153.

249. *Ibid.*, 153. In this context it is important to see the difference between panentheism and pantheism. Although both, pantheism and panentheism are concerned with how God is present in the world, its understandings are different. Panentheism (*pan*=all; *en*=in; *theós*=God), which Boff traces back to Karl Christian Frederick Krause (1781-1832), is advanced further by Whitehead, Schillebeeckx and Piet Fransen. Panentheism "starts from the distinction between God and the creature, yet always maintains the relation between them. The one is not the other. Each of them has his/her/its own relative autonomy yet is always related. Not everything is God, but God is in everything. ... God flows through all things; God is present in everything and makes of all reality a temple. And then, vice versa, everything is in God." On the other hand "Pantheism (*pan*=all; *theós*=God) claims that all is God and God is all. It holds the view that God and world are

Boff applies the perichoretic relationship of the Trinity to his panentheistic worldview. He notes: "By way of perichoresis (the essential interrelatedness of the Divine Persons) creation has a trinitarian character."[250] He even considers that the Trinitarian conception of God can offer important and relevant possibilities to the ecological discourses.[251] For him, panentheism is "a most appropriate way of embracing and encompassing the universe, for it means that we are always in a state of approaching one and the same trinitarian God. This experience gives rise to a new integrative and holistic spirituality that can unite heaven and earth." For him, "[t]he world is not only a bridge to God. It is also the place where God is honored and worshiped, and the place where we meet God." He even considers panentheism as "a very old and noble Christian concept that can strengthen our spirituality and enrich our theological understanding of ecology."[252] Applying "the unique experience of God as communion" to ecological discourse, Boff argues:

> Ecological discourse is structured around the web of relationships, interdependencies, and inclusions that sustain and constitute our universe. Together with unity (a single cosmos, a single planet Earth, a single human species, and so forth) diversity also flourishes (galaxy clusters, solar systems, biodiversity, and multiplicity of races, cultures and individuals). This coexistence between unity and diversity opens an area where we may consider our understanding of divinity in terms of trinity and communion.[253]

Furthermore, Boff considers that "the Trinity emerges as one of the most suitable representations of the mystery of the universe."[254] In his opinion, the trinitarian view of the universe "helps us to delve deeper into

identical. "Pantheism maintains that everything is God, and that primordial energy, atoms, stones, mountains, stars, and human beings form part of the deity. Then things, living beings, and persons are but different manifestations of the same unique substantial reality, which is God. According to pantheism, things are not things in themselves, possessing autonomy, but concretizations and synonyms of the same reality, that is, the cosmic and universal God." Boff, *Ecology and Liberation*, 50-51. Panentheism differs from the primitive people, who are naïve pansacramentalists, and have seen everything in a fully sacramental matter. For them, each thing and each function points to their ultimate source, God, manifesting the holy. Boff also notes how this attitude of the primitive people becomes important in varying degrees for Francis, Bonaventure, Teilhard. Boff, *Die Kirche*, 130-131.

250. Boff, *Cry of the Earth*, 166.

251. *Ibid.*, 154. He also underscores that such a trinitarian concept is not limited to Christianity alone.

252. Boff, *Ecology and Liberation*, 51.

253. Boff, *Cry of the Earth*, 154-155.

254. *Ibid.*, 156. More details on trinity in this context, *ibid.*, 155-157.

understanding our common home, planet Earth, the universe, and its future, because they are all woven of the most intricate and open relationships, in the likeness of the Trinity. The blessed Trinity constitutes the common sphere of all beings and entities: the theosphere."[255]

3.1.2. The Spirit in Creation

Similar to Boff's understanding of God in cosmogenic principles, he explores the presence of the Holy Spirit within the scope of the New Cosmology that expresses reality as energy and life. He also notes how the category of Spirit in all human cultural traditions can contribute to understand the cosmos as cosmogenesis and to comprehend reality as energy fields and intricate web of relationships.[256]

The etymological meaning of the Hebrew word for spirit, *ruach*, itself considers Spirit as "the energy giving reality that fills the expanding cosmic spaces." This *ruach* fills the entire universe, as the scripture says (Wis 1:7)."[257] *Ruach*-spirit often means vital breath and is not restricted to human beings. The Earth is also a living being, and the wind is the breath of the earth, hence, *ruach*-spirit. It is the "originating cosmic power permeating all and giving it life."[258] It takes particular forms as energy in the cosmos, in the physical world, in the living world, in human beings and in God. In the cosmos spirit is seen in energy in its most elementary components. In the physical world, it is seen behind all its movements, and in the living world, it is seen in the life of plants and animals. In human beings it is the inner spirit, in various forms, and finally, in God as the true life. What he underscores in all these realities is that "the spirit is present from the beginning of the universe, permeating

255. *Ibid.*, 157.

256. *Ibid.*, 158. He cites such expressions seen in various cultures, for example, behind animism and shamanism. *Ibid.*, 158-159. In this context, "The word *spirit* conceals a primordial experience to be found in the archaeology of the great religions and at the bases of Western and Oriental philosophy. We experience the spirit not as a mere part of the human being, but as a vital whole. *Spirit* is then the term for the energy and vitality of all manifestations of being human." Boff, *Ecology and Liberation*, 165.

257. The feminine word *ruah* "appears 389 times in the Hebrew scriptures. Recent studies have shown that in all Semitic languages (Syriac, Punic, Akkadian, Samaritan, Ugaritic, and Hebrew) the verbal root of *ruah* is *rwh*, whose original meaning is not 'breath' or 'wind', as usually given, but 'the atmospheric space between heaven and earth', which can be calm or turbulent. By derivation it also means 'unfolding and spreading,' 'expansion and extension of living space'. Properly speaking, *ruah* means the vital sphere where the human being, the animal, or any other living thing imbibes life." Boff, *Cry of the Earth*, 159.

258. Boff, *Ecology and Liberation*, 50.

it, emerging in a series of forms until it reaches its highest expression: the divine Spirit."[259]

Boff's understanding of the Spirit has an integrating character. In this sense the Spirit in human beings is not 'a part' as opposed to another part as body and soul, but rather spirit is a totality of being.[260] God is spirit means "to seek to give expression to God in the framework of life, of irruption, communication, transcendence of whatever is given, overflowing abundance, passion, and fiery love." It is not a static force of a metaphysical nature, rather, the "spirit-as-cosmic-force and vital energy blows where it wills and energizes the entire cosmogenesis. It is the *ubique diffusus, transfusus, circumfusus* of the church fathers, that is, that which fills all things and is spread throughout all spaces and times."[261] This understanding of God as Spirit directs our experience to the interplay of relationships and subjectivity. The deepening of these experiences helps us to come up against the absolute Spirit, who enlivens the whole universe (*Spiritus vivificans*)."[262]

The Trinitarian conception of God explains the role of the Spirit in relation to Creation. The cosmos "created in the likeness and image of the God Trinity" denotes the interplay of relationships. Thus in co-creation all things possess a mysterious depth coming from the mystery of the Father, its light and its wisdom by the Son, but the perspective of communion and love is revealed in the Holy Spirit. "By the joining of the three persons in creating (perichoresis), everything comes interwoven with relationships, interdependencies, and webs of intercommunion." The specific role of the Spirit lies in the keeping of this union. It is clear from the fact that "creation is projected and created in the Spirit" revealing the unique features of the Person of the Holy Spirit.[263]

While underscoring the presence of the Spirit in the cosmos, Boff criticizes Christianity for not giving due emphasis to the presence of the

259. Boff, *Cry of the Earth*, 160.

260. The human spirit is that which seeks to express the "vital drive embodied in the human being. It is not ... something in the human being, but the proper and unique way of being of man and woman." It is 1) a force for synthesizing and creating unity, 2) a force for socialization and communication, 3) the power of meaning and 4) the power of transcendence. Boff, *Cry of the Earth*, 160-161.

261. *Ibid.*, 161. He also underscores how the Fathers of the Church, both Greek and Latin, express the idea of "*Spiritus ubique diffusus* (the universally diffused Spirit)." In particular Boff refers to Fathers like Gregory of Nazianzus, Gregory of Nyssa, St. Basil and St. Peter Damian. Boff, *Ecology and Liberation*, 50.

262. Boff, *Cry of the Earth*, 162. Boff speaks about the different dimensions of how the Spirit reveals: e.g. ecstasy, enthusiasm, inspiration, communication and presence of reasonability and order in the universe.

263. *Ibid.*, 167.

Spirit in the world compared to the Incarnation and the cosmic presence of the risen Christ in the world. He criticizes Greek theology for tending towards monarchianism. It speaks of the monarchy of the Father, with respect to the order of intratrinitarian relations. For them "it is the Father who upholds the divine substance and communicates it differently to the Son and to the Holy Spirit." He also criticizes Latin theology rooted in Christomonism. For them, "Christ is all, centralization in Christ, yesterday, today, and forever, as though there were no Father and Spirit." In his opinion both lack the Spirit.[264] He observes the same in modern trends like that of Teilhard de Chardin who affirmed the cosmic presence of the risen Christ in the process of evolution in his work on the cosmic Christ. All these theologies failed to do justice to the reality of the Spirit's indwelling in creation.[265] For Boff, as much as the incarnate Son, the Spirit is concerned with the mystery of Creation.[266]

3.1.3. Cosmic Christology

In the section on Christ as sacrament, we saw how Jesus becomes a sacrament. In particular, we have seen how the divine-human encounter in Jesus is central to the understanding of the sacramentality of Jesus. Although we have underscored the cosmic dimension inherent in Boff's theology of the sacramentality of Jesus, we shall now go deeper into it. In particular we will see how Boff delineates "the cosmic relevance of Jesus Christ and how the story of universe is interwoven with the story of Christ." As we have already noted, he goes beyond the historical context of the Mediterranean and the person of Jesus to other revelations in various cultural contexts. He even suggests to "transcend the anthropocentrism ... common in all Christologies, for Christ has divinized and liberated not only human beings but all beings in the universe."[267]

First of all, Boff's Christology emerges from Christogenesis. Accordingly, humanity and divinity are simultaneously present in Jesus. He compares this to all beings who are seen to be simultaneously in the form of energy wave and material particle. In this sense the entire universe is united with God. This is clearly manifested in Jesus' relation to God. By calling God Abba he took the entire universe to the status of the sons and daughters of God the Father. Furthermore, the title 'Christ' that was given to Jesus also shows that in Jesus "the mystery of God has been made supremely manifest." In this sense, "the *Christ* has taken shape and

264. *Ibid.*, 165-166.
265. Boff, *Ecology and Liberation*, 49.
266. *Ibid.*, 152.
267. Boff, *Cry of the Earth*, 174.

consciousness in Jesus" because he "already existed in the cosmogenic and anthropogenic process."[268] Boff considers the Christic element as "part of evolution until it breaks forth in consciousness and is internalized and assumed by persons of faith. It then becomes Christological and Christic as contained in consciousness."[269]

Secondly, the Christ of faith stems from Christogenesis. Here, the Christic becomes Christological in the incarnation of Jesus. Therefore, although Incarnation was present from Creation, "the crystallization of the Christic" or its personalization took place with an *ad extra* intervention by God. In his opinion, the transition from Christic to "Christological presupposes a whole labor of the cosmos in terms of creating a consciousness, and indeed consciousness attaining levels of universalization, internalization, and achievement of higher synthesis." He is also convinced of the need of a convergence in order "to attain an omega point" for moving from the Christic to the Christological. Here faith becomes crucial. "Faith sees in the omega point of evolution the Christ of faith, he who is believed and announced as head of the cosmos and of the church, the meeting of all beings."[270] In other words, faith helps us to have access "to the ultimate innerness of the world, where it reveals itself as the temple of God and of the transfigured cosmic Christ."[271]

Finally Boff delineates how the Christ of faith is rooted in the historical Jesus, who is linked to the history of the universe and made up of the cosmogenic principles. In this sense he even says that Jesus' body "had the same ancestral origin and even materials from the cosmic dust that may be older than our solar and planetary system."[272] As Cosmogenesis

268. *Ibid.*, 77. Boff traces a resemblance to this in Teilhard de Chardin's words: "In nature there is a 'Christic element'." Chardin also noted its objective character linked to the structure of the universe itself and he calls it "pan Christism."

269. *Ibid.*, 177. He even suggests that we can use other terms such as *sophia-wisdom, Krishna, Karma*, or *Karisma*, for Christ to be understood within the ecumenical context. For him these are terms that have a cosmic dimension. He also draws our attention to Jung's use of Christ in the realm of archetype of the collective unconscious. *Ibid.* For Boff the significance of Buddha, Chuang-Tzu, Socrates and Plato "is fully revealed in the light of Christ. Jesus accomplished in reality what they had in mind. They are sacraments of Christ." Boff, *Sacraments of Life*, 41. See also: M. Fox, "Is the 'Cosmic Christ' a Term That Is Anti-Ecumenical?," *The Coming of the Cosmic Christ* (San Francisco, CA: Harper and Row, 1988) 241-244.

270. Boff, *Cry of the Earth*, 178.

271. Boff, *The Path to Hope*, 39.

272. Boff, *Cry of the Earth*, 179. He even notes that "[t]he iron that ran in his veins, the phosphorus and calcium that strengthened his bones, the sodium and potassium that allowed signals to travel through his nerves, the oxygen making up his body, and the carbon, all this had the effect of making his incarnation truly cosmic." *Ibid.*

has subjectivity and interiority that accompanies the evolution of matter, "the subjectivity of Jesus is inhabited by the more primitive movements of consciousness, by the more archaic dreams, by the more basic passions, by the deeper archetypes, by the more ancient images and ideas."[273] Furthermore, the incarnation is not limited to Jesus alone but is extended to all human beings. It is shared by all human beings because the humanity common to all belonged to God. It reached its peak in Jesus.[274] Although the incarnation roots Jesus in the cosmos, it limits him to space and time, which draws limitation to Incarnation. For example, Jesus is a Jew, not a Roman; a man not a woman. In this sense Incarnation is still a process on its way. Thus, "The Word continues to emerge from the matter of the world and from the human mass to verbify the whole universe and bring it into the Reign of the Trinity."[275]

Boff understands the passion of the world in the same way. For him, Jesus is crucified from the beginning of the world and participates in the sufferings of all people.[276] The redemption and, thus, the resurrection are sensible only against the background of Christ's cross and passion. His suffering for others is extended to all those crucified in cosmogenic history. Like in the Creation Jesus' suffering for others is not limited to human beings, but extended to all creation. This enables Jesus to go beyond the space-time limitation of His incarnation. In other words His limits are equated to "the dimensions of the cosmos," making Him "truly the cosmic and universal Christ."[277] It also enables faith communities to extend "the meaning of Jesus to all realms of salvation history including the history of the world."[278]

In this context it seems important to note that Boff considers the incarnation, descending of God, and resurrection, the ascent of Creation to God, are the two fundamental aspects of Christian faith.[279] At the same

273. *Ibid.*, 79. In this context it is good to note the Chalcedonial affirmation that "Jesus in his humanity is consubstantial with us, in body and soul." From the new cosmology perspective it "means that Jesus is a product of the initial great explosion and inflation, that his roots are in the Milky Way, his homeland is the solar system, and his house is planet Earth. He took part in the emergence of life and the formation of consciousness. Like any human being, he is a child of the universe and of Earth. He belongs to a human family. And the human being is that one by whom the cosmos itself comes to its own self-awareness and the discovery of the Sacred, the biological site where divinity breaks into matter." *Ibid.*

274. *Ibid.*, 179.

275. *Ibid.*, 180.

276. *Ibid.*

277. *Ibid.*, 181.

278. *Ibid.*, 176.

279. While Francis "valued Incarnation over Resurrection, as if one included the

time along with many scholars Boff delineates the transcendent meaning of Jesus, based on the resurrection event. Through the resurrection, the earthly life of Jesus was transfigured into "God's mode of being." It gives wider meaning to the earthly Jesus who emerges into the new human with the resurrection. It makes him go beyond the limits of the body in order to be present in the cosmos and in communion with all reality.[280] In Resurrection, Christ becomes "the paradigm and exemplar of what will happen to all humans and the totality of creation."[281] Resurrection is "full liberation from all the obstacles standing in the way of the lordship of God and the full realization of all the dynamic forces of life and glory placed by God within human beings and the whole of creation."[282] Therefore, he argues that "Resurrection must be understood as a total, exhaustive realization of human reality in its relationship with God, with others, and with the cosmos. Resurrection is therefore the eschatologization of a human being who has arrived at the end of the evolutionary process and been inserted into the divine reality."[283] Furthermore, when go deeper from "analyzing the world with creation *in illo tempore* as our starting point" to "comprehend it with eschatology, the future present in Jesus resurrected, as our point of departure."[284] Resurrection shows that death and entropy are not the last word. "Life comes back transfigured and at an incomparably higher level" displaying "the eschatological dimension of the cosmos."[285] Through the Resurrection, "Jesus revealed in

other," following the Scotist tradition, Boff argues that, "The Son is not just the supreme revelation of the Father, his Word and perfect Image within the circle of the Trinity. He is all these within creation too." Payne, *Sacramentality in the Writings of Leonardo Boff*, 83. For Scotus, "since the Christ was the "first thought of" in relation to creation, creation itself has a primary christic dimension. Hence creation, as sacrament, points to Christ since its raison d'être is Christ, God the Son become human. The historical Incarnation of Christ reinforces this link between Christ and creation." *Ibid.*, see also pp. 15-17.

280. Boff, *Cry of the Earth*, 175. Jesus' coming back to life was first explained using apocalyptic terminology as elevation and glorification. Later, the eschatological framework using resurrection terminology. And this latter expression, continued in the Church. In Boff's opinion, beyond the expression of elevation or resurrection, it is important to see the message: the new life of Jesus. *Ibid.*

281. Boff, *Jesus Christ Liberator*, 260.

282. L. & C. Boff, *Introducing Liberation Theology*, 54-55.

283. Boff, *Jesus Christ Liberator*, 207. "[R]esurrection entails such an intensity of life that death no longer exists, nor is any entropy at work. Jesus has been transported, as it were, to the end of history and whatever was latent in the billions of years of cosmogenesis and anthropogenesis has been made open. Stated more technically, Jesus' fate has been 'eschatologized'." Boff, *Cry of the Earth*, 175-176.

284. Boff, *Jesus Christ Liberator*, 208.

285. Boff, *Cry of the Earth*, 81. Eschatological means "the happy ending, the revelation of the end of the cosmogenic process is anticipated in time. The future is brought into

himself the anticipated goal of the world and the radical meaning of all creation,"[286] and opens "the possibility of a complete reconciliation." It is a reconciliation that "includes the past and the victims. It is not just the future that is assured; the past is also rescued." It means that the cosmic Christ "emerges as the moving force of evolution; he is its liberator, and the one who brings it to fulfillment." In this sense a "Cosmic Christology seeks to provide an integrating and balanced vision."[287]

As already noted, the cosmic Christology is grounded on the Trinitarian dimension of God. "The cosmic root of Christ is found at the heart of the inner life of the Trinity. All things are marked by the Son, just as they are permeated by the Spirit."[288] The incarnation and salvific mission of Jesus stem from the immanent Trinity.

> In the very act in which God communicates and expresses Godself within the interplay of the immanent Trinity – it is the Son in the power of the Spirit – God also expresses all the possible imitations that are not God but will be creatures of God. The cosmogenesis, biogenesis, and anthropogenesis are present in this internal and eternal divine plan, including that conscious and free being who can receive the Son in itself to the maximum degree, becoming the incarnate Son and, as such, loving God in a supreme and divine manner.[289]

The Trinitarian mission of salvation is exercised in history through the economic Trinity. "Thus creation has emerged in the specific way in which it has come to us in the form of cosmogenesis, biogenesis, anthropogenesis, and Christogenesis. And within Christogenesis, Jesus was that one intended to receive the Son maximally within all human reality, and with him all other humans."[290] Hence, the incarnation of Jesus became the most important means to know the Trinity's intention for us. The Incarnation "shows the Trinity's eternal design: to bring all beings into its communion through the mediation of the Son and the driving force of the Holy Spirit."[291] "[T]he Father wanted the individual Jesus of Nazareth, hypostatically united to the Son... to root the Trinity in the midst of the human race and all of creation."[292] Thus he says:

the present." *Ibid.*, 181-182.

286. Boff, *Jesus Christ Liberator*, 211.
287. Boff, *Cry of the Earth*, 82.
288. *Ibid.*, 185.
289. *Ibid.*, 184.
290. *Ibid.*, 185.
291. *Ibid.*, 186.
292. *Ibid.*, 187.

> [T]he ultimate foundation on which all subsists and exists is Jesus Christ. He is the savior and universal liberator. In him salvation is incarnated and offered universally to all. Through him we also have access to ultimate mystery of creation, the holy Trinity, which dwells in the world and in the heart of the just human being. In the mystery of the Trinity God's universal salvific will attains its full, transcendent meaning. We find that human salvation is the presence of the Father, Son, and the Holy Spirit in the world, and the presence of the world in the Father, the Son and the Holy Spirit. This is the meaning of all creation, which is the precondition for self-communication of the Trinity and the celebration of that communication. While the creator and creature preserve their distinctive identities, God ultimately becomes all in all.[293]

Boff applies the Trinitarian image of God, in particular cosmic Christology to address issues on ecology. The interrelation of Creation amongst itself and towards God stems from its relation to the Trinity through Christ. Thus, we see "[t]he christic structure that pervades all reality took concrete form in Jesus of Nazareth because he, from all eternity, was thought of and loved as *the* focal being in which the total manifestation of God within creation would take place for the first time. This manifestation signifies the finished interpretation of human beings and God, unconfoundable and indivisible unity, the goal of creation now inserted into the trinitarian ministry."[294] Moreover, Boff contends that "creation is inserted into the very mysterious depths of the Triune God. Creation is not exterior to God, but one moment of his complete manifestation."[295] For him, "[t]he entire universe emanates from this divine relational interplay and is made in the image and likeness of the Trinity."[296] Therefore Boff argues that the creatures reveal the self-communication of the Trinity. "They show trinitarian communion opening outwards, giving itself, revealing itself. No created being is opaque and closed in on itself; each participates in a structure of meaning."[297]

Boff further notes how cosmic Christology takes a sacramental form in the Eucharist for the Christians.[298] In his opinion, World and Christ

293. Boff, *Liberating Grace*, 123.
294. Boff, *Jesus Christ Liberator*, 260.
295. *Ibid.*, 259.
296. Boff, *Ecology and Liberation*, 11.
297. Boff, *Trinity and Society*, 187.
298. Boff, *Cry of the Earth*, 183. Here Boff recalls Chardin, for whom "the eucharist prolongs in some fashion the incarnation and maintains Christ's connection to the elements of the cosmos in an ongoing manner. The host is not simply the piece of bread on the altar. The whole universe becomes host in order to be the cosmic body of Christ." *Ibid.* He also underscores the cosmic vision of Christ, present in the Eucharist, and is

form a sacramental unity. It is a communion of both, first, in that the world shows the external side of God and, then, God shows the inner side of the world. In this sense the world is transparent.[299] "The material elements are sacraments that put us in communion with him, because they, in the most intimate part of their being, pertain to the very reality of Christ."[300]

Based on cosmic Christology, Boff argues that "the incarnation of Son was not due to human sin."[301] According to him, "[a] theology of creation helps us to understand the meaning of a theology of redemption. Redemption presupposes a drama, a degeneration of creation, a failure of human vocation that has affected all human beings and their cosmic environment."[302] Based on 'the cosmo- and verbocentric view', he argues that "the incarnation belongs to the mystery of creation."[303] In this sense, he criticises the overemphasis on the mystery of redemption to the detriment of the mystery of Creation.[304] "The incarnation, which encompasses the entire universe ... signifies the supreme glorification of God."[305] In his opinion, "[s]in has not destroyed the original plan of the Trinity but rather has given it the unique way it comes into being, in the form of the suffering Servant and the Crucified One who shares in the passion of the world."[306] Thus, redemption is a recovery of Creation's original nature. "This means that biblical revelation, the church, the magisterium, and the sacraments ... exist in relation to the creation and serve its recovery. ... The Hebrew and Christian revelation is intended to recover and not to replace the revelation of creation."[307]

In short, Boff, by using different theories, tries to elucidate God's presence in the world, and basically explains this with a Trinitarian perspective. Through all the three spheres, Boff underscores the sense of mystery. This sense of mystery, which speaks of the sacred presence of the transcendent in the world, necessitates a human response to it.

forwarded by philosophers like Leibniz and Maurice Blondel. *Ibid*, 184.

299. Boff, *Die Kirche*, 156.

300. Boff, *Jesus Christ Liberator*, 212.

301. Boff, *Cry of the Earth, Cry of the Poor*, 185.

302. Boff, *Ecology and Liberation*, 47.

303. Boff, *Cry of the Earth*, 185. This is basically a Scotist tradition. See J. B. Carol, *The Absolute Primacy and Predestination of Jesus and His Mother* (Chicago, IL: Franciscan Herald Press, 1981).

304. Boff, *Ecology and Liberation*, 45.

305. Boff, *Cry of the Earth*, 185.

306. *Ibid*.

307. *Ibid*., 47-48. For Boff, forgetting creation, we tend to exaggerate the importance of the Bible (fundamentalism), inflate the role of the Church (ecclesiocentrism), and exaggerate the function of the sacraments (sacramentalism). *Ibid*.

3.2. Human Beings in relation to God and World

Having seen how Boff delineates God's presence in the world, now we shall see how Boff demonstrates human response to God. In order to explain this, it is important to see how the human being is placed in Creation. Hence, in this section we shall first see the place of the human being in Creation, and in the second section, we delineate the human's response to it.

3.2.1. Role of Human Being in the Creation

Human beings have an important role to play in Creation. In order to understand the human role in Creation, three things seem important: the role assigned to humanity, the Trinitarian basis for human action and finally the ethical and sacramental nature of the human being.

3.2.1.1. Human Being: Co-Creator of God

According to the priestly tradition the human being was presented as a representative of God who carries out God's creative work. This is well expressed through the terms "image and likeness." Even the terms such as 'dominion' and 'subdue' are to explain the responsibility given to the human being to continue God's work. As sharers of the 'image and likeness' of God they are called 'sons and daughters of God'. They "share in the nature of the Father-creator, which is wisdom and goodness." In this sense it goes beyond simple participation in his creative work as a responsible representative of God to rest on the Sabbath. It denotes "celebration made actual in terms of the perfection and goodness of all creation (Gen 2:2-3). At the summit of the human mission we find, not work, but leisure, not struggle but gratuitousness and joyful rest."[308] This participation in God's leisure explains well the mystery character of Creation. According to Boff, unfortunately, however, the Christian theology of Creation has helped to undermine this mystery character of the world. This happened because the Christian myth placed men and women at the center of the universe. Therefore, he considers this image behind the present ecological crisis.[309] The words 'dominion' and 'subdue' are reinterpreted literally in line with Descartes and Bacon that "the human being is intended to dominate and harness the forces of nature for the individual and social welfare of humanity."[310] He even exclaims that due to the ag-

308. Boff, *Ecology and Liberation*, 44.

309. Boff, *The Path to Hope*, 7; Id., *Ecology and Liberation*, 43-45.

310. Boff, *Ecology and Liberation*, 44. He underscores that "the understanding of reality behind the scientific and technological notion of modernity confirms this same will to dominate. Descartes, Galileo, Newton, and Bacon taught that knowledge is power and

gression of the human being towards other creatures, humans, then, missed the transparency of Creation.[311]

The second version presents the human being as some one who "is a friend of nature, works with the earth (which he or she is to till), and acts as the good angel of the earth, in order to safeguard it." Here also one sees the same spirit of celebration as in the first. Boff even suggests that "[t]his meaning should have qualified the first." At the same time, it "was obscured or spiritualized" in order to exploit Creation. He criticizes it and calls us to "recover the original and profoundly ecological meaning of the biblical message."[312] Along with this he also notes that "a certain theological tradition dominant in some ecclesiastical circles encouraged suspicion of physicality, disdain for the world, rejection of all forms of pleasure, and contempt for sexuality and femininity. It favoured the idea of a God detached from the world, thus promoting the formation of a world separate from God."[313] At the same time, he underscores the efforts in the current theological discussions to appropriate creation and redemption in a line with Francis of Assisi, Bonaventure, Duns Scotus and William of Ockham. He also underscores the efforts of some trends in modern theology of earthly reality and the entire theology of the Orthodox church."[314]

In short, both in the Priestly and Yahwist versions of Creation, human beings are presented as "custodians of other beings, and ... responsible for their integrity." In this sense, they are co-creators with God.[315] Thus,

that power is dominion; that it means developing the capacity to subject all creatures with their brute strength to slavery in our service, as Descartes put it." In Boff's opinion, this conception is seen behind all sorts of aggression against the eco-system right from the beginning of the modern era. The same ideology was under work in the process of colonization, slavery and cultural distortion. In his opinion, Latin America, Africa and Asia were "victims of the aggression by European countries in which the agenda of the modern age was worked out. The same will to overpower and subject is focused on other human beings and nature." *Ibid.*, 85-86.

311. *Ibid.*, 77.

312. *Ibid.*, 44-45.

313. *Ibid.*, 45. Here Boff is pointing to certain trends that prevailed in the medieval period as some sort of a particular piety. At the same time Boff underscores some of the positive trends that too have found place in this period. For example, he draws our attention to St. Francis, St. Clare, and their followers.

314. *Ibid.*, 46.

315. *Ibid.*, 86-87. In his opinion, there is no fixed central point, rather, "We all exist thanks to others, with others, and through others. Together we make up the biosphere as a great integrated and integrating whole." *Ibid.*, 87. He even says that "The christian myth of creation, unlike the Greek myth of Prometheus, has always maintained that the human being is made a creator in order to prolong the creative act of God, and, being given the responsibility of a son or a daughter, to shape the creation with creativity and in freedom.

Boff emphasizes the participatory role of human beings in Creation. "Humans are made for participation and creation; we want not only to receive bread but help to produce it, so that we may emerge as agents of our own history. We hunger for bread but also for participation and beauty."[316] This participatory role of human beings points to the responsibility entrusted to them, because they belong to nature as nature belongs to humankind and depends on human care and labor. In this sense human beings are ethical beings and "are able to express care and concern for nature, to give expression to their care and its inward ascendant thrust, and to bring degradation and destruction to an end."[317] For him, the human relationship to Creation is one of responsibility and he terms it ethical relationship.[318]

3.2.1.2. Trinitarian Life in Human Being

Boff compares the communitarian dimension of human life to the life of the Trinity. Here again it is important to note that unlike the Greek model that "proceeds from the monarchy of the Father and seeks the unity in him" or the Latin model that "proceeds from the unity of the divine nature," Boff offers a third model, which is rooted in the *perichoresis* of the divine persons.[319] God, the communion of the Father, the Son, and the Spirit "are co-existent and dwell together eternally without any hierarchy among themselves. The interrelationship of life and love among them (*perichoresis*, in theological terminology) is so profound and radical that it is the means by which they are, so to speak, unified and constitute one God."[320] Two paradigms are important in his *perichoreic* understanding of Trinity: "the idea of God as divine community and the Trinity as the basis and paradigm of human community."[321]

God is present in *homo sapiens et faber*, not in person, but in and behind free and creative human activity." *Ibid.*, 79.

316. Boff, *Cry of the Earth*, 9.

317. Boff, *Ecology and Liberation*, 26.

318. *Ibid.*, 46-47.

319. John O'Donnell, "The Trinity as Divine Community: A Critical Reflection upon Recent Theological Developments," *Gregorianum* 69 (1988) 5-34, p. 18.

320. It "is neither an absurd mystery nor a mathematical contradiction, but the supreme expression of the experience of love and human communion. ... It is not enough to have a *tête-à-tête*, as it were, of an 'I' (the Father) and a 'Thou' (the Son), for that would amount to dual narcissism. The 'I' and the 'Thou' have to meet in an "us" (the Holy Spirit), like a third person overcoming the isolation of two separate individuals. Thus there is a perfect dialectic not merely of two but of three persons, who are distinct but always interrelated." Boff, *Ecology and Liberation*, 153. See also Id., "Trinitarian Community and Social Liberation," *Cross Currents* 38 (1988) 289-308.

321. O'Donnell, "The Trinity as Divine Community," 18. It seems that there are a lot

Boff grounds his theory of ecology on the Trinity's "complex and complete interplay of relations." Thus, he argues that "[t]he ecclesial community must feel part of the human community, and the human community has to feel that it is part of the cosmic community. They all form part of the trinitarian community of Father, Son, and Holy Spirit."[322] Therefore, like in the Trinity, which affirms on the one hand the one nature of the Godhead and, on the other hand, maintains the diversity of the divine persons, the universe is a reproduction of diversity and of union. In his opinion:

> [The world] is complex, diverse, one, united, interrelated, because it is a reflection of the Trinity. God invades everything, enters into every relationship, erupts into every ecosystem. But God especially sacramentalizes the life of every human individual, because there we find intelligence, will, and sensibility as distinct concretizations of our one humanity, whole and entire. We are a unique life and form of communion realized distinctly. We are one and at the same time multiple, like the mystery of the triune God.[323]

3.2.1.3. Ethical and Sacramental Human Beings

The theology of Creation that underscores the continuing responsibility of human beings in Creation serves as the basis for Boff's theory of ecological and social justice.[324] For him, it is not merely an aspect of the responsibility entrusted to human beings, but it stems from their concern to "make the world as good as possible."[325] In this sense it is important to note that "the human race is part of nature and the biosphere, not the center of the universe. It exists in profound communion with all other beings. It is distinguished not by biological superiority but by the character of human beings as moral entities."[326] The ethical dimension is inscribed in

of similarities with Moltmann in his theology of the Trinity. In this sense it is worth noting the study of Stephanie Hartmann, *Trinitätslehre als Sozialkritik? Das Verhältnis von Gotteslehre und Sozialkritik in den trinitätstheologischen Entwürfen von Jürgen Moltmann und Leonardo Boff* (Frankfurt/M: Lang, 1997).

322. Boff, *Ecology and Liberation*, 48.

323. *Ibid.*, 49.

324. *Ibid.*, 77. Ecological justice means respect for the otherness of beings and things as well as their right to continue to exist. Social justice means respect and concern for people, as well as the abrogation of those forms of oppression that are exercised through social relations. *Ibid.*

325. *Ibid.*, 81.

326. *Ibid.*, 86. Based on recent researches in biology and etiology he argues that "we can act beyond our interests ... assuming the responsibility for preserving nature and promoting all forms of life, especially those that are oppressed." For example, these studies show that "the laws that have governed the process of building ecosystems comprise

their nature.[327] For him, the human being is "the sole creature in creation conceived and conceiving itself as an ethical being" and "the destiny of the whole earth system can depend on the ethical choice made by humanity."[328] Human beings are capable of acting freely and of making judgements. They are guided by the principles of solidarity, compassion and love, along with personal interests. Boff considers this character of responsibility as that which makes humans an "ethical being."[329]

Our relation to Creation poses questions of responsibility towards the "otherness, of anything that concerns some people and others. Ethics enters at this point."[330] The "otherness of all that exists in creation" becomes foundational in Boff. In his opinion, "All beings, especially living beings, deserve to be accepted and even respected in their otherness." Acceptance and respect becomes obligatory for humankind because "[o]nly human beings can bless this otherness, live freely with it, or wickedly destroy it. This is what grounds our ethical responsibility."[331] According to Boff, "[t]o be truly ethical, humankind has to be able to understand the urgent need for ecological balance" by being human together with nature and with all other human beings.[332]

Considering the importance assigned to human beings, Boff characterizes the essential vocation of human beings as to become 'sacramental human beings'.[333] In this sense one has to see everything in terms of God and perceive the entire world as one grand sacrament. It is this quality of human beings that enables them to turn "an object into a symbol and an action into a rite."[334] For this he urges "to recapture the religious richness contained in the symbolic and sacramental universe that inhabits our daily life."[335] This is because for him, "everything is, or can become, a sacrament" depending "on human beings and the way they look at things. The world will reveal its sacramental nature insofar as human beings look

not the struggle for the survival of the fittest (Darwin), but a huge synergetic process based on collaboration and solidarity among creatures (James Lovelock, D. Sagan).

327. *Ibid.*, 32.

328. *Ibid.*, 31.

329. Leonardo Boff, "Social Ecology: Poverty and Misery," *Ecotheology: Voices from South and North*, ed. David G. Hallman (Geneva: World Council of Churches, 1994) 235-263, p. 243.

330. Boff, *Ecology and Liberation*, 81.

331. *Ibid.*, 87-88.

332. *Ibid.*, 31.

333. Boff, *Sacraments of Life*, 32.

334. *Ibid.*, 3-4. He explains it with the Brazilian example of offering coffee or tea to a visitor.

335. *Ibid.*, 7.

at it humanely, relating to it and letting the world come inside them to become their world."[336]

For the sacramental human being "everything and every historical event appear as sacraments of God and God's divine will."[337] For this, he calls for an "inner human view of things that transmutes them into sacraments."[338] In Pauline terms, he notes that "all human beings ... are called to reflect deeply on the works of creation. ... The world, without ceasing to be world, will be transmuted into an eloquent sacrament of God" (Romans 1:19-20).[339]

> Humans are not simply beings who manipulate their world. They are capable of reading the message that the world carries within it, that is written in all the things making up the world. ... In the ephemeral they can read the Permanent; in the temporal, the Eternal; in the world, God. Then the ephemeral is transfigured into a sign, the presence of the permanent, the temporal into a symbol of the reality of the Eternal, the world into a great and grand sacrament of God.[340]

Here sacramental thinking becomes an imperative. It helps one to think that everything in this world is unique and incomparable.[341] He criticizes the modern attitude that fails to see the sacramentality of things. Although the modern person lives "in the midst of sacraments," s/he "does not have the open eye to visualize them reflectively." S/He sees "things only as things. It views them only from the outside. When we look inside them, we perceive that they have a crack through which a higher light enters. The light illuminates things, making them clear and transparent."[342]

This serves as the basis for a proper ecological mentality.[343] He even says that for an appropriate ecological mentality, we need "to realize that Mystery is involved in everything, penetrates everything, shines in everything." He criticizes the Western Church for presenting the view that "we may one day experience the Mystery that we call God, everything is a

336. *Ibid.*, 18.

337. *Ibid.*, 30. He illustrates this with the example of Francis of Assisi. "All things are sacraments when viewed in God's perspective and light. The world, human beings, and things are signs and symbols of the transcendent." *Ibid.*, 38.

338. *Ibid.*, 17.

339. *Ibid.*, 32.

340. *Ibid.*, 1-2.

341. *Ibid.*, 18.

342. *Ibid.*, 11.

343. Boff considers "ecological mentality" as one of the five ways to make the option for the poor. Boff, *Saint Francis: A Model for Human Liberation*, 58-63.

way and all living creatures are sacraments and gates to a meeting with God."[344] He then argues that since we all proceed from the same Creator "there is a universal brotherhood and sisterhood among all beings." He contends that since all creatures are sacramental they bear traces of the divine.[345]

3.2.2. Ecocentric Ethical Order

As we have seen, human beings are fundamentally endowed with the responsibility of celebration; nevertheless, such "celebration is made actual through perfection and goodness of creation."[346] At this point we are confronted with the ethical responsibility of human beings in their relation to Creation. This is coupled with the transformation that human beings are required to make of themselves.

3.2.2.1. Challenging Paradigms

In our first part, we observed the changing worldviews from theocentrism to anthropocentrism and then to new cosmology. Further, we noted how God's presence is seen in the new cosmic order, and underscores the immanent presence of God in the world. Even so in concrete human life, we encounter the exploitation of both human beings and Creation. From the paradoxical experience of the presence of the divine in the world and the experience of negativity in life, we are compelled to look for a new ethical order.

Boff criticizes utilitarian and anthropocentric ethics, which upholds human dominion over others and nature. He explores the pitfalls of the utilitarian ethics of the existing social system from three perspectives. First, by using the criticism of liberation movements, he criticizes the utilitarian mode of ethics. In such a system society's main concern is not "built on life, the common good, participation or solidarity among human beings, but on economy, the powers and instruments that create wealth through the ravaging of nature and the exploitation of human being."[347] He also acknowledges their critique of utilitarian ethics for using human beings and natural resources as raw materials in the pursuit of accumulating wealth. Boff also criticizes it for favoring only the wealthiest in the society.[348]

344. Boff, *Ecology and Liberation*, 43.

345. *Ibid.*, 77.

346. *Ibid.*, 44.

347. Boff, "Social Ecology: Poverty and Misery," 235.

348. *Ibid.*, 236. The liberation movements that arose from the awareness of economic inequality in society are concerned with "a culture of citizenship, democracy, participa-

Secondly, he explores the pacifist and active non-violence groups' observations of violence that is generated because of the unequal development of the society. There are different faces of violence such as that of class, ethnic, gender and religious conflicts. They are concerned about their rights and engage in competition. "Human potential for sensitivity towards others, tenderness towards life and wholehearted co-operation are set aside to make way for the baser sentiments of exclusion and class or personal advantage." He also notes that "the development of peace and active nonviolence movements who propose models of society that seek justice through social democracy" are developed to combat the aforementioned problems.[349]

The above two schools are concerned mainly with the injustice to human beings undermining the damage done to creation at large. Therefore, he delineates the third one based on the ecological movements that criticize and fight against the ravaging of the environment. In his opinion, the awareness of the ecological crises gave birth to the responsibilities of human beings "for the survival of the planet and of animal and plant life." Furthermore, it underscores human responsibility "for the misery and poverty in the world and for promoting relationships that allow life and well-being for all human beings and all of nature."[350]

In short, the utilitarian, or anthropocentric ethic, of the present systems undermines the rights of other 'beings in creation'. For this reason, he calls our attention to the ecological and cosmic rights along with human and social rights. In this sense he argues for a new ethical order, which is ecocentric and its main concern should be to seek "the equilibrium of the earthly community."[351] For a genuine ecology, he underscores the need to go beyond the anthropocentric viewpoint of the West. He calls for "the integrity of creation" and in particular to safeguard all forms of life, including the most threatened."[352] His concern for the good of all in the society and the preservation of nature is expressed in his commitment for social ecology.

tion, solidarity and liberation." *Ibid.*

349. *Ibid.*, 236-237.

350. *Ibid.*, 237.

351. Boff, *Ecology and Liberation*, 29-30. In this context he calls our attention to other cultural traditions such as Buddhism and Hinduism in the East, Francis of Assisi, Schopenhauer, Albert Schweitzer and Chico Mendes in the West, which developed an ethics of universal compassion. Their interest was to seek harmony, respect and concern among all creatures than promoting the advantage of the human race. *Ibid.*

352. *Ibid.*, 85.

3.2.2.2. Social Ecology

Boff's concern for ecology[353] made him to emphasize the need for social ecology.[354] "Social ecology seeks to study the relationships that a society establishes between its members and its institutions and between these and nature."[355] He relates social injustice to ecological injustice because the human race is part of the environment. Therefore, he argues that "social injustice goes hand-in-hand with ecological injustice." Hence option for the poor should "include an option for the most threatened of other beings and species."[356]

Boff suggests an ethic, which is both social and environmental. He proposes to overcome two types of injustices: social-economic-political injustice, which affects the human person directly and environmental injustice that affects human beings indirectly, but nonetheless directly affects the entire planet. Furthermore, he suggests to overcome naturalism and anthropocentrism that disrupts the ecological equilibrium.[357] He also

353. His concerns are not limited to some general norms, such as the conservation of species that are threatened by extinction, the preservation of natural parks or regions so as to promote ecological tourism, political environmentalism. Above all, he is concerned about social justice that is, he is concerned about the human being and nature. Boff, "Social Ecology: Poverty and Misery," 238.

354. Social ecology deals with the concerns of ecology and poverty. These concerns emerged in the UN conferences on the environment held at Stockholm (1972) and at the Rio Earth Summit (1992). In these conferences, while the representatives from the Northern Hemisphere took an environmentalist stand giving insufficient consideration to human beings, the representatives from the Southern Hemisphere from a political and social point of view focused on the human being in interaction with the environment. It was an effort to combine social and environmental injustices. Leonardo Boff with Virgil Elizondo notes: "A minimum of environmental justice is essential for a minimal social justice as well as for the preservation of the *dignitas terrae*." Furthermore: "Today, nature's most threatened creatures are not the whales or the giant pandas of China, but the poor of the world, condemned to die of hunger and disease before their time." Leonardo Boff and Virgil Elizondo, "Ecology and Poverty: Cry of the Earth, Cry of the Poor" (Editorial), *Concilium* (1995), n. 5, ix-xii, x-xi. See also Boff, "Social Ecology: Poverty and Misery," 239.

355. Boff, "Social Ecology: Poverty and Misery," 237. Social ecology is "the study [of] social systems in interaction with ecosystems," acknowledging the way human well-being and nature's well-being are mutually dependent. Boff, *Ecology and Liberation*, 26. Further he notes: "Social ecology studies human historico-social systems in interaction with environmental systems. Human history is inseparable from that of our environment, and from the type of relationships that we have interwoven with it, in a dynamic interplay of mutual involvement." *Ibid.*, 88.

356. Boff, *Ecology and Liberation*, 88. Here, he calls attention to the Kaiapo, the Yanomani and other tribes and animals, who are threatened with extinction.

357. Boff, "Social Ecology: Poverty and Misery," 243. "Naturalism understands nature as a hypostatic subject, with sacred and unchangeable laws to which human beings

criticizes current theologies, including liberation theology, for not addressing the social contexts as conventional ecology did. Therefore, he suggests that ecological perspectives should be complemented with a coherent and holistic vision.[358]

In order to solve the problems of ecology he advocates an 'ecologico-social democracy'. Such a democracy "accepts not only human beings as its components but every part of nature, especially living species."[359] In other words: "[d]emocracy must become socio-cosmic: that is, the elements of nature such as mountains, plants, rivers, animals and atmosphere must be the new citizens who share in the human banquet, while humans share in the cosmic banquet. Only then will there be ecological justice and peace on planet Earth."[360] For this, he suggests "to develop an attitude of respect, of veneration, of compassion, of brotherhood and sisterhood, and of tenderness and fellowship with the whole of creation."[361]

3.2.2.3. Mental Ecology: An Integral Approach

From a social ecology, he goes further to develop a mental ecology in order to overcome the dominant nature of humankind. In his opinion, mental ecology provides human beings with positive psychic energy to overcome the consumerist dominant nature in them.[362] For this he suggests the need for spirituality and mysticism.[363] It is grounded on the

must submit. Anthropocentrism, by contrast, treats human beings as the sovereigns of creation."

358. *Ibid.*, 245.

359. Boff, *Ecology and Liberation*, 89. From the ethical and political standpoint, he draws our attention to the need to find the *best* possible form of government. For him, the democratic form of governing is the best form of organizing a society. He lists different forms of democracy such as: direct democracy, representative democracy, participatory or social democracy and democracy as a universal value. Apart from these, he notes the emergence of a democratic way of living. It is "either as a universal value or as a more integrative way of organizing society. This new form is ecological-social democracy." For him, we "need to ask for a democracy that is not only participatory and social, but ecological." *Ibid.*, 82-84.

360. Boff, "Liberation Theology and Ecology," 74.

361. Boff, *Ecology and Liberation*, 90.

362. *Ibid.*, 32-36. This has to be understood in light of Francis who made a synthesis "between internal and external ecology," leading to a "form of cosmic mysticism." Francis expressed the outward, or external, ecology through the tender and loving concern which is extended to all others than himself. He placed *eros* and *pathos* over the *logos* (the structure of understanding reality). In this sense, he placed the heart at the center of knowing. For him, "knowledge of the heart was not estranged from reality but instead reinforced communion and friendship with actuality." He also developed an inward ecology (mental ecology) through his writings, prayers, and songs. *Ibid.*, 52-53.

363. *Ibid.*, 36. By mysticism he means, "a fundamental and all-inclusive experience."

mystical dimension of everything. In this sense, it is part of nature that something is known and at the same time it is able to remain mysterious.[364] He also underscores the importance of the dimensions of ethics, mind and spirit for new eco-systemics. The particularity of this ethical order is its ecocentric nature rather than anthropocentrism. Thus "[m]ental ecology tries to reconstruct the intimate thrust of humankind toward the correct valuation of, and appropriate entry into, the cosmos. The human mind and heart have a special place for those promptings of the spirit that urge humankind to a mystical relation with the universe as a whole."[365] He exhorts us towards "a new theological worldview that sees this planet as a great sacrament of God, the temple of the Spirit, the place of creative responsibility for human beings, a dwelling place for all beings created in love."[366]

It is a spirituality that becomes mysticism in its mature stage.[367] Mystery is the depth dimension found in every person, creature and reality as a whole.[368] The experience of mystery is to be found at the root of all

It is connected to spirituality. Spirituality, which comes from spirit. Spirit is not only in all living beings, such as human beings, animals and plants, but also in the whole earth and the universe. They "are experienced as bearers of spirit, because they are sources of life and furnish all the elements that are needed for life, yet also sustain the thrust of creation." *Ibid.* "Spirituality does not start from power, or from the accumulative instinct, or from instrumental reason. It relies on the movements of sacramental and symbolic reason, on the gratuitousness of the world, on relationships, on deep stirrings within, on the sense of communion that all things possess, and on a vision of the vast cosmic organism, shot through and permeated with signs of and allusions to a higher and a fuller reality." *Ibid.*, 37.

364. *Ibid.*, 144. At the same time he suggests the absence of any specific confession for such spirituality. He notes that "[t]his is not so much a matter of adhering to a religious faith as of professing a cosmic spirituality, like Albert Einstein." *Ibid.*, 42-43. "Albert Einstein ... believed that the cosmic religious feeling was the strongest and highest motive of scientific research." *Ibid.*, 51. It is also worth noting that "eminent scientists such as Niels Bohr, Werner Heisenberg, Max Planck, David Bohm, and Albert Einstein, among others, testify to the experience of mystery. *Ibid.*, 144-145.

365. *Ibid.*, 137-138.

366. Boff, "Social Ecology: Poverty and Misery," 245.

367. Boff, *Ecology and Liberation*, 138. According to Boff, the term mysticism is related to mystery and has many meanings. In everyday usage it is used as "an idea beyond reason and to suggest intentions or a reality concealed from ordinary mortals. Mystery can also mean the atmosphere of interest, curiosity, and fascination surrounding a certain person." Originally, in the cultic religions, it was used to mean the religious experience that was gained through initiation rites. In philosophical speculation, it became separated from experience and came to be used to mean the rational aspect of a doctrine or revelation. In this sense one speaks of the Christian mystery of the Trinity, of the incarnation, of grace, and so forth. *Ibid.*, 142-143.

368. *Ibid.*, 143. "Every individual is a mystery. We may come to know him or her

religions. It is not a mere matter of ecstasy, rather it is an experience of wonder at the sacred aspect of reality and life. He even says that all are mystics in a certain sense. For example, "when we become conscious of a deeper level of the self, when we try to study the other side of things, when we become aware of the inward richness of the other, and when we confront the grandeur complexity, and harmony of the universe," then we become mystics.[369] Hence, "[r]eligious life is a specific way of being in the world: it is a matter of seeing everything and living everything as shot through with God's presence."[370] It is a life in the Spirit and means that the Spirit "is not opposed to body, but includes it. The body is always vitalized, that is, spiritualized. Spirit is, however, opposed to death. The main contrast is not between spirit and matter, or between soul and body, but between life and death." From this we see that for Boff, spirituality "means living according to spirit, in accordance with the dynamism of life." It is something that affirms, protects and promotes life.[371] Its main concern is to "promote solidarity with all living beings."[372]

through long acquaintance, in the intimacy of love, by recourse to the sciences, or in the light of various human traditions. Yet, whatever concept or setting we choose, no one can really spell out in full the precise meaning ... Ultimately, to himself or herself, and to everyone else, an individual is a mystery, a secret. We know only what a person may freely reveal in the course of his or her life, what may be seen from without, and what may be gleaned from various forms of understanding that we have developed. Nevertheless, in spite of all this, the living, personal mystery of the individual always confronts us anew" (p. 144).

369. *Ibid.*, 147-148.

370. Boff, *The Path to Hope*, 16.

371. Boff, *Ecology and Liberation*, 165. It means, life seen in its integrity both in terms of its outward aspects such as relations with others, with society and with nature as well as inward aspects such as dialogue with the inner self. "This dialogue is conducted by means of contemplation, reflection, and inwardness; in short through the power of subjectivity." *Ibid.* For more details on the outward and inward aspects experiencing the Spirit, see: *ibid.*, 166-172.

372. *Ibid.*, 37. For this, he suggests to use science and technology as ways of helping us to guarantee, preserve, and even reconstruct ecological equilibrium. This is pertinent in the context of some thinkers who have strayed from the path of equilibrium. For example, Descartes, epistemologically (i.e., "Discourse on Method") maintains that the human vocation consists in being "masters and proprietors of nature." Bacon also expresses the meaning of knowledge in these dubious terms: "Knowledge is power." Power or nature, according to Bacon, is a prime necessity: "Now we govern nature in opinions, but we are thrall to her in necessity; but if we would be led by her invention, we should command her by action" (*In Praise of Human Knowledge*)." In contrast Boff suggests to "go back to those old masters ... who inaugurated a new kind of tenderness in the face of nature, following the examples of Francis of Assisi, Teilhard de Chardin and the entire great Augustinian, Bonaventurian, Pascalian, and existentialist tradition. None of these masters believed that knowledge was a form of appropriation and of domination of things, but rather

The experience of mystery is the experience of God. Faith comes afterwards. Moreover, for Boff, faith is not an "adhesion to a teaching that gives access to revelation and the supernatural." When this happens, faith is a mere ideology, which leads to fundamentalism. Religion becomes meaningful and becomes a truth "only when it represents a response to an experience of God made personally and communally." Therefore faith is "an expression of an encounter with God which embraces all existence and feeling – the heart, the intellect and the will. The occasion and times of such encounters become sacraments, points of reference to a form of experience that is overwhelmingly, irrefutably significant." Accordingly, a truly religious person "possesses a mystical form of knowledge. This is an experiential knowledge imbued with the evidence of encounters with God."[373]

In the Old Testament, Israel experienced God in the struggle of the oppressed in Egypt and in Babylon. In this sense Boff notes that Judaic and Christian understanding of mystery and God is identified with the history of the people, in particular with the "history of the oppressed." Thus the "God of history is presented as an ethical God." From this perspective Boff argues that "the mysticism of the Bible is a mysticism of open eyes and of active hands. The follower and servant of God is the one committed to justice; the one who stands up for the weak; and the one brave enough to denounce a purely celebratory religion without the mediation of neighbourly love."[374] Furthermore, in the New Testament, Jesus' mission was also a mission of liberation. Boff suggests that this "mystique of ethical commitment ... is accompanied by a mystique of contemplation." Thus, human beings are representatives of God, and therefore, "divine agents in their being and in their action." They "observe the signs of God's hand in everything: in all created things and in the spiritual and physical reality of humankind."[375]

In Christianity, as we have seen, this encounter took place through Jesus' incarnation. Jesus was not incarnated in a royal family, or in the

a form of love and of communion with things." *Ibid.*, 38.

373. *Ibid.*, 148. "Theology emerges from this kind of experience. It represents an attempt to translate a fundamental experience into terms proper to reason (doctrine), practice (ethics), and celebration (liturgy). The very names given to God originate in a primordial experience. Yahweh, for example, means the accompanying God, present in the life of the people; Elohim means the God who illuminates the way and shines forth into existence." "The present crisis in the church and in the historical religions consists in the painful absence of a profound experience of God. Church offices are occupied by ... religious power. They are not interested so much in the truth of God as in the security of their religious system." *Ibid.*, 148-149.

374. *Ibid.*, 149-150.

375. *Ibid.*, 150.

priestly family, but rather his divinity was revealed through the image of oppression and suffering. This suffering is followed by his resurrection as "a sign of reaffirmation of the primacy of justice and of life." Christian mysticism, following the path of Jesus "implies a commitment to solidarity with the poor, for Jesus wishes to be one of them." Therefore, it "implies a commitment to personal and social change, and to the ... kingdom of God."[376]

Based on the contemplative and mystical aspect of Christian scriptures Boff affirms that both the incarnate Son and the Spirit are concerned with the mystery of creation, which are in the process of ascension toward the reign of Trinity. Furthermore, he argues that "[t]he assurance of the general resurrection ... enabled the early Christians to speak of the cosmic Christ and of the Spirit's dwelling in the energy of the universe and of life."[377] He considers Christian mystique as the mysticism of the spirit, which is cosmic and open to the future. In this sense the Christian mystique "seeks unity in all differences, searching for it as the divine thread that runs through the entire universe and all consciousness and human action, until it unites ahead and above in the prospect of supreme synthesis with God, the omega-point of evolution and creation."[378]

Boff also highlights mysticism, or its cognate *mystique*, that appears in the social and political scene. Its basis is already seen in Judeo-Christian mysticism, which has a "politico-liberational-contemplative character."[379] Likewise, he considers the radical commitment of certain movements as a process of mysticism. It helps them "to disclose the various dimensions of the mystery of life and the various levels of human commitment. ... In this context spirituality and God become truly mean-

376. *Ibid.*, 150-151.

377. *Ibid.*, 151-152. This omnipresence of Christ and the Spirit, which we have already seen, is an important motif of St. Francis of Assisi. He "saw all created things and beings, from the sun and the moon to birds and snails, as sacraments of God and as brothers and sisters." Teilhard de Chardin has introduced this "in the context of modern cosmology and tried to identify the emergence of consciousness and the unequivocal sign of God's presence in the movement of matter toward ever greater complexity. Cosmogenesis, which in its turn gives way to theogenesis, ends in a state of ultimate fulfilment, the culmination of entire process, when all things are gathered up in God." *Ibid.*, 152.

378. "This mysticism of union and unity is clearly indebted to the powerful current which descends from Greek Fathers (Gregory of Nyssa and Gregory of Nazianzus) passes down through the Platonic and Augustinian tradition, pauses at St. Bonaventure with his wonderful *Itinerarium Mentis ad Deum* (*Journey of the Soul to God*), and carries on only to culminate in St. John of the Cross (*Ascent to Mount Carmel*) and St. Teresa of Avila (*The Interior Castle*). It then flows out into Teilhard de Chardin's ardently mystical texts *The Divine Milieu* and *Silence and Christ*." *Ibid.*, 152-153.

379. *Ibid.*, 154.

ingful in everyday events, in major decisions, in achievements, and in setbacks."[380] "Spirituality and mysticism form part of life in its wholeness and in its sacredness. They support the thrust of resistance and the persistent longing for liberation."[381] Here mysticism "is a combination of deep convictions, noble visions, and strong passions, which stir and spur people and movements to show their will to struggle, or which inspire procedures capable of controlling this or that problem and of sustaining hope in the face of historical setbacks." It is a form of mysticism because it refuses to accept the *status quo* and aims to construct a better future. Mysticism "is the secret motor of all commitment, the enthusiasm which continually powers the militant. It is the interior fire arousing the individual in spite of the monotony of everyday tasks."[382] Boff underscores the need to integrate personal characteristics such as "subjectivity, gratuitousness, celebration, good humor, and play" along with politics.[383]

4. Conclusion

Our discussion on the sacramentality of creation and the human response to it, from the perspective of Leonardo Boff, has helped us to see a different horizon. Boff, as an heir of Latin theology, makes his evaluation of the theme from the perspective of the Latin West. Within the Western tradition, he belongs to the Franciscan tradition of doing theology. Therefore, one can legitimately say that in Boff we observe the Franciscan strand of Western theology in dialogue with unjust systems in Latin America. This context has shaped his theological horizons. His basic concern is the impact of an unjust system not only on human beings but also on Creation at large.

380. *Ibid.*, 140-141.

381. *Ibid.*, 142.

382. *Ibid.*, 155. This mysticism, in his opinion, will help one to accept defeat with honor rather than with victory with shame. Leonardo Boff, *Ecology and Liberation: A New Paradigm*, 156. "Human beings prefer to go without bread rather than surrender their freedom. Bread eaten in conditions where oppression is tolerated is bitter and dishonorable." *Ibid.*, 157.

383. *Ibid.*, 158. Boff considers celebration as fundamental and essential. In his opinion, "Without celebration, which is accompanied by festivity, music, and aesthetic beauty, and by purification of body and mind (a feast is only festive when it is ready and waiting), mystery runs the risk of becoming a formula, and mysticism and the mystique mere transient psychological uplift." In celebration "we live out symbolically something that history actually denies us. Consequently, celebration has an irrefutably anticipatory nature. When celebrating we already sing of the victorious revolution, we already rejoice ritually at the achievement of liberation, and we already feel that we are sitting down to a banquet with God as guests or as sons and daughters in our Father's house." *Ibid.*, 160.

Boff's sacramentology and worldview already indicate a different style in the development of these themes. Boff attempts to go deeper into the traditional understandings of both. In the case of sacramentology, his main contribution seems to be mainly on sacramental thinking, which helps one to see the presence of the Transcendent in the immanent world through transparency. Moreover, transparent presence of God manifested in history and in the experience of the people is essential to understanding his theology as a whole. We also demonstrated how the idea of a transparent God is manifested in Creation, Christ and in the Church as sacraments. With respect to his worldview, Boff clearly explained the transition from a theocentric worldview to an anthropocentric one and finally to the new cosmology, where cosmos is at the center. Although he criticizes theocentrism and anthropocentrism of the earlier worldviews, his cosmos centered worldview of the new cosmology did not negate either. Both the transparent presence of God, in his sacramental understanding, and cosmos centered new cosmology further enables us to deepen the sacramental presence of God in the world and the place of human beings in it.

Finally, in the third part, we saw the transparent presence of God in the world from the perspective of theology, science, culture etc., without ignoring God's presence from a Trinitarian perspective. Moreover, we illuminated the role of the human being as an ethical and sacramental being with respect to the whole of Creation. For Boff, a mystical approach to Creation with one's deep ethical responsibility to it is of paramount importance. The mystical approach here is not detachment from the world, but it is the result of a deep commitment to the world. In this sense, he emphasizes social ecology, which insists upon an ethical responsibility to everything in Creation. Furthermore, he highlights the necessity of a mental ecology, with its emphasis on an integral approach. This integral approach clearly affirms the sacramentality of the world and the sacramentality of the human being.

Chapter Three

WORLD AS SACRAMENT IN ALEXANDER SCHMEMANN
A LITURGICAL RESPONSE TO
THE SACRAMENTALITY OF CREATION

Alexander Schmemann,[1] liturgical theologian par excellence, was one

1. Alexander Schmemann was born in 1921 in Reval, Estonia, into a Russian emigrant family. When he was seven, the family moved to Paris, where he received his schooling in the Russian schools. Having completed his high school studies, he enrolled at St. Sergius Theological Seminary [St. Sergius Theological Seminary was established in 1925 with a view to the theological formation of Russian Orthodox Church members in the Diaspora]. Schmemann completed his degree in 1945, and in the same year he became an instructor of Church History in St. Sergius. Schmemann was ordained to the priesthood in 1946. He defended his doctoral dissertation in 1959 at St. Sergius, Paris. After emigrating to the United States in 1951, he joined the staff at St. Vladimir's Theological Seminary in New York. Later, in 1962, he assumed the post of dean of theology, which he held until his death on Dec.13, 1983. Schmemann held positions such as a member of the study and planning committee of the standing conference of the Orthodox Bishops in America (SCOBA), of the Metropolitan Council of the Orthodox Church in America (OCA) and the American Theological Society (ATS). He also broadcasted nearly 3000 talks to Soviet Russia over Radio Liberty, which are published in three volumes under the title *Celebration of Faith* (Crestwood, NY: St. Vladimir's Seminary Press, 1991-1995). For a short sketch of Schmemann's life and theology among others see John Meyendorff, "A Life Worth Living," *SVTQ* 28/1 (1984) 3-10; Robert Slesinski, "The Theological Legacy of Alexander Schmemann," *Diakonia* 29 (1984-1985) 87-95; Peter Scorer, "Alexander Schmemann (1921-83)," *Sobornost* 6/2 (1984) 64-68; Bernard Dupuy, "Un témoin de l'Orthodoxie Contemporaine: le Père Alexandre Schmemann (1921-1983)," *Istina* 30 (1985) 117-130; Michael Plekon, "The Church, the Eucharist and the Kingdom: Towards an Assessment of Alexander Schmemann's Theological Legacy," *SVTQ* 40/3 (1996) 119-143; Thomas Fisch, "Introduction: Schmemann's Theological Contribution to the Liturgical Renewal of the Churches," *Liturgy and Tradition: Theological Reflections of Alexander Schmemann*, ed. Thomas Fisch (Crestwood, NY: St. Vladimir's Seminary Press, 1990) 1-10; Mathai Kadavil, "A Journey from East to West: Alexander Schmemann's Contribution to Orthodoxy in the West," *Exchange* 28 (1999) 224-246.

among the pioneers who made a significant contribution in asserting the sacramentality of the World in the present time.[2] His inquiry into the sacramental meaning of the world becomes strident in the face of a widening dichotomy between sacred and profane.[3] As he notes, on the one hand, there is a great concern for the world in the Church and on the other hand there is a great effort to rediscover the sacramental nature of Christian life with renewed insistence on the particular sacramental acts in the life of the individual.[4] He maintains that these were already present in the two world-views that were predominant in the early Church. On the one hand the New Testament speaks of God's great concern for the world, so much so that He gave His only-begotten Son in order to save the world. In this sense Schmemann considers the Eucharistic sacrifice as "an act of giving for the sake of the world; that the world is an object of divine love, divine creation, divine care; that is to be saved, transfigured and transformed." But on the other hand the New Testament speaks negatively of the world, in the sense that we must leave it for the kingdom of God. It is in this paradoxical situation that he tries to discover the resonance that traditionally justified both world-views. "Acceptance of the world is more than justifiable, it is necessary. There can be no Christianity where the world is not seen as an object of divine love. On the other hand, there is every justification for that detachment, that abandonment of the world so heavily stressed in the ascetical tradition."[5]

2. The paper he presented in 1964, entitled "The World as Sacrament" at the Catholic Art Society, Georgetown University, could be considered as a pioneer work in this line, at least from the liturgical theology perspective. Alexander Schmemann, "The World as Sacrament," *Church, World, Mission*, ed. Alexander Schmemann (Crestwood, NY: St. Vladimir's Seminary Press, 1979) 217-227, p. 217.

3. Schmemann even says that the fundamental opposition of 'spiritual versus material', 'sacred versus profane', 'supernatural versus natural' were for centuries the only accepted moulds and categories of religious thought and experience. He was mainly concerned to overcome this opposition. Alexander Schmemann, *Sacraments and Orthodoxy* (New York: Herder and Herder, 1965) 14. The same book is published also under the titles *The World as Sacrament* (London: Darton, Longman & Todd, 1966); *For the Life of the World* (Crestwood, NY: St. Vladimir's Seminary Press, 1976).

4. Schmemann, "The World as Sacrament," 218. As part of the great concern for the world he underscores the trends like liberation theology which shows interest for the liberation of society, and therapeutic theology which offers various sorts of assistance for individuals. The latter is some sort of escapism by which they show total indifference towards the world. See Alexander Schmemann, "Liturgy and Eschatology," *Sobornost* 7/1 (1985) 6-14, pp. 7-8.

5. Schmemann, "The World as Sacrament," 219-220. Here, Schmemann refers, on the one hand to the mystical and ascetical tradition of the Church, and on the other hand, he refers to the institutional Church that was in constant touch with the needs of the people. Chryssavgis traces its root to the early Christian tradition and notes: The root of the two

However, in the face of a dichotomy between the concern for the world and detachment from the world, Schmemann calls for a synthesis. His main theological concern made him sum up his life and theology in one simple phrase: "two 'nos' one 'yes' and eschatology." The two 'nos' are secularism and religion. The one 'yes' is the sacramental vision of the world redeemed and glorified by Christ, holding out for man already in this world an anticipation of the kingdom of God, to come at the end of time.[6] Schmemann with his eastern background and western education, as well as his work as a theologian and pastor, suggests an alternative to this dilemma that could be termed as 'the sacramental world-view'. He propounds to "see the world as sacrament, and ourselves and our whole created environment in sacramental terms."[7] He stunned both secularism and religion, both of which in his opinion distort the message of Jesus Christ. According to him, Jesus, by His incarnation and redemption, put an end to the division between the sacred and the profane and opened a new way.[8] Schmemann asserts that Christianity is that new way that helps us to look at the world from the sacramental perspective. This vision of 'the world as sacrament,' he claims, gives us a hermeneutical key to look at the world positively and to interpret its problems.[9]

The aim of this chapter is to expound Schmemann's proposed solution to extreme views on spirituality and materiality by looking at his interpretations of the world from a sacramental perspective. It is beyond our scope to critically assess the patristic and post-patristic tools Schmemann employed in developing his thesis. Our study begins by sketching out the theological context of Alexander Schmemann. It will be followed with his notions of sacramental symbolism and world-view. Finally, we see his theology of the sacramental vision of the world.

divergent world-views, spiritualistic and materialistic, needs to be understood in the early Christian background. The Greeks showed a cosmological interest and "sought truth in the harmony and beauty of the world – even if the material and historical were ultimately but an image of the spiritual and eternal." On the other hand, the early Christian community showed an eschatological orientation. Their main concern, was "the final revelation of God in history." Fathers made a creative synthesis of the cosmological interest of the Greeks and the eschatological concern of the Jews. John Chryssavgis, "The World as Sacrament: Insights into an Orthodox World-view," *Pacifica* 10 (1997) 1-24, p. 3.

6. Thomas Hopko, "Two 'Nos' and One 'Yes'," *SVTQ* 28/1 (1984) 45-48.

7. Schmemann, "The World as Sacrament," 220.

8. In this sense Schmemann even says that Jesus put an end to religion and opened a new way of life. Schmemann, *Sacraments and Orthodoxy*, 21.

9. John Chryssavgis says the same when he noted: "If there exists today a vision able to transcend and transform all national and denominational tensions, it may well be that of our world understood as sacrament." John Chryssavgis, "The World as Sacrament: Insights into an Orthodox World-view," 1.

1. Theological Horizons of Alexander Schmemann

Schmemann's theological heritage seems to be very important to understand his presuppositions in doing theology. What is important for us to consider is his Russian heritage, his diaspora context both in Paris and later in the United States, and his encounters with theologians of the liturgical and ecumenical movements.

1.1. Russian Heritage

The Russian Orthodox Church, to which Schmemann belonged, had to undergo tremendous changes at the beginning of the past century with the First World War and the communist revolution.[10] The Revolution of 1917 heralded an era of religious persecution, many people left Russia, marking the beginning of the Russian Diaspora in Europe. In the beginning, the Russian émigrés "dreamt of a return home."[11] Gradually, they began to accept their tragic fate as permanent immigrants. The anguish and confusion of the people in the Diaspora became the focus of theologizing among the Russian Orthodox theologians, already in the third and the fourth decades of the twentieth century. The Russian Orthodox Church in Paris received many of them. From different parts of Russia, they sought asylum at St. Sergius in Paris. According to Schmemann: "[t]he center of theological work shifted then from Russia to the Russian Diaspora. Some theologians of both traditions – 'academic' and the 'free' – were invited to teach at the Orthodox theological faculties of Belgrade, Sofia, Bucharest, and Warsaw. In 1925 a center of higher theological learning was established in Paris, which became the 'capital' of the Russian emigration."[12] During this period theological works were

10. Schmemann compares the situation of Orthodoxy at the end of the First World War with the crisis that followed the collapse of Byzantium in 1453. Schmemann, "Trying the Spirits," *SVSQ* 1(1957) 3-4, p. 3.

11. Meyendorff, "A Life Worth Living," 3. For a detailed discussion of Russian emigrates in Paris see: Aidan Nichols, *Theology in the Russian Diaspora: Church, Fathers, Eucharist in Nikolai Afanas'ev (1893-1966)* (Cambridge: Cambridge University Press, 1989).

12. Alexander Schmemann, "Russian Theology: 1920-1972: An Introductory Survey," *SVTQ* 16 (1972) 172-194, 175. The two traditions are the two religious revivalist traditions of the pre-Revolutionary Russia. The academic tradition stems from the four pre-Revolutionary academies, those of Moscow, St. Petersburg, Kiev, and Kazan. Their emphasis was on patristics, liturgics and Church history. The 'free' traditions stem from lay circles, who returned to Orthodoxy on the eve of the revolution. Their emphasis was on speculative dogmatics. See Lewis Shaw, "John Meyendorff and the Heritage of the Russian Theological Tradition," *New Perspectives on Historical Theology*, ed. Bradley Nassif (Grand Rapids, MI: Eerdmans, 1996) 10-42, p. 11.

made available in exile and a new generation of theologians was trained, capable of taking over the tradition of their teachers.[13] Schmemann benefited from the heritage of the modern trends in Russian Orthodox theology.[14]

The renewal movement was fostered in Paris, in interaction with the renewal movements in the West. Gradually St. Sergius, the Orthodox Theological Seminary in Paris, became the center of theological work for the Russian Diaspora.[15] The theological arena of St. Sergius was very decisive in shaping Schmemann as an Orthodox theologian. Furthermore, it is important to note that following the revivalist movement, there were

13. St. Sergius eventually published twelve volumes of *Pravoslavnaya Mysl* (Orthodox thought). Another important theological and philosophical periodical, *Put* (The Way), was edited in Paris by N. A. Berdyaev & B. P. Vysheslavetzeff (sixty-one issues, 1925-40). Since 1953, St. Vladimir's faculty has published from New York its own *SVSQ/SVTQ* (in English). See Schmemann, "Russian Theology: 1920-1972: An Introductory Survey," 175-176.

14. The modern trend began with the religious revivalism of the nineteenth century. In the post-Byzantine period, due to the absence of higher theological schools, Orthodox students sought their theological training in the West. Theologians educated in Roman Catholic and Protestant universities, consciously or unconsciously adopted theological categories, terminology and forms of argument foreign to their own Church tradition. [Georges Florovsky termed this transition 'pseudomorphosis'. Georges Florovsky, *The Ways of Russian Theology (Part I)*, gen. ed. Richard S. Haugh (Belmont, MA: Nordland Publishing Co., 1979) 85.] The radical change they brought to their own ethos and theological tradition resulted in the foundation of theological schools that were alien to the traditional forms of Orthodox piety and spirituality. The entire history of modern Orthodox theology was a long attempt to overcome this "alienation," to recover its independence from western patterns and to return to its own initial sources. Russian Orthodox theology started a process of renewal from the second half of the nineteenth century. Schmemann, "Russian Theology: 1920-1972: An Introductory Survey," 173. In reaction to the westernizing trend in Russia emerged 'slavophilism', which attempted a reconciliation between Hegelian Philosophy and Orthodox Christianity. Later, a second trend evolved known as 'sophiological school', which attempted to solve the problems of the relation between God and the world by the concept of "divine wisdom" or "Sophia." It seems that the discussions centered around the sophiological school had a great impact on Schmemann, especially in his effort to look at the world from a sacramental perspective, which we shall later see.

15. With the Revolution (1917), many leading theologians of the pre-Revolutionary "renaissance" period went into exile. And they continued their revival mission in the Diaspora. Many of them began their career at the Orthodox theological faculties of Belgrade, Sofia, Bucharest, and Warsaw. In 1925, with the beginning of St. Sergius, a higher theological learning in Paris, it became the 'capital' of the Russian emigration." Schmemann, "Russian Theology: 1920-1972: An Introductory Survey," 175. Paul Meyendorff notes, St. Sergius Theological Institute gathered some of the greatest Orthodox minds of the 20th century, including Sergius Bulgakov, Anton V. Kartashev, Vasihi V. Zenkovski, Cyprian Kern, Nicholas Afanassieff, and Georges Florovsky. See Paul Meyendorff, "The Liturgical Path of Orthodoxy in America," *SVTQ* 40 (1996) 43-64, p.49.

two theological schools prevalent among the Russian Orthodox theologians. First, the 'sophiological speculations' of Sergius Bulgakov, the then dean of St. Sergius, and secondly, the "historical theology" of Georges Florovsky.[16] At St. Sergius there was not a unified school of thought, nor a commonly accepted program. About this Schmemann writes: "Schematically, we should distinguish two main streams or trends, two different types of theological approach."[17] Though never attracted by the sophiological speculations of Bulgakov, Schmemann had great respect for him.[18] Apart from Bulgakov and Florovsky, other brilliant professors were A. V. Kartashev, Cyprian Kern, and Nicholas Afanassieff. Each of these had a great influence on him. Later, the 'Eucharistic Ecclesiology' of Afanassieff became the central guiding force of his speculative vision and pastoral activity.[19] His experience of the diaspora and theologians laid the foundations for Schmemann's liturgical theology which undergirded his theological methodology. Meyendorff even says that Schmemann's theological world-view was shaped during his Paris years.[20]

1.2. The Encounter with the West

The second phase of his diaspora experience was rooted in American soil. Along with Florovsky, Meyendorff and others Schmemann continued his pursuit, which he began in Paris, at St. Vladimir's Seminary in America.[21] Although the beginning of Orthodoxy in America goes back to the Alaskan mission of the Russian Orthodox Church, their missionary endeavor among the natives of Alaska and the Aleutian Islands did not directly affect the growth and development of Orthodoxy in the United

16. Bulgakov and Florovsky represent the 'free' and 'academic' traditions respectively of pre-Revolutionary Russia in Paris. See Shaw, "John Meyendorff and the Heritage of the Russian Theological Tradition," 11. For a brief discussion on Bulgakov and Florovsky see: Alexander Schmemann, *Ultimate Questions: An Anthology of Modern Russian Religious Thought* (Crestwood, NY: St. Vladimir's Seminary Press, 1977) 135-136 and 297-298.

17. See Alexander Schmemann, "Roll of Honour," *SVTQ* 10/1-2 (1966) 7-8. According to Robert L. Nichols, "It would be more correct to speak of two emphasis within Russia's recent theological past which continued to grow and flourish even in emigration after 1917 rather than speak of two groups," Robert L. Nichols, "Translator's Note" *The Ways of Russian Theology (Part I)*, xi-xv, xv.

18. Slesinski, "The Theological Legacy of Alexander Schmemann," 88; Meyendorff, "A Life Worth Living," 4.

19. See Slesinski, "The Theological Legacy of Alexander Schmemann," 88; Meyendorff, "A Life Worth Living," 4-5. Scorer, "Alexander Schmemann (1921-83)," 65.

20. Meyendorff, "A Life Worth Living," 5-6.

21. For details of the works of St. Vladimir's in the first twenty-five years see: Alexander Schmemann, "Thoughts for the Jubilee," *SVTQ* 13/1-2 (1969) 95-102.

States.[22] The second stage of Orthodoxy in America begins with the emigrations.[23] The real growth, however, of the diocese in the United States began with the mass return of Catholic Uniates to Orthodoxy as well as the increase of Greek, Syrian, and Slavic immigration.[24]

Orthodoxy faced a totally new situation in America that was alien to Orthodox culture. In Grigorieff's opinion, the Orthodox Church was not ready to meet the challenges of the West, especially in the cultural context of the New World. He gives two reasons: First, the national character of the Church in Russia and its close connection with the state. Second, the rigidly conservative makeup of the Russian clergy, which made it difficult for them to integrate themselves into a foreign milieu.[25] The migration of Easterners to American soil also raised serious pastoral problems. It was even more complex with the presence of the Alaskan missions and the multi-jurisdiction of the diaspora. Because they were now living in a constantly changing world, assimilation and integration of Orthodoxy to the contemporary needs was one of the primary diasporic concerns. It was into this milieu that Schmemann arrived. He became

22. The Aleutian Island and Alaska were discovered by the captains of the Russian Imperial Navy, Behring and Chirkov, in 1741. Later, at the request of Gregory Shelehov and Ivan Golikov, the partners of a Russo-American company, petitioned Empress Catherine II and the Holy Synod to send missionaries. A mission of eight monks, under the leadership of Archimandrite Joasaph Bolotov, reached Kodiac Island in Alaska on September 24, 1794. It was the beginning of the Russian Orthodox Church in America. In 1867 the Russian government sold Alaska to the United States, with the clause that the United States Government would respect the property and rights of the Russian Orthodox Church. See Dimitry Grigorieff, "The Historical Background of Orthodoxy in America" *SVSQ* 5/1-2 (1961) 3-54, p. 6.

23. Orthodox parishes were begun for the emigrants in the United States; the first three came into being almost simultaneously and absolutely independent of each other in the late sixties of the nineteenth century. These churches were established for the spiritual needs of various Orthodox nationals who came to the New World. See Grigorieff, "The Historical Background of Orthodoxy in America," 7.

24. Toward the end of the nineteenth century, many Carpatho-Russians and Galicans from Russia Rubra in the Austro-Hungarian Empire emigrated to America. Among them, a large number settled in Minneapolis, Minnesota, organized a parish and engaged a priest (Fr. Toth) from their native country. Even though they belonged to the Catholic Church (Uniates), the Roman Catholic Archbishop, John Ireland of St. Paul, did not grant them permission, and refused to recognize Father Toth as a valid priest on account of his marriage. Because of this refusal, they joined the Eastern Orthodox Church. According to Grigorieff, in 1891 Father Toth and his parishioners, numbering 361 members, were reunited to the Russian Orthodox Church. This event laid the foundation for the mass return of the Uniates in America to Orthodoxy. In the following decades, over 225,000 Carpatho-Russian and Galican Uniates became Orthodox. See Grigorieff, "The Historical Background of Orthodoxy in America," 9.

25. Grigorieff, "The Historical Background of Orthodoxy in America," 7-8.

instrumental, along with others, in transmitting the Russian émigré heritage to new generations,[26] and was a pioneer who also alarmed many Orthodox believers about the tasks facing them in their changing context. Schmemann's three consecutive articles on the problems of Orthodoxy in America[27] are classical examples of his involvement in the pastoral situation of the Orthodox Church there. Within the context of the cultural transition of Orthodoxy, he tried to keep the Orthodox principles intact, while at the same time, he interpreted them for the present existential context.

Schmemann distinguished the spread of Orthodoxy into different cultures since the Byzantine era, and its spread in the American context as very different.[28] According to Schmemann "'America' is a *culture*, i.e., a complex of habits, customs, thought forms, etc., many of which are either new or alien to Orthodoxy, to its history and tradition and it is impossible simply to 'transpose' Orthodoxy into the American cultural categories."[29] The alien nature of the Orthodox tradition is not the result of "her 'orientalism' or a difference in ethnical background, but, because of her fundamental theological and spiritual presuppositions, of her whole 'world view'."[30] In his opinion the American culture is marked with religious pluralism. The religious "neutrality" of American culture prevents a total "integration" of religious culture. He observes a deep dichotomy between the religious and secularist viewpoints. On the one hand, America sincerely proclaims the need for religion. On the other hand, it does not alter the fundamental dichotomy between religion and daily life.[31] His awareness of the dichotomy between religious and secular world-views, and his effort to remedy this problem, allows us to delineate his theology of the sacramentality of the world.

26. Rowan Williams, "Eastern Orthodox Theology," *The Modern Theologians. An Introduction to Christian Theology in the Twentieth Century*, ed. David F. Ford (Oxford: Basil Blackwell, 1995) 152-170, p. 167.

27. Alexander Schmemann, "Problems of Orthodoxy in America: The Canonical Problem," *SVSQ* 8/2 (1964) 67-85; "Problems of Orthodoxy in America: The Liturgical Problem," *SVSQ* 8/4 (1964) 164-185; "Problems of Orthodoxy in America: The Spiritual Problem," *SVSQ* 9/4 (1965) 171-193.

28. Schmemann, "Problems of Orthodoxy in America: The Canonical Problem," 76-77.

29. Schmemann, "Problems of Orthodoxy in America: The Spiritual Problem," 192-193.

30. Schmemann, "Problems of Orthodoxy in America: The Liturgical Problem," 172.

31. Schmemann, "Problems of Orthodoxy in America: The Canonical Problem," 77-78.

1.3. Dialoguing with Liturgical and Ecumenical Movements

Schmemann's theological genius is expressed mainly in the context of liturgical theology. Two things are to be noted in this context: first, his relation to the liturgical movement; second, his concern for the renewal of the Orthodox liturgy.

Schmemann acknowledges his deep indebtedness to the liturgical movement,[32] and highlights two merits. First, the liturgical movement helped to break the division between the eastern and western churches. According to Schmemann, for several centuries the East and West lived in ecclesial and doctrinal separation from one another. During this period they developed, within each of their separated "worlds," a sense of self-sufficiency which led to a narrowing of spiritual vision and an impoverishment of theological perspective. Schmemann notes that the liturgical movement, even before the organized ecumenical movement began, was the first to break through the ignorance and indifference. Secondly the liturgical movement helped to renew the ecclesial and theological understandings of both churches. Schmemann acknowledges the contributions of people like Odo Casel and Lambert Beauduin, J. A. Jungmann and Louis Bouyer, Romano Guardini and H. A. Reinhold. They not only helped the West to understand its liturgical and spiritual heritage better, but also to understand better his own *lex orandi.*[33] Schmemann even suggests that the liturgical movement developed in the West as an "Orthodox trend in a non-Orthodox context." Moreover, he notes that the western

32. Schmemann, *Sacraments and Orthodoxy*, 7. Schmemann is, in Peter Scorer's words, "indebted to the entire spiritual and liturgical revival that was so widespread in the West at the time and to the leading exponents of the 'liturgical movement'." Scorer, "Alexander Schmemann (1921-83)," 66. Thomas Fisch observes: "[T]he value of Alexander Schmemann's contribution to the liturgical renewal of the Churches of East and West can be assessed only within the context of the history of the liturgical movement." Fisch even notes that "[s]ince at least the time of Beauduin, the western liturgical movement has tended to turn toward the East. Similarly, Orthodoxy in Russia has a long history of contact with the West. In Paris in the 1940s, Orthodox emigrates to the West encountered Catholic reforms looking Eastward, and so began a stimulating and fruitful dialogue which continues today." Fisch, "Introduction: Schmemann's Theological Contribution to the Liturgical Renewal of the Churches," 1. See also Slesinski, "The Theological Legacy of Alexander Schmemann," 88. The culmination of such an encounter is seen behind the Seventh International Liturgical Study Week held in Germany in 1960 which had taken as its theme "The Eucharistic Celebration in the East and West." Virgil C. Funk, "The Liturgical Movement (1830-1969)," *The New Dictionary of Sacramental Worship*, ed. Peter E. Fink (Collegeville, MN: Liturgical Press, 1990) 695-715, p. 710.

33. Schmemann, *Sacraments and Orthodoxy*, 8.

interest in liturgical tradition helped the Orthodox to overcome the 'Western' defects and the deviations of Orthodox theology.[34]

The ecclesial, theological and liturgical developments of the Orthodox churches were the main focus of Schmemann's writings. Metropolitan Philip considers him as "the father of Liturgical Theology in the Orthodox Church," and notes that his "emphasis on the eucharistic experience as a journey to the kingdom, created a spiritual renaissance in thousands of parishes throughout the Orthodox world."[35] Likewise, Paul Meyendorff observes that, "it is Schmemann who is credited, or blamed, for many of the liturgical changes that we in America have experienced in recent decades."[36] According to Peter Galadza, Schmemann's 'trialogue' with Dom Bernard Botte and Jardine Grisbrooke[37] marked the "most seminal and significant exchange of a virtual flood of articles and proposals" regarding the Eastern Christian Liturgical reform.[38]

Schmemann made a distinction between liturgical renewal in the West and in the East.[39] According to him, the liturgical revival in the West was first of all a return to the corporate idea of worship. From the Orthodox point of view, however, other dimensions of the liturgy must be rediscovered or brought back into its corporate experience of worship.[40]

Furthermore, Schmemann underscores a crisis in the liturgical life of the Orthodox Church, where there is an experience of alienation of the *lex orandi* from the *lex credendi*. He criticizes professional theologians who constitute a kind of *Lumpenproletariat*. In their hands theology

34. Alexander Schmemann, "Liturgical Theology: Its Task and Method," *SVSQ* 1 (1957) 16-27, p. 19.

35. Metropolitan Philip, "I have fought the good fight," *SVTQ* 28/1 (1984) 37-39, p. 38 (Homily delivered at the funeral service of Schmemann on December 15, 1983).

36. Meyendorff, "The Liturgical Path of Orthodoxy in America," 49.

37. Bernard Botte, "On Liturgical Theology," *SVSQ* 12 (1968) 170-173; Alexander Schmemann, "A Brief Response," *SVSQ* 12 (1968) 173-174; W. Jardine Grisbrooke, "Liturgical Theology and Liturgical Reform: Some Questions," *SVTQ* 13 (1969) 212-217; Alexander Schmemann, "Debate on Liturgy: Liturgical Theology, Theology of Liturgy, and Liturgical Reform," *SVTQ* 13 (1969) 217-224.

38. Peter Galadza, "Restoring the Icon: Reflections on the Reform of Byzantine Worship," *Worship* 65 (1991) 238-255, p. 238. In this article Galadza has given an extensive bibliography of the literature concerning liturgical renewal in the Byzantine Churches that followed the 'trialogue'.

39. Against the general presumption that "the Orthodox Church needs no liturgical renewal because it has preserved intact the great liturgical prayer of the early church," Schmemann notes: "we all need a liturgical revival, and the 'liturgical' Churches may be in need of it even more than the non-liturgical ones." Alexander Schmemann, "The Liturgical Revival and the Orthodox Church," *Liturgy and Tradition: Theological Reflections of Alexander Schmemann*, 101-114, p. 101.

40. Schmemann, "The Liturgical Revival and the Orthodox Church," 102.

ceased to be the conscience and the consciousness of the Church.[41] Elsewhere he characterizes Orthodox theology by two words: confusion and awakening. By confusion he means, lack of unity among Orthodox theologians concerning the unity of theological language, method, the nature of questions and the mode of their solution. He criticizes the way in which Orthodox theology is developed using a plurality of theological 'keys' within several mutually exclusive intellectual frameworks. At the same time he considers this confusion as a sign of awakening for a new search based on a genuinely Orthodox theological perspective.[42]

Schmemann is also concerned about the nominalism and minimalism in the liturgical life and practice of the Church, again a result of the alienation of the *lex orandi* from the *lex credendi*. He firmly believed that there is a growing discrepancy between the demands of tradition on the one hand, and the nominalism and minimalism of liturgical piety and practice on the other hand.[43] Another aspect of this crisis is the encroachment of secularism that alienates liturgy from the life of the faithful. According to him the liturgy, which was connected to all aspects of the Church's life, shaped its consciousness as well as the Christian "world view," has lost its influence on the faithful.[44] Instead, the pressures of secularism brought about a dichotomy between the sacred and the profane. In Schmemann's opinion: "[L]iturgical pietism fed by sentimental and pseudo-symbolical explanations of liturgical rites results, in fact, in a growing and all-pervading secularism. Having become in the mind of the faithful something 'sacred' *per se*, liturgy makes even more 'profane' the real life which begins beyond the sacred doors of the temple."[45] Schmemann was always engaged in a fight against the nominalis-

41. Alexander Schmemann, "Liturgy and Theology," *Liturgy and Tradition: Theological Reflections of Alexander Schmemann*, 49-68, p. 50. In order to keep theology relevant in the life of the Church he suggested three tasks (pastoral responsibility, missionary task and prophetic task) for Orthodox theology in America. See Alexander Schmemann, "The Task of Orthodox Theology in America Today," *SVSQ* 10/4 (1966) 180-188.

42. Alexander Schmemann, "Theology and Eucharist," *SVSQ* 5 (1961) 10-23, p. 10. A typical example of this confusion could be seen in the debate on 'the Western rite'. See Alexander Schmemann, "The Western Rite," *SVSQ* 2/4 (1958) 37-38; "Some Reflections Upon 'A Case Study'," *SVTQ* 24/4 (1980) 266-269.

43. In Schmemann's opinion, the liturgical traditions which are preserved in books are disappearing from practice. The selection of certain elements and rejection of other elements are based not on the principle of the lex orandi but on other considerations which are totally alien to it. Schmemann, "Liturgy and Theology," 51.

44. *Ibid.*

45. *Ibid.*, 52.

tic and secularist tendencies that endangered the life of Orthodoxy in the Western context.[46]

Schmemann has involved himself in the activities of the ecumenical movements and wrote innumerable articles on the different aspects of ecumenism.[47] Schmemann's ecumenical approach could be analysed from two angles. First, his ecumenical concern within the Orthodox Churches and secondly, with other Christian traditions. At this point, we must note his attitude towards ecumenical thinking. It was mainly a response to the initial confusion towards ecumenism of Orthodox theologians who were confused about the nature of leadership within the Orthodox traditions and the theological nature of their response.[48] Schmemann notes the two different approaches to the very phenomenon of the ecumenical movement and to the nature of Orthodox participation, from the development of Russian theology amongst the emigrants, in the 1920s. For some, the ecumenical movement is "an ontologically new phenomenon in Christian history requiring a deep rethinking and re-evaluation of Orthodox ecclesiology as shaped during the 'non-ecumenical' era." Sergius Bulgakov, Leo Zander, Nicholas Zernov, and Paul Evdokimov were the proponents of this group. The other group, "without denying the need for ecumenical dialogue and defending the necessity of Orthodox participation in the Ecumenical Movement, reject the very possibility of any ecclesiastical revision or adjustment and who view the Ecumenical Movement mainly as a possibility for an Orthodox witness to the

46. In Paul Meyendorff's opinion Schmemann's warning against secularism has become a reality today. He writes: "The Eucharist has lost its connection to the Orthodox liturgical corpus, of which it is supposed to be the climax – something akin to reducing a fifteen-course banquet to dessert alone. And, all too often, our people reduce Christianity only to attending Sunday liturgy, making little connection between this liturgical assembly and their daily life. This is precisely the triumph of that 'secularism', about which Fr Schmemann warned us some thirty years ago." Meyendorff, "The Liturgical Path," 54.

47. Alexander Schmemann, "Rome, the Ecumenical Council and the Orthodox Church (I): Possibilities and Impossibilities," *SVSQ* 3/2 (1959) 2-5; "The Orthodox Church, the World Council and Rome," *SVSQ* 3 (1958) 40; "Rome, the Ecumenical Council and the Orthodox Church (II): Possibilities and Impossibilities," *SVSQ* 3/3 (1959) 45-46; "The Unity of Orthodoxy," *SVSQ* 1/4 (1957) 2-3; "Episcopatus Unus Est: On the Standing Conference of Canonical Orthodox Bishops in the Americas," *SVSQ* 4/4 (1960) 26-29; "Father Alexander Schmemann Replies to the 'Sorrowful Epistle'," *Diakonia* 5 (1970) 89-94; "Theology or Ideology?," *Technology and Social Justice*, ed. Ronald H. Preston (London: SCM, 1971) 226-236; "The East and the West May Yet Meet," *Against the World for the World: the Hartford Appeal and the Future of American Religion*, ed. Peter L. Berger & Richard John (New York: Neuhaus Seabury Press, 1976) 229-231.

48. Schmemann, "Rome, the Ecumenical Council and the Orthodox Church (I): Possibilities and Impossibilities," 2.

West."[49] Along with Florovsky and others, Schmemann became a staunch supporter of this trend.

As already noted, one of his main concerns was the unity of various Orthodox churches, and he observes the problem of multijurisdiction of different national churches in America as early in 1900. There were many efforts to bring different churches into one fold.[50] Schmemann criticized the disunity in the sense that the empirical Orthodox Church is divided with respect to St. Ignatius of Antioch's definition of the Church as a "unity of faith and love." For Schmemann, unity is not the absence of divisions, disagreements and schisms; rather, it is the presence of unity as the very essence of the Church.[51] In this context his contributions to the establishment of the Federation of Orthodox Churches of America (1943) and his involvement and contribution to the Pan-Orthodox Conferences (1961) are expressions of his great concern. According to Schmemann, the first expression of the union of the Orthodox Church of different jurisdictions is seen with the formulation of the standing conference of Orthodox Bishops in America which started in 1960.[52]

Schmemann was also concerned with the Orthodox churches' relations with other churches. He criticized two prominent attitudes of the Orthodox Church towards its stance to the Catholic Church: first, those anti-Catholics who reject all that is Roman, and secondly, those who reduce all problems to the question of papacy. Differing from both, he suggests "an extensive, sober and consistent evaluation of Roman Catholicism taken as a whole, a study of its spiritual and theological ethos."[53] Leaving the polemical attitude of the past Schmemann came to a dialogical attitude that is characteristic of modern ecumenism. He strongly advocates that "from the emotional, historical, cultural and all the other roots of our 'anti-Romanism,' we must go back to the only real, the only valid one: *the doctrinal*... Unity, reunion, conversion – for the Orthodox all these terms can mean but one thing – agreement in faith, unity in dogma."[54] According to him there is a possibility of a new dialogue. He

49. Schmemann, "Russian Theology, 1920-1972," 190-191.

50. George Papaioannou gives a detailed study of different effort to bring the Orthodox Churches in America. See George Papaioannou, "Efforts toward Orthodox Unity in America: A Historical Appraisal," *Orthodox Theology and Diakonia*, ed. Demetrios J. Constantelos (Brookline, MA: Hellenic College Press, 1981) 273-304.

51. Schmemann, "The Unity of Orthodoxy," 2.

52. Schmemann, "Episcopatus Unus Est," 26.

53. Schmemann, "Rome, the Ecumenical Council and the Orthodox Church (I): Possibilities and Impossibilities," 2. In this context Schmemann's article entitled: "The Idea of Primacy in Orthodox Ecclesiology," *SVSQ* 4/2-3 (1960) 49-75 is of particular importance.

54. Schmemann, "Rome, the Ecumenical Council and the Orthodox Church (I): Pos-

noted such a trend already in the "re-sourcement" movement. In his opinion, return to the real sources: i.e., the Bible, the Fathers and the Liturgy, has deeply marked the theological life of both Orthodox Church and the Roman West and has given them a new spirit of dialogue.[55] His positive attitude towards ecumenism was well expressed in his response to the announcement of the Second Vatican Council. He wrote: "[A] reaction of Orthodox theology, even at this early stage, is not only possible but positively necessary. Whether an invitation or an offer is to come from or not, whether its general tenure is acceptable or not, a clarification of our own position regarding Roman Catholicism is overdue."[56] Moreover, he participated at the Second Vatican Council as an observer and representative of the Russian Orthodox Church. He also worked as the vice-chairman of the WCC youth department and was a member of the Faith and Order Commission.

In short, Schmemann's theological thinking was shaped by the ideas of Russian Orthodox revival, his life in the diaspora in Paris and America as well as his dialogue with the liturgical, patristic and ecumenical movements of the Catholic and Protestant churches. All the above factors contributed to make him a theologian who maintained a harmonious blend of both the East and the West. In particular, we would also like to underscore the fact that Schmemann continued the path of Russian religious revival leaders by dialoguing with various theological trends. To a certain extent this tradition gave a great impetus for a critical engagement with various cultures. However, his critical engagement with the western theologians on liturgy and sacraments helped him to articulate liturgy and sacraments in the contemporary situation. Finally, his encounter with the secular culture of the West contributed to his reflection on bridging the gap between the sacred and profane. Having seen his theological horizons, now we shall see how Schmemann opened up the notion of sacraments and the world towards the contemporary world.

2. Sacrament and World in Schmemann

Before entering into the discussions on the sacramentality of the world, it seems important to clarify the key notions: sacramental symbolism and

sibilities and Impossibilities," 3. (emphasis is from the original) He is critical of any effort to discard the doctrinal aspects. See Schmemann, review of *Eastern Christiandom – A Study of the Origin and Development of the Eastern Orthodox Church*, by Nicholas Zernov, *SVSQ* 7/2 (1963) 96-97.

55. Schmemann, "Rome, the Ecumenical Council," 4-5.

56. *Ibid.*, 2.

world-view in Schmemann. It is significant to note that he comes to his own interpretations by way of a critical analysis of both western and eastern perspectives.

2.1. Sacramental Symbolism

As we have already seen in the first chapter, Schmemann is one of the pioneers who made significant contributions to retrieve liturgy as a source for doing theology. Using the hermeneutics of liturgical theology, which sees liturgy as the *locus theologicus*, Schmemann argues that the sacramental celebrations themselves are liturgical celebrations and *vis à vis*.[57] This inter-relation of liturgy and sacraments is often seen in his writings.[58]

Schmemann underscores the importance of 'symbol' as a key term in contemporary sacramentology. He attempts to build a bridge between, on the one hand, the experience and worldview of the Fathers and, on the other hand, the "aspirations doubts and confusions of our age." He emphasizes the centrality of this approach, for both religious and secular thought, because of the complete disruption and breakdown in "communication" of a "unitive principle;" the *symbol*, however, brings together human existence and knowledge.[59] Although he emphasizes the importance of symbolism in sacraments, he cautions against the efforts of sacramentologists who undermine the uniqueness of Christianity in their study of symbolism. For example, he criticizes Eliade for his effort to bring together the symbolic worlds of the East and West. For him, "any religion without Christ (even Christianity and Orthodoxy) is a negative phenomenon, even frightening. Any contact with such a religion is dangerous. One can study it to better understand Christianity, or Christ. But by itself, it can not be salvation, however one understands this world."[60] Schmemann rather proposes the idea and experience of symbol based on the early Christian tradition.[61]

57. Schmemann, "Liturgy and Eschatology," 10; Idem, "Theology and Eucharist," 19.

58. Fagerberg underscores this in his study of Schmemann and points out that sacramentology must be rooted in liturgy as lex credendi is rooted in lex orandi. David W. Fagerberg, *What is Liturgical Theology? A Study in Methodology* (Collegeville, MN: Liturgical Press, 1992) 165.

59. Alexander Schmemann, "Sacrament and Symbol," *For the Life of the World* (Crestwood, NY: St. Vladimir's Seminary Press, ²1973) 135-151, pp. 146-147.

60. Alexander Schmemann, *The Journals of Father Alexander Schmemann 1973-1983*, trans. Juliana Schmemann (Crestwood, NY: St. Vladimir's Seminary Press, 2000) 30-31.

61. For Schmemann's view on 'sacramental symbolism' see Mathai Kadavil, "Sacramental-Liturgical Theology: A Critical Appraisal of Alexander Schmemann's Sacramen-

2.1.1. Eschatological Symbolism

Schmemann grounds the sacramental symbolism of the early Christian tradition on the eschatological teaching of Jesus.[62] This understanding, which he called 'eschatological symbolism,' shaped the fundamental *ordo* of Byzantine worship.[63] One of his major contributions lies in his study of the cultic mode of expressing the *Escathon*, i.e. the holy, the sacred, or otherness. He argued that the early Church used the forms and language of the cult to transcend the cult.[64] At the same time, he demar-

tology of 'Eschatological Symbolism'," *QL* 82 (2001) 112-127; Id., "De Sacramentologie van Alexander Schmemann: Een kritische beschouwing," *Het Christelijk Oosten* 52 (2000) 5-27.

62. Theological books of the 1960's were flooded with discussions on eschatology. Orthodox theologians also contributed to the growing interest of the topic. Although Orthodox theologians place a lot of importance to this topic, Schmemann's emphasis on 'eschatology' has to be read within this particular context. This eschatological emphasis is to be seen in all areas of his theological work.

63. Alexander Schmemann, "Symbols and Symbolism in the Byzantine Liturgy: Liturgical Symbols and their Theological Interpretation," *Liturgy and Tradition: Theological Reflections of Alexander Schmemann*, 115-128, p. 125. "The Ordo is the collection of rules and prescriptions ('rubrics' in the language of western liturgics) which regulate the Church's worship and which are set forth in the Typicon [Typicon is the official and written ordo] and various other books of rites and ceremonies." Alexander Schmemann, *Introduction to Liturgical Theology*, trans. Asheleigh E. Moorhouse (London: Faith Press, 1966) 28. He uses the same word "ordo" for "the fundamental structure of the eucharist." Alexander Schmemann, *The Eucharist: Sacrament of the Kingdom*, trans. Paul Kachur (Crestwood, NY: St. Vladimir's Seminary Press, 1988) 13.

64. Alexander Schmemann, "Theology and Liturgical Tradition," *Liturgy and Tradition: Theological Reflections of Alexander Schmemann*, 11-20, pp. 17-18. The debate on the cultic nature of Christian worship must be understood within the context of the debate on the influence of mystery cults on Christian worship. The comparative school in the history of religions, based on parallels between Christianity and pagan religions, argued that Christian worship was influenced from the very outset by mystery cults that were widespread in the Hellenistic world. Against this "thesis" came the "antithesis" that denied any genetic connection between the Christian cult and the pagan mysteries, based on the scientific study of the Jewish roots of the Christian cult and exegetical study of the New Testament. In Schmemann's opinion, however, though the antithesis successfully refuted this theory, they could not answer the question of the essential nature of the Christian cult. Dom Odo Casel proposed a synthesis reconciling and removing the conflict between the "thesis" and "antithesis," by underscoring the mystery character of Christianity. For him, mystery is "a sacred ritual action in which a saving deed is made present through the rite; the congregation, by performing the rite, takes part in the saving act, and thereby wins salvation." Odo Casel, *Das christliche Kultmysterium* (Regensburg: Putset, 1960) 79. Schmemann criticizes Casel's basic assertion concerning the mysteriological nature of the Christian cult. Even though he accepts many of his views, he parts company with Casel on his interpretation of cult. Casel understood cult as that which makes present the act of the past. Schmemann, however, draws our attention to the transposed meaning

cated the Christian cult from the cults of mystery religions and of the Jews. For example, in the mystery religions 'cult' in its very essence presupposes a radical distinction between the 'sacred' and the 'profane'. Similarly, the Jewish understanding of worship, though opposed to pagan cults, continued to demarcate the 'sacred' from the 'profane'. A clear example of this is demonstrated by the temple worship, based on a priestly order.[65] But Schmemann considers Christian worship different from both pagan and Jewish worship. In it the dichotomy between the sacred and the profane is absent. Christian worship is not a sacred action, or rite, performed in order to establish contact between the community and God, rather, it should be understood as a "way" in the path of Jesus making Christian worship non-cultic.[66] This does not mean that it was totally different from Jewish worship. Christianity continued the Jewish worship with its cultic character; however, it acquired a new meaning within the Christian tradition. It is a "radical transformation of the spirit of worship" in the sense of attaching new meanings to the structures and forms of this worship.[67]

> The Old Testament cult was viewed by Christians not only as a providential preparation for and prototype of the new, but also as its necessary foundation, since only by the 'transposition' of its basic categories – Temple, priesthood and sacrifice – was it possible to express and reveal the newness of the Church as the revelation of what had been promised, as the fulfilment of what had been hoped for, as an eschatological fulfilment.[68]

Christian worship is neither a sacred action, nor rite, performed in order to establish contact between the community and God, nor is it a natural community that is sanctified through the cult.[69] In his opinion, "the

attributed to the cults in Christian worship. Schmemann, *Introduction to Liturgical Theology*, 81-82.

65. Schmemann, "Theology and Liturgical Tradition," 16. This is very clear from the "old" cult of Moses. There were three fundamental "categories" of Old Testament worship: the temple, the priesthood and the institution of sacrifices. This was a "cult" and a "religion" in the sense of its contact and relationship with God. Schmemann, *Introduction to Liturgical Theology*, 79.

66. He even argues that by abolishing the sacred-profane dichotomy, i.e. cult, Jesus abolished religion. Hence the New Testament has not presented Christianity as a cult or as a religion. "Religion is needed where there is a wall of separation between God and man. But Christ who is both God and man, has broken down a wall between man and God. He has inaugurated a new life, not a new religion." Schmemann, *Sacraments and Orthodoxy*, 21.

67. Schmemann, "Theology and Liturgical Tradition," 15.

68. Schmemann, *Introduction to Liturgical Theology*, 80.

69. Schmemann, "Theology and Liturgical Tradition," 16.

regeneration of the Hebrew cult within Christianity" is not "the regeneration of its external forms;" rather, its regenerative significance lies in the Church's own faith and ecclesiological consciousness. It is a "new liturgical piety wholly determined by the faith of Christians in the ontological newness of the Church as the eschatological beginning in this world, in this aeon, of the Aeon of the kingdom."[70] The Church's purpose is not the sanctification of its members, but the creation of the people of God as the Body of Christ. Regeneration is not experienced as a repetition of the saving fact, rather as the proclamation of the saving nature of this fact.[71] He underscores this transition of the cult as sacrament.[72]

The non-cultic character is clear from the term *leitourgia*, which was used for early Christian worship, especially for the Eucharist. The Greek word *leitourgia* had no cultic connotation; rather, it meant a public office, a service performed on behalf of a community and for its benefit. It acquired a religious meaning in the Septuagint, but not a "liturgical" one. "It implied the same idea of service, applied now to the chosen people of God whose specific 'leitourgia' is to fulfil God's design in history, to prepare the 'way of the Lord'." Therefore, Schmemann argues that the Christian *leitourgia* cannot be reduced to, or expressed, in terms of 'cult'. In his opinion, unlike in cultic religions, where worship or cultic acts were the only content of religion, in the Christian "cult," *leitourgia* has a functional meaning that transcends the categories of cult as such.[73]

Christian *leitourgia* serves as the key to understand the innate antinomy[74] of the Christian *lex orandi*: its unquestionable continuity with Jewish tradition and its equally unquestionable newness. He interprets the sacrament in terms of a fundamental Christian dichotomy between the old and the new, or better, as the *passage* from the "old" into the "new." The mode of its presence is the Church. In it there is a tension "between this world and the world to come, between being in this world, yet also not of this world." This tension, in his opinion, is what constitutes the

70. Schmemann, *Introduction to Liturgical Theology*, 80

71. *Ibid.*, 85.

72. Schmemann, "Theology and Liturgical Tradition," 17-18.

73. Schmemann, "Theology and Eucharist," 17.

74. Antinomy is a notion that was often used to interpret the meaning of sacraments in the Orthodox tradition. It is a notion used in Greek philosophy in the context of law. Immanuel Kant is to be credited for bringing this notion into philosophy and to theology. In theology it is used to explain the truth that is expressed through contradiction. Pavel Florensky, *The Pillar and Ground of the Truth: An Essay in Orthodox Theodicy in Twelve Letters*, trans. Boris Jakim (Princeton, NJ: Princeton University Press, 1997) 106-123. It seems that Schmemann uses this expression to explain the presence of the other world already in this world. In other words, it is a tension between being in this world, yet, not of this world.

basis of the early Christian worship, in particular, of Baptism and Eucharist.[75] For Schmemann, "liturgical tradition of the Church is fundamentally antinomical in its nature. It is a cult which eternally transcends itself because it is a cult of a community which eternally transcends itself by realizing itself, as the body of Christ, as the Church of the Holy Spirit, as ultimately, the new *aeon* of the Kingdom."[76]

From this description, we can see that the essential particularity of eschatological symbolism is that in it there is no distinction between the sign and the signified. The sign and that which it signifies are one and the same reality. The liturgy is something that happens to us. It means that through the liturgical entrance, the liturgical community or rather the Church enters into heaven. There, we join the angels in their unceasing glorification of God. In this sense, our offering to God the gifts of bread and wine is the sacrifice of ourselves. This is possible because we are *in Christ.*[77]

This also points to the ecclesial, cosmic and eschatological dimensions of Christian *leitourgia*. It "is the action of the Church itself, or the Church *in actu*, it is the very expression of its life. It is not opposed to the non-cultic forms or aspects of the *ecclessia*, because the *ecclesia* exists in and through the *leitourgia*, and its whole life is a *leitourgia*." In this sense, one could say that "the Church belongs to the age to come, but dwells in 'this world' and its proper mission is to witness the *eschaton*." Furthermore, "the sacraments of Baptism and Eucharist, and the sacraments according to the early Christian understanding are precisely the means of the escathological life of the Church."[78] Thus, the essential function of the liturgy is to reveal "the *eschatological* character of the Christian cult whose essential 'function' is to *realize* the Church by revealing it as the epiphany of the Kingdom of God."[79] The "absolute newness of Christian sacrament is not in its ontology as sacrament but in the specific '*res*' which it symbolizes," i.e., Christ and His Kingdom. Thus,

75. Schmemann, "Symbols and Symbolism in the Byzantine Liturgy," 125-126.

76. Schmemann, "Theology and Liturgical Tradition," 18.

77. Schmemann, "Symbols and Symbolism in the Byzantine Liturgy" 127.

78. Schmemann, "Theology and Liturgical Tradition," 17-18.

79. Alexander Schmemann, "Liturgical Theology: Remarks on Method," *Liturgy and Tradition: Theological Reflections of Alexander Schmemann*, 137-144, p. 142. It means in this tradition "the relationship between the sign in the symbol (A) and that which it "signifies" (B) is neither a merely semantic one (A means B), nor causal (A is the cause of B), nor representative (A represents B). He called this relationship an epiphany. "A is B" means that the whole of A expresses, communicates, reveals, manifests the "reality" of B (although not necessarily the whole of it) without, however, losing its own ontological reality, without being dissolved in another "res." Schmemann, "Sacrament and Symbol," 141.

he argues that "the '*mysterion*' of Christ reveals and fulfils the ultimate meaning and destiny of the world itself."[80]

2.1.2. Symbolism in Patristic Sacramentology

As we have seen the Fathers continued the early tradition of explaining sacramentology in and through the liturgy.[81] Nevertheless, Schmemann also notes certain shifts in the understanding of the sacramental symbolism of the Fathers. Although the early Fathers continued the antinomical character of the early Christian experience of the Kingdom, the emphasis was shifted from the experience of the Kingdom to the knowledge of the Kingdom, by learning and reflecting more on the *mysterion*. Later, this knowledge is imparted through illustration.

The first shift in sacramental symbolism started with the mystical commentary addressed to the faithful. Unlike the catechetical instructions, which dealt almost exclusively with the rites of initiation,[82] the focus of the mystagogical commentary was primarily on liturgy. It aimed to prepare the Church for proper participation in the Church's worship by explaining the *mysterion*.[83] According to St Maximus the Confessor, the symbol is inseparable from and subordinated to the central notion of the theology of *mysterion* that refers to the mystery of Christ and to His saving ministry. In this sense it is both the "content of faith, the knowledge of the divine mystery revealed in Christ, and the saving power communicated through and in the Church." For him, liturgy is the "locus of the symbol." It is "the mode of the presence and action of the *mysterion*." Hence, symbol is "the very reality of that which it symbolizes. By representing, or signifying, that reality it makes it present, truly represents it."[84] For Maximus, through symbolism, the liturgy gives us, both the *theoria*, or the knowledge and the contemplation of the saving mysteries and *theosis*, or the ascension of the human soul to God and communion with Him. These two realities cannot be separated: knowledge and communion. Schmemann notes:

80. Schmemann, "Sacrament and Symbol," 140.

81. *Ibid.*, 146.

82. The pre – and post – baptismal initiation reflects the two main traditions of scriptural exegesis: the Alexandrian, represented by Origen, Gregory of Nyssa and Pseudo-Dionysius, who emphasised theoria, and the Antiochene, represented by Cyril of Jerusalem, John Chrysostom and Theodore of Mopsuestia, who affirmed the notion of historia. Both traditions consider liturgy, like Scripture, a source of gnosis, the knowledge of God revealing Himself in His saving acts. Schmemann, "Symbols and Symbolism in the Byzantine Liturgy," 119-120.

83. *Ibid.*, 120.

84. *Ibid.*, 122-123.

> The symbol is means of knowledge of that which cannot be known otherwise, for knowledge here depends on participation – the living encounter with and entrance to that "epiphany" of reality which the symbol is. But then theology is not only related to the "mysterion" but has in it its source, the condition of its very possibility. Theology as proper words and knowledge *about* God is the result *of* God – and in Him of all reality.[85]

The Fathers considered symbol as a key to sacrament "because sacrament is in continuity with the symbolical structure of the world in which 'omnes...creaturae sensibiles sunt signa rerum sacrum'. [Thomas Aquinas, *Summa Theologica*, *Quest*. 60, Art. 2,1.] And the world is symbolic – 'signum rei sacrae'" because of "its being created by God." From this we can see that the symbolic belongs 'to its ontology'. It is not only a means "to perceive and understand reality, [rather] a means of *participation*."[86] The merit of this understanding of symbol is that it maintains the three dimensions of the Christian vision of reality in tension: the Church, the world and the Kingdom. Holding these three realities together in a tensive unity, "it made them *known* ... as both understanding and participation. It was the source of theology – knowledge *about* God in His relation to the world, the Church, and the Kingdom – because it was knowledge *of* God and, in Him, of all reality. Having its beginning, content and end in Christ, it at the same time revealed Christ as the beginning, the content and the end of all that which exists, as its Creator, Redeemer, and fulfilment."[87]

According to Schmemann, the value of Maximus' theology of *mysterion* is that "the liturgical symbol is validated by a consistent theology of the liturgy, which, in turn, applies to liturgy a comprehensive and consistent theological vision." This leads to different strands of mystagogical symbolism among the Fathers. For example, the symbolic interpretations of the liturgy of Gregory of Nyssa, Pseudo-Dionysius, and Maximus are substantially different from one another in emphasis, even though they uphold the same general, mystical, and mysteriological orientation. "The reason for this is that they apply to the liturgy their particular vision rather than seek in the liturgy the vision implied in its own *ordo*, in its own structures and texts."[88] Schmemann, however, criticizes the Fathers

85. Schmemann, "Sacrament and Symbol," 141; Id., "Symbols and Symbolism in the Byzantine Liturgy," 123.

86. Schmemann, "Sacrament and Symbol," 139-140.

87. *Ibid.*, 144-145.

88. Schmemann, "Symbols and Symbolism in the Byzantine Liturgy," 124-125. John Meyendorff underscores this difference more vividly. According to him, the early Christians understood the Eucharist as a mystery of true and real communion with Christ. For example, Chrysostom observes that in the Eucharist "Christ even now is present, even

for their emphasis on theological contemplation of the *mysterion* and viewing the liturgy as a means for it. In his opinion, this shift from liturgical participation in the mystery to the contemplation of the mystery is violence done to the very essence of the liturgy.[89] Schmemann explains this by examining the principle of continuity and discontinuity. In his opinion, there is continuity in the meaning of liturgy of the *ordo*, but there is a discontinuity in its comprehension. That is, the word means one thing for Maximus the Confessor, but a different thing for Germanus of Constantinople. This difference "served as the main source for the later illustrative symbolism. The discontinuity, the difference here is, above all, of a theological nature. It is a difference between two understandings of the symbol in its relationship to theology."[90]

Following the period of mystagogical catechesis, there began a new tradition of liturgical symbolism called "illustrative symbolism." By "illustrative symbolism" Schmemann means "the later symbolic identification of each liturgical act with one precise event of Christ's earthly life."[91] He considers the various Byzantine and post-Byzantine liturgical

now operates." *Epistolam Secundam ad Timotheum Commentarius*, II: 4, *PG* 62, 612. Gregory of Nyssa presents the Eucharist as a mystery of real "participation" in the glorified Body of Christ, the seed of immortality. John Meyendorf traces its origin to the pastoral needs of the post-Constantine Church. According to him, in the theological rationalization of this new situation, the Fathers began to explain the Eucharist as a system of symbols to be contemplated. Gradually, sacramental participation was replaced with intellectual vision. He considers Pseudo-Dionysius as the most important proponent of this symbolical understanding. Reducing the Eucharistic synaxis to a moral appeal, Pseudo-Dionysius calls his readers to a higher contemplation. "Let us leave to the imperfect these signs which, as I said, are magnificently painted in the vestibules of the sanctuaries; they will be sufficient to feed their contemplation. As far as we are concerned: let us turn back, in considering the holy synaxis, from the effects to their causes, and, thanks to the lights which Jesus will give us, we shall be able to contemplate harmoniously the intelligible realities in which are clearly reflected the blessed goodness of the models." *Ecclesiastica Hierarchia*, III, 3/1-2, *PG* 3, 428 AC. John Meyendorff, *Byzantine Theology. Historical Trends and Doctrinal Themes* (New York: Fordham University Press, [2]1983) 201-202.

89. Schmemann, *Introduction to Liturgical Theology*, 99-115.

90. Schmemann, "Symbols and Symbolism in the Byzantine Liturgy," 121-122.

91. *Ibid.*, 123. He also notes that "the divine liturgy by Germanus of Constantinople (eighth century), an explanation which Bornert rightly defines as the quasi official or at least the most commonly accepted interpretation, and which without any doubt served as the main source for the later illustrative symbolism." Alexander Schmemann quoted this from René Bornert, *Les Commentaires byzantins de la divine liturgie, du VIIe au XVe siècle* (Paris: Institut Français d'Études Byzantines, 1966) 162. Elsewhere René Bornert observes that, since Theodore of Mopsuestia (350-428), all commentators on the Byzantine liturgy consider the Divine Liturgy as a representation of the earthly life of Christ. *Ibid.*, 81. For Schmemann "since Cabasilas, [b. c. 1322] the Eucharist is a symbolical representation of the life of Christ, serving as a framework for the double sacrament of

commentaries, which interpret liturgy as a symbolic representation of the life and ministry of Christ from His birth to His ascension, in this category. Here, the symbols are reduced to an illustration, and its purpose is pedagogic or educational.[92] Schmemann criticizes illustrative symbolism that in it there is no relation between the symbols and the symbolic meanings attributed to the liturgy. In other words, liturgical symbolism is reduced to a narration of the life of Jesus in the liturgical context, discarding the theological content of the liturgy. Schmemann sees a danger in this understanding, because, in his opinion, the external celebration of liturgy is considered to be a "sacred play." Therefore, the "dramatic" character of the Byzantine liturgy is often falsely referred to as being rich in symbolism.[93]

2.1.3. Post-Patristic Sacramentology

Sacramentology took a new turn in the post-patristic period. Schmemann criticizes the West for mainly two reasons: the alienation of the sacraments from liturgy and a rational approach to sacramentology. The former could be regarded as the beginning of the distortion of patristic sac-

consecration and communion, yet not essential for its 'validity' and 'efficacy'." Schmemann, "Theology and Eucharist," 19.

92. According to Schmemann, "There exists a substantial number of Byzantine and post-Byzantine – Greek, Russian, Serbian etc. – commentaries in which all liturgical acts, as well as the liturgy in its totality, are interpreted as being above all symbolic representations, i.e., as acts 'representing', 'signifying', and thus 'symbolizing', something else, be it an event of the past, an idea, or a theological affirmation." Schmemann, "Symbols and Symbolism in the Byzantine Liturgy," 115-116. See also Schmemann, *The Eucharist: Sacrament of the Kingdom*, 30-31. Paul Meyendorff observes that the illustrative symbolism which was already in the Fathers was developed in the context of iconoclast controversy. He notes, against the iconoclasts rejection of any images and the acceptance of the Eucharist as the only valid image of Christ, the Orthodox began to make a more realistic approach along Christological and soteriological lines. This led to the depiction of Christ in iconography as man and not as a lamb. [Concilium in Trullo, canon 82 in Sacrorum conciliorum nova et amplissima collectio, ed. Giovanni D. Mansi, vol. 11, 977-980]. Thus, in the late Byzantine liturgy, the anagogical approach by the Alexandrians was supplemented by the more historical, representational interpretation of the Antiochene school. See Paul Meyendorff, "Liturgy and Spirituality I: Eastern Liturgical Theology," *Christian Spirituality*, ed. Bernard McGinn & John Meyendorff, World Spirituality, 16 (New York: Crossroad Publishing Company, 1985) 350-363, p.359.

93. Schmemann, "Symbols and Symbolism in the Byzantine Liturgy," 117. For example, Symeon of Thessalonica writes that the seven items of the bishop's liturgical vestments correspond to the seven actions of the Holy Spirit, that his mantle symbolizes the "providential and almighty and all-preserving grace of God," and then goes on explaining in the same manner the whole liturgy. This sort of explanation, in the opinion of Schmemann, is radically different from that of Maximus and the other mystagogical commentators. *Ibid.*, 123-124.

ramentology and the latter as its natural outcome. The alienation of theology and sacramentology from liturgy, coupled with the rational approach led to the development of a certain conceptual system to explain the meaning of sacraments.

Schmemann criticizes scholastic theology[94] mainly because it sought to discover the meaning of the sacraments outside the context of the actual liturgical celebration. He accuses the medieval *De Sacramentis* for isolating the "sacrament" from its liturgical context. Instead of beginning from the concrete liturgical tradition, the scholastics began with "a priori and abstract categories and definitions."[95] He observes:

> The medieval *De Sacramentis*, however, tends from its very inception to isolate the 'sacrament' from its liturgical context, to find and to define in terms as precise as possible its *essence*, i.e., that which distinguishes it from the 'non-sacrament'. Sacrament in a way begins to be opposed to liturgy. It has, of course, its ritual expression, its 'signum,' which belongs to its essence, but this sign is viewed now as ontologically different from all other signs, symbols, and rites of the Church. And because of this difference, the precise sacramental sign alone is considered, to the exclusion of all other 'liturgy,' the proper object of theological attention.[96]

The alienation of sacraments from liturgy automatically led the medieval theologians to look for new interpretations of symbols. Schmemann identifies two problems in the post-patristic understanding of symbols. Primarily, they identified symbol with a "means" of knowledge. Consequently, there occurred a separation of knowledge from *mysterion*. Secondly, they reduced "knowledge to rational and discursive knowledge *about*, rather than *of*. It can be a revelation about the 'res,' but not the epiphany of the 'res' itself." In this scheme, knowledge and participation have become two separate realities.[97] Although the tradition affirmed that the sacrament is real, they found it increasingly difficult to comprehend

94. Schmemann defines "scholastic theology" not as a definite school or period in the history of theology, but as a theological structure which existed in various forms, both in the West and in the East. See Schmemann, "Theology and Liturgical Tradition," 13. He criticizes the effort to look at the roots of Byzantine scholasticism in the West. In his opinion, it arose gradually on Byzantine soil and in specifically Byzantine conditions. Alexander Schmemann, "St. Mark of Ephesus and the Theological Conflicts in Byzantium," *SVSQ* 1/1 (1957) 11-24, p. 18.

95. Schmemann, *The Eucharist: Sacrament of the Kingdom*, 13. In particular he notes that "the sacrament of the eucharist is inseparable from the divine liturgy." *Ibid.*, 161.

96. Schmemann, "Sacrament and Symbol," 137. In his opinion, it came to the point that one could read and understand the elaborate treatment given in St. Thomas' Summa to the sacraments, without knowing much about the liturgical celebration.

97. *Ibid.*, 141-142.

the symbol as the mode of sacrament. They resolved this problem "by a mere reinforcement of one terminology – the 'symbolical' – by another one – th e 'realistic'. The sacrament is both 'figura et res, veritas et figura,' it is 'non solum mystice sed etiam vere'."[98] Soon, however, they realised that the two terms had become opposed to each other. This opposition is clearly seen in the Eucharistic controversies which were mainly focused on "real presence." The discussion on Christ's real presence in the Eucharist logically implied the possibility of another type of presence that was *not* real. This "other presence" was then symbolic.[99] Schmemann demonstrates this through the example of Berenger of Tours. For Berenger, "the Body and Blood of Christ in the Eucharist are not real because they are symbolical." Simultaneously, in 1059 the council of Lateran condemned him saying: "[the Body and Blood] are real precisely because they are not symbolical."[100] It resulted in the dissolution of the holistic view of sacraments as symbol and reality. Here, we see the disconnection and the opposition of the two terms: *verum* and *mystice*, the acceptance, on both sides, that they are mutually exclusive. Schmemann considers it as the collapse of the fundamental Christian *Mysterion* that antinomically held together "the reality of the symbol, and of the symbolism of reality."[101] Thereafter, theologians accepted sacraments in terms of either *signum* or *res* instead of both *signum* and *res*.

This new understanding, of course, led to other problems with respect to the relation between the *signum* and the *res*. The theologians tried to resolve the problem by defining *signum* as *cause*. Hence, another great misunderstanding of sacramentology was created. The causality linking the institution to *signum* and to *res* became viewed as extrinsic and formal. Besides denying the ontological continuity between sign and reality, also all continuity between the institution and the normal order of things was rejected. Thus, Schmemann observes: "Considered as the 'causa principalis' of the 'signum' as 'causa secunda,' institution becomes now an absolute starting point of a sacramental system entirely *sui generis*." In his opinion, the efforts "to bring back into the notion of 'signum' the 'richness of traditional symbolism' concern the 'accidents,' not the 'sub-

98. *Ibid.*, 142-143.

99. *Ibid.*, 138. He even observes that "in the common theological language as it takes shape between the Carolingian renaissance and the Reformation, and in spite of all controversies between rival theological schools, the 'incompatibility between symbol and reality', between 'figura et veritas' is consistently affirmed and accepted." *Ibid.*, 138.

100. *Ibid.*., 142-143; Id., "Worship in a Secular Age," 11-12.

101. Schmemann, "Worship in a Secular Age," 11-12. See also Id., "Sacrament and Symbol," 143.

stance' in the doctrine and understanding of sacraments."[102] The principle of causality also led to the subordination of the Eucharist as "effect" and to the Church as "cause."[103]

This change in understanding slowly led to viewing the Church as the 'distributor of grace' and for limiting "the theological study of the Eucharist to only two problems: that of the transformation of the bread and wine into the Body and Blood of Christ and that of communion." This very significant shift in the understanding of sacraments made sacraments private services for the personal sanctification of individual Christians.[104] It makes the Church to remain "mainly as a 'power' – to perform the transformation, to give communion. The priest is the minister (the 'performer') of the sacrament, the elements of bread and wine – its 'matter' the communicant – its recipient."[105]

He further criticizes the theologians for reducing the sacraments to the categories of 'form' and 'matter,' 'causality' and 'validity,' and for excluding the liturgical tradition from their theological speculations.[106] The rational approach only deepened the disintegration of liturgy from sacraments. Liturgy was considered as a non-essential, symbolical "frame work" for the minimum of action and words necessary for validity. The whole liturgical action ceased to be understood as *sacramental*, i.e., as a series of transformations ultimately leading the Church into the fullness of the Kingdom, the only real "condition" of the transformation of the elements.[107] Finally, since theology, by focusing on certain aspects of the Eucharist, "imperceptibly relegated all other elements of the eucharistic

102. *Ibid.*, 144.

103. Schmemann, "Theology and Eucharist," 16.

104. *Ibid.*, 18. For example, the "sacrament of penance, which was originally an act of reconciliation with the Church is understood today as mere 'power of absolution'. Matrimony, which at first had even no special 'liturgy' of its own and was performed through the participation of a newly-wed couple in the Eucharist is replaced with a 'blessing' bestowed upon husband and wife, as a simple Christian action of marriage. The Eucharistic cup is replaced in it by a cup 'symbolizing' common life." Schmemann, "Theology and Eucharist," 18. In his opinion, today, sacraments are generally existing first and primarily in the form of a particular and fixed number of sacraments and associated mainly with the personal needs of the individual Christian. In the process of systematizing we lost the sacramental sense in general. Instead the number, institution, validity and so on became our concerns. Everything is measured. For example the amount of grace one receives through a sacrament etc. Schmemann, "The World as Sacrament," 220-221.

105. Schmemann, "Theology and Eucharist," 18-19.

106. Schmemann, "Worship in a Secular Age," 5. He considers the reduction of entire teaching on sacraments to the question of 'validity' and 'objectivity' as the fundamental "defect of any scholasticism, or any theological rationalism" (emphasis added). Schmemann, *The Eucharist: Sacrament of the Kingdom*, 116.

107. Schmemann, "Theology and Liturgical Tradition," 19-20.

celebration into the category of 'non-essential' rituals," it gradually opened the way to the so-called *liturgical symbolism*.[108]

Not only does Schmemann criticize "the theologians" but also the historians of theology, who interpret these changes as the progress of "scientific theology" and the growth of a "more precise" theological method.[109] In his opinion, theology's alienation with the liturgy also influenced the study of theology. Thus, the very discipline "liturgics" dealt mainly with a practical study of the Church services, together with an explanation of liturgical symbolism and the theological and historical aspects of worship. "Liturgics" main concern is to teach aspiring priests how to perform services in conformity with the rubrics and canonical requirements. It discards the real meaning of *leitourgia* and its communal experience, the meaning of the Church, and the relationship between the Church and her cult.[110] It does this by beginning with a general theory of sacraments, and then by applying this theology to each particular sacrament.[111]

To conclude our discussion, we could underscore two of Schmemann's contributions to sacramentology. First, the importance of liturgy in the study of sacraments and, secondly, his focus on the eschatological symbolism of the early Christian tradition. The latter is of particular importance to our study. Although eschatology is often misunderstood as world denying and futuristic, Schmemann draws our attention to its positive meanings. For him, eschatology is nothing but experiencing the Kingdom of God in this world itself. In this sense, eschatology is "an emphatic *yes* to the world with an equally emphatic *no*."[112] For him, it is

108. Schmemann, "Theology and Eucharist," 19. In particular he criticizes the scholastic overemphasis on "transubstantiation" as the focal point of the Eucharistic conversion. This reduction of a certain part of the Eucharist as important and the other as non-essential made him to call each part of the liturgy "sacrament." For this reason, all the twelve chapters of his The Eucharist: Sacrament of the Kingdom begins with "the sacrament of... ." According to him: "[T]he divine liturgy is a single, though also 'multifaceted', sacred rite, a single sacrament, in which all its 'parts', their entire sequence and structure, their coordination with each other, the necessity of each for all and all for each, manifests to us the inexhaustible, eternal, universal and truly divine meaning of what has been and what is being accomplished." Schmemann, *The Eucharist: Sacrament of the Kingdom*, 160-161.

109. Schmemann, "Sacrament and Symbol," 137. See Id., *The Eucharist: Sacrament of the Kingdom*, 66-69; 142-143.

110. Schmemann, "Liturgical Theology: Its Task and Method," 16.

111. Latin *De Sacramentis* begins "from a general definition of sacraments as 'visible means of the invisible grace' he will proceed to the distinction in them between 'form' and 'matter', their institution by Christ, their numbering and classification and, finally their proper administration as their condition of their validity and efficacy." Schmemann, "Sacrament and Symbol," 135.

112. Alexander Schmemann, "The 'Orthodox World', Past and Present," *Church,*

"to be fully *in* the world ... at the same time totally *not* of this world."[113] The positive attitude of early Christian eschatology helps us to see the world in Christ. It also critically analyses the monastic interpretation that seeks to withdraw from the world as an escape from the world.[114] The "antinomical" character of Schmemann's eschatological symbolism serves as an important key to interpret the world as sacrament. It brings together the Church, the world and the Kingdom, by bridging the gap between the sacred and the profane.

2.2. Christian World-View

Before entering into a discussion on the 'Christian world-view,' it is important to clarify the framework in which Schmemann develops the Church's understanding and relation to the world. First of all, the very question how Orthodox churches view the world, and the relation between Church and the world, is the result of a systematisation in theology. As noted earlier, the rational approach in theology has forced theologians to make such distinctions. Understood from this perspective, Schmemann tries to evince the Church's worldview based on the early Christian experience. Accordingly, the early Church did not distinguish between the Church and the world because "the Christian *oikoumene* which grew out of the reconciliation between the Church and the Graeco-Roman Empire ... remained the only self-evident expression and experience of the Church's 'presence' in the world."[115]

It is also important to note that the theological worldview is significant to understand the theological difference between the East and the West. Schmemann even argues that if Western culture is alien to the Eastern culture, it is "not because of her 'orientalism' or a difference in ethnical background, but, because of her fundamental theological and spiritual presuppositions, of her whole world-view."[116] Significantly, the theological difference on sacramental symbolism between the West and the East is the result of their different worldview.[117]

In the following section we look forward to delineate how Schmemann maps out the development of changing worldviews along with its impact in the understanding of the sacraments. From the very outset, it is

World, Mission (Crestwood, NY: St. Vladimir's Seminary Press, 1979) 25-66, p. 29.

113. *Ibid.*, 64.

114. *Ibid.*, 30.

115. Alexander Schmemann, "The Problem of the Church's Presence in the World in Orthodox Consciousness," *SVTQ* 21 (1977) 3-17, p. 4.

116. Schmemann, "Problems of Orthodoxy in America: The Liturgical Problem," 172.

117. Schmemann, "Sacrament and Symbol," 139.

important to note that it is very difficult, and rather confusing, to make a clear demarcation of changing worldviews. In general, we discover three worldviews in Schmemann: conflict between the Church and the State, reconciliation between the two in the post-Constantine era and, finally, a divorce between them in the post-Christian era.[118] Since the post-Constantine era both East and West approached Church and State differently, we shall observe four perspectives in this section: the early Christian, eastern, western and modern ones.

2.2.1. Early Christian World-View

As noted earlier, Schmemann makes it clear that there was no distinction between the Church and the state. In this sense he denied the criticism that there was a conflict between the Church and the Empire, in early Christianity, based on the conflicting view of the expectation of the immanent *Parousia.* He also denied that "the later reconciliation with world, state, society and culture" was the result of "its progressive liberation from the eschatological obsession of the earlier period."[119] On the contrary he demonstrates two reasons for the conflict.

First of all, the Christian conflict between the Church and the state in the early period is due to "their refusal to honor the Emperor with the title of *Kyrios*, Lord." This is clear from the fact that their fight was not against any other defect of the Empire like "*injustice* (slavery), *colonialism* (the regime of imperial *versus* the senatorial provinces), or *imperialism* (expansion at the expense of other states and nations)." At the same time the very denial of "the emperor the divine title Kyrios implied in fact much more than all this, for it challenged once and for all the self-proclaimed divinity of the state, its claim to be an absolute value, a divine 'end in itself'. And it implied not only a negation, but also an affirmation."[120] Positively this denial meant the affirmation of Jesus Christ as true Kyrios. Secondly, it also affirmed the dependence of the state "to the dominion of the one Kyrios, Jesus Christ. In a deep sense it rejects the 'separation' of Church and state." Finally, it affirmed the antinomical reality of the "Kingdom in 'this world,' as criterion for both its negation and its affirmation, as the source of true charity and justice, as above all the criterion enabling men to 'discern the spirits – whether they are from God.'"[121]

118. Schmemann, "The 'Orthodox World', Past and Present," 27.
119. *Ibid.*.
120. *Ibid.*, 31-32.
121. *Ibid.*, 32-33.

Secondly, the conflict is the result of the confusion on the understanding of truth and authority. The Roman attitude to "authority" and "truth" is clearly seen in Pilate's enquiry into "the truth." It implies, first of all, "a distinction and a separation between Truth on the one hand and Authority on the other." Secondly, it "implicitly denied the possibility for man to know the Truth and to be guided by it. Hence the absolutization of authority and the divinization of Caesar." In other words for them "Authority is truth." On the other hand, for Christians "Truth is Authority." This conviction was seen behind the early Christians' readiness for martyrdom.[122]

Furthermore, Schmemann observes that the early Christian worldview was criticized based on a negative understanding of eschatology of later origin. On the contrary, he tries to demonstrate the positive dimension of eschatology by showing that the eschatological outlook of the early Christians was not a denial of the world but a positive way of looking at the world and experiencing it. This positive outlook is rooted in the fact that 'the world' for the early Christians refers to the Kingdom of God. Therefore the denial of the world is not the result of an 'anti-world' outlook, rather it was the result of a 'pro-Kingdom' attitude.[123]

For the early Christians, the Kingdom of God was a reality that is already present in this world. It was the result of the incarnation, death, resurrection, and ascension of Jesus and the descent of the Holy Spirit on the day of Pentecost. Therefore, God's Kingdom continues in the Church. This belief is the basis of their antinomical relation to the world with "an emphatic *yes* to the world" and equally with an "emphatic *no*." The Christian "no" to the world and their proclamation of the end of *this* world exhorts believers to become "dead with Christ." However, it is also proclaimed that the world is redeemed in Christ. "This means that for those who believe in Christ and are united to Him, this very world, – its time and matter, and even death – have become 'means' of communication with the Kingdom of God, the sacrament, i.e. the mode, of its coming and presence among men." It means to say that "the early Christian eschatology, rather than rejecting the world, posits the foundation of a world-view which implies a 'positive' attitude towards the world in general, and towards the state in particular."[124]

However, Schmemann acknowledges that the early Christians understanding started to change with the conversion of Constantine. In the post-Constantine period, the opposing view of his conversion made east-

122. *Ibid.*, 33.
123. *Ibid.*, 28-29.
124. *Ibid.*, 29-30.

ern and western Fathers appropriate the early Christian worldview from within their own socio-cultural and religious contexts.[125]

2.2.2. Eastern World-View

In the post-Constantine period, the eastern churches generally followed the eschatological worldview of the early Church. For them, eschatological faith is the starting point and the ultimate term of reference to the entire 'eastern experience'.[126] In this sense, Schmemann compares the relation between Church and state in terms of organic unity. This unity for Schmemann resembles the union of soul and body.[127]

Schmemann traces the origin of the definition of the eastern 'eschatological experience' to the conversion of Constantine which formed the spiritual and psychological foundation of Byzantine theocracy.[128] For them, Constantine's conversion was an election by God. Through the election of the emperor, "the empire itself is called to accept Christ and to become His *politeuma.*" It "means that in the person of the emperor, the empire acknowledges as its own Kyrios the Lord of heaven and earth, places itself in the perspective and under the dominion of His Kingdom. Thus *ab initio* the alliance between Church and state is based ... on *faith.*" Therefore, his conversion and its acceptance by the Church meant "no change in faith, no alteration of its eschatological content."[129] The Church's acknowledgement of the emperor means its surrender to the care and protection of him whom Christ Himself chose and appointed to serve His Kingdom.[130] Schmemann demonstrates three examples for the eschatological worldview of the eastern Christian tradition.

First, Schmemann notes how the Christian attitude is different in Christian and non-Christian contexts. In a non-Christian state, the Church has one possibility "to 'be herself,' i.e. to preach and to confess Christ, the unique Kyrios, and His Kingdom, to offer salvation to all men everywhere." Here, the Church retains her identity in contrast to the political

125. This had its impact in their understanding of theology especially ecclesiology. While the Easterners viewed the Church "as a sacramental organism whose function and purpose is to reveal, manifest and communicate the Kingdom of God," the Westerners viewed the Church from a juridical perspective. *Ibid.*, 38-39.

126. *Ibid.*, 34.

127. Schmemann, "The Problem of the Church's Presence in the World in Orthodox Consciousness," 5; Id., "Orthodoxy," *The Study of Spirituality*, ed. Cheslyn Jones, Geoffrey Wainwright & Edward Yarnold (London: SPCK, 1986) 519-524, p. 520.

128. Schmemann, "The 'Orthodox World', Past and Present," 35.

129. *Ibid.*, 35-36. The notion of 'state' in Schmemann could be understood as 'world' in general. For him the term "world" encompasses state, society, culture, etc. *Ibid.*, 61-62.

130. *Ibid.*, 37-38.

identity. On the other hand, in a Christian state, since the state shares Christian values with the Church, it has no difficulty in leaving its 'management' to the care and administration of the state. This is possible because both the Church and the state "are rooted precisely in the same 'eschatological ecclesiology,' in the same fundamental experience of the Church."[131]

Second, the Church-state relationship in the East is not based on a juridical principle, but on the notion of *Truth.*[132] This means to say that the Easterners understood the relationship between Church and state as the acceptance of the faith of the Church by the empire. It was this truth that, in the eyes of the Church, guaranteed her real independence, the fulfillment by her of her mission.[133] Therefore, Schmemann argues that Byzantine Christianity was not merely an example of "Caesaropapism," i.e., a surrender of Church to the state, because in it we miss "the psychological 'make-up' of a society of a world."[134]

Finally, Schmemann demonstrates this based on the monastic tradition of the eastern Christians. The eastern experience of the eschatological worldview is seen behind the "paradoxical mutual acceptance of monasticism by the empire and of the empire by monasticism." This paradoxi-

131. *Ibid.*, 40.

132. The concept of 'Truth' is the basis of the Byzantine theory and practice of the Church-state relationship. It has to be understood from three perspectives: doctrinal, liturgical and ascetical. First, the doctrinal aspect does not mean a mere rigid doctrinal formulation, rather, it is something that permeates the whole of life. Accordingly, Christianity is the revelation of divine Truth, which is to be known and received and to be appropriated and to be transformed into life. Thus the theological controversies of the early Church are not merely 'abstract' or 'intellectual', but had a soteriological and existential significance. It is something that deals with "the nature of man, with the meaning of his life, with the goals of his praxis." In this way, the patristic theology always kept an existential character by keeping the balance between 'theoretical' and 'practical'. For example, the Byzantine debates on enhypostaton, or the two wills and two energies in Christ, which may appear as the very example of the irrelevant, is the result of the appropriation of the great theandric mystery and the basis of Christian 'humanism', or a Christian vision of the world. The second aspect of 'Truth' is the expression and the embodiment of Beauty, expressed mainly through the liturgy. As we have seen, it is not merely worship or cult, rather, it is a way of life. Here, there is no place for a dichotomy between sacred and secular. It is the experience of the Kingdom of God, an experience of "heaven on earth, of a Presence which transcends all human experience and categories, yet relates all of them to itself and reveals the world as Cosmos, in which heaven and earth are truly full of divine glory. This experience of 'the world to come' in this world "assumes the whole of creation – matter, sound, color – and transfigures all of it in its sacramental passage and ascension into the glory of God's presence." The third aspect of Truth is the Byzantine Christian culture as ascetical. *Ibid.*, 47-49.

133. *Ibid.*, 40.

134. *Ibid.*, 42.

cal situation was manifested in their life. On the one hand, the monks did not reject the 'Christianization' of the world; yet, on the other hand, they left the world. In their flight they are not giving up their concern for the Church or for the world.[135] This is because for Schmemann, their renunciation is also "based on the same eternal Christian antinomy: '*in* the world but not *of* the world'."[136] The acceptance of this monastic attitude by the empire and the society is reflected in bringing monasticism from the deserts to the outskirts of cities. Slowly the monastic liturgy started reshaping the liturgy of the whole Church. Moreover, the acceptance of monasticism was the result of "the recognition of the ultimate *freedom* of man." It is not understood in secular terms, rather, it comes from "his belonging to God and to His Kingdom."[137]

At the same time Schmemann delineates its degeneration among the eastern Christians in the later period. In the post-Byzantine period, the 'eastern experience' continued in countries like Bulgaria, Russia, Serbia.[138] Nevertheless, this does not mean that the 'eschatological worldview' of early Christianity was continued throughout the East. For example, the southern Slavs failed to appropriate the 'Byzantine theocratic consciousness' under the Turkish regime. This impacted a change, though not 'dogmatically' but psychologically, in the Church's universal mission, in its cosmic and historical scope and finally in its dynamic relationship with this world. It was "replaced with a kind of non-historical 'quietism' which came to be viewed, by the Orthodox and non-Orthodox alike, as the 'essence' of Orthodoxy." From this period onwards we see a change in outlook from the earlier understanding of eschatology as "openness to history and to God's action in it" to a "particular situation of the past."[139]

Although the Russian Orthodox Church continued the 'eastern experience,' it also underwent a change through Westernization.[140] Schmemann

135. *Ibid.*, 43-44. Asceticism is not the result of fear or pessimism, but must be understood as "theosis, a deification of man by the grace of the Holy Spirit." The rejection of asceticism today by many in the name of 'anti-human' or 'anti-social' is the result of a lack of understanding of their concept of man and his goals. He notes, "long before the vague terms 'freedom' and 'liberation' became the passe-partout slogans of modernity, they stood ... at the very heart of an entire civilization, as its ultimate aspiration and goal." *Ibid.*, 50.

136. *Ibid.*, 45.

137. *Ibid.*, 46.

138. *Ibid.*, 51-52.

139. *Ibid.*, 52-53.

140. It seems that the radical 'Westernization' which Schmemann refers goes back to the 'Westernization' imposed on Russia by Peter the Great in the eighteenth century. *Ibid.*, 53.

considers this as the result of the non-critical acceptance of the 'Western idea'.

> The acceptance of the specifically Western eschatology without the "eschaton," of the Kingdom without the King, which reduced man to matter alone, society alone, history alone, which closed his spiritual and intellectual horizon with "this world" alone. This reduction of man, his progressive alienation from his divine and transcendent destiny began in the West at the time of the Renaissance, continued through the Enlightenment, and found its fulfilment in the "this worldly" enthusiastic utopianism of the nineteenth century.[141]

One reason for the success of the Western idea in Russia is "the initial acceptance by many Russians of the Revolution as fulfilling the 'eschatological' aspirations of the Russian people, the interpretation of the 'western' idea in 'eastern' terms."[142]

But from the nineteenth century we see the emergence of many Russian thinkers opposing this 'western idea'. Even though, throughout the entire nineteenth century the most creative and original Russian thinkers from Chaadaiev to Dostoyevsky engaged in criticizing the West, the westernized Russian intelligentsia endorsed it more enthusiastically.[143] This renewal resulted in the emergence of "a trend, a spiritual and intellectual perspective which permeates and unifies, inspite of all its internal diversity and even polarity, the Russian culture of the nineteenth century and which Berdiaev termed 'the Russian idea'."[144] Though there is no consensus regarding the content of the 'Russian idea,' the general orientation is seen as a move towards a new synthesis between *eschatology* and *history*, towards a reintegration of this world into the perspective of the Kingdom of God. According to him, "It was in Russia indeed that after many centuries of acute 'Westernization' Orthodox theology recovered its genuine sources: the patristic thought, the liturgical tradition, the mystical realism of the spiritual *theoria*."[145]

141. *Ibid.*, 55-56.

142. *Ibid.*, 56-57.

143. The "westernized" Russian intelligentsia, as Berdiaev well put it, "busied itself not with politics but with saving mankind without God. This is exactly the scope and content of western "secularism" which today begins to engulf western Christianity itself. It is time to realize that the Russian Revolution and the pseudo-messianic totalitarianism, which grew out of it, was the triumph on Russian soil of a "Western" idea, the reductio ad absurdum of a Western dream, the literal application of a Western program." *Ibid.*, 56.

144. *Ibid.*, 53.

145. *Ibid.*, 54.

2.2.3. Western World-View

The conversion of Constantine marked a shift in the western worldview. It was the beginning of a new relationship between the Church and the state. It seems that Schmemann understood the western interpretation of Constantine's conversion as a loss of independence at the hands of the Emperor,[146] and as an alliance between Church and state.[147] He interprets this shift as the result of the rejection of the eschatological experience of the early Church, and recognizes this movement as the beginning of secularization. Schmemann contends that even before secularization, the term 'world' was secularized by Christian thought in the West. He considers the abandonment of the eschatological perspective as the rejection of the world's real sanctification by the West.[148] Schmemann calls the transposition in the West from the eschatological perspective of the early Church to the post-Constantine period, 'juridical'. He posits that it is characteristic of western ecclesiastical development that the relationship between Church and state were initially formulated in juridical or legal terms.[149] By appropriating the relation in juridical terms, the West eliminated the antinomy and the tension inherent in the patristic notion of *mysterion* "from its approach to faith, from its ultimate 'intuition' of God and creation, from ecclesiology and soteriology."[150] He characterizes the western world-view as *non-eschatological:*

> The West rationalized the *mysterion,* i.e. deprived it precisely of its antinomical or eschatological character. It replaced the tension, essential in the early Church, between the 'new' and the 'to come,' between the 'old' and the 'new,' with an orderly, stable and essentially extra-temporal distinction between the 'natural' and 'supernatural,' between 'nature' and 'grace;' and

146. *Ibid.*, 38.
147. *Ibid.*, 35-36.
148. *Ibid.*, 61.
149. *Ibid.*, 33, 38.
150. *Ibid.*, 59. It is important to note here that Schmemann is using mysterion from a strictly sacramental point of view. Schmemann even considers this as the basic principle behind all controversies between the East and the West. In his opinion, controversies like "Filioque, original sin, created grace, essence and energies, purgatory, and even the papacy – [...]which to so many today appear totally irrelevant, were transformed into an 'existential' key, explained in terms of their 'practical' significance, it would become clear that their 'common denominator' in the Eastern mind is, first of all, the rejection by the West of the mysterion – the holding together, in a mystical and existential, rather than rational, synthesis of both the total transcendence of God and His genuine presence. But this mystery is precisely that of the Kingdom of God, the faith and the piety of the Christian being rooted in the experience now of that which is to come, in communion by means of 'this world' with Him who is always 'beyond', in truly partaking of 'the joy and the peace of the Holy Spirit" (p. 60).

> then, in order to assure God's total transcendence, it viewed grace itself not as God's very *presence* but as a created 'medium'. Eschatology thus became exclusively 'futuristic,' the Kingdom of God a reality only 'to come' but not to be experienced now as the new life in the Holy Spirit, as the real anticipation of the new creation. Within this new theological framework, 'this world' ceased to be experienced as *passage,* as 'end' to be transfigured into 'beginning,' as the reality where the Kingdom of God is 'at hand'. It acquired a stability, almost a self-sufficiency, a *meaning* of its own, guaranteed to be sure by God *(causa prima, analogia entis),* yet at the same time an autonomous object of knowledge and understanding. For all its 'other-worldliness,' the Latin medieval synthesis was based in fact on the alienation of Christian thought from its eschatological source ... on its own 'secularization'.[151]

He further notes a second "secularization," an inevitable result of the past, which began at the Renaissance and continued in the modern era. This secular worldview was dominant both in the political and intellectual world. Politically the Church "claimed a power superior to that of the state, and intellectually a source of knowledge superior to human reason." He considers both claims as essentially 'juridical' in the sense that it is "extrinsic to the nature of that which they claimed to dominate." The impact of this secularization is a change in relationship of *power* rather than of *essence*. It means that what the 'world' "rejected was an extrinsic submission to the *authority* of the Church, the Church's ultimate 'jurisdiction' over them, but not an essentially 'Christian' idea of state, culture, etc."[152]

Schmemann goes further to a third level of secularization in the West. The main characteristic of the third civilization "lies not in 'secularization' as the world's autonomy from the Church's power and not even in 'secularization' as culture's autonomy from 'religious values'." On the contrary, it lies in the acceptance that Schmemann termed "the *secular eschatology* of the modern secular world."[153] He observes that the west-

151. *Ibid.*

152. *Ibid.*, 61-62. The juridical relationship of the Church and the world means that "as a connection in which those who are connected remain ontologically extrinsic to one another. Within this type of relationship, the Church may dominate and govern the world, as she did in medieval society, or she may be legally separated from it, as she is in our modern era. In both cases and situations, the world as such remains essentially 'secular'." p. 61. He even considers the medieval struggle between the Papacy and the western emperors, Luther's doctrine of the two kingdoms, and the modern theories of the separation of Church and state are ultimately the result of such a juridical approach (pp. 33-34).

153. *Ibid.*, 62. He blames the Church for this change and notes that "it was Christian faith that 'poisoned' the human mind with a certain vision and experience of cosmos and time, of matter and history, that made the 'world' a notion, an experience correlated to

ern Christians, Catholic as well as Protestant, seem to consider 'secularised eschatology' as the criterion of Christian faith, and action as the reference for all Christian renewal, and as the valid framework and content of Christian eschatology. He criticizes the modern trend in theology that emphasizes some form of eschatological faith. According to him:

> [Their interest in eschatology] is based not on an interest in the early eschatology in which the transcendent Kingdom of God and not the world is the *eschaton,* but on the desire to find a common language with the secular world. Even where an attempt is made to preserve the transcendent Kingdom, it is preserved as a vague "horizon of hope" and not as the radical *reality* of all Christian experience. The obsession with "relevance" and "involvement," the incredible discovery of Christ's social and political "radicalism," the enthusiastic "rethinking" of Christianity within the categories of secular utopian ideologies – it all looks as if having at first "secularized" the world for the sake of a totally transcendent God, the Christian West is about to give up the "transcendent" as the very content of Christianity.[154]

He also criticizes the growing interest of the West in the Church's reorientation towards the needs and problems of the world. In his opinion, this "secular" character lies behind the inner motivation, and criterion of all Christian "renewal."[155] In his opinion, it is not faith, but rather "ideology and utopian escapism" that are determining the Christian worldview. He accuses the "theologies of liberation" of making sure that "[i]ssues relating to economics, politics and psychology have replaced a Christian vision of the world at the service of God."[156] Thus, he warns against the current discussions on the Church and its relationship to the world, where themes like religion, politics, justice and development are

that of the Kingdom of God and challenged man with a kind of 'impossible possibility'. And it was the Church in the West that 'gave up' that vision and replaced it with a universe in which no room was left for history and movement, for the historically unique and irreversible, for the dynamic and disturbing ruah of the Spirit" (pp. 62-63).

154. *Ibid.*, 63.

155. *Ibid.*, 58. The Orthodox reaction to this situation "is split between, on the one hand, so radical a rejection of the Western approach that it distorts and vitiates Orthodoxy itself by reducing it to a fearfully "apocalyptic" rejection of the world, and, on the other hand, the search for a compromise which, as all compromises, only increase confusion. There is thus an urgent need to transpose this "feeling" into a more articulate and constructive critique, and this can be done only by referring the present Western trend to the Eastern "experience" in its totality" (p. 59).

156. Schmemann, *The Eucharist: Sacrament of the Kingdom*, 10. According to him, in such trends, it is "Not God, but man has become the measure of all things." Against this he suggests a "eucharistic renewal of the Church" which we shall see later.

dominant.[157] According to him, in the quest for meaning and relevance we missed the transcendent God. In our eagerness to "participate in the struggle of millions of people for greater social justice and for world development," we have lost the soteriological dimension and content of Christian faith.[158]

2.2.4. Critical Dialogue between West and East

Schmemann looks at the Christian worldview of today from a different perspective. First of all, he realizes the problem of distinguishing it between the West and the East. Even before globalization, he noted the existence of different cultures together in one society. As we have already noted the Russian Revolution, the First and Second World Wars and the on-going wars in the Middle-East forced many of the adherents of the eastern Church to abandon their homelands. The dramatic difference in the worldviews between the East and the West has become a very pertinent issue in the context of their integration in the West. The East in the West has been one of Schmemann's important concerns in his theological reflection. He believes that "the culture into which the Orthodox Church was 'exiled' ... were essentially shaped by *secularism* ... whose meaning can and must be found in itself, independently from any reference to the 'transcendent'."[159] Thus, he finds it difficult to transpose Orthodoxy into the cultural categories dominated by Western secularism.[160]

Schmemann defined secularism as a negation of worship. It is the negation of man as a worshipping being, as *homo adorans*.[161] He defines it elsewhere "as the *autonomy* of the secular, i.e. worldly life of man and society from religion and its scale of values, a radical distinction between the religious and the secular 'sectors' of life."[162] Though Schmemann defines secularism as a negation of worship, he also points out that it is not identical with atheism. "A modern secularist quite often accepts the idea of God. What, however, he emphatically negates is precisely the *sacramentality* of man and world. A secularist views the world as con-

157. In presenting a paper in an international symposium on the 'Social and Economic Teaching of the World Council of Churches from Geneva 1966 to Uppsala 1968' Schmemann severely criticized some of the modern trends in linking various social issues with theology: "Theology or Ideology?," 227.

158. Schmemann, "Theology or Ideology?," 229.

159. Schmemann, "Orthodoxy," 521.

160. Schmemann, "Problems of Orthodoxy in America: The Spiritual Problem," 192-193.

161. Schmemann, "Worship in a Secular Age," 4.

162. Schmemann, "Problems of Orthodoxy in America: The Liturgical Problem," 172.

taining within itself its meaning and the principles of knowledge and action."[163] In this sense, he even considers secularism as one of the most dangerous tragedies for Orthodoxy in the West. Furthermore, he calls secularism as the great heresy of our time.[164]

Nevertheless, he blames Christianity for the development of secularism and even calls secularism a "stepchild" of Christianity. It means that unlike the heresies of the patristic age, which were provoked by the encounter between Christianity and Hellenism, secularism "is the result of a 'breakdown' within Christianity itself, of its own deep metamorphosis."[165] At the same time he claims that the Orthodox worldview is beyond such secular view. According to him, Orthodoxy still claims "that the whole life not only belongs to God, but is to be made God-like and God-centered, transformed into communion with God." In this sense there is no activity in the Church which "can be neutral, not capable of being *sanctified*, i.e., transformed into communion with God."[166] He also notes how religious neutrality, that belongs to secular culture, prevents religion from a total "integration" within culture.[167] From this perspective, he always rejected the adaptation of Orthodoxy to the secularist and nominalistic needs of the society.

Although there is much discussion about the Kingdom of God in theological discourse on social justice today, he remains critical. This is because discussions on development tend to limit its goal to 'society' and forget the person in his unique and eternal *hypostasis*.[168] At the same time, Schmemann detects an eschatological longing in the midst of the Christian search for justice:

> While Christians, in their eagerness to be 'relevant,' shift the emphasis from the 'transcendent' to the 'immanent,' one detects in the world a growing thirst for and hunger for that which can *transcend,* i.e. fill life with the ultimate meaning and content. Behind the sometimes cheap and romantically naive rebellion against 'systems' and 'establishment,' behind the rhetoric of 'revolution' and 'liberation,' there is a genuine longing not only for the Absolute but for *communion* with it, for its true possession. Behind the 'juridi-

163. Schmemann, "Worship in a Secular Age," 8. Emphasis added.

164. *Ibid.*, 11. Alexander Schmemann, "The Underlying Question," *Church, World, Mission: Reflections on Orthodoxy in the West*, ed. Alexander Schmemann (Crestwood, NY: St. Vladimir's Seminary Press, 1979) 7-24, p. 22.

165. Schmemann, "Worship in a Secular Age," 11.

166. Schmemann, "Problems of Orthodoxy in America: The Liturgical Problem," 172-173.

167. Schmemann, "Problems of Orthodoxy in America: The Canonical Problem," 77.

168. Schmemann, "Theology or Ideology?," 234.

cal,' it is for the 'eschatological' that the modern man is longing, and this means for the Kingdom of God.[169]

Schmemann criticizes secular approaches that are used in the quest for social justice. He considers the eschatological worldview and experience as the only answer to the world's agonizing problems:

> [W]ithout the recovery of that experience no clear pattern of Christian thought and action can be detected. As long as the Church is imprisoned by the world and its ideologies, as long as she accepts and views all "problems" facing humanity in their secular and worldly formulations, we remain within a vicious circle without any hope of breaking through it. Before it can be put to any "use," the notion of the Kingdom of God is to be purified of all "utilitarianism."[170]

Concluding our discussion on the Christian worldview at various stages in history, one could observe how strongly Schmemann presents the positive aspects of an eschatological worldview and the pitfalls of a secular worldview. The antinomical holding of this world and the world to come is the basis to uncovering his attitude towards the world. As we have noted in the case of sacraments, this tension between being in this world, yet not of this world's, underpins his understanding of the sacramentality of the world.

3. The World as Sacrament

Having seen Schmemann's theological horizon, his notions of sacramental symbolism and worldview, in this section, we look forward to see the sacramentality of Creation and the appropriate Christian response to it. In the first part we shall look at the sacramentality of Creation, based on Schmemann's interpretation of the Creation-Fall-Redemption paradigm. Secondly, we shall see the human response to the sacramentality of Creation.

3.1. Sacramentality of Creation

The sacramentality of Creation must be seen from the Creation-Fall-Redemption paradigm. Often Schmemann claims that the Christian worldview holds these three fundamental principles of Christian faith: Creation, Fall and Redemption in unity.[171] They are considered as the

169. Schmemann, "The 'Orthodox World', Past and Present," 65.
170. *Ibid.*
171. These themes appear several times in Schmemann's writings. See Schmemann,

three fundamental acclamations of Christian faith.[172] Stuhlman observes that this scheme of thought is mainly found in Schmemann's narrative writings on the sacraments rather than in his systematic writings on theological themes.[173]

3.1.1. Creation

Creation[174] is considered as "positive in its origin as well as in its essence."[175] According to Stuhlman, Schmemann works out the goodness of Creation from the perspective of Irenaeus.[176] Accordingly, Schme-

Sacraments and Orthodoxy, 14-22; "The World as Sacrament," 223; "The Problem of the Church's Presence in the World in Orthodox Consciousness," 10-11; "Liturgy and Eschatology," 12-13.

172. Chryssavgis even says that "[w]hen one of these is isolated or violated, the result is an unbalanced and destructive vision of the world." Chryssavgis, "The World as Sacrament: Insights into an Orthodox World-view," 6.

173. Byron Stuhlman, "The Theme of Creation in the Liturgical Theology of Alexander Schmemann," *La Maison Dieu* (1995) 113-127, p. 119.

174. It seems that the discussion on Creation Theology initiated by Vladimir Soloviev (1853-1900) in the Russian Orthodox Church, which led to the beginning of the 'sophiological' School, had an influence in Schmemann in developing his view on the sacramentality of Creation. Influenced by Jacob Boehme, Spinoza, Schopenhauer, Fichte and Hegel, Solovyov sought to combine pantheism with the Christian doctrine of Incarnation. He interpreted the Incarnation as the fulfillment of an ontological and preexisting "becoming of the world into the Absolute." In order to explain this he used the existence of a female principle, 'Sophia' or the world soul. Paul Florensky (1882-1943), Sergius Bulgakov (1871-1944) and Nicholas A. Berdyaev (1874-1948) continued this line of thought, of course, with slight variations. The 'neo-patristic school' of Georges Florovsky, Vladimir Lossky, Meyendorff and Schmemann criticized their approach. Lossky and Meyendorff compared the first to Origen and to Origeneism, and they claimed themselves to that of Athanasius. Schmemann, an ardent member of the neo-Patristic School, although he did not actively participate in these debates delved into these themes from the liturgical and sacramental perspectives. For a short survey of the contemporary discussions on the theology of Creation in the Orthodox tradition see: John Meyendorff, "Creation in the History of Orthodox Theology," *SVTQ* 27 (1983) 27-37.

175. Schmemann, "The Problem of the Church's Presence in the World in Orthodox Consciousness," 10-11. Thus, the Fathers underscore "that even the devil is good by nature and evil only through the misuse of his free will." Schmemann, "Liturgy and Eschatology," 13.

176. For Irenaeus, "the goodness of creation, its original perfection, is understood as a potential for the realization of God's purposes rather than as the accomplished realization of those purposes." Stuhlman, "The Theme of Creation in the Liturgical Theology of Alexander Schmemann," 118-119. Ireneaeus presented a 'Trinitarian theology of Creation' against Gnostics who divided God between the imperfect God of the material creation and the God of salvation who liberates the materiality of created existence. Against this view, he argued that since the world was created through the Son, it is real and good. Furthermore, based on the Incarnation of Jesus, he argued that "there is a continuity be-

mann interprets the goodness of Creation as already present in the first chapter of Genesis. As a sacrament, the Creation is "in itself an essential means both of the knowledge of God and communion with Him."[177] It is these two qualifications, God's revelation and our communion with him, stand as the central notions in understanding the sacramental nature of the world.

Firstly, the revelatory character of God's Creation means that the world, both as cosmos and as time and history, "is an *epiphany* of God" revealing His presence and power.[178] Based on the notion of the world as an epiphany of God, rooted in the thought of Saint Dionysius the Areopagite,[179] he notes that "the world was created as a matter of a sacrament."[180] The goodness of Creation, specifically the world and its his-

tween creation and redemption, between all the will and works of God in and towards the world. It is therefore, according to Irenaeus, the material world as a whole which is destined for redemption, and indeed already participating in it by virtue of the work of the eschatological Spirit." Colin E. Gunton, "Relation and Relativity: The Trinity and the Created World," *Trinitarian Theology Today: Essays on Divine Being and Act*, ed. Christoph Schwöbel (Edinburgh: T & T Clark, 1995) 92-112, p. 97. Irenaeus employed the trinitarian logic of faith "to assert the unity of the divine economy: the God of creation is the God of salvation and the final consummation, and this God is the Father working through his 'two hands' the Son and the Spirit." Christoph Schwöbel, "Christology and Trinitarian Thought," *Trinitarian Theology Today*, 113-146, p. 129. "This trinitarian emphasis on the unity of the divine economy is underpinned by the doctrine of the anakephalaiosis according to which Christ repeats the story of Adam and thereby realizes the image of God that Adam in his immaturity forfeited." Irenaeus, *Adversus Haereses* 5.16.2f. Irenaeus clearly expresses this when he says that the Son and the Spirit are the 'two hands' of God the Father (Irenaeus, *Adversus Haereses* 5.1.3) and "through the Spirit, man ascends to the Son, and through the Son to the Father." Irenaeus, *Adversus Haereses* 3.15.3.

177. Schmemann, "The World as Sacrament," 120.

178. Schmemann, "Worship in a Secular Age," 5. Here it is important to underscore that the cosmic understanding of Schmemann cannot be equated with the pagan understanding of cosmos as nature. On the contrary, from a Christian perspective, he understands it historically.

179. Dionysios the Areopagite is one among the prime exponents of the Orthodox sacramental vision of reality. Eric Justin David Perl, "Symbol, Sacrament, and Hierarchy in Saint Dionysios the Areopagite," *GOTR* 39 (1994) 311-356, p. 321. Perl argues that the "departure from Dionysian apophaticism and cosmic sacramentalism lies at the root of most of the west's vagaries in all areas of theology and, as Father Schmemann has so clearly shown ('Worship' and 'Sacrament', passim), leads inevitably to secularism." *Ibid.*

180. Schmemann, "The World as Sacrament," 223. Victor de Waal observes that God has chosen the created world to communicate Himself sacramentally. Victor de Waal, "Review of *The World as Sacrament*, by Alexander Schmemann," *Sobornost* 5/5 (1967) 374-375. Dionysius regards creation as theophany, the manifestation of God. Perl, "Symbol, Sacrament, and Hierarchy in Saint Dionysios the Areopagite," 313. "From the doctrine that creation is theophany, it follows that the entire cosmos is a symbol of God in the

tory, is a sacrament of the favor of God. It means that through creation "God blessed the world, blessed man, blessed the seventh day (that is, time), and this means that He filled all that exists with His love and goodness, made all this 'very good'."[181] In this regard he argues that our very createdness is an affirmation of God's goodness. Therefore, when we say that we are God's creation, we are affirming that "God's voice is constantly speaking within us and saying to us, 'And God saw everything that he had made, and behold, it was very good' (Gen 1:31)."[182]

Secondly, the purpose of this revelation manifested in Creation is to keep human beings in communion with Him. In this sense, Schmemann argues that God's Creation is His gift to human beings "to make man's life communion with God."[183] This is because "[t]he world was God's gift to us, existing not for its own sake but in order to be transformed, to become life, and so to be offered back as man's gift to God."[184] Human beings are responsible to make this offering possible. From this perspective Schmemann argues that "[m]an was created as a priest."[185] He notes:

> [A]ll rational, spiritual, and other qualities of man, distinguishing from other creatures, have their focus and ultimate fulfillment in this capacity to bless God. ... '*Homo sapiens*', '*homo faber*', ... yes, but first of all, '*homo adorans*'. The first, the basic definition of man is that he is the *priest*. He stands at the centre of the world and unifies it in his act of blessing God, of both receiving the world from God and offering it to God – and by filling the world with this eucharist, he transforms his life, the one that receives from the world, into life in God, into communion.[186]

Schmemann believes that "the unique position of man in the universe is that he alone is to *bless* God for the food and the life he receives from

realist sense of 'symbol'" (p. 320).

181. Schmemann, *Sacraments and Orthodoxy*, 15.

182. Schmemann, "Liturgy and Eschatology," 13.

183. Schmemann, *Sacraments and Orthodoxy*, 14.

184. Schmemann, "The World as Sacrament," 223.

185. *Sacraments and Orthodoxy*, 15.

186. *Ibid.*, 16. According to Schmemann, "in the mythology of creation, man is created a hungry being; that is why God made the world as his food. Man is dependent; dependence is an objective slavery. But if God is the master and we are just slaves, what can He receive from a universe where everything depends on Him? This is where sacrifice centers, and priesthood. The priest is first and foremost the sacrificer ... and so he is the man who can freely transform that dependence: he is the man who can say thank you. For the moment when the slave whom God has created can thank Him for his life and for his food, he is liberated; sacrifice, the thank-offering, is liberating." Alexander Schmemann, "Sacrifice and Worship," *Liturgy and Tradition: Theological Reflections of Alexander Schmemann*, 129-135, p. 132.

him." Moreover, from a biblical perspective, he argues that "to bless God is not a 'religious' or a 'cultic' act, but the very way of *life*."[187] Hence, "[t]he natural dependence of man upon the world was intended to be transformed constantly into communion with God. Man was to be the priest of a eucharist, offering the world to God, and in this offering he was to receive the gift of life."[188]

Thus he considers sacrifice as a natural movement of life.[189] For Schmemann worship is an essential act of the human being and through worship, he enters into communion with God. "[T]he very notion of worship is based on an intuition and experience of the world as an 'epiphany' of God, thus the world – in worship – is revealed in its true nature and vocation as 'sacrament'."[190]

> It is the 'natural sacramentality' of the world that finds its expression in worship and makes the latter the essential ἔργον of man, the foundation and the spring of his life and activities as man. Being the epiphany of God, worship is thus the epiphany of the world; being communion with God, it is the only true communion with the world; being knowledge of God, it is the ultimate fulfilment of human knowledge.[191]

He considers this "*sacramental* character of the world and of man's place in the world" as the basis that determines and shapes worship in general and Christian *leitourgia* in particular.[192]

3.1.2. Fall

The Fall of Creation means the fall of the human being "from the awareness that God is all in all."[193] This means that the Fall is not only alienation from God, but also a failure to accept God's revelation in all Creation. Adam's failure is not the lack of awareness *about* God. On the other hand it is failure "to *know God*, and his life ceased to be that meeting with God, that communion with him – and in him with all of God's creation."[194] Here one could observe how Schmemann makes a distinction

187. Schmemann, *Sacraments and Orthodoxy*, 15.
188. *Ibid.*, 17.
189. Schmemann, "Sacrifice and Worship," 130.
190. Schmemann, "Worship in a Secular Age," 5-6.
191. *Ibid.*, 6.
192. *Ibid.*, 5. Here, he acknowledges the contributions of the 'phenomenology of religion'. In his opinion, "Religionwissenschaft seems to have known more about the nature and meaning of worship than the theologians who kept reducing sacraments to the categories of 'form' and 'matter', 'causality', and 'validity'."
193. Schmemann, *Sacraments and Orthodoxy*, 17.
194. Schmemann, *The Eucharist: Sacrament of the Kingdom*, 175.

between knowledge *about* God and knowledge at an experiential level, i.e. knowledge *of* God.[195] For him, knowledge about God comes under the categorization of the fallen world.[196] Hence, the result of the Fall is mainly the inability to *know God* and a departure from His communion.

The Fall is not only a separation of the human being from communion with God; it is also the separation of the world from God.[197] According to him, "[t]he fall is not that he preferred world to God, distorted the balance between the spiritual and material, but that he made the world *material*, whereas he was to have transformed it into 'life in God,' filled it with meaning and spirit."[198] In other words, what Schmemann tries to underscore is that the Fall is the result of a loss of communion.

And the loss of communion impact human beings' unique role as priest. Schmemann therefore notes that by the Fall the human being lost his "desire to be a priest." Instead of being a priest, he becomes a 'consumer' and considers the world as his right.[199] In particular, in the fallen world, man lost the priestly power to offer the whole world to God.[200] "Man forgot the priesthood which was the purpose and meaning of his life."[201] The experience of the fallen world is that human activities are not in communion with God, and people forget that breathing can be a source of communion with God.[202]

This separation between God and man is the cause of original sin. In other words, sin means "*man has forgotten God.*" This forgetting is not simply to "stop thinking about God," rather, "[i]t is precisely a *falling away* from him, from life, ceasing to live through him and in him." Instead of turning one's love to God, it turned to himself.[203] Hence, "sin is not guilt," but "the rupture from God of life itself." It is not an individual action, but the whole life.[204]

According to Schmemann, the religion of the fallen world cannot redeem the world, "for it has accepted the reduction of God to an area called 'sacred' ('spiritual,' 'supernatural') – as opposed to the world as

195. See how Schmemann has made a similar distinction in the case of sacramental symbolism. See no. 96.

196. Schmemann, *The Eucharist: Sacrament of the Kingdom*, 175.

197. Schmemann, "The 'Orthodox World', Past and Present," 31.

198. Schmemann, *Sacraments and Orthodoxy*, 20.

199. Schmemann, "Sacrifice and Worship," 132.

200. Schmemann, *Sacraments and Orthodoxy*, 17.

201. Schmemann, "The World as Sacrament," 223.

202. Schmemann, *Sacraments and Orthodoxy*, 18.

203. Schmemann, *The Eucharist: Sacrament of the Kingdom*, 126. In this sense he criticises the faithful who, in his opinion, "seek in religion everything imaginable, but not God." *Ibid.*

204. *Ibid.*, 103.

'profane'."[205] It means that in the fallen world "man saw the world as one thing, secular and profane, and religion as something entirely separate, private, remote and 'spiritual'. The sacramental sense of the world was lost."[206] However, Schmemann argues that the Fall "cannot destroy and annihilate the essential goodness of God's creation."[207] Still human beings cannot achieve goodness through their own efforts. Schmemann even says that only "God can save – precisely *save* – us."[208] It is for this reason that God "gave his only-begotten Son for the salvation of the world, in which the Son of God, having become the Son of man, offered himself as the sacrifice for the life of the world."[209]

3.1.3. Redemption

Redemption is the restoration of the human being and the world from the state of the Fall. Through redemption the human being is redeemed to return to the awareness of God and to His communion. Through redemption "Christ restored to creation its potential of being sacrifice to God and restored to humanity its vocation as *homo adorans* to offer it." In "Christ the whole world has become sacrament and sacrifice, for in the whole world ... God's grace is encountered."[210] In the place of the Old Testament religion, Jesus abolished religion and opened a new way of life. It is a life in union with Jesus.[211] For him "religion is nothing other than *thirst for God*."[212] This desire for God comes from our knowledge of God. The knowledge of God, which Jesus speaks of, is eternal life.[213] It is this knowledge that allows the human being to love and to strive for God in order to have communion with God. Therefore, there is only one sin: "not wanting God and being separated from him."[214]

205. Schmemann, *Sacraments and Orthodoxy*, 17.

206. Schmemann, "The World as Sacrament," 223. The dichotomy between sacred and profane originated in this context.

207. Schmemann, "The Problem of the Church's Presence in the World in Orthodox Consciousness," 11.

208. Schmemann, *The Eucharist: Sacrament of the Kingdom*, 103.

209. *Ibid.*, 103-104.

210. Fagerberg, *What is Liturgical Theology?*, 269.

211. Schmemann, *Sacraments and Orthodoxy*, 21.

212. Schmemann, *The Eucharist: Sacrament of the Kingdom*, 102. This thirst is something very deep as the Psalmist says: "'My soul thirst for God, for the living God' (Ps 42:2) ... than contemporary man does, with all his 'spiritualized' religion, abstract 'moralism' and dried-up intellectualism." *Ibid.*

213. *Ibid.*, 175. "This is eternal life, that they know thee the only true God." Jn 17:3.

214. *Ibid.*, 102.

The ultimate experience of redemption is "the salvation of the world."[215] Redemption of the world means "to place it in the perspective of the Kingdom of God as its end and ultimate term of reference, to make it transparent to the Kingdom as its sign, means and 'instrument'."[216] As we shall see this is the experience of the Church in the liturgy and the experience that guides the human beings in their mission.

In this case, it is also important to note that redemption is not only the work of Jesus; rather, it is the manifestation of the kenotic love of the Trinity. The kenotic love of Christ, which reached its climax on the Cross, is the manifestation of the Trinitarian love for all. In Schmemann's words:

> [I]n Christ 'God so loved the world that he gave his only Son,' and in Christ man so loved God that he gave himself totally, and in this twofold giving nothing remains not given, and love regains in all – 'the crucifying love of the Father, the crucified love of the Son, and love of the Spirit triumphing through the power of the cross'.[217]

This kenotic love comes to its climax in Jesus. In Jesus, we see the descent of God's love towards mankind and the ascent of human love towards God. This love becomes the basis of Christianity. Thus, he notes: "The newness of Christianity lies not in the commandment to love, but in the fact that it has become possible to fulfil the commandment. In union with Christ we receive his love and can love with it and grow in it."[218]

In short, Schmemann believes that these triune intuitions we received from God, i.e. world as created, fallen, yet redeemed are "our key to all the problems which today trouble the world."[219] It also means to say that "[o]n the one hand, sacrament is rooted in the nature of the world as created by God: it is always a restoration of the original pattern of things. On the other hand, it is rooted in Christ personally. Only through the perfect man can the broken priesthood of humanity be restored."[220]

215. Schmemann, "The Problem of the Church's Presence in the World in Orthodox Consciousness," 11.

216. Schmemann, "The 'Orthodox World', Past and Present," 31.

217. Schmemann, *The Eucharist: Sacrament of the Kingdom*, 104. The last quote within the quote is from Filaret (Drozdov), Metropolitan of Moscow, Homily on Holy Friday, in Sermons and Discourses, 1 (St Petersburg, 1873).

218. *Ibid.*, 136.

219. Schmemann, "Liturgy and Eschatology," 13.

220. Schmemann, "The World as Sacrament," 224.

3.2. *Christian* Leitourgia *and Celebration of the Kingdom of God in the World*

The Creation-Fall-Redemption paradigm is celebrated in Christian *leitourgia.* In other words the Christian *leitourgia* is the celebration, or thanksgiving, of God's gift to humanity in Creation. In this sense Schmemann notes that it is "the liturgical experience and the liturgical testimony which enables us to sing, 'Heaven and earth are full of thy glory'; it is here that we restore, or at least have the possibility of restoring, the essential Christian vision of the world."[221] Human beings who are raised back to priesthood are now in a position to experience God and the world in their celebration. Thus, Christian *leitourgia* brings together, within one symbol, the three levels of Christian faith and life: the Church, the World, and the Kingdom.[222] It is for this reason that we shall unfold how the three levels – ecclesial, cosmic and eschatological – of Christian faith are demonstrated in the writings of Schmemann.

3.2.1. Church as Sacrament

The sacramental meaning and experience of the Church is a central point in Alexander Schmemann. Although it is central to Schmemann, a clear definition, or even discussion of ecclesiology had a late origin in the Orthodox churches. Applying the hermeneutical principle of context in the development of a doctrine,[223] Schmemann argues that the absence of doctrinal development of the Church in the Orthodox tradition marks the absence of any doctrinal crisis, such as the Reformation or Counter-Reformation in the West.[224] The absence of clear definitions or dogma,

221. Schmemann, "Liturgy and Eschatology," 12.

222. Schmemann, "Sacrament and Symbol," 151.

223. This is applicable in the case of any doctrinal development. In the case of sacramentology, for example, the magisterial teaching on sacraments appeared in the context of abuses or errors in its practice. This is very clear in the doctrinal formulation of Tridentine teaching on the sacraments. Rather than positively asserting what a sacrament is, Trent was preoccupied in answering the criticisms and also in avoiding its misuse. Secondly, the ecclesial and personal contexts of the authors are also important. Kevin W. Irwin, "Sacramentality and the Theology of Creation: A Recovered Paradigm for Sacramental Theology," *LS* 23 (1998) 159-179, pp. 159-161.

224. Alexander Schmemann, "The Missionary Imperative," *Church, World, Mission,* ed. Alexander Schmemann (Crestwood, NY: St. Vladimir's Seminary Press, 1979) 209-216, p. 210. Schmemann traces the origin of such a need to the 1920s (Stockholm 1925 and Lausanne 1927) when the Orthodox Church became involved in the ecumenical movement. "[F]or the first time the Orthodox were requested not only to state their ecclesiological beliefs, but also to explain them, i.e., to express them in consistent theological terms." *Ibid.*, 210-211. Although he claimed that it was difficult to do so, due to theological presuppositions that make it difficult to agree on common theological terms and lan-

however, does not exclude the importance of ecclesiology. On the contrary, as from the very beginning, the Orthodox Church understood ecclesiology as the experience of the Church in the liturgy. In speaking of the sacramentality of the Church, three things are important: the liturgical experience, the celebrant and mission of the Church.

3.2.1.1. Church as Liturgical Experience

The centrality of liturgy, which Schmemann applies to sacraments, theology etc., should also be seen in relation to the Church.[225] According to Schmemann, Christian *leitourgia* remains at the centre of the expression of the Church. Christianity is the "*sui generis* experience of the Church,"[226] and "is primarily the experience given and received in the Church's *leitourgia* – in her lex orandi."[227] Elsewhere, he notes that the Church "creates, manifests and fulfils herself in and through the sacraments."[228] This is because "the *ecclesia* exists in and through the *leitourgia*, and its whole life is a *leitourgia*."[229] Hence, the Easterners use description rather than mere propositions to express faith. Their criteria lie not in formal and autonomous 'authorities,' but in adequacy to and consistency with the inner life and experience of the Church.[230] Orthodoxy's uniqueness is that it expresses its faith in and through the worship of the Church that gives meaning and definition to Orthodox ecclesiology.

This experience of the Church in the liturgy is demonstrated in its fullness in the Eucharist. Therefore, the Orthodox theologians generally

guage, one could see various efforts in articulating the divergent views thereafter.

225. We have seen already the importance Schmemann placed on the inter-relation of liturgy and sacraments and liturgy/sacraments and theology in the first chapter. We also delineated the importance of leitourgia in understanding sacramental symbolism. Although not fundamentally different from the earlier references, the focus of this section is on the Christian experience of being Church. In other words, we will discuss the ecclesial dimension of the Church. Paul Meyendorff observes that the experience of the liturgy, as the "source for the knowledge of God and for participation in divine life itself," is the most perfect expression and realization of theosis or divinization. Meyendorff, "Liturgy and Spirituality I: Eastern Liturgical Theology," 351.

226. Schmemann, "The Underlying Question," 20. For him, experience as unique and sui generis means the experience that cannot be reduced to the categories of the "subjective" and "objective," "individual" and "corporate." It is the experience of the Church as new reality in terms of "creation and life renewed and transformed in Christ, made into the knowledge of and communion with God and His eternal Kingdom."

227. Schmemann, "Liturgy and Theology," 54-55.

228. Schmemann, *The Eucharist: Sacrament of the Kingdom*, 35-36.

229. Schmemann, "Theology and Liturgical Tradition," 17.

230. Schmemann, "Liturgy and Theology," 54. He also calls the Eucharist 'the sacrament of the Church'. Id., "Theology and Eucharist," 12.

classify it in terms of 'eucharistic ecclesiology'.[231] It means that the Church is not that "generates" the liturgy, whilst, it is the Eucharist that "'generates' the Church, makes her to be what she is."[232] As we have already noted, it is in the liturgy, in particular in the Eucharist, "the Church accomplishes the *passage* from this world into the world to come."[233] And this passage constitutes the very essence of the Church's life.[234] The Eucharist is the very celebration of this passing from the old to the new. In his words:

> The basic act of this fulfillment, and therefore the true 'form' of the Church, is the Eucharist: the sacrament in which the Church performs the passage, the *passover*, from this world into the Kingdom, offers in Christ the whole creation to God, seeing it as 'heaven and earth full of His glory', and partakes of Christ's immortal life at His table in His Kingdom.[235]

The Church, as a passage from this world to the other world, denotes the cosmic and eschatological dimensions. It is in this sense that he calls

231. It seems that Afanassieff develops his "eucharistic ecclesiology" from this perspective. See Schmemann, "The Idea of Primacy in Orthodox Ecclesiology," 55. [For a detailed study on eucharistic ecclesiology of Afanassieff see: Nichols, *Theology in the Russian Diaspora: Church, Fathers, Eucharist in Nikolai Afanas'ev (1893-1966)*; M. Edmund Hussey, "Nicholas Afanassiev's Eucharistic Ecclesiology: A Roman Catholic Viewpoint," *JES* 12 (1975) 235-252.] As Michael Plekon observes, Schmemann along with his professors Frs Kern, Afanasiev and Bulgakov, rediscovered the Church as a eucharistic community. In his opinion, "the eucharistic ecclesiology or ecclesial sense of the Eucharist becomes the unifying thread of all his writing and teaching." Michael Plekon, "The Church, the Eucharist and the Kingdom: Towards an Assessment of Alexander Schmemann's Theological Legacy," *SVTQ* 40/3 (1996) 119-143, p. 130. It seems to us that Schmemann went beyond Afanassief and developed the notion of 'eucharistic theology'. "The term 'eucharistic eccelesiology' has been recently introduced into our theological vocabulary. One can speak of even greater reasons for eucharistic theology." He also claims "that Orthodox theology is by its very nature 'eucharistic'. ... It means that in the life of the Church the Eucharist is the moment of truth which makes it possible to see the real 'objects' of theology: God, man and the world, in the true light, which, in other words, reveals both the objects of theology as they really are and gives the necessary light for their understanding'. Alexander Schmemann, "Theology and Eucharist," 22. It confirms the dictum of St Irenaeus: "Our teaching is confirmed to the Eucharist, and the Eucharist confirms our teaching." *Adversus Haereses*, 4.18.5, *PG* 7, 1027-1029. (Nostra autem consonans est sententia, et Eucharistia rursus confirmat sententiam nostram.) This definition appears often in Schmemann's writings. For example see "Theology and Liturgical Tradition," 12; "Theology and Eucharist," 23.

232. Schmemann, "Theology and Eucharist," 17.

233. Schmemann, "The Missionary Imperative," 212.

234. Alexander Schmemann, "Towards a Theology of Councils," *SVSQ* 6 (1962) 170-184, p. 172.

235. Alexander Schmemann, "Ecclesiological Notes," *SVSQ* 11 (1967) 35-39, p. 37.

the Eucharist the "sacrament of the Church" and the "sacrament of the Kingdom." It means "Kingdom, which for 'this world' is *yet to come* and forms the ultimate horizon of its history, is already present ... in the Church. And it is the liturgy which accomplishes this presence and *parousia*."[236]

Moreover, Schmemann criticizes the West for reducing worship "as a function of the Church" and Church "as a function of worship."[237] Schmemann calls the former *leitourgia* and the latter cult. In this understanding we miss "the very epiphany of the cosmic and eschatological 'content' of the Church's faith and thus of the Church herself."[238] The reduction of liturgy into cultic categories weakened its ecclesial vision. Accordingly, "[w]orship has become the only *content* of Church life, an end in itself." By reducing worship into the content of Church life, "it has lost its real power: to express, edify and fulfil the Church."[239] In other words, "worship has ceased to be the self-expression of the Church."[240] Because of this reduction Schmemann argued for:

> [T]he rediscovery of the 'leiturgia' in its relation to the Church, as the *expression* of the Church, as the act which actualizes and fulfils the Church – 'makes her what she is'. ... it was a return from the pietistic and individualistic conception of worship to its understanding as the self-revelation of the Church. It was a return – through the 'leiturgia' – to the Church, and through the Church to the 'leiturgia'.[241]

The liturgy or the Eucharist as the expression of the Church also underscores the priestly role of the human being. To understand this, we must look at the notion of the "sacrament of the assembly."

3.2.1.2. Church and Its Institutional Character

The understanding of the Church (liturgy and in particular Eucharist), as a passage from this world to the other world, stands at the center of the understanding of the Church. "Essential as it is for the Church as *sign* and *sacrament*, the institution cannot be simply identified with the Church. As institution the Church is of 'this world,' as fulfillment she is of 'the world to come'."[242] Therefore, the Church is understood as "the mystery

236. Schmemann, "Liturgical Theology: Remarks on Method," 142-143.
237. Schmemann, *Introduction to Liturgical Theology*, 23.
238. Schmemann, "Liturgy and Theology," 58.
239. Schmemann, "Liturgical Theology: Its Task and Method," 26.
240. *Ibid.*, 25.
241. *Ibid.*, 18.
242. Schmemann, "The 'Orthodox World', Past and Present," 38-39.

of the new creation and … the mystery of the Kingdom."[243] "It is the mystery of the Church as new creation in its two dimensions – the cosmic and eschatological – that reveals to us the meaning and structure of the Church as *institution*."[244]

For Schmemann, "[t]he Church is a divine institution, founded not by men, but by Christ, receiving her life from God and having one specific goal: to save people by introducing them into the life of grace, forgiveness, love and truth, by uniting them to the life of Christ Himself."[245] He observes:

> In the patristic perspective, the Church is primarily the gift of new life, but this life is not that *of the Church*, but the life of Christ in us, our life in Him. For the Church is not a 'being' in the sense which God or man may be called 'beings' ('hypostasized natures' to use the ancient terminology), she is not a new 'nature' added to the existing natures of God and man, she is not a 'substance'. The term *new* applied to her – new life, new creation – does not mean an ontological newness, the appearance of a 'being' which did not exist before, it means the redeemed, renewed and transfigured relationship between the only 'substantial' beings: God and His creation.[246]

Hence, the Church as the Body of Christ is not merely symbolic, but expresses the very nature of the Church.[247] The Church in its structure as hierarchical, sacramental or liturgical "has no other function than to make the Church ever capable of fulfilling itself as the Body of Christ, as the Temple of the Holy Spirit, to actualize its very nature as grace."[248]

He criticizes the recent trend of understanding the Church from the secular perspective as a society or an organization.[249] He sees this as the

243. Schmemann, "Liturgy and Theology," 57.

244. Schmemann, "Ecclesiological Notes," 36-37.

245. Schmemann, "The Church is Hierarchical," *SVSQ* 3/4 (1959) 36-41, pp. 36-37.

246. Schmemann, "Theology and Eucharist," 14-15. For this reason Schmemann notes that in the iconographical tradition of Orthodoxy there is "no icon of the Church, because an icon implies necessarily a 'hypostasized nature', the reality of a substantial and personal 'being' and in this sense the Church is not a 'being'. Yet, on the other hand, each icon – that of Christ, of the Theotokos, of any saint – is always and essentially an icon of the Church, because it manifests and reveals the new life of a being, the reality of its transfiguration, of its passage into the 'new eon' of the Holy Spirit, this being precisely the manifestation of the Church. Therefore, the concepts of 'organism' or 'body' can be utterly misleading if, in a definition of the Church, they precede and give foundation to, that of 'life'. It is not because she is an 'organism' that the Church gives us the 'new life', but the new life given in her, or rather, the Church as new life, makes as an organism, transforms us into the Body of Christ, reveals us as 'new being'" (p. 15).

247. Alexander Schmemann, "The Idea of Primacy in Orthodox Ecclesiology," p. 52.

248. Schmemann, "The Missionary Imperative," 212.

249. Schmemann, "Problems of Orthodoxy in America: The Spiritual Problem," 173.

result of its reduction to certain categories and the use of some philosophical and theological clues.[250] He observes a tendency in "westernizing" theological systems to reduce ecclesiology to the question of the institutional aspect of the Church. Thus the post-Tridentine *De Ecclesia*

> focuses the attention almost exclusively on the 'institution,' and away from its cosmic and eschatological nature and goal. It makes 'institution' a kind of end in itself, and in doing this, in apparently exalting the Church, it, in fact, tragically mutilates her; making her as we see it today more and more 'irrelevant' for the world, less and less 'expressive' of the Kingdom of God.[251]

It does not mean that the institutional aspect of the Church is secondary and non-essential. Rather, he understands the institution as the means of her expression and actualization in 'this world,' of her identity with, and participation in, the reality of the new being.[252] In order to bring this about, Schmemann suggests a theological rediscovery of the Eucharist. It means "the rediscovery of the Church *in actu*, the Church as the sacrament of Christ, of His 'parousia' – *the coming* and *presence* of the Kingdom which is *to come*."[253]

According to Schmemann, the "eucharistic conversion" of theology helps the theologian to liberate himself from the dead authority of pseudo-traditional systems, puts him into direct contact with the whole of

250. Schmemann, "Theology and Eucharist," 13. He observes, "If, in the past, the Church was identified too exclusively with hierarchy and institution, there is a tendency now to just as exclusively identify her with an 'organism'. The Fathers, we are told, have not left with us any precise definition of the Church's nature or essence. Consequently, theologians reconstruct what seems to them to be the patristic ecclesiology, not discerning too often that, in fact, this overwhelming 'organic' ecclesiology reflects some contemporary philosophical and sociological doctrines more than the experience of the early Church."

251. Schmemann, "Liturgy and Theology," 57. Schmemann classifies the post-Tridentine De Ecclesia as mother and pattern, not only of modern western ecclesiology, but of the eastern one as well.

252. Schmemann, "Towards a Theology of Councils," 172. This does not mean that he is not concerned about the organizational Church. In the context of Diaspora, Schmemann argues for the local Orthodox Church avoiding any ethnic barriers. According to Meyendorff: "[T]ogether with most representatives of the 'younger' generation of Orthodox theologians, Fr. Schmemann saw no other answer and no other meaning for the existence of the 'Diaspora' than the establishment of the territorial, eventually French-speaking local Church in France." Meyendorff, "A Life Worth Living," 6. He further adds, "if there was any commitment which was constant in his life, already in France, it was the hope that the uncanonical overlapping of 'jurisdictions', which was the single most obvious obstacle to Orthodox witness in the West, would be replaced by local Church unity in conformity not only with canons, but with the most essential requirements of Orthodox ecclesiology." *Ibid.*, 8.

253. Schmemann, "Theology and Eucharist," 22.

reality: God, man and the world.[254] He also underscores the need for a "eucharistic renewal of the Church," against secularist tendencies that dominate Christian thinking.[255] Schmemann even notes that the "[r]eturn to Bible, return to Fathers ... means, above all, the return to the Church through the Eucharist and to the Eucharist through the Church."[256]

3.2.1.3. Sacrament of the Assembly and Priesthood

The mission of the resurrected Christ is continued in the Church. In this sense, Jesus' call "to abide in his love" (Jn 15:4,5,9) "means to be and to live in the Church."[257] Therefore, "[t]he essence of the Church lies in the manifestation and presence in the world of love as life and life as love."[258] This is manifested primarily in the act of liturgy, and it is clear that all liturgies emphasize an "indispensable correlationship between the Liturgy and an assembly, between the Eucharist as the actualization of the Church, as *ecclesia*, as a gathering."[259] It is in this sense that Schmemann calls the Eucharist the 'sacrament of the assembly' in line with the fifth-century author of the *Areopagitica*.[260] For Schmemann, gathering of the faithful "was always considered the first and basic act of the Eucharist."[261] It is "a function or 'ministry' of a man or of a group on behalf of and in the interest of the whole community."[262]

Christian *leitourgia* underscores the corporate nature of worship and, therefore, the involvement and participation of the whole community in the liturgy and in the making of the Church. This corporate nature of

254. *Ibid.*, 21.

255. Schmemann, *The Eucharist: Sacrament of the Kingdom*, 10.

256. Schmemann, "Theology and Eucharist," 23.

257. Schmemann, *The Eucharist: Sacrament of the Kingdom*, 136.

258. *Ibid.*, 137.

259. Schmemann, *Introduction to Liturgical Theology*, 99.

260. Schmemann, *The Eucharist: Sacrament of the Kingdom*, 12. [Ecclesiastical Hierarchy 3.] Schmemann elaborates this theme in the first chapter entitled "Sacrament of the Assembly" in The Eucharist: Sacrament of the Kingdom, 11-26. The Orthodox tradition places the Eucharist in high esteem and it is even called the 'sacrament of sacraments' (teleton telete). *Ecclesiastica Hierarchia*, III, I, *PG* 3, 423-424C.

261. *Ibid.*, 15.

262. Schmemann, *Sacraments and Orthodoxy*, 28. The idea of assembly and concelebration is also expressed in the setting of the Church. In this sense, Schmemann recalls the idea of the original Christian temple as "domus ecclesiae, the site of gathering of the Church together and the eucharistic breaking of bread." It is not only the gathering of baptised Christians, but of the whole Creation. In his opinion, the Church, which assembles in the Temple as *sobor* (in Russian it means: assembly or council and cathedral) is "the gathering together of heaven and earth and all creation in Christ – which constitutes the essence and purpose of the Church." Schmemann, *The Eucharist: Sacrament of the Kingdom*, 19.

worship underscores not only the importance of the participants, but it also contributes a great deal in the understanding of the Church.[263] This is clear from the fact that our purpose of going to Church is not "for individual prayer but to *assemble together as the Church*" and, together with the faithful, "*to constitute the church.*"[264] He also notes that "the *assembling as the Church* is above all the sacrament of love. We go to the church *for love*, for the new love of Christ himself, which is granted to us in our unity. We go to the church so that ... *constituting* the body of Christ, we can abide in Christ's love and manifest it in the world."[265] In this sense the priesthood of the Church is to share in "the priesthood of Christ, ... who through his own offering of himself sanctified the Church and granted her participation in his priesthood and in his sacrifice."[266] Therefore, "the eucharistic sacrifice was offered not only on behalf of all and for all, but *by all*, and therefore the real offering by each of his own gift, his own sacrifice, was a basic condition of it."[267] "We are ordained so that, together constituting the Church, we may offer his sacrifice for the sins of the world, and in offering it, witness to salvation."[268]

He emphasizes the "person" of Christ "for Christ's priesthood consists in his *personal* self-sacrifice to God and to mankind." Thus "the calling to the priesthood itself is directed to the *person* of the one called and is inseparable from it." Therefore, Jesus' "teaching is inseparable from his *person*." From this sense he argues that it is false to distinguish between "priesthood" and "personality." In his opinion, such distinguishing will distort "the essence of priesthood as the continuation in the church of the priesthood of Christ."[269]

Furthermore, the Eucharist denotes the meeting of divine-human dimensions. This meeting of divine and human makes it a sacrament. The Church and liturgy are at the same time a 'God-centered' and a 'human-centered' reality. On the one hand, the Church is a gift from God. It is primarily "a God-created and God-given reality, the presence of Christ's new life, the manifestation of the new 'aeon' of the Holy Spirit." On the other hand, the Church is a "*human response* to the divine gift, its acceptance and appropriation by man and humanity." While the Church, as a God-centered reality, denotes "the mystical nature of Christian life, as life 'hidden with Christ in God,'" the Church as a world-centered reality

263. Schmemann, *Of Water and the Spirit: A Liturgical Study of Baptism*, 8.
264. Schmemann, *The Eucharist: Sacrament of the Kingdom*, 23.
265. *Ibid.*, 138.
266. *Ibid.*, 115.
267. *Ibid.*, 107.
268. *Ibid.*, 92.
269. *Ibid.*, 117.

denotes "the understanding of the Church as being left in this world, in its time, space and history, with a specific task or mission."[270] This meeting or encounter between God and human in the Church is the center from where one moves to God and to the world. As a God-centered reality, the Church acknowledges God's gift and returns to God. This we express in the Eucharist with the ascension to God. It is "the sacrifice of the whole world to God, the intercession for the whole world before God." Its human-centeredness exhorts us to return to the world with the grace we received. It begins where the first movement ends – that of "return into the world." According to Schmemann, "The Eucharist is always the End, the sacrament of the *parousia*, and yet it is always the *beginning*, the *starting point*: now mission begins." The objects and goals of mission are man and world.[271]

The entire life of the Church is based on the conjoining of two seemingly contradictory affirmations. "On the one hand the Church, like Christ, and because of she is Christ's, is directed to the whole world, to all of creation, to all humanity. ... He is the *Saviour of the world.* On the other hand, the Church affirms that through his saving love Christ is turned to each human being, for each human being." Christian prayers reflect this theme as well. Therefore, on the one hand, the prayers "call man to the unity of love and faith, in order to fulfil the Church as the body of Christ." On the other hand, it is "directed to the whole – to the entire creation, the whole world, all mankind – and to each unique and unrepeatable human person."[272]

As noted above, Schmemann's interpretation of the 'sacrament of the assembly' offers a better place for the participation of the laity in the liturgy. According to him "ordo is entirely ... constructed on the principle of correlation – the mutual dependence of the celebrant of the service and the people. One may even more precisely define this bond as a *co-serving* or *concelebration*."[273] Already in 1957, he wrote: "It is in the liturgy, i.e., in the priestly function of the church that the participation of the laity is the most active. Father Afanassiev terms this participation *concelebration of the laos with the celebrant*. The function of the clergy implies that of the laity, and although they cannot be confused, neither can exist or be fulfilled without the other."[274] Furthermore, "[t]he eucharistic celebra-

270. Schmemann, "The Missionary Imperative," 212-214.

271. *Ibid.*, 215.

272. Schmemann, *The Eucharist: Sacrament of the Kingdom*, 82.

273. *Ibid.*, 14. He acknowledges Nicholas Afanassiev for the expression co-serving or concelebration.

274. Alexander Schmemann, "Review of *The Service of the Laity in the Church* (in Russian), by Nicholas Afanassief," *SVSQ* 1/1 (1957) 41-44, pp. 42-43.

tion is not something performed by the clergy for the benefit of the laity who 'attend'. Rather it is the ascension of the Church to the place where she belongs *in statu patriae*. It is also her subsequent return to this world: her return with power to preach the Kingdom of God."[275] This passing from this world to the other world is not limited to the clergy, but extended to all.

Although Orthodox theology strongly emphasizes the corporate nature of worship, Schmemann is aware of the changes that took place due to the western and secular attitude that dominates the Church. "The experience of worship has long ago ceased to be that of a corporate liturgical act. It is an aggregation of individuals coming to Church, attending worship in order to satisfy individually their individual religious needs, not in order to *constitute* and to *fulfil* the Church."[276]

He also criticized the reduction of priesthood into 'clericalism' and '*laicism*'. In his opinion, "the reduction of 'ministry' to the clergy alone and the consequent atrophy in the consciousness of the laity, led to the gradual demise of the *sacrificial* perception of the Church- the eucharist."[277] He also criticizes the laity, who perceives "the Church as existing for themselves," rather than "themselves as the Church transformed and eternally being transformed into a sacrifice and offering to God, into participants in the sacrificial ministry of Christ."[278]

Although Schmemann criticizes the overemphasis on the ministerial priesthood, he upholds the uniqueness of priesthood in that "[i]t is *only* the priest who is called and ordained to affirm this identity, to manifest and fulfil it in the mystery of the eucharist." In this ministry we share "the same indivisible priesthood of Christ, which eternally lives and is eternally fulfilled in the Church, the body of Christ."[279] For him the priest "is called and appointed in the Church, the body of Christ, to be the *image* of the Head of the body – Christ – and this means to be the one

275. Schmemann, "Liturgy and Eschatology', 12.

276. Schmemann, "Theology and Eucharist," 13.

277. Schmemann, *The Eucharist: Sacrament of the Kingdom*, 114.

278. *Ibid.*

279. *Ibid.*, 115. He also criticises the Latin reduction of sacraments to *ex opere operato* and to *ex opere operantis*. Nevertheless, "[i]n the Orthodox perception of the Church, both the absolute non-dependence of the gift that God has given on any earthly, human 'causality' whatsoever, and the personal character of this gift, whose reception depends, consequently, on the person to whom it is given, are equally self-evident." p. 116. It means "[t]he crude popular expression 'as is the priest, so is the parish' has greater truth than all the cunning reasoning about *ex opere operato* and *ex opere operantis*" (p. 117).

through whom the *personal* ministry of Christ is continued and realized."[280]

3.2.2. Cosmic Dimension of Christian Leitourgia

The cosmic dimension of Christian *leitourgia* – Church – explicates how the Church "manifests in 'this world' the genuine world of God, as he first created it."[281] It is the awareness of the renewed nature of Creation manifested in the Church. In this sense, Schmemann underscores the importance of the "*correlation* of the Church and the world." For him, "'assembly as the Church' is above all the joy of the regenerated and renewed creation, *the gathering of the world*." He further notes that "the sacrament of the Church – the eucharist" is "the sacrament of the world."[282] In other words, "what is being redeemed, renewed and transfigured through her is not the 'Church,' but the old life itself, the old Adam and the whole of creation."[283]

The goodness of Creation is celebrated in the Eucharist. It is expressed in the eucharistic anaphora by raising the offerings to God. "The divine liturgy – the continual ascent, the lifting up of the Church to

280. *Ibid.*

281. *Ibid.*, 35. It is important to note that the cosmic dimension is not based on the observation of nature as seasons or cyclical movement of stars but on history. It is an event beginning with Creation and culminating in the Parousia. Zizioulas makes a clear distinction of this. In his opinion, "Humanity's relation with God did not pass through nature but through obedience to the will of God, a fact that gave to Christian spirituality an ethical character ("doing the truth") and a strongly personalist dimension: it was through personal relationships that the human person's union with God was realized." John D. Zizioulas, "The Early Christian Community," *Christian Spirituality*, ed. Bernard McGinn & John Meyendorff, World Spirituality, 16 (New York: Crossroad, 1985) 23-43, p. 23. In Zizioulas' opinion, the cosmic dimension of the Church is neither to be understood in the sense of cosmic mysticism that has the danger of absorbing Creation into the divine and can lead to paganism, nor "in the sense of Teilhard de Chardin's vision of things which implies that the entire cosmos ... develops ... into the reality of Christ." Conversely, it has to be understood from an anthropocentric view of the cosmos and from an anthropological approach to the mystery of Christ. John D. Zizioulas, "The Mystery of the Church in Orthodox Tradition," *One in Christ* 24 (1988) 294-303, pp. 302-303.

282. Schmemann, *The Eucharist: Sacrament of the Kingdom*, 53. It seems that the early Church emphasised Eucharist as the sacrament of the world from a soteriological sense based on the Pauline understanding of the Eucharist. As Petros Vassiliadis notes, it is a shift from "the (eucharistic) experience to the (Christian) message, from eschatology to Christology (and further and consequently to soteriology), from the event (the Kingdom of God), to the bearer and centre of this event (Christ, and more precisely his sacrifice on the cross)." Petros Vassiliadis, "Eucharistic and Therapeutic Spirituality," *GOTQ* 42 (1997) 1-23, p. 5.

283. Schmemann, "Theology and Eucharist," 15.

heaven, to the throne of glory, to the unfading light and joy of the kingdom of God – is the focus of this experience, simultaneously its source and presence, gift and fulfilment."[284] According to Schmemann, our offering of bread and wine is not only an act that makes it relevant to Christ's offering, but it also relates "that offering to the facts, the physical basis of our human condition as it has existed from the very beginning."[285] The bread and wine symbolize Creation.

> These things [bread and wine] placed upon the altar acquire thereby a separate and sacred character. They stand close to the veil that separates our world, our daily experience from God's life, and soon they pass through that veil. But it is bread and wine that make that transition, and they do so not merely as fruits of this world – of this cornfield, that vineyard – but as symbols and even as vehicles of the whole world itself in its entirety.[286]

The bread and wine offered in the Eucharist represent the whole world in Jesus being offered to the Father.[287] "[O]ur initial offering in the Eucharist is not merely of two things but also of our whole world, our whole life in all its dimensions."[288] For him these gifts are holy and divine in the same way "as the humanity of Christ is divine and holy, the beginning and gift of the 'new creation,' the new life."[289] The whole world is considered sacramental because of its transformation into real life.[290] In this sense, he even says: "[T]he bread and wine is what is to

284. Schmemann, *The Eucharist: Sacrament of the Kingdom*, 164.

285. Schmemann, "The World as Sacrament," 223. Chryssavgis expresses it well that "a sacrament remains – in all its transcendence – an historical event, demanding material expression. When God is manifest in time and space, and the Eucharist is God's revelation in bread and wine, then the world becomes the historical and material sacrament of the presence of God, transcending the ontological gap between created and uncreated. The world relates in very tangible terms the cooperation between divine and human in history, denoting the presence of God in our very midst." Chryssavgis, "The World as Sacrament: Insights into an Orthodox World-view," 5.

286. Schmemann, "The World as Sacrament," 222. The bread and wine acquire sacred character because they symbolizes creation. According to him, "the wine is a eucharistic gift not because it looks like blood, but because blood is life, and wine is something which makes the heart of man glad." Schmemann, "Sacrifice and Worship," 130-131.

287. Schmemann, "The World as Sacrament," 224.

288. *Ibid.*, 222.

289. Schmemann, *The Eucharist: Sacrament of the Kingdom*, 118.

290. Schmemann, "The World as Sacrament," 223. Schmemann also considers the transforming quality of Creation in explaining the sacramentality of the world. He notes: "Our world breeds life; by the chemistry of growth, bread is nourished up out of dead minerals; our own life depends upon that bread; the 'dead' world becomes our body, our life. If we are to consider the whole world as something sacramental, it must be initially because of this transformation which is happening all the time." *Ibid.*

become *my* body and *my* blood."[291] The transformed Creation, which is the divine gift and sacrifice, is "carried up to heaven and become the gift of the divine life and communion in the body and blood of Christ." The "creation is transformed into a gift and sacrifice" so that the Church can manifest and fulfil the new life in this world.[292]

"Orthodox ecclesiology traditionally sees the beginning of the Church in paradise and her life as the manifestation of the Kingdom of God."[293] Although the communion that existed between God and human beings in paradise was lost, it is given back with Jesus' redemption. In the Eucharist, we are brought back to the experience of paradise. The paradise experience is characterized as the experience of thanksgiving. "We were created in paradise and for paradise, we were exiled from paradise, and Christ "leads us again to paradise."[294] The Fathers understood and experienced the Church

> as the new life of the new creation and the presence, the '*parousia,*' of the Kingdom. Their attention is not focused on the 'institution' because the very nature and purpose of that institution is not to exist 'in itself' but to be the 'sacrament,' the *epiphany* of the new creation. In this sense, their whole theology is ecclesiological for it has the Church, the experience of the new life, the communion of the Holy Spirit as its source and context.[295]

This transition, inaugurated by Christ and sanctified by the Holy Spirit, continues in the Church. "The Church is the continuing presence of Pentecost as power of sanctification and transfiguration of all life, as *grace* which is knowledge of God, communion with Him and, in Him, with all that exists. The Church is creation as renewed by Christ and sanctified by the Holy Spirit."[296] In his opinion, the purpose of the Church is "to reveal and manifest the true meaning of creation as fulfillment in Christ, to announce to the world its end and the inauguration of the Kingdom."[297]

3.2.3. Eschatological Dimension of Christian Leitourgia

The eschatological dimension of the Church denotes the anticipation of the experience of the Kingdom in the Church.[298] The Church is eschato-

291. Schmemann, "Sacrifice and Worship," 130-131.
292. Schmemann, *The Eucharist: Sacrament of the Kingdom*, 118.
293. Schmemann, "Ecclesiological Notes," 35-36.
294. Schmemann, *The Eucharist: Sacrament of the Kingdom*, 174.
295. Schmemann, "Liturgy and Theology," 57.
296. Schmemann, "Ecclesiological Notes," 36.
297. *Ibid.*, 37.
298. By the term eschatological, Schmemann means, "the unique Christian experi-

logical means that "its essential function is to manifest and to actualize in this world the *eschaton*, the ultimate reality of salvation and redemption. In and through the Church, the Kingdom of God is made already present, is communicated to men."[299] The purpose of the Church as a sacramental organism "is to reveal, manifest and communicate the Kingdom of God, to communicate it as Truth, Grace and Communion with God and thus to fulfil the Church as the Body of Christ and the Temple of the Holy Spirit."[300]

As we have already indicated, eschatological reality is made present to us in the Church through the liturgy. Therefore, Fisch is right in saying that "[i]t is Schmemann's insight that eschatology ... is in fact what defines the liturgy. The 'specificity' of the Christian liturgy 'consists in its eschatological character'."[301] The Church as a *leitourgia* is "a calling to act in this world after the fashion of Christ, to bear testimony to him and to his kingdom."[302] Thus Schmemann notes:

> Church is the presence, the actualization in this world of the "world to come," in this *aeon* – of the Kingdom. And the mode of this presence, of this actualization of the new life, the new *aeon*, is precisely the *leitourgia*. It is only within this eschatological dimension of the Church that one can understand the nature of the liturgy: to actualize and realize the identity of the *ecclesia* with the new *aeon*, of the 'age to come'.[303]

According to him, "The Church lives on two levels, has two 'states'. She is waiting for, but she also possesses already, the object of expectation."[304] It is for this reason that he considers the experience of the King-

ence of the Kingdom of God, as, on the one hand the Kingdom 'to come', and, on the other hand, as that same Kingdom present and actualized in the Church." Schmemann, *Celebration of Faith.* Vol. III: *The Virgin Mary*, 73. We have already discussed at length eschatology in relation with sacramental symbolism and also in relation to world-view. Here our focus will be more on the eschatological experience.

299. Schmemann, "The Missionary Imperative," 212. As Zizioulas notes, instead of considering eschatology "as the end of the Church's pilgrimage ... we must think of the eschata as the beginning of the Church's life, the arche, that which brings forth the Church, gives her her identity, sustains and inspires her in her existence." In other words the Church exists not because of the death and resurrection of Christ but because of the Kingdom that has come. Therefore it reflects the future more than the historical fact. Zizioulas, "The Mystery of the Church in Orthodox Tradition," 296.

300. Schmemann, "The 'Orthodox World', Past and Present," 38-39.

301. Fisch, "Introduction: Schmemann's Theological Contribution to the Liturgical Renewal of the Churches," 8.

302. Schmemann, *Sacraments and Orthodoxy*, 28.

303. Schmemann, "Theology and Liturgical Tradition," 16-17.

304. Alexander Schmemann, "Fast and Liturgy: Notes in Liturgical Theology," *SVSQ* 3 (1959) 2-9, p. 7.

dom as an experience of the Church, even writes that the Church "has no other experience than that of the Kingdom."[305] According to Schmemann, the expression 'heaven on earth' is considered to be the fundamental experience of the Church in the Orthodox theology. In this sense, the Eucharist is not only thanksgiving to God, but also the experience of the Kingdom. Schmemann notes:

> [T]he Eucharist is not simply a way of discharging our duty of thanks to God .... It is rather the only possible holding together ... of the *whole* truth about God and man. It is the sacrament of the world sinful and suffering, the sky darkened, the tortured man dying: but it is also the sacrament of the change, His transfiguration, His rising, His Kingdom. In one sense we look back, giving thanks for the simple goodness of God's original gift to us. In another sense we look forward, eschatologically, to the ultimate repair and transfiguration of that gift, to its last consummation in Christ.[306]

This eucharistic and eschatological dimension helps us to realize the futility of the world. He observes that "the more deeply we think in eucharistic and therefore in eschatological terms, the more acutely we shall be aware that the fashion of this world passeth away, that things only acquire point and meaning and reality in their relationship to Christ's coming in glory."[307]

This eschatological dimension helps the Church to transcend the institutional meaning of it. "In the Eucharist, the Church transcends the dimensions of 'institution' and becomes the Body of Christ. It is the 'eschaton' of the Church, her manifestation as the world to come." This means "[a]s institution the Church is in *this world* the sacrament of the Body of Christ, of the Kingdom of God and the world to come."[308] In other words, Schmemann considers that the Church as a structure "is to be an 'epiphany,' to manifest and to fulfil the Church as expectation and fulfilment, as pilgrimage and anticipation."[309] This centrality of the Kingdom of God in Christian theology, that is present in the Eucharist, allows him to call the Eucharist the "sacrament of the Kingdom."[310]

305. Schmemann, "The Problem of the Church's Presence in the World in Orthodox Consciousness," 16-17.

306. Schmemann, "The World as Sacrament," 225.

307. *Ibid.*, 226.

308. Schmemann, "Theology and Eucharist," 16.

309. Schmemann, *Celebration of Faith.* Vol. III: *The Virgin Mary*, 64.

310. Schmemann has given "sacrament of the Kingdom" as the sub-title to his classical work on the Eucharist and he dealt with the theme in detail in the second chapter entitled "sacrament of the Kingdom." *The Eucharist: Sacrament of the Kingdom*, 27-48.

Schmemann often criticizes the obliteration of the eschatological dimension of Christian liturgy of the post-patristic period. According to him, "[e]schatology was relegated to the end of the theological manuals into a chapter *De Novissimis* which was exclusively personal and futurist."[311] According to him, an "individualistic and almost exclusively futuristic reduction of eschatology ... which deprived even the sacraments, the Eucharist itself, of their eschatological dimension ... into the future alone, made it more into a mere doctrine of rewards and punishments after death."[312]

Schmemann considers the loss of the eschatological dimension of liturgy that was fundamental to the Christian experience of faith itself, as the result of the divorce between theology and the liturgical experience of the Church. Eventually theology came to define the sacraments as no more than 'channels of grace'. He even notes that in the modern secularized theology it has gone further and considers them as 'channels of help'. Nevertheless, he notes that "in reality the sacraments are to be seen as the *locus*, the very centre of the Church's eschatological understanding and experience. The whole liturgy is to be seen as the sacrament of the Kingdom of God, the Church is to be seen as the presence and the communication of the Kingdom that is to come."[313] He applies the same eschatological approach "to all aspects of liturgical celebration."[314]

Schmemann considers the obliteration of the eschatological dimension of Christian *leitourgia* as not something theoretical, but realized it in the experiential level. He characterizes this change that took place at the subconscious level as the greatest tragedy of Christianity.[315] This awareness forced him to return to the original meaning of eschatology as an essential objective of the liturgical movement. According to Schmemann:

> [N]o theological reflection on the world will be possible unless we rediscover, make truly ours again, that reality which alone constitutes the Church and is the source of her faith, of her life and therefore of her theology: the reality of the Kingdom of God. The Church is *in statu viae*, in pilgrimage through 'this world,' sent to it as its salvation. But the meaning of that pil-

311. Schmemann, "Liturgical Theology: Remarks on Method," 143. He observes that in this understanding the "sacraments were defined and understood as so many means of personal sanctification. Ecclesiology was reduced to a total institutionalism, and piety to an individualism complete in and closed upon itself." *Ibid.*

312. Schmemann, "The Problem of the Church's Presence in the World in Orthodox Consciousness," 14. Id., *Celebration of Faith.* Vol. III: *The Virgin Mary*, 73.

313. Schmemann, "Liturgy and Eschatology," 10.

314. *Ibid.*, 12.

315. Schmemann, "The Problem of the Church's Presence in the World in Orthodox Consciousness," 14.

grimage, as indeed the meaning of the world itself, is given and revealed to us only when the Church fulfils herself as being *in statu patriae*, truly at home at Christ's table, in His Kingdom.[316]

Despite his criticisms, Schmemann is optimistic of this task of the liturgical movement and noted that it was liturgical theology that succeeded to bring out "the *eschatological* character of the Christian cult whose essential 'function' is to *realize* the Church by revealing her as the epiphany of the Kingdom of God."[317]

> It is possible to say that liturgical theology has as its proper domain or 'object' eschatology itself, which is revealed in its fullness through the liturgy. And if today it is necessary for us to 'rediscover' all of this, that is because the essential tragedy within the history of the Church has been the nearly total eclipse of the eschatological 'content' and inspiration which are so evident in the faith and life of the primitive church.[318]

Schmemann argues that, the problems of the world need to be sought from this perspective. In his opinion, " [w] hat is required, [to answer the world's problems] is a return on our part to that source of energy, in the deepest sense of the word, which the Church possessed when it was conquering the world. What the Church brought into the world was not certain ideas applicable simply to human needs, but first of all the truth, the righteousness, the joy of the Kingdom of God."[319] Schmemann thus ascertains the positive meaning of eschatology and notes: " [t] he eschatological nature of the Church is not the negation of the world, but, on the contrary, its affirmation and acceptance as the object of divine love." In other words, the "Church is nothing but the sign and the reality of the love of God for this world, the very condition of the Church's mission to the world."[320]

The eschatological experience that one receives in the Eucharist needs to be made present to the world. According to him, the Church's mission is the proclamation and communication of the *eschaton*. From the Orthodox perspective, mission is the communication of what God has given us

316. *Ibid.*, 16.

317. Schmemann, "Liturgical Theology: Remarks on Method," 142. He even notes that "it is accordingly high time that the experience of the liturgical movement, although regrettably short-lived, be translated and consolidated into a liturgical theology which alone today can restore to us that unique eschatological energy and perspective which makes us the people of God, acquainted with the true sense of the ancient formula: 'in this world but not of this world'." Id., "Liturgical Theology: Remarks on Method," 144.

318. *Ibid.*, 143.

319. Schmemann, "Liturgy and Eschatology," 13.

320. Schmemann, "The Missionary Imperative," 213-214.

in the Eucharist to the world. "Nothing reveals better the relation between the Church as fullness and the Church as mission than the Eucharist, the central act of the Church's *leitourgia*, the sacrament of the Church itself. There are two movements in the eucharistic rite: *the movement of ascension* and the *movement of return*."[321] This experience is possible because the people of God become as Paul Evdokimov puts it, "liturgical beings."[322] Schmemann further posits that:

> the whole perspective of sacrifice depends on the starting point. The beginning is before there is any sin or evil, with something that belongs to the real life. Then comes the second stage: evil, betrayal, suffering, death. Sacrifice remains there, but it acquires a new energy, and goes on finally to the third stage, the eschatological meaning: the end of all things, the fulfilment of all things in the perfect sacrifice, the perfect communion, the perfect unity. These are the three dimensions of sacrifice ... to be restored for a balanced view and theology of sacrifice ... all these aspects are essential: thanksgiving, communion, giving up, sharing, transformation.[323]

To conclude this section, we should say that the equal emphasis that Schmemann accorded to the ecclesial, cosmic and eschatological dimensions of Christian *leitourgia* are to be seen as his chief theological merit.

> What is important for us at this point is the relationship between this cosmic and eschatological nature of the Church and her *leitourgia*. For it is precisely in and through her liturgy – this being the latter's specific and unique "function" – that the Church is *informed* of her cosmic and eschatological vocation, *receives* the power to fulfil it and thus truly *becomes* "what she is" – the sacrament, in Christ, of the new creation; the sacrament, in Christ, of the Kingdom.[324]

The main focus in this section has been on the ecclesial, cosmic and eschatological dimensions of Christian *leitourgia*. Schmemann argued that the liturgy, celebrated ecclesially, has cosmic and eschatological dimensions. Our ecclesial worship that holds the world and then offers it to the Creator, enables us to enter into the *eschaton*. The unified view of the Church, the world and the Kingdom is fundamental for formulating any genuine theology. Schmemann remarks:

321. *Ibid.*, 214.

322. Paul Evdokimov, *Les âges de la vie spirituelle*, Paris, Desclée de Brouwer, 1964, 209-226. See Michael Plekon, "The Church, the Eucharist and the Kingdom: Towards an Assessment of Alexander Schmemann's Theological Legacy," 136.

323. Schmemann, "Sacrifice and Worship," 131.

324. Schmemann, "Liturgy and Theology," 57.

> The liturgy of the Church is cosmic and eschatological because the Church is cosmic and eschatological; but the Church would not have been cosmic and eschatological had she not been given, as the very source and constitution of her life and faith, the *experience* of the new creation, the experience and *vision* of the Kingdom which is to come. And this is precisely the *leitourgia* of the Church's cult, the function which makes it the source and indeed the very *possibility* of theology.[325]

According to Schmemann, distinguishing these dimensions, ecclesial – cosmic – eschatological, on the one hand, and seeing them in their mutual interdependence on the other hand, is the failure of contemporary Christian thought. This failure is responsible for the various 'reductions' and 'surrenders' in theology. In his opinion, "there have always existed three fundamental types of 'heretical temptations' for Christian theology, all of which consist precisely in the 'reduction' of one of the dimensions."[326] Detecting the emphasis on one or the other, which ultimately led to the distortion of the holistic view of Christian theology, impelled him to emphasise a more unified vision.

> A Christian vision and understanding of the world is simply impossible without it being seen in the light of the church and the kingdom of God. An ecclesiology that is not rooted in cosmology and eschatology is a radically wrong one. And finally, the ultimate reality of Christian faith, hope and love, the kingdom of God, cannot be 'known,' and thus believed in, hoped for and be the content of our love, except by means of 'this world' and the church.[327]

In short, along with many others,[328] it seems that the equal emphasis given to the ecclesial, cosmic and eschatological dimensions of Christian *leitourgia* is Schmemann's great contribution to Christian thought.

325. *Ibid.*, 58.

326. Schmemann, "Theology or Ideology?," 234.

327. *Ibid.*, 235.

328. Thomas Fisch considers this unified view of Church, world and the Kingdom as Schmemann's great contribution to theology. In his opinion, "Amid the many studies produced in recent years on the Church, on the eucharist, and on the early church's eschatological consciousness, Schmemann alone perceives and enunciates the interconnection of these three things within the living Church's experience and its celebration of the liturgy." Fisch, "Introduction: Schmemann's Theological Contribution to the Liturgical Renewal of the Churches," 8. Michael Pelkon also notes that the "pervasive sacramental view of the world and of the Church's mission in it are perhaps the most radical part of Schmemann's theological contribution." Plekon, "The Church, the Eucharist and the Kingdom: Towards an Assessment of Alexander Schmemann's Theological Legacy," 137.

4. Conclusion

Our discussion on Schmemann has helped us to unravel the problem of the so-called sacred-profane dichotomy. As we have seen, travelling with 'Orthodoxy' from East to West, Schmemann along with other contemporary Orthodox theologians has tried to make the transition smooth. His open yet critical approach was not limited to the West, but extended to the East. In this process, he always referred back to the early Christian tradition, whose faith is rooted in eschatology. This eschatological belief guided Schmemann in explaining sacramental symbolism and the Christian worldview as 'eschatological'.

In the second part, we first demonstrated how human beings stand at the center of reality and maintain communion with God with a sacramental view of Creation. In particular, we have seen the priestly role that was given to them as from the beginning. Secondly, we have shown how the tension of elevating this world to the other world, and the other world descending to this world is held together in the Church through its liturgy.

What is underscored in all of these sections "is not merely a renewed insistence upon the importance of particular sacramental acts in the life of the individual." Moreover, we have tried to show the "sacramental character in the whole of life."[329] This sacramental character of human living helps one to bridge the gap between sacred and profane keeping the eschatological tension of being concerned of the world and yet detached from the world. This open but critical attitude to the world is the result of a life in faith. Although a vision of this kind could be negatively interpreted as "mystical" in nature, Schmemann has tried to show that it is a positive view of the world that seeks to transcend the limits of time and space.

329. Schmemann, "The World as Sacrament," 218.

Chapter Four

WORLD AS SACRAMENT IN SAINT EPHREM A COMBINATION OF ETHICAL AND LITURGICAL RESPONSE

In our discussions on Boff and Schmemann we have tried to delve into their theology of the sacramentality of Creation and their response to it in two different ways. Boff, belonging to the Western tradition, emphasizes the ethical responsibility towards Creation, whilst, Schmemann, rooted basically in the Greek-Byzantine tradition, emphasizes the liturgical response to Creation. To mediate between these two viewpoints, we will now look at the Syrian tradition. Although the Syriac tradition is rooted in the Judeo-Christian tradition, it originated outside of the ambiance of the Greco-Roman world.[1] This historical setting of the Syrian tradition is very relevant in shaping a theology to the multi-religious context of today's world. Therefore, our focus in this chapter will be to investigate the notion of sacraments, world and the sacramentality of Creation in the Syrian tradition.[2]

1. By this demarcation, we do not intend to say that they are mutually exclusive. Contrarily, our interest here is to focus on the distinctiveness of these three basic Christian traditions. In particular, although it seems difficult to cordon off the guard Syriac Fathers from any Greek influence, we will try to bring out the specific Semitic elements and the influence of Mesopotamian religious tradition that make the Syriac tradition different from the Latin *sacramentum* and the Greek *mysterion*. For its origin outside the Greco-Roman world, see Leslie W. Bernard, "The Origins and Emergence of the Church in Edessa during the First Two Centuries A.D.," *Vigiliae Christianae* 22 (1968) 161-175.

2. There are different Christian churches that share Syriac liturgical tradition (East Syriac and West Syriac). The East Syrian Churches are: Assyrian Church of the East (old), Assyrian Church of the East (new), Chaldeans and Malabar Church. The West Syrian Churches are: Malankara Orthodox Syrian, Syrian Orthodox, Maronite and Malankara Catholics. Churches like the Marthoma Church, Independent Church of Thozhiyoor, Church of South India, though they share the Syrian tradition, they are not included in the

The Syriac churches, though they share a common language, respect differences depending on their particular cultural contexts. The differences are seen in the canons, the patristic foundations, and even in the emphasis on liturgical and sacramental celebrations. Despite the differences, there are many early Church Fathers who are acceptable to all Syrian traditions. We limit the scope of this study mainly to Saint Ephrem the Syrian.[3] At the same time, as we discuss the liturgical and sacramental traditions, we shall also make use of other sources.

1. Theological Horizons of Saint Ephrem

In the first part, we shall begin our discussion by looking into Ephrem's life and epistemological foundations for an adequate understanding of his theology of sacraments and worldview. This will be followed by a study on the sacraments from the Syrian tradition. In this second part, we do not limit our study to Ephrem alone; rather we will view it from the Syrian tradition in general. Finally, we shall delineate how Ephrem expressed a Christian worldview amidst the cosmological disputes of his time.

main stream Syrian Churches because of their Protestant leanings.

3. Ephrem (306-373) was born in the area of Nisibis. There are many legends about his parental heritage and of his childhood. While some scholars speak of him as the son of a pagan priest, others speak of his origin from a Christian family. Regarding his life, one comes across two traditions in particular, based on Greek and Syrian sources. Sidney Griffith calls the two images as "the icon of Ephraem Byzantinus and the portrait of Ephraem Syrus." Sidney H. Griffith, "St Ephraem the Syrian," *Sobornost* 20/2 (1986) 21-40, p. 23. While the Byzantine tradition presents the image of a monastic Ephrem, the Syriac tradition presents him as a poet theologian. Griffith, "St Ephraem the Syrian," 25. See also Edward G. Mathews, Jr., "The Vita Tradition of Ephraem the Syrian, the Deacon of Edessa," *Diakonia* 22 (1988-89) 15-42; Sidney H. Griffith, "Images of Ephraem: the Syrian Holy Man and His Church," *Traditio* 45 (1989-90) 7-33; Joseph P. Amar, "Byzantine Ascetic Monachism and Greek Bias in the Vita Tradition of Ephrem the Syrian," *OCP* 58 (1992) 123-156. Ephrem's works contain both poems and prose. His genius is mainly expressed in his poems, which contain *memrê* and *mãadrashź*. *Memrê* are verse homilies and poetical meditations on scriptural passages that are to be mainly sung on feast days. *Mãadrashź* are hymns of praise. His prose works too are two types: his commentaries on Genesis, Exodus and the Diatessaron and his polemical texts, *Prose Refutations*. There is an enormous amount of literature on the study of Ephrem. Edmund Dom Beck (1902-1991) is credited for his great contributions on the edition and translations of Ephrem's original works to German. Besides this, he authored a number of books and articles on Ephrem. Koonammakkal has divided Ephremic studies into two: pre-Beck and post-Beck era. The pre-Beck studies are to be valued for being limited to the collection of Ephrem's original works. Contrarily, Beck's German editions, on the complete works of Ephrem, gave a new shift to later Ephrem studies. Thomas Koonammackal, "Changing Views on Ephrem," *Christian Orient* 14 (1993) 113-130, p. 114.

1.1. Knowledge of God

The early Syrian traditions, in particular of Ephrem and Aphrahat, are said to be beyond the impasse of Hellenistic influence. Although there are theories that establish the influence of Greek philosophy in the writings of Ephrem,[4] mostly Ephrem's writings participate in Semitic thought. This is clearly seen in his prose and poems. His prose writings are for the most part responses to the heretics. In these one observes usage of Greek philosophical categories to answer his opponents. His poems, however, are exhortations he gave to the faithful. These poetical writings contain a paradoxical narration of Christian doctrines. They clearly shows that the Greek categories seen in Ephrem's writings have not made any significant change to his semitic thinking. Rather, along with other Syrian Fathers Ephrem gave a new flavor to Christian thinking. Our concern here is to highlight Ephrem's approach to understanding God that makes him distinct from the Latin or Greek tradition. We shall see this from three different perspectives: intellectual investigation (rational approach), dialectic between apophatism and cataphatism, as well as the sacramental approach.

1.1.1. Intellectual Investigation

Before entering into the discussions on the epistemology of Ephrem, it is important to note his teaching on the 'ontological chasm' that exists between Creator and Creation.[5] The chasm that exists is mainly from the part of Creation. It is because of the createdness. From Creator to Creation, there is no chasm. On the contrary, there is a movement of love from the Creator to Creation.[6] The human difficulty of comprehending God makes it difficult for them to speak of Christ's nature.[7] Human beings pursuit to know God comes in this context.

The fourth century Syria of Ephrem's time was full of heresies and controversies. The proponents of various theories from the Greco-Roman world were often sent out from their land and came to places like Syria. It was a fertile land for them to introduce their teachings. In particular there

4. Ute Possekel's recent study on Ephrem shows the depth of this problem. Ute Possekel, *Evidence of Greek Philosophical Concepts in the Writings of Ephrem the Syrian*, CSCO, 580 (Louvain: Peeters, 1999).

5. For details see Thomas Koonammakkal, "Ephrem's Imagery of Chasm," *OCA* 256 (1998) 175-183.

6. *Ibid.*, 177.

7. Ephrem's tenth hymn in the collection of *Hymns on the Faith* speaks of Christ's nature in the first four stanzas. In the following two stanzas he speaks of the "gospel examples of timidity in approaching Christ." Robert Murray, "A Hymn of St Ephrem to Christ on the Incarnation, the Holy Spirit, and the Sacraments," *ECR* 3 (1970) 142-150, p. 142.

were different attempts that tried to rationalize God in order to comprehend the Divine.[8] But Ephrem insisted strongly upon the incomprehensibility of the Creator by human beings.

Ephrem criticizes people who engage in intellectual 'prying' or 'investigation'. He characterizes them as people who have "renounced their faith and annulled their baptism."[9] He also cautions against preconceptions that can also lead us astray. He uses the Jewish rejection of Christ in the New Testament as the best test example of this. The Jewish authorities had their own preconceived idea of what the Messiah should be like; so, they rejected the true Messiah.[10] The choice between these approaches is left to the individual's free will. The denial of Jesus is the outcome of pride and preconceptions, while acceptance of Jesus stems from an attitude of faith, openness and love.

Our investigation to come to know God is to bring Him down to the level of creatures. According to Murray, Ephrem's use of 'prying' '*ûqqabâ* (speculative enquiry) always refer to Arians. He mainly criticizes them, not for their false teachings, but rather for making the Godhead subject to all human enquiries.[11] Like other Syrian Fathers, Ephrem never sought to understand God through theological definitions. He even considered theological definitions as dangerous, as well as potentially blasphemous. Ephrem considers this the 'poison of Greek wisdom'.[12] This is one of the main themes in *Hymns on Faith*. In Murray's opinion, Ephrem rather suggests a symbolic and analogical approach to theology.[13] Elsewhere we read Murray's comment: "Ephrem refuses to answer the Arians by developing speculative theology on the orthodox side, as both Athanasius and the Cappadocians did; he sticks to his symbolism

8. According to Paul S. Russell, Ephrem's *Hymns on Faith* and *Sermons on Faith* are "directed clearly against opponents who seem to him to claim too much knowledge of God." It also seems to be against the "Neo-Arian" writers. Paul S. Russell, "Ephraem the Syrian on the Utility of Language and the Place of Silence," *Journal of Early Christian Studies* 8/1 (2000) 21-37, p. 24. The knowledge of God was not a topic of discussion in the early stages of the Arian Controversy. See Michael E. Butler, "Neo-Arianism: Its Antecedents and Tenets," *SVTQ* 36 (1994) 355-371. It arose in the context of the Aëtaian and Eunomian stages of the Arian controversy. See Paul S. Russell, *St. Ephraem the Syrian and St. Gregory the Theologian Confront the Arians* (Kottayam: Saint Ephrem Ecumenical Research Centre, 1994) 121-145. For Sidney H. Griffith, the followers of Arius or Aetius are the ones who "measure the disclosures of biblical revelation solely by the logic of the 'Hellenic' canons of reason." Sidney H. Griffith, "A Spiritual Father for the Whole Church: St Ephrem the Syrian," *Sobornost* 20/2 (1998) 21-40, p. 30.

9. *Hymnen de Fide* 9: 10; 23: 2.

10. *Hymnen de Fide* 44: 9-10.

11. Murray, "A Hymn of St Ephrem," 149.

12. *Hymnen de Fide* 2: 24.

13. Murray, "A Hymn of St Ephrem," 149.

and demands that the mystery remain veiled. Not *fides quaerens intellectum* but *fides adorans mysterium*."[14] Since God remains incomprehensible, Ephrem argues that any effort to define God is setting limits on Him,[15] and could be even counter-productive.[16] Hence any effort to define God ultimately is the result of an effort to contain the uncontainable, to limit the limitless.

1.1.2. Dialectic between Apophatism and Cataphatism

Ephrem's arguments against intellectual investigation do not mean that he opposes any form of knowledge and prefers ignorance. On the contrary, he is critical of ignorance and suggests a moderation of 'intelligence' between rational investigation and ignorance.[17] For him, "The way of intelligence is to be observant, analytical and carefully precise but not dogmatically definitive, absolutist, arrogant, or rigid. ... Knowledge is the ability to describe the what but not to dominate the inward workings (the how and why) of God, man and salvation."[18] Therefore, instead of doing theological inquiry through definitions as in the Greek tradition, Ephrem applies a method that uses paradoxes and symbols. In this regard, his poetical writings are more important than his prose.[19] For him, the awareness of not knowing is the greatest of all knowledge.[20] In order to

14. Murray, *Symbols of Church and Kingdom: a Study in Early Syriac Tradition* (Cambridge: Cambridge University Press, 1975) 89. According to Brock, the issue of the incomprehensibility of God lay at the very centre of the controversy between Eunomius and the Anomoeans on the one side, and Basil and Gregory on the other. Sebastian Brock, *The Luminous Eye: The Spiritual World Vision of Saint Ephrem the Syrien* (Kalamazoo: Cistercian Publications, 1992) 180.

15. Kathleen McVey (ed.), *St. Ephrem the Syrian: Selected Prose Works*, trans. Edward G. Mathews, Jr. & Joseph P. Amar (Washington, DC: Catholic University of America Press, 1994) 49-50.

16. David D. Bundy, "Language and Knowledge of God in Ephrem Syrus," *PBR* 5 (1986) 91-103, p. 99. *Prose Refutations* I, viii.

17. Bundy, "Language and Knowledge of God in Ephrem Syrus," 99. *Prose Refutations* I, vii.

18. Bundy, "Language and Knowledge of God in Ephrem Syrus," 100. In this sense he criticises Arians and Manichaeans for going beyond the limits of what can be known. Their investigations resulted in the loss of faith, instead they acquired certain "theories about God, the world, man and the salvific process." They are compared to Eve, who aspired to know everything. *Prose Refutations* I, vii.

19 Brock, *The Luminous Eye*, 23-24. For a short study on the poetical method of Ephrem in doing theology see Sebastian Brock, "The Poet as Theologian," *Sobornost* 7/4 (1977) 243-250, pp. 244-245.

20. *Prose Refutations* I, xvi-xvii.

overcome this ignorance and to enter into the deeper structures of reality, Ephrem advocates meditation and contemplation.[21]

His 'methodology' is brilliantly expressed between the dialectic of 'apophatism' and 'cataphatism'. This dialectic is to be pursued by all Christians and should remain balanced. In this sense, as traditionally understood, one can speak of God analogically.[22] Theologically, "the debate is between the apophatic (negative) and the cataphatic (affirmative) approaches to the attempt to talk about God." According to Murray, in Ephrem, "[r]eason insists – almost brutally – that the attempt to penetrate the nature of God is both folly and blasphemy, while Love simply has to praise and respond to the revelation and experience of himself which God himself has given."[23]

Ephrem's understanding of the transcendence and immanence of God within Creation that holds in a continual state of tension, is spoken of as that which is 'hidden' and 'revealed'. These terms are used in two totally different perspectives: human and divine.

The human perspective is the human experience of God's hiddenness (*kasyuta*). This experience relies on "God's various instances of self-revelation." At the same time, it is important to note that such experience of God's self-manifestation is never a full revelation of God's hiddenness, rather, it is always only a partial revelation. Hence, human perspective is essentially subjective and their approach to God's hiddenness depends on different sets of revelation (*galyata*). What is not revealed and kept hidden (*kasyātā*) are "those things pertaining to His own nature, to the generation of the Son, and to the Holy Spirit."[24] God's revelation to each individual varies from person to person depending on one's quality.[25] Ephrem argued that human knowledge is limited. This affects "his awareness of himself, his feelings, desires and motivations." We are not certain about how we know, yet our knowledge "is a series of images and words which are sorted in the mind. One does not possess the reality itself."[26] He even asks, if one cannot know oneself, how can we know of

21. *Prose Refutations* I, iv.

22. Robert Murray, "St Ephrem's Dialogue of Reason and Love," *Sobornost* 2/2 (1980) 26-40, p. 26.

23. *Ibid.*, 27.

24. *Hymnen de Fide* 44: 7; 19: 7; 51: 2-3. See G. Noujaim, "Anthropologie et économie de salut chez S. Ephrem: autour des notions de ghalyatâ, kasyatâ et kasyâ," *ParOr* 9 (1979-80) 313-315.

25. "The Watchers as Watchers saw Him; according to the degree of his knowledge each person saw Him. Everyone according to the measure of his discernment thus perceived Him, that One greater than all." *Hymnen de Nativitate* 4: 199-200. Kathleen E. McVey, *Ephrem the Syrian: Hymns* (New York/Mahwah, NJ: Paulist, 1989) 32.

26. *Hymnen de Fide* 57: 1-5.

God.[27] Elsewhere, he notes, "Let us know how small our knowledge is, too contemptible to scrutinise the Knower of All."[28]

The second perspective is that of divine reality that Ephrem calls 'truth' (*shrara, qushta*). This goes beyond the human experience of God to God's actual Being (*ituta*). This reality of God's Being "which objectively exists, ... can only be experienced in a hidden and ... subjective way." In this sense, types and symbols are not instances of divine self-manifestation (*galyata*) through visible Creation, but are rather something hidden that points to something that will be revealed later. For example, "what is 'hidden' in the symbols of Nature and of Scripture is revealed in Christ at the Incarnation; what lies hidden in the Sacraments will be revealed at the eschaton, in Paradise." According to Brock, the tension between these two poles, hidden and revealed, "is none other than the tension between the transcendence and immanence of God."[29] For Ephrem "God's Being belongs to an area of hiddenness and silence."[30]

1.1.3. Sacramental Approach

The incomprehensibility of God or better the tension between transcendence and immanence leads to a sacramental attitude towards God and Creation. For Ephrem, Scripture possesses two kinds of meaning, the outer historical meaning, and the inner spiritual meaning (hidden power). In his opinion, both intimately coexist, as humanity and divinity coexist in Jesus. Brock compares the presence of the 'hidden power,' in Ephrem to the traditional doctrine of divine inspiration in Scripture. To master this 'hidden power' one needs the inner eye and faith. Moreover, the continuous inspiration of the Holy Spirit is needed for an individual to see the 'hidden power' with this inner eye.[31] Ephrem even notes that Creation gives birth to Christ in symbols, as Mary did in the flesh.[32] It is observable only by the eye of faith; the clearer the eye, the more symbols will become visible and each symbol will become more meaningful. The existence of hidden symbols provides a cohesive substructure of strands that link and connect together every part of Creation. Since symbols point to divine reality, their presence in God's two witnesses, Scripture and Nature, gives new meanings to the natural world and the Bible. In this

27. *Hymnen de Fide* 1: 16.

28. *Hymnen de Fide* 15: 3.

29. Brock, *The Luminous Eye*, 28-29, 67.

30. *Ibid.*, 145. In this regard Brock notes certain similarities between Ephrem and Gregory of Nyssa. See also Paul S. Russell, "Ephraem the Syrian on the Utility of Language and the Place of Silence,"25.

31. Brock, *The Luminous Eye*, 162.

32. *Hymnen de Virginitate* 6: 8.

sense one can say that Ephrem's understanding of symbols offers an essentially "sacramental understanding of the world." Furthermore, it is in this sense that "the plural of *raza*, 'symbol', is frequently used in the sense of 'sacraments'."[33]

Creation is of full of mysteries and points towards the hidden power of the Creator.[34] Towards creation we must have a sense of wonder and gratitude.[35] For Ephrem, anyone can learn something about God, because He has come down to the level of our understanding. Once we understand this about God, it "will result in an attitude of wonder (*tehra*)." The emphasis on intellectual investigation is the result of the absence of this sense of wonder.[36] The "sense of wonder gives rise to faith, and faith is the prerequisite if any knowledge of God is to be attained."[37] Therefore, one could say with McVey that Ephrem's poetry aims "not to explain the system of the universe nor to impose any rigid ideas of his own about the Christian message on others." It, however, aims "to give birth in God's creatures to that true worship of the Creator of all, to instill a desire to live the mystery of God's love toward humanity. Types and symbols are but a simple invitation to the one who perceives them to participate in the divine life offered to all; they are not proof texts to coerce the unbeliever."[38]

If the intention of Ephrem's writings is not to explain the mystery of the universe, then, what are his intentions? It is very clear from above that instead of explaining the mysteries of God, Ephrem's aim is "to give birth in God's creatures to that true worship of the Creator of all, to instill a desire to live the mystery of God's love toward humanity."[39] It is grounded on "a vision of the world as a vast system of symbols or mysteries."[40]

33. Brock, *The Luminous Eye*, 56.

34. *Hymnen de Virginitate* 6: 8.

35. *Hymnen de Fide* 41: 7; 84: 2.

36. He explains it by giving the biblical example of Baalam, who failed to 'wonder' when his donkey spoke (*Hymnen de Fide* 41: 7). Brock, *The Luminous Eye*, 69.

37. Brock, *The Luminous Eye*, 69-70. For Ephrem, faith is the 'second soul' to the body. The life of the soul depends on faith. And when the soul denies faith or becomes divided by doubt, it becomes a mere corpse. *Hymnen de Fide* 80: 1. Ephrem also depicts faith as the eye that enables one to see hidden things. *Hymnen de Ecclesia* 24: 3. Faith needs to be accompanied by love and prayer. *Hymnen de Fide* 4: 11. God's love wishes to be met by a response of human love and desire for Him. Love has the key to the divine treasure house. *Hymnen de Fide* 32: 3.

38. McVey (ed.), *St. Ephrem the Syrian: Selected Prose Works*, 55. See *Hymns on Nisibis* 16: 6.

39. McVey (ed.), *St. Ephrem the Syrian: Selected Prose Works*, 55.

40. *Ibid.*, 41.

2. Sacrament and World in Ephrem and in the Syrian Tradition

2.1. Sacramentology

The Syrian Christian tradition of sacramentology, rooted in *rāzā* is to be understood in the light of Hebrew *sôd*. This root of Syriac *rāzā*, in the Hebrew tradition, can be better conceived within the framework of the Semitic background of *mysterion*.[41] Hence, we focus on the Semitic and Hebrew tradition of *rāzā*. In this section, we shall first clarify the notions: *sôd* and *rāzā*. This will then be followed by the theology of sacraments in the Syriac tradition.

2.1.1. Clarification of Notions

2.1.1.1. Sôd

The Hebrew noun *sôd* is an "etymological crux."[42] The Oxford Old Testament Lexicon gives two meanings for *sôd*. First, "council" in familiar conversation is given. This could be a circle of familiar friends or an assembly, or company. Second, "counsel" that are taken by those in familiar conversation. This could mean counsel itself or secret counsel that may be revealed in familiar converse with God.[43] Similarly, the Hebrew Aramaic dictionary gives three meanings: confidential discussion both in the assembly of Yahweh and of the people, a secret of God towards people through prophets and among people as well as a circle of confidents.[44] Brown discovers a similar meaning in South Arabic, for example, "council, assembly." He also notes the use of *mśwd*, a performative of the root *śwd* in the Minean inscriptions as "a smaller council consist-

41. As we have already seen in our first chapter, unlike the school of comparative religions that focused on the influence of the mystery religions in the development of the theology of *mysterion*, theologians like Raymond Brown traced its roots to the Semitic background. This study sheds some light on the importance of sacramentology in the Syrian tradition. Perhaps Raymond E. Brown's research on the Semitic concept of "mystery" stands as a good example of this. Raymond E. Brown, "The Pre-Christian Semitic Concept of 'Mystery'," *CBQ* (1958) 417-443.

42. M. Sœba, "סוֹד *sôd* secret," *Theological Lexicon of the Old Testament*, ed. Ernst Jenni & Claus Westermann, trans. Mark E. Biddle, Vol. 2 (Peabody, MA: Hendrickson, 1997) 793-795, p. 793. According to Sœba, apart from making references to other Semitic languages, scholars often make no suggestions regarding possible derivations.

43. Francis Brown, S. R. Driver & Charles A. Briggs, *A Hebrew and English Lexicon of the Old Testament: With an Appendix Containing the Biblical Aramaic*, trans. Edward Robinson (Oxford: [1]1907, 1959) 691.

44. Ludwig Koehler, Walter Baumgartner & Johann Jakob Stamm, *The Hebrew and Aramaic Lexicon of the Old Testament*, tr. & ed. under the supervision of M. E. J. Richardson (Leiden/New York/Köln: Brill, 1995) 745.

ing of the king, nobles and privileged classes."[45] The above references seem to agree on the general meaning of *sôd* as "council" and "counsel." For a more concrete meaning, we must refer to its use in the Old Testament.

The Hebrew term *sôd* although it appeared 21 times in the Old Testament with varied meanings it was never used as an equivalent to *mysterion* in LXX.[46] It was used as a possible rendering of *mysterion* in the pre-exilic use of "the heavenly assembly and its secrets."[47] The use of *sôd*, in the sense of 'council' or 'assembly,' can mainly be seen in passages dealing with the heavenly *sôd*.[48] Looking at the many passages in the Bible that describes the heavenly council, Brown argues that the heavenly *sôd* exercised authority "to enact decrees concerning the conduct of the world." He also notes that the heavenly advisors "are no longer equal gods, but angels, 'the sons of God'." In these assemblies, Yahweh renders the final decree and the angels' role is to suggest and to carry out the decrees. The decisions "were made known to the people by the prophet who was introduced by vision into the sessions of the *sôd*."[49] It seems that the prophets were introduced into the heavenly assembly to gain knowledge of its secret decrees in the preexilic periods and it played an important role in the later period. Thus, in postexilic Jewish literature, the knowledge of heavenly mysteries is extended to the privileged individuals through visions in the secrets of God.[50]

45. Brown, "The Pre-Christian Semitic Concept of 'Mystery'," 418.

46. Günther Bornkamm, "μυστήριον, μυέω," *Theological Dictionary of the New Testament*, ed. Gerhard Kittel, trans. & ed. Geoffrey W. Bromiley, vol. IV (Grand Rapids, MI: Eerdmans, 1967) 802-828, p. 814. However, in the Hexapla translation *sôd* is used as the Hebrew equivalent for *mysterion*. *Sôd* here means "'confidential speech or advice,' 'secret,' then the 'circle of confidants who are consulted'. Only where the sense is 'secret' or 'secret plan' is "μυστήριον a possible rendering." *Ibid.*

47. Brown, "The Pre-Christian Semitic Concept of 'Mystery'," 417-427.

48. *Ibid.*, 418. This notion of "heavenly assembly" is very important in Semitic thought. H. Wheeler Robinson made a thorough study on this. H. Wheeler Robinson, "The Council of Yahweh," *JTS* 45 (1944) 151-157; Idem, *Inspiration and Revelation in the Old Testament* (Oxford: Clarendon, 1946) 167-170. Brown calls attention to two aspects of this divine assembly in pagan (Babylonian and Ugaritic) literature. First, he notes the "similarities in the expressions used of these divine assemblies and those which occur in biblical references to the heavenly council of God and His angels." Secondly, "the terminology used to describe the divine assemblies is that of the governing and judicial national assemblies." Brown, "The Pre-Christian Semitic Concept of 'Mystery'," 418-419.

49. Brown, "The Pre-Christian Semitic Concept of 'Mystery'," 419-420.

50. *Ibid.*, 421. The knowledge of the heavenly mysteries is expressed through *rāz* or *sôd*, and more rarely by *nistār*.

Furthermore, Brown notes references to the earthly *sôd*, which means an "assembly of righteous (Ps 111:1; Ez 13:9) or of the evil (Jer 15:17, 16:11; Ps 64:3; Gn 49:6)." *Sôd* also denotes "the circle of village men getting together every night at the entrance of the town." Besides these meanings *sôd* also conveys the notion of "intimate friendship."[51] It is also "used for the secret decision rendered at councils and for counsel in general." This meaning of "secret decision" or "counsel" is of particular importance. It is in this sense that "the Hebrew represented by Prv 15:22; Ps 83:4 and Qumran, *sôd* is used simply for secrets or mysteries."[52]

In short, *sôd* is used as heavenly or earthly assembly, for a council and for counsel. These assemblies are in conversation with God and for the good of the world. Thus, we could rightly argue that *sôd*, understood as the council or as counsel, speaks of revelation. In this sense Sœba says: "Since *Sôd* refers to Yahweh's heavenly 'council' and his divine 'decision/plan/secret' and thus directly to his action and being, it acquires essential significance for the development and content of the Old Testament God."[53]

Another significant development in the use of *sôd* is the gradual inclusion of people into the council. Thus, in the pre-exilic books where the secrets of God's vision were reserved for God, angels and to certain privileged prophets, in the post-exilic period where righteous are also included. Here, we see how slowly God's revelation is extended to a wider circle of righteous people.

2.1.1.2. Rāzā

Sôd is often translated as *rozo* in the Peshitta.[54] It is a Persian loan word in Aramaic and Hebrew.[55] Though Kuriakose Luke accepts its frequent use in Middle Persian or Pahlavi and recognizes its entry into the Aramaic and Hebrew world from Cyrus' conquest of Babylon (538 B.C.), he traces its origin to Old Iranian and further to its Proto-Aryan origin. In his

51. *Ibid.*, 421. See also Thomas Poovathanikunnel, *The Sacraments: The Mystery Revealed* (Kottayam: OIRSI, 1998) 56-57.

52. Brown, "The Pre-Christian Semitic Concept of 'Mystery'," 421. *Sôd* is used both as human secret and heavenly mysteries.

53. Sœba, "dîs *sôd* secret," 795.

54. Brown, "The Pre-Christian Semitic Concept of 'Mystery'," 418. In the West Syrian tradition the term is used as *rozo*, while *rāzā* in the East Syrian tradition. In this section we use the term, depending on the context of the text.

55. *Ibid.*, 421. He also notes that the term *rāz* does not appear until the phalavi period. S. Telgedi, "Essai sur la phonétique des emprunts Iraniens en Araméen talmudique," *Journal Asiatique* 226 (1935) 177-265, pp. 254-255 (This article deals mainly with loanwords from Iranian into Jewish Aramaic). In the modern Persian, it is used as "hidden," "secret," etc.

opinion, *rāzā* is a modification of the Proto-Aryan *rahas* (post-vedic) which survives unchanged in Sanskrit and means "solitude, lonely place, secret, what is hidden."[56] In this context, it is worth noting that the "Thomas Christians" of West and East Syrian traditions use the Malayalam word *rahasyam*, which is a rendering of the Sanskrit *rahas*.[57]

The Syriac dictionaries give various meanings to the word *rāzā*, for example: "1) a secret; cf. *B^eraza'* "in secret, secretly;" 2) agreement, council; 3) conspiracy; 4) anything having a secret or mystical meaning, a type, figure, sign, symbol; ... 5) a mystery, sacrament, the Holy Eucharist, the sacred species; 6) pagan rites."[58]

The Biblical use of the term *rāzā* was first used in Hebrew with Jesus ben Sira 8:18; 12:11. Here, it acquired a secular use. It also obtained a theological significance in the book of Daniel and in the Dead Sea Scrolls.[59] In Daniel, who interpreted the dreams of Nebuchadnezzar concerning the end of days, it is used in reference to the establishment of the future kingdom that cannot be destroyed. Even though it is used in connection with various kings and kingdoms, its usage has strong religious overtones,[60] and with an eschatological meaning.[61] The basic meaning of

56. Luke, "The Technical Term *Raza*," 114-115. Kuriakose Luke gives various meanings of *rāzā* in Syriac. It is a denominative verb from the stem *razzez*. Its meaning is "to signify mystically, teach by types or mysteries." Its reflective form *'etrazzaz* means "to be instructed in the mysteries, be made familiar with them, be signified in mysteries or sacraments. There is the simple reflexive stem *'et'erez* (also *'eter'ez*), which means 'to be initiated into the mysteries, be mystically signified, receive secret information'." Its causative stem *'ārez* (also *'ar'ez*) means to "initiate into mysteries, instruct, declare through mysteries and symbols, signify, imply." The verb has a specifically Christian sense and often refers to catechesis and Christian initiation. From this we see that the verb came into existence within the setting of liturgical worship (*ibid.*, 113-114). Besides the works cited by Brown, Luke refers to K. Hoffmann, "Altiranisch," *Iranistik Linguistik*, Handbuch der Orientalistik, I. Abt., IV. Bd., I. Absch. (Leiden: Brill, 1958) regarding its Iranian origin. For its use in Pahlavi see: Henrik Samuel Nyberg, *A Manual of Pahlavi* (Wiesbaden: Harassowitz, 1964-74), Vol. II, 169. For its proto-Aryan use see J. Wackernagel & A. Debrunner, *Altindische Grammatik*, 3 vols., in 4 parts (Göttingen: Vandenhoeck & Ruprecht, 1954) II, 221.

57. Jose Poovannikunnel, *The Concept of "Mystery" (rāzā) in the Syro-Malabar Qurbana: A Study on the Biblical and Theological Dimensions of the Liturgical Theology of the Eucharistic Celebration* (Kottayam: OIRSI, 1989) 6.

58. Joseph Brim, *Dictionarium Syriaco-Latinum* (Soc. Jesu Beryti Phoneniciorum, 1911) 630; R. Payne Smith (ed.), *Thesaurus Syriacus*, Vol. 2 (Oxford: Clarendon, 1901) 3874.

59. Luke, "The Technical Term *Raza*," 115. It occurs eight times in the Aramaic Daniel: Dn 2:18, 19, 27, 28, 29, 30, 47; 4: 9. For the use of *rāz* in the book of Daniel see Poovathanikunnel, *The Sacraments*, 53-54. In Targums *rāz* even replaced *sôd*.

60. Brown, "The Pre-Christian Semitic Concept of 'Mystery'," 423.

61. Bornkamm, "μυστήριον, μυέω," 814.

rāz in the Biblical context is Revelation. Revelation here means "the disclosure of God's saving plans through God's own agents which otherwise would remain hidden from his people."[62] In this sense *rāz* remains closely connected to the heavenly *sôd*.

In the Qumran documents, *rāz* often occurs in connection with God's secret counsels and plans.[63] Here, *rāz* often means "divine mysteries having cosmological emphasis about the creation of the world and the luminaries. God's *rāz* in its eschatological aspect involves an unfathomable and inscrutable decree of the divine will which affects angels, men and the future of Israel." There is a resemblance to the Qumran usage in the writings of Paul. Thus, in Paul, one observes a connecting link between the Aramaic *rāz* and the Greek *mysterion*. For the *mysterion* that is used in Ephesians and Colossians reflects the eschatological presuppositions that was seen in the Qumran usage of the term *rāz*.[64] Both terms also bespeak the restoration of the entire cosmos into a harmony as is understood in Eph 1:9-10. In reference to the Old Testament types, *raz* was used to mean God's secret plan.[65]

Gregorios Yohanna Ibrahim goes beyond the meaning of rozo/mystery expressed in the Gospels and in the Epistles of Paul (Mk 4:11; 1 Tim 3:16; Rom 16:25; 1 Cor 15:51; Rom 11:25; Eph 5:32) as the 'hidden' or 'secret'. In his opinion, it has a deeper meaning, and is similar to the use of the seven sacraments.[66] He also notes how the Syrian Fathers distinguished between mystery and secret as did St Paul. In his opinion, the word *rozo* "signifies a visible Holy Rite that produced an invisible grace in the soul of the person to whom it is administered and from which he/she receives spiritual strength."[67]

62. Poovannikunnel, *The Concept of "Mystery"*, 6-7.

63. L. Sabourin, "The Parable of Kingdom," *Biblical Theological Bulletin* 4 (1976) 126. It occurs 55 times in the Qumran documents.

64. Markus Barth, *Ephesians, Introduction, Translation and Commentary on Chapters 1–3* (New York: Doubleday & Company Inc., 1974) 19, 124, 329. Barth translates the Greek *mysterion* as 'secret' rather than 'mystery' in Ephesians and in Colossians. To see the similarities of the use of 'mystery' in Paul and Qumran see, Joseph Coppens, "'Mystery' in the Theology of Saint Paul and Its Parallels at Qumran," *Paul and Qumran: Studies in New Testament*, ed. J. Murphy O'Connor (London: Geoffrey Champan, 1968) 132-158.

65. Pauly Maniyattu, *Heaven on Earth: The Theology of Liturgical Spacetime in the East Syrian Qurbana* (Rome: Mar Thoma Yogam, 1995) 7.

66. Mar Gregorios Yohanna Ibrahim, "Introduction to the Sacraments: An Oriental Orthodox Perspective," *Syriac Dialogue: Fourth Non-Official Consultation on Dialogue within the Syriac Tradition*, ed. Johann Marte & Gerhard Wilflinger (Vienna: Pro Oriente, 2001) 107-117, p. 108.

67. *Ibid.*, 109.

2.1.2. *Sacramentology*

Before entering into the discussion on *rāzā/rozo* as sacrament, it seems important to note two different areas where the term *rozo* is used in the Syrian tradition. It is clearly stated in the joint communique of the fourth non-official consultation of Pro-Oriente of the representatives of various Syrian Churches on sacraments.

> Although Syriac *raza/rozo* can just mean 'secret' (as in the Aramaic of the Book of Daniel), there are two main religious contexts where it has a technical sense: in exegesis it corresponds approximately to 'type,' 'symbol' (in the patristic sense of the word where an ontological link is understood as existing between the symbol and the reality it symbolizes), and in liturgy, where the (plural) *raze/roze* are par excellence the Eucharistic Mysteries. In both cases *raza/rozo* denotes visible sign endowed with a 'hidden power' (St Ephrem) which, in the case of *raze/roze* in Scripture and in the natural world, serves as a vehicle for the disclosure of a divine reality, and, in the case of the Eucharistic Mysterie/*Qurbana/Qurbono*, as a means and vehicle of salvation.[68]

Murray notes the overlapping of these two meanings. In Ephrem's typology, which is drawn from the world around him, he notes how "this world of natural symbols in its turn overlaps with the sacramental theology." At the same time, he observes this aspect, even though "comparatively underdeveloped in Ephrem, is already an important aspect of his theology of symbols and their force."[69]

2.1.2.1. *Rozo* as Sacrament

The Christians of the Syriac tradition use the term, *rozo*, for sacramental rites, and it was widely used in Syria by the fourth century.[70] *Rozo* is a technical term commonly used in the Syrian liturgical traditions for the sacramental rites in general, and in particular, the plural is used for the Eucharist.[71] The singular, *rāzā*, also means the universal salvific plan of

68. *Syriac Dialogue*, ed. Marte & Wilflinger, 119.

69. Robert Murray, "Symbolism in St. Ephrem's Theology (I)," *ParOr* 6-7 (1975-76) 1-20, p. 2.

70. For a detailed study on *razâ* in sacramentology see Irénée-Henri Dalmais, "Raza et Sacrament," *Rituels: Mélanges offerts au Père Gy o.p.*, ed. Paul de Clerck & Eric Palazzo (Paris: Institute Catholique de Paris, 1990) 173-182. See also Wilhelm de Vries, *Sakramententheologie bei den syrischen Monophysiten*, OCA, 125 (Rome: Pontificium Institutum Orientalium Studiorum, 1940); Idem, *Sakramententheologie bei den syrischen Nestorianern*, OCA, 133 (Rome: Pontificium Institutum Orientalium Studiorum, 1947).

71. Murray, *Symbols of the Church and Kingdom*, 21. Among the Syro Malabar Christians, the singular form is used for the most solemn form of the Eucharistic Liturgy. However, in the Syrian Antiochean tradition, the singular form is used to mean the Church-procession. See Varghese Pathikulangara, *Resurrection, Life and Renewal* (Ban-

God.[72] "Sacraments are celebrations of *mdabranutha/mdabronutho* (Economy of Salvation), namely God's plan in Jesus Christ to save humanity by offering his divine grace through those rites which the Church recognizes as holy *raze/rozo*."[73] Along with its other uses, Brock also agrees to its use in the sense of 'sacraments'.[74] *Rāzā* can also denote all material things used for sacraments.[75] Furthermore, the word for sacraments in the Syro-Malankara tradition is *qudosho*. It comes from the root *qadesh* and it means to sanctify, hallow or consecrate.[76]

Both Aphrahat and Ephrem use *raze* in terms of sacraments, especially to the sacrament of initiation and to the Eucharist.[77] Beck notes the different typological terms used by Ephrem such as: *Râzâ* = Symbol, *t'upsâ* = typus, *dmūtā* = image (Bild), *âtâ* = sign (Zeichen).[78] According to Nabil El-Khoury, Ephrem uses *raze* "interchangebly with *demutâ* (picture) or *peleta* (simile, parable), but can still carry the meaning of *tupsâ* τύπος or *juqnâ* (icon)." He also notes that in the case of "the sacraments of the New Testament, Baptism, the Holy Eucharist and Extreme Unction, Ephraim quite frequently uses the term *nisâ*, which actually has more the sense of 'sign'. It can, however, be used interchangeably with

galore: Dharmaram Publications, 1982) 157. In the Malankara tradition, that follows the Antiochene tradition, the Church-procession is still called *rāzā*. On the previous evenings of the parish feast, people gather together in the parish, or one of its sub-stations (in some places people even gather in some particular houses), for the evening prayer. After the evening prayer, people go around the village finally reaching the parish. People of all religions will decorate their houses and will greet the procession with reverence. The celebrant will bless the houses on both sides of the way and the people will kiss the Cross. The procession has a cosmic dimension and serves to bless all of the villagers, animals and fields.

72. Edmund Beck, "Symbolum-Mysterium bei Aphraat und Ephräm," *OC* 41-42 (1957-1958) 19-40, p. 22; Pierre Yousif, *L'Eucharistie chez s. Éphrem* (Rome: Pontificium institutum orientale, 1984) 271; *Razâ* in the sense of *tupsâ* is of particular importance in this regard. P. Tanios Bou Mansour, *La Pensée symbolique de S. Éphrem le syrien* (Kaslik: Bibliothèque de l'Université Saint-Esprit XVI, 1988) 28. For a general study on *razâ* and *tupsâ*, see 26-35.

73. *Syriac Dialogue*, ed. Marte & Wilflinger, 119.

74. Brock, *The Luminous Eye*, 56.

75. de Vries, *Sakramententheologie bei den syrischen Monophysiten*, 32.

76. Paul Verghese, "Relation between Baptism, 'Confirmation' and the Eucharist in the Syrian Orthodox Church," *SL* 4 (1965) 81-93, p. 84.

77. Murray, "Symbolism in St. Ephrem's Theology (I)," 4. Aphrahat alludes *râzâ* to the sacrament of Baptism, Eucharist and Confirmation. Beck, "Symbolum-Mysterium bei Aphraat und Ephräm," 23. Ephrem also uses it for three sacraments: Confirmation (*myron*), Baptism and Eucharist, the latter being the centre of all (*ibid.*, 31).

78. Beck, "Symbolum-Mysterium bei Aphraat und Ephräm," 20. Yousif, *L'Eucharistie chez s. Éphrem*, 271. These words and other similar words are studied in detail by Bou Mansour, *La Pensée symbolique de S. Éphrem le syrien*, 26-71.

razâ."[79] Although there are different words used in different contexts, one could say with Murray that Ephrem's use of the various words, symbols, types and mysteries are renderings of the word *raza.*[80] Brock agrees with him and notes that although Ephrem employs a variety of different words, including the Greek word *tupos*, the common term used is *raza* (plural: *raze*), which "is used to express the divine reality hidden in the types or symbols. Symbol and reality (*shrara*, literally 'truth') are intimately linked, for inherent in the symbol, or *rāzā*, is the 'hidden power', or meaning (*hayla kasya*) of the reality."[81] The meaning of *rāzā* can be summarized as that which "signifies a means to understanding which can be perceived by the senses, but which nevertheless leads the understanding to the abstract ideal which is hidden from the material eye."[82]

One remarkable thing in the study of *rāzā* is that unlike the Greek *mysterion*, it is not used in the cultic sense. Murray notes that there is only "one development of μυστήριον in the Greco-Roman world in which the early Syriac fathers shared little or not at all is that which from the time of Clement of Alexandria on, but above all in the 4th century, was borrowed from the mystery religions."[83] Dom Beck also finds only one possible instance of such use in Ephrem.[84] However, Paul Verghese does not rule out the possible connection to the mystery cults. At the same time he points to its specific meaning in ecclesiastical Syriac as "an act of the chosen community, either initiating into the community, or instructing the baptized, or performing the 'great mystery of the upper room'."[85]

2.1.2.2. Mystery of Jesus' Redemption

The sacramentology of the Syrian tradition, rooted in the *rozo*, is closer to '*mysterion*' (mystery) than to '*sacramentum*' (sacred). It underscores the symbolic and mysteriological understanding of sacraments at a deeper level. The understanding of sacraments as mystery helps one to go beyond its restricted use, referring to seven particular sacraments.[86] It

79. Nabil El-Khoury, "Hermeneutics in the Works of Ephraim the Syrian," *OCA* 229 (1987) 93-99, p. 94. *Contra Haereses* 27: 3; *Hymnen de Fide* 13: 5; 74: 22; *Hymnen de Virginitate* 7: 6.

80. Murray, "Symbolism in St. Ephrem's Theology (I)," 3.

81. Brock, *The Luminous Eye*, 41. For the use of *rāzā* as symbol in Ephrem see *Hymnen de Virginitate* 8: 6.3.

82. Nabil El-Khoury, "Hermeneutics in the Works of Ephraim the Syrian," 94.

83. Murray, "Symbolism in St. Ephrem's Theology (I)," 4.

84. Beck, "Symbolum-Mysterium bei Aphraat und Ephräm," 39.

85. Verghese, "Relation between Baptism, 'Confirmation' and the Eucharist in the Syrian Orthodox Church," 82.

86. There are disputes regarding the number of sacraments in the Syrian tradition. For

covers all areas of salvific mystery. It is for this reason that the Syrian Christians call different religious and liturgical tradition *rozo*. It is the celebration of the mystery of Jesus' redemption of mankind. As Verghese notes, *rozo* is "primarily an act of Christ through His Body the Church. It is a mystery in so far as it penetrates into the eternal order of reality and thus transcends our timespace logic." From this perspective, he criticizes discussions on what happens to the elements and how.[87] Bawai Soro similarly notes that *rāzā*, understood as mystery, means the Church and "transcends the existential moment. It both 're-presents' the past redemptive act of Jesus Christ on the Cross, and points to the future eschatological expectation of his Second Coming. In the Church's 'Mysteries' the believer is given participation in the Death and Resurrection of Christ, and in the life of the Kingdom to come."[88]

2.1.2.3. Liturgy and Sacraments

Rāzā underscores the importance of liturgy in the study of sacraments. It also helps to explain the absence of any systematic explanation of sacraments in the writings of the Syrian Fathers.[89] Unlike the Greco-Antiochean Fathers, who wrote catechetical and mystagogical homilies, the early Syriac Fathers didn't write anything of the sort and the liturgy remained at the center of their theology. The first Syriac commentary on sacraments seems to be from Narsai, which is rooted in the homilies of

a detailed study on the number of sacraments, accepted by various Fathers at various stages, see de Vries, *Sakramententheologie bei den syrischen Monophysiten*, 29-32. See also Murray, *Symbols of Church and Kingdom*, 21-23. Mar Bawai Soro, "Understanding Church of the East Sacramental Theology: The Theodorian Perspective," *Syriac Dialogue*, ed. Marte & Wilflinger, 22-43, pp. 39-41. Soro lists three traditions regarding the number of sacraments prevalent in the Assyrian Church of the East. *Ibid.*, 43. For the discussions on sacraments, based on various Syrian traditions, see the same book 48-52. Paul Verghese also justifies the broader view of sacraments going beyond seven in the Malankara tradition. Verghese, "Relation between Baptism, 'Confirmation' and the Eucharist in the Syrian Orthodox Church," 83-84. For a discussion on the number of sacraments in the East Syrian tradition, see Pierre Yousif, "The Sacrament of Marriage in the Tradition of the Church of the East (Assyrian, Chaldean, Malabar)," in a paper presented at the fifth Syriac Consultation (Vienna: Pro Oriente, February 26 – March 1, 2002) 1-12, pp. 10-11. The discussions on the number of sacraments are still a burning issue and there is no unanimous agreement on this topic. The recent synod of the Assyrian Church, convened in Chicago in 2001, has reconsidered this topic and decided to exclude marriage from the list of sacraments.

87. Verghese, "Relation between Baptism, 'Confirmation' and the Eucharist in the Syrian Orthodox Church," 82-83.

88. Mar Bawai Soro, "Understanding Church," 22-23.

89. de Vries, *Sakramententheologie bei den syrischen Monophysiten*, 29.

Theodore of Mopsuestia.[90] He is considered to be the first one of the Church of the East who presented a complete exposition of the sacramental beliefs of the Church.[91] Moreover, the Syriac translations of the liturgical homilies of the Greek Fathers provided a basis for the development of sacramentology in the Syrian traditions.[92] Here one cannot ignore the fact that beginning with Theodore of Mopsuestia and Narsai one notes a strong influence of Greek theology in Syrian Christian tradition. Therefore, for a genuine study of the Syrian tradition one has to consider the early period prior to Theodore of Mopsuestia.

Although the Syriac Fathers did not produce commentaries on the sacraments, they produced *mêmré*, or metrical homilies, on the important feasts of the liturgical year. These are poetical meditations of scriptural inspiration that are to be sung at the offices on feast days. Besides *Mêmré*, Ephrem developed another poetical genre, namely hymns (*madrāšê*). While the *mêmré* were recited, the *madrāšê* contain stanzas and are intended for singing. Hence, any study of the sacraments must consider the whole gamut of liturgical texts. In order to understand the liturgical theology of the Syrian tradition, we are forced to include, not only the liturgical texts of the respective sacramental celebrations, but also the liturgical texts of the daily, weekly and yearly cycle.[93]

2.1.2.4. Sacraments and Theology

A proper understanding of sacraments as *rāzā* undergirds the importance of liturgy and sacraments as *locus theologicus*. This does not mean to say that liturgy provides the various themes for the different branches of theology. Rather, as we have seen, it points to a fundamental approach to theology that acknowledges the liturgical experience for developing and doing theology. Thus, Bawai Soro suggests that a proper study of sacramentology must be done in relation to Christian anthropology, Christology and soteriology.[94]

According to Soro, the redemption of human beings by Jesus Christ is the context and foundation of Christian sacramental life. Against the background of man's fall to sin, the sacramentology of the Church of the East rests upon Jesus, the High Priest of the order of Melchizedec.[95] Ac-

90. Baby Varghese, "Some Aspects of West Syrian Liturgical Theology," *SL* 31 (2001) 171-178, p. 171.

91. Mar Bawai Soro, "Understanding Church," 22.

92. Varghese, "Some Aspects of West Syrian Liturgical Theology," 171-172.

93. Elie Khalifé-Hachem, "Maronite Sacramental Theology," *Syriac Dialogue*, ed. Marte & Wilflinger, 53-61, p. 53.

94. Mar Bawai Soro, "Understanding Church," 22.

95. *Ibid.*, 23. The sacrifice of Melchizedec "replaces the cultic rituals of the Old Tes-

cording to the New Testament understanding Jesus Christ "established his own sacrifice on the Cross as the atonement for our sins and brought about the reconciliation of all creation with God, thus bringing God's forgiveness and redemption to the world, and renewing God's covenant with all humanity."[96]

Coupled with the Christological understanding, the role of the Holy Spirit is similarly emphasised in the Syrian tradition. Verghese notes that "All the mysteries are related integrally to the great mystery of the Incarnation and its continuation in the Body of Christ. All of them are equally related also to the operation of the Holy Spirit in Christ's Body the Church."[97]

In short, our study, on the notions of *sôd*, *rāzā*, and the sacramentology of the Syrian tradition, points to a wider meaning compared to *sacramentum* and *mysterion*. Besides what we have discussed, *rāzā* is also used to explain the mystery of Revelation. This is of particular importance for our discussion on the sacramentality of Creation.

2.2. World-View

Ephrem's worldview has to be understood based on his theology of *rāzā*. It is the result of an effort to understand the dialectic between Creator and creation. In order to understand this, it seems important to understand the theology of Creation in Ephrem.

2.2.1. Theology of Creation

Ephrem's theology of Creation is to be drawn in the background of his teachings against the various controversies prevalent at his time. It is in this background he defended his theology of Creation rooted in the Judeo-Christian tradition. Here, we limit our survey of these controversies to their relationship to cosmology.

2.2.1.1. Philosophical Background

One of the central concerns of fourth century Syria was cosmology. During this period the discussions in the intellectual circles was mainly on

tament's Aaronic priesthood, which mediated the presence of God through rituals and sacrifices, but which, in the fullness of time, was brought to fulfillment in and through the priesthood of Jesus Christ." *Ibid.* For details see Theodore of Mopsuestia, *Commentary on the Lord's Prayer and on the Sacraments of Baptism and the Eucharist*, ed. Alphonse Mingana, Woodbrooke Studies, 6 (Cambridge: Heffer, 1933) 18.

96. Mar Bawai Soro, "Understanding Church," 23.

97. Verghese, "Relation between Baptism, 'Confirmation' and the Eucharist in the Syrian Orthodox Church," 84.

"the questions of the nature of God, the nature of matter, the process of creation, the organization of the creation and the structure and the function of the non-visible world."[98] These questions and discussions are reflected in the writings of Arian, Bardasian, Mani and Marcion as well as their followers. Ephrem's *Prose Refutations of Mani, Marcion and Bardaisan*[99] and *Hymns against Heresies*[100] refer to the magical and astrological practices at Edessa and reflect his teachings against the controversies raised by Mani, Marcion and Bardaisan.[101] Ephrem's *Commentary on Genesis* also "sustains the polemic against heresies of Marcion, Bardaisan, and Mani."[102] Similarly McVey notes that his *Hymns on Virginity* contain a variety of polemics against these three.[103] The teachings of all the three heretics contain "the idea, in one form or another, that the world was fashioned out of various preexistent substances."[104]

Although Ephrem's refutations are directed mainly against Bardaisan, Mani and Marcion, he also expressed concern against the questions raised by the Arians. In particular, his *Hymns on Faith* is directed against the Arians.[105] Arius was primarily concerned to find a rational explanation of the mystery of God. In particular, his main focus was on the eternal generation of the Son from the Father,[106] and presented the generation of the

98. Bundy, "Language and Knowledge of God in Ephrem Syrus," 97.

99. Charles W. Mitchell, *Saint Ephrem's Prose Refutations of Mani, Marcion and Bardaisan*, Vol. I *The Discourses Addressed to Hypatius* (London: Williams and Norgate, 1912); Vol. II, *The Discourse called "Of Domnus" and Six Other Writings* (London: Williams and Norgate, 1921).

100. Edmund Beck, *Des Heiligen Ephraem des Syrers Hymnen contra Haereses*, CSCO.S 76-77, 169-170 (Louvain: Peeters, 1957).

101. H.J.W. Drijvers, *Cults and Beliefs at Edessa* (Leiden: Brill, 1980) 36. His *Prose Refutations* are aimed at intellectual elites. However, the hymns are aimed at ordinary people though the arguments are taken from Bardaisan. H. J. W. Drijvers, *Bardaisan of Edessa* (Assen: Van Gorcum & Comp. N. V., 1966) 128-129. In general, all his works seem to be pastoral in nature intending the ordinary members of the Church. Russell, "Ephraem the Syrian on the Utility of Language and the Place of Silence," *Journal of Early Christian Studies* 8: 1 (2000) 21-37, 22. See also Sidney H. Griffith, *"Faith Adoring the Mystery": Reading the Bible with St. Ephraem the Syrian* (Milwaukee, WI: Marquette University Press, 1997) 8ff.

102. McVey (ed.), *St. Ephrem the Syrian: Selected Prose Works*, 64.

103. *Ibid.*, 40. For example: "The pagans err in worshipping the works of God rather than God their Creator. Conversely the Marcionists err in claiming to worship God while denying the goodness and beauty of God's creation. Both Judaism and Marcionism are pointedly rejected because they deny the presence of Christ in the Jewish Scripture and in nature. The only correct path is through nature to the revelation of God in scripture."

104. *Ibid.*, 61.

105. Edward G. Mathews, Jr., "St. Ephrem, Madrase on Faith, 81-85 Hymns on the Pearl, I-V," *SVTQ* 38 (1994) 45-72, p. 48.

106. For examples of Arian quotations in Ephrem see Russell, "Ephraem the Syrian

Son within time. By putting the ontological gap (chasm) between the Creator and created inside of time, the Arians deemed it possible for the human intellect to investigate it. Ephrem, along with other Orthodox theologians, considered this a double blasphemy. On the one hand "they located the Son on the wrong side of the ontological gap." On the other hand, they attempted to find "a rational definition of the Son's Generation from the Father."[107] Their rationalistic approach "tends to make the divine Persons into what Ephrem calls 'bound natures' (that is, determined and predictable) instead of free."[108] Ephrem criticizes the Arians in the sense that they failed "to respect the transcendence of God as they argued about the relations of Father and Son."[109]

According to Marcion all things in Creation come from an eternal primal matter, which he calls *hūlź*.[110] Marcion also "established a dualism: a good God (the Maker) and the divine Stranger, the Just God who disputed the universe which had been formed from already existing matter."[111] Since matter (the world) contains evil, human beings are to be purified. Thus, Marcionites advocate asceticism and sexual rigorism. Their dualistic worldview led them to develop a docetic Christology and to deny the physical resurrection of the body, soul and spirit.[112]

The Bardaisanin cosmology is another important instigator.[113] Besides

on the Utility of Language and the Place of Silence," 23, no. 8.

107. Brock, *The Luminous Eye*, 24. Ephrem in the poem, *Hymnen de Fide* 31: 1-7, makes it clear that "since humanity cannot cross the ontological chasm and so approach God, God has to cross it in the opposite direction first." And "the whole aim of this divine descent into human language is to draw humanity upto God." Brock, *The Luminous Eye*, 69: 11-13.

108. Murray, "St Ephrem' Dialogue of Reason and Love," 30.

109. *Ibid.*, 27.

110. McVey (ed.), *St. Ephrem the Syrian: Selected Prose Works*, 49. For Marcion's influence of *hūlź* on Ephrem see, Edmund Beck, "Die Hyle bei Markion nach Ephräm," *OCP* 44 (1978) 5-30. For Ephrem's teaching against Marcion, see B. Aland, "Marcion: Versuch einer neuen Interpretation," *ZTK* 70 (1973) 420-447; H.J.W. Drijvers, "Marcionism in Syria: Principles, Problems, Polemics," *The Second Century* 8 (1987-88) 167; David D. Bundy, "Marcion and the Marcionites in Early Syriac Apologetics," *LM* 101 (1988) 21-32.

111. *Prose Refutations* II, 50-142; trans. xxiii-lxv. Bundy, "Language and Knowledge of God in Ephrem Syrus," 94-95.

112. *Hymnen contra Haereses* 52: 5-13.

113. Drijvers even considers Ephrem as "one of the principal sources for our knowledge of Bardaisan's ideas." Drijvers, *Bardaisan of Edessa*, 128. For Ephrem's treatment on Bardaisan see *ibid.*, 133-143; Idem, *East of Antioch: Studies in Early Christianity* (London: Variorum, 1984); Edmund Beck, "Bardaisan und Seine Schule bei Ephräm," *LM* 91 (1978) 271-333; Idem, "Ephräms Rede gegen eine philosophische Schrift des Bardaisan," *OrChr* 60 (1976) 24-68; B. Ehlers, "Bardesanes – ein Syrische Gnostiker," *ZKG* 81 (1970) 334-351; H. Kruse, "Die 'mythologischen Irrtümer' Bar-Daisāns," *OrChr* 71

the works referred to at the beginning, there are many other works in which Ephrem refers to Bardaisan, although its authority as Ephrem's work is under dispute.[114] Bardaisan considered God as an organizer, rather than as Creator; Creation is the result of an accidental union of five entities (*'ityê*),[115] and also uses the word to refer to the planets.[116] At the same time, it is important to note that there are disputes, among Bardaisan and his followers regarding how the world was ordered from the mixture of various elements.[117] The basic problem of Ephrem is that if God is just an organizer of matter, will Bardaisan and Mani "not give the name of God to matter also, matter having been the occasion of the work of God the Creator."[118]

For Ephrem, Mani was full of heresy.[119] Mani's cosmology includes

(1987) 24-52. Jansma even says that Ephrem's arguments against astrological determinism are borrowed from the armoury of Bardaisan's, *The Book of the Laws of Countries*. T. Jansma, "Ephraem on Exodus II, 5: Reflections on the Interplay of Human Freewill and Divine Providence," *OCP* 34 (1973) 5-28, p. 16. It is also important to note that against Bardaisan, Ephrem wrote his literal commentary on the creation of six days. T. Jansma, "Ephraems Beschreibung des ersten Tages der Schöpfung," *OCP* 37 (1971) 300-305; A. Guillaumont, "Genèse 1, 1-2 selon les commentateurs syriaques," *In principio: Interprétations des premiers versets de la Genèse*, Études augustiniennes, série antiquité, 51 (Paris: Études augustiniennes, 1973) 115-132. For his treatment on Bardaisan in his hymns, see Edmund Beck, "Bardaisan und Seine Schule bei Ephräm," *LM* 91 (1978) 271-333 271-333.

114. For the details of such works see Drijvers, *Bardaisan of Edessa*, 129.

115. *Hymnen contra Haereses* 3: 1(-7); 41: 7; 49: 6; *Commentary on Genesis* 1: 2. Bardaisan's five entities are water, wind, fire, light and darkness. For Ephrem "they were fundamental elements (*kyānē*) which were created by God." He considers the first four as created elements, darkness, however, has no real existence on its own. See *Commentary on Genesis* 1: 16. McVey (ed.), *St. Ephrem the Syrian: Selected Prose Works*, 76, see note 27. Elsewhere Ephrem speaks of six entities including God himself and also of seven entities. Having considered the fact that different authors give various numberings of entities, Drijvers concludes that "in Bardaisan's system Ephrem knows, beside God, of four pure elements, light, wind, fire and water, while darkness represents impurity." Drijvers, *Bardaisan of Edessa*, 136. For details of the discussion, see *ibid.*, 131-136. In *Hymnen contra Haereses* 3: 7, it says that Bardaisan's error is from the Greeks. Further in 14: 7 he says that Bardaisan, Mani and Marcion took the concept of matter from the Greeks. *Ibid.*, 131.

116. *Hymnen contra Haereses* 51: 13.

117. Drijvers, *Bardaisan of Edessa*, 139-141.

118. *Ibid.*, 137.

119. *Hymnen contra Haereses* 22: 13-22; 41: 8; 51: 14; *Prose Refutations* I, 9. Bardaisan is considered to be the teacher of Mani, particularly of his cosmology. See *Prose Refutations* I, 122 (text) xc (tran). For detailed study on Mani's cosmology see Samuel N. C. Lieu, *Manichaeism in the Later Roman Empire and Medieval China* (Manchester: Manchester University Press, 1988) 7-32; David D. Bundy, "Ephrem's Critique of Mani: The Limits of Knowledge and the Nature of Language," *Gnosticisme et monde hellénis-*

the eternal *hylē*, a doctrine which was originally derived from Marcion.[120] He conceived reality as divided into the "kingdom of light" and the "kingdom of darkness." This dichotomy is also called "truth" and "lie," "God" and "matter." In order to redeem oneself from the powers of darkness, he suggested a strict asceticism, and proposed two levels of ascetic life. The lower morality, which was suggested for ordinary people, must keep the ten Manichaean commandments, along with other practices like fasting and prayer. The higher morality was suggested for the righteous elect. Besides adhering to the commandments, they must also abstain from marriage, possession of property, meat, wine etc.[121]

Ephrem criticizes Bardaisan and Mani for allegorizing the biblical account of creation in six days to develop their cosmology.[122] According to Ephrem "*'ityê* of Bardaisan and the *hūlź* of Mani and Marcion are nothing more than elements or created natures (in Syriac, *kyānź*), created by the sole Being who created all that is not Himself."[123] The Bardaisan and Manichean cosmology agrees on the ordering of the world and the need for purification to eliminate the powers of darkness. However, they disagree on how the purification should be accomplished. For Mani, it is through a rigorous ascetical life. Bardaisan, on the other hand, proposes to strive "after good through an active attitude in the world." For him, knowledge and faith are not in fundamental opposition, moreover, they are prerequisites to achieve participation.[124]

tique: Actes du Colloque de Louvain-la-Neuve (11-14 mars 1980), ed. J. Ries, et al., Publications de l'Institut Orientaliste de Louvain, 27 (Louvain-la-Neuve: Institut Orientaliste de Louvain, 1982) 289-298; idem, "Language and Knowledge of God in Ephrem Syrus."

120. *Hymnen contra Haereses* 22: 17.

121. W. Stewart McCullough, *A Short History of Syriac Christianity to the Rise of Islam* (Chico, CA: Scholars, 1982) 104-105.

122. *Commentary on Genesis* 1: 1. See also Nabil El-Khoury, *Die Interpretation der Welt bei Ephraem: Beitrag zur Geistesgeschichte*, Tübinger theologische Studien, 6 (Mainz: Grünewald, 1976) 49-62; Tryggve Kronholm, *Motifs from Genesis 1–11 in the Genuine Hymns of Ephrem the Syrian, with Particular Reference to the Influence of Jewish Exegetical Tradition*, Coniectanea Biblica. OT Series, 11 (Lund: Gleerup, 1978) 41-43. On the other hand, Ephrem's approach is that of a meditation of the six days in their relation to the Incarnation. *Hymnen de Nativitate* 26.

123. See *Hymnen contra Haereses* 14: 7-10; *Commentary on Genesis* 1: 2.

124. Drijvers, *Bardaisan of Edessa*, 141-142. Drijvers also notes Bardaisan's vagueness on how this is achieved.

2.2.1.2. Ephrem's View of Creation

Ephrem remained within the Judaeo-Christian interpretation of the biblical concept of Creation. Accordingly, he affirmed the creation of everything out of nothing.[125] Creation is the free and loving act of God (*ad extra*) from nothing.[126] It is not an accidental event in time, but a willful act of God.

Ephrem viewed God as the only true self-subsistent being (*itūtā*).[127] This word is rooted in the expression "I am who I am" of Exod 3:14. This word is transliterated and associated with *'ityâ* or *'itutâ*.[128] Ephrem uses the term *'ityâ* (and its deritative *'itūtā*), only for God. He is the only *'itūtā*, or 'Being'. For Ephrem, to give a created thing the name, *'ityâ*, is more blasphemous than any idol-worshipping committed in the Old Testament.[129] Thus, he criticises Bardaisan, who speaks of different *'ityê*.[130]

For Ephrem, God (*'ityâ* or *'itutâ*) is the uncreated Being.[131] He is a God 'without beginning and end'. For him there is only one *'ityâ*, and to accept several *'ityê* means to accept several things with the same nature.[132] There is no similarity or connection between the eternal *'itutâ* and Creation. To find any resemblance between the two is an error,[133] because what we see in Creation are the works of God.[134] Furthermore, he distinguished the essence of the Creator from the essence of Creation.[135] The distinction between Creator and creature is infinite[136] and the

125. *Hymnen contra Haereses* 28: 8; 3. See El-Khoury, *Der Interpretation der Welt bei Ephraem*, 65-81.

126. *Hymnen de Fide* 26: 1; 45: 3.9.

127. *Hymnen de Fide* 63: 6; 37: 24; 45: 3. Although Ute Possekel uses the untranslated words, he explains *'itutâ* as '(divine) being' or '(divine) essence,' while *'ityâ* as either 'entry,' 'God,' or 'eternal principle'. Possekel, *Evidence of Greek Philosophical Concepts in the Writings of Ephrem the Syrian*, 59.

128. Possekel, *Evidence of Greek Philosophical Concepts in the Writings of Ephrem the Syrian*, CSCO, 580 (Louvain: Peeters, 1999) 57.

129. See *Hymnen contra Haereses* 53: 11-12. See also *Hymnen contra Haereses* 16: 9; *Hymnen de Fide* 63: 6.

130. Possekel, *Evidence of Greek Philosophical Concepts in the Writings of Ephrem the Syrian*, 57.

131. *Hymnen de Fide* 73: 21; 49: 3; *Prose Refutations* I, 37; *Hymnen contra Haereses* 16: 3-9.

132. Possekel, *Evidence of Greek Philosophical Concepts in the Writings of Ephrem the Syrian*, 58.

133. *Hymnen de Fide* 26: 7.

134. *Hymnen de Ecclesia* 22: 3. See also *Memrê on Faith* 2: 413-418.

135. *Hymnen de Fide* 1: 3; 3: 13; 26: 7.

136. See *Prose Refutations* II, 219 (text), civ (translation). Regarding the unity of Creator see Kronholm, *Motifs from Genesis 1–11 in the Genuine Hymns of Ephrem the Syrian*, 35-39.

"'*ityâ* is unchangeable, as God is unchangeable."[137] The created universe however, is liable to change.[138]

The distinction between Creator and Creation is very important in Ephrem, and it helped him to criticize the efforts of heretical teachers who looked upon Creation as God. Ephrem clearly expresses this by drawing an analogy between how Moses criticized those who considered created things to be gods.[139]

Ephrem uses the word *kyânâ* for nature. Possekel offers three meanings for this word.[140] First, it designates all created things. Sometimes it even includes human creations, yet on other occasions, it is used to contrast human beings, who are the only ones endowed with a free will, with other beings in Creation.[141] In this sense it is used to designate the order God gave to Creation itself.[142] Secondly, it refers to the inner nature of Creation. It denotes a thing's substance, and determines its qualities and actions. Thus, Ephrem describes enormous qualities of things that are incomprehensible to human beings.[143] It includes the nature of human beings.[144] In some places where he describes human nature, he speaks of particular persons such as Mary and Zachariah.[145] However, about the nature of the heretics, Ephrem claims that they are bound natures (*kyânâ* or *'asirâ*). This relates to the fixed inner nature of something, which is an essential character of a "thing." In contrast to a thing, he makes a distinc-

137. Possekel, *Evidence of Greek Philosophical Concepts in the Writings of Ephrem the Syrian*, 59.

138. *Prose Refutations* II, cxv, *Hymnen de Fide* 3: 13; 26: 7.

139. *Commentary on Genesis*, prologue, 2. See also *Hymnen contra Haereses* 48: 2.

140. Beck has demonstrated only two meanings. This partly is because his study of this word was mainly based on the *Mêmre on Faith* and *Hymns on Faith*. Possekel goes further and looks for meanings in the *Prose Refutations* and the *Commentary on Genesis*. Possekel, *Evidence of Greek Philosophical Concepts in the Writings of Ephrem the Syrian*, 60, see note 35. Possekel's basic argument here is to see the possible influence of Greek Philosophy in the writings of Aphrahaat and Ephrem. See particularly pages 62-64. However, it is not our concern here to enter into such a discussion; our interest is limited to see how this notion is important to distinguish between Creator and Creation.

141. Possekel, *Evidence of Greek Philosophical Concepts in the Writings of Ephrem the Syrian*, 60-61. According to Possekel, in *Hymnen de Fide* 35: 5(6) nature includes the human being. However, in *Hymnen de Fide* 28: 4 and in *Hymnen contra Haereses*, there are differences.

142. Possekel, *Evidence of Greek Philosophical Concepts in the Writings of Ephrem the Syrian*, 60. See *Hymnen de Nativitate* 10: 7; *Memrê on Faith* 2: 477.

143. *Ibid.*, 60. Descriptions of this kind occur mainly in the *Hymns on Faith*.

144. See *Hymnen de Ecclesia* 6: 14; 9: 1. Possekel, *Evidence of Greek Philosophical Concepts in the Writings of Ephrem the Syrian*, 61.

145. *Hymnen de Nativitate* 2: 20. Possekel, *Evidence of Greek Philosophical Concepts in the Writings of Ephrem the Syrian*, 61.

tion for the human being. For him, "the human body is bound by its nature, but the human will is free."[146] This is also true of the nature of God. When speaking of God, however, *kyânâ* is associated with *'ityâ*, but of course not synonymously.[147] Finally, the word can be used to refer to elements such as fire and air, which Bardaisan considers as *'ityê*. By calling these elements *kyânâ*, he puts into question Bardaisan's use as eternal principles.[148]

The three usages of *kyânâ* make the differences in the created natures of Creation clear. The human being, endowed with free will, remains the highest created being of all Creation.

2.2.2. God's Revelation

Although God remains incomprehensible for human beings, God reveals himself to humanity in different ways. God's manifestations in the world are made available through the Scriptures and nature. For Ephrem, Scripture and nature (*ketaba* and *kyana*) constitute God's two witnesses.[149] Ephrem even considers the created world and the two testaments as three harps upon which the divine musician plays.[150]

According to Brock, "the Syriac original calls this world a 'school'."[151] Types (in Syriac, *tupsê*; in Greek, τύπος) and symbols (in Syriac, *râzê*; in Greek, σύμβολα) are to be found everywhere in Creation.[152] The created world is praised not only for its beauty and order;

146. *Hymnen de Nativitate* 1: 98. See also *Hymnen de Ecclesia* 6: 16. Possekel, *Evidence of Greek Philosophical Concepts in the Writings of Ephrem the Syrian*, 61.

147. *Hymnen de Nativitate* 1: 97; God's nature as Creator *Hymnen contra Haereses* 37: 2; the unchanging nature of God *Hymnen contra Haereses* 36: 6; the divine nature older than the universe *Hymnen de Nativitate* 4: 147; the incomprehensibility of God's nature, *Hymnen de Nativitate* 3: 5; *Hymnen de Fide* 70: 14. Possekel, *Evidence of Greek Philosophical Concepts in the Writings of Ephrem the Syrian*, 61.

148. Possekel, *Evidence of Greek Philosophical Concepts in the Writings of Ephrem the Syrian*, 61-62.

149. See *Paradise* 5: 2; *Hymnen de Virginitate* 20: 12; *Hymnen contra Haereses* 28: 11-12; *Hymnen de Fide* 41: 7; 84: 2; *Paschahymnen* 4: 22-24.

150. *Hymnen de Virginitate* 27-30.

151. Sebastian Brock, "Humanity and the Natural World in the Syriac Tradition," *Sobornost* 12/2 (1990) 131-142, 138. For Isaac of Nineveh, "the first book which was given to rational beings was the natural created world." Isaac of Niniveh, *On Ascetical Life*, tr., Mary Hansbury (Crestwood, NY: St. Vladimir's Seminary Press, 1989) 81.

152. "Wherever you look, God's symbol is there; wherever you read, there you will find His types. For by Him all creatures were created, and He stamped all his possessions with His symbols when He created the world." *Hymnen de Virginitate* 20: 12. "Creation gives birth to the symbols of Christ, as Mary gave birth to His limbs." *Hymnen de Virginitate* 6: 7.

rather it contains symbols that speak of the identity of the Creator.[153] It is important to note that "certain material things enjoy a privileged place because they link the world of nature to the world of scripture."[154]

"For Ephrem, both Scripture and Creation are replete with God's symbols and mysteries, symbols which may point vertically, as it were, to his trinitarian Being, or horizontally to his incarnate Son."[155] The harmony that exists between God and His Creation is very clearly seen in the formulation of Ephrem's theology.[156] God's presence is both in Scripture and in nature. This serves as the basis for Ephrem's symbolic theology.[157]

As Brock observed, Ephrem's approach to Scripture and the world is sacramental. Brock, however, distinguishes Ephrem's scriptural exegesis from modern biblical scholars, whose primary concern is with historical truth. Rather, Ephrem's "object of enquiry is not historical truth but spiritual reality – a different sort of truth, possessing a different mode of objectivity."[158] To embark on such an enquiry what is important is to have "the experience of faith," and faith is essential to understand God.[159] This helps us to understand why Ephrem often uses typology to explain various realities. Accordingly, he tries to give nuances of meaning for biblical persons and events. For Ephrem "biblical types do not stand on their own as a special, isolated mode of revelation. He never treats the biblical text as a world on its own: rather the Bible, as a work of God in human imagery and language, is a part, as well as a special interpreter, of the whole world and its history. The Bible contains *raze*, revelatory symbols of Christ, because the whole world does."[160]

Furthermore, Ephrem is considered to be a representative of the *Theoria* of the school of Antioch. Ephrem's use of Scripture and "his treatment of two economies of salvation and the two Adams places him in a position much closer to the Antiochean tradition" than to the Alexandrian

153. McVey, *Ephrem the Syrian: Hymns*, 41. For example, see *Hymnen de Virginitate* 20: 12.

154. McVey, *Ephrem the Syrian: Hymns*, 46. An example of such an importance accorded to nature is illustrated in the hymns on oil. See *Hymnen de Virginitate* 4-7.

155. Brock, *The Luminous Eye*, 42.

156. McVey, *Ephrem the Syrian: Hymns*, 48.

157. *Ibid.*, 40.

158. Brock, *The Luminous Eye*, 161.

159. Faith has two aspects: positively given in Creation, Bible and faith equal an "analogical and descriptive value." Negatively, it is "the acceptance of not being able to know the what, how and why of God." Bundy, "Language and Knowledge of God in Ephrem Syrus," 99.

160. Murray, "Symbolism in St. Ephrem's Theology (I)," 5.

allegorical tradition.[161] Murray explicates: "In his exegetical prose works Ephrem expounds Old Testament episodes as they occur, writing soberly as an exegete of Antiochene type, with typology as currently used in that tradition, but in his hymns he constantly interweaves biblical and 'natural' symbols."[162] Cayré also says that Ephrem represents the Antiochene School. While Ephrem explains the Bible textually, his hymns are allegorical.[163] Nevertheless, Yousif seems to disagree that Ephrem is dependent on the Antiochene school, although he agrees on the similarity. In his opinion:

> [I]t is more exact if we see in him a view corresponding to that of Antioch, since there is no historical evidence of any dependence of Ephraem on that school even if its supposed founder, Lucian (†AD 312) is earlier than Ephraem, but Lucian himself studied in Edessa. But if the school was founded by Diodore of Tarsus (†392), how can we attribute an earlier scholar to a later school?[164]

Besides this Kronholm sees a possible influence from Syriac asceticism, *Odes of Solomon*, and the rabbinical exegetical method.[165] Brock also agrees that Ephrem's commentaries on Genesis and Exodus show "intriguing familiaritiy with Jewish exegesis."[166] Leloir, however, seems to reduce Ephrem's exegesis to the law of symbolism and parallelism between the two testaments.[167] Bundy, on the other hand, suggests that

161. McVey (ed.), *St. Ephrem the Syrian: Selected Prose Works*, 47.

162. Murray, "Symbolism in St. Ephrem's Theology (I)," 5. For example, *Hymnen de Virginitate* 20: 12; *Hymnen de Paradiso* 5: 2.

163. Fulbert Cayré, *Précis de patrologie et d'histoire de la théologie* (Paris: Desclée, 1927), vol. 1, 370.

164. Yousif, "Exegetical Principles of St Ephraem of Nisibis," 298.

165. Kronholm, *Motifs from Genesis 1–11 in the Genuine Hymns*, 25-27.

166. Sabastian Brock, "An Introduction to Syriac Studies," *Horizons in Semitic Studies*, ed. John H. Eaton, Semitics Study Aids, 8 (Birmingham: University of Birmingham, 1980) 1-33, p. 8. It is even noted that at some parts of his commentary, he "preserves Targumic traditions against the reading of the Peshitta version." McVey (ed.), *St. Ephrem the Syrian: Selected Prose Works*, 62-63 (no. 17-18). For the Jewish background of Ephrem's exegetical method, see among others D. Gerson, "Die Commentarien des Ephraem Syrus im Verhältnis zur jüdischen Exegese: ein Beitrag zur Geschichte der Exegese," *Monatsschrift für Geschichte und Wissenschaft des Judentums* 17 (1868) 15-33, 64-72, 98-109, 141-149; Sebastian Brock, "Jewish Traditions in Syriac Sources," *Journal of Jewish Studies* 30 (1979) 212-232, p. 219; Robert Murray, *Symbols of Church and Kingdom*, 301-310; N. Sed, "Les hymnes sur le Paradis de Saint Ephrem et les traditions juives," *LM* 81 (1968) 455-501.

167. Louis Leloir, "Symbolisme et parallélisme chez Saint Ephrem," *À la rencontre de Dieu: mémorial Albert Gelin*, Bibliothèque de la faculté catholique de théologie de Lyon, 8 (Le Puy: Mappus, 1961) 363-374. The same analysis is seen in Hidal. Sten Hidal,

Ephrem avoids the literal and fundamentalist explanation of Scripture and proposes a symbolic understanding of Scripture.[168] According to Murray, Ephrem analyses the Bible's language; his method is symbolic rather than merely factual statement.[169]

Ephrem admits the dynamic convergence of the Old and the New Testaments and focuses on "the inner sense of the words and sets them in their typological context within the rest of the sacred text."[170] Sebastian Brock explores the typology in Ephrem as a Poet.[171] Ephrem's "theological method, often labelled symbolic theology, is an intricate wave of parallelism, typology, names and symbols." He uses these tools "to express the various paradoxes of the Christian mystery."[172] His "works are pregnant with biblical phrases, metaphors, images and symbols."[173] "Ephrem's poems are filled with paradox and wonder, and he uses typological exegesis in an imaginative way.[174]

Nevertheless, the ontological chasm, which in Ephrem's view cannot be bridged by human knowledge, can be crossed by love.[175] Ephrem suggests three ways of divine self-revelation: types and symbols; names or metaphors; and the Incarnation. These three primary means in Ephrem

Interpretatio syriaca: die Kommentare des Heiligen Ephräm des Syrers zu Genesis und Exodus mit besondere Berücksichtigung ihrer Auslegungsgeschichtlichen Stellung, Coniectanea Biblica, OT Series, 6 (Lund: Gleerup, 1974) 25.

168. It is against Arianism and Manichaeism that Ephrem reacts against the literal and "fundamentalist" explanations and opts for a symbolic understanding of Scripture. Bundy, "Language and Knowledge of God in Ephrem Syrus," 101. See note 44.

169. Murray, "Symbolism in St. Ephrem's Theology (I)," 6.

170. McVey (ed.), *St. Ephrem the Syrian: Selected Prose Works*, 47. The unity between the two texts is so strong that there is no incident where a typological parallel is not present in the other.

171. Brock, "The Poet as Theologian," 244-245. "Ephrem's poetical theological method is not fully described by reviewing only how he handles types, natural symbols and sacramental 'mysteries'. All these are elements in his theology of revelation which is based on a grand conception of the harmony between God and all the orders of his Creation. God has filled Creation with his traces, inadequate yet valid pointers to himself; he has given man a mind and the faculty of language which can appreciate these pointers, express them and follow them by the light of the gift of faith." Murray, "Symbolism in St. Ephrem's Theology (I)," 2. See also Robert Murray, "Der Dichter als Exeget: der hl. Ephräm und die heutige Exegese," *ZKT* 100 (1978) 484-494.

172. McVey (ed.), *St. Ephrem the Syrian: Selected Prose Works*, 48.

173. David D. Bundy, "Ephrem's Exegesis of Isaiah," *SP* 18 (1990) 234-239, p. 234.

174. Both Brock and Murray compare Ephrem to the writings of Paul Ricœur. Brock, "An Introduction to Syriac Studies," 5; Id., *The Luminous Eye*, 181; Murray, "Theory of Symbolism," 3.

175. Griffith, "A Spiritual Father for the Whole Church," 31. See *Hymnen de Fide* 49: 12-13. For the image of 'bridge,' see Edmund Beck, "Zwei ephrämische Bilde," *Christianus* 71 (1987) 1-9.

are referred to as 'changes' (*šuhlâpê*).[176] These 'changes' do not affect the divine brightness for the sake of humanity, but God Himself loses absolutely nothing of His nature or His majesty.[177] According to Brock, the Bible and world witness God essentially by means of symbols and types. These revelations culminate in "God's revelation of himself to man, a revelation which in one sense culminates in the Incarnation, but in another awaits its final fulfillment until the Second Coming – an ambivalence between the temporal and eschatological that is recurrent, especially in early Christian thought."[178]

2.2.2.1. Types and Symbols

Symbols and types play a central role in Ephrem. Types and symbols, along with mysteries, are renderings of the word *rāzā*. It is also rendered by the same words: by τύπος in Greek and *tupsa* in Syriac.[179] As noted, Ephrem draws both types and symbols from Scripture and nature. According to Brock, Ephrem's use of symbol has a lot of similarity with many of the Greek and Latin Fathers. He also notes the difference with modern English usage, where a symbol is usually differentiated from what it symbolizes.[180] Murray has also made a similar observations in that Ephrem stands close to the primitive Church for his theology of types and symbols, yet, looks forward to the theology of icons.[181]

Ephrem, in his typological approach presents Jesus as the fulfilment of the Old Testament types and symbols.[182] The term Μυστηριον/*rāzā* was used to typify the 'Christ-bearing' sense concealed in the Old Testament figures.[183] The remarkable thing is that the types and symbols point both to His existence (*ousia*) and to His activity (*energeia*) as Creator.[184]

The purpose of types and symbols available in Nature and Scripture is to entice humanity back from its fallen state to the state of perfection. From the perspective of divine reality, "symbols and types can be said to serve as a veil to protect humanity from the overpowering brightness of

176. See *Hymnen de Virginitate* 28: 11; *Hymnen de Fide* 5: 7; 11: 9; 31: 5; and *Hymnen de Paradiso* 11: 6-7.

177. McVey (ed.), *St. Ephrem the Syrian: Selected Prose Works*, 51.

178. Sebastian Brock, "World and Sacrament in the Writings of the Syrian Fathers," *Sobornost* 6/10 (1974) 685-696, p. 687.

179. Murray, "Symbolism in St. Ephrem's Theology (I)," 3-4.

180. Brock, *The Luminous Eye*, 41.

181. Murray, "Symbolism in St. Ephrem's Theology (I)," 3.

182. Antony George Kollamparambil, *From Symbol to Truth: A Syriac Understanding of the Paschal Mystery* (Roma: CLV – Edizoni Liturgiche, 2000) 105.

183. Murray, "Symbolism in St. Ephrem's Theology (I)," 3-4.

184. McVey (ed.), *St. Ephrem the Syrian: Selected Prose Works*, 48, 49.

God's full revelation."[185] They reveal some aspect of the divine hiddenness.[186] However, humans are given the choice to accept this or reject it based on their free will. To accept is always a choice, guided by the freedom of faith as much as by the compulsion of proof.[187]

It is also important to note that symbols are multifaceted. For example, Ephrem uses "pearl" to express the Kingdom, of faith, of Christ, his virgin birth, his crucifixion etc. Therefore, one meaning does necessarily exclude the other. Thus, "the pearl simply serves as a window opening into all sorts of different aspects of 'Truth', it is an invitation and starting point for mediation."[188] "Ephrem sees a continuous dialectic between the one divine reality and the many symbols."[189] "First we have the movement from One to the many ... And then we have the movement from each of the many symbols to the One."[190]

Both types and symbols point to an objective reality that Ephrem calls 'Truth' (*rārā*).[191] According to Brock, symbol and reality (*shrara*, literally 'truth') are intimately linked in the sense that symbol, or *rāzā*, contains the "'hidden power,' or meaning (*hayla kasya*) of the reality."[192]

185. Brock, *The Luminous Eye*, 54.

186. *Ibid.*, 41.

187. *Ibid.*, 54. It is important to note the importance of the free will to understand God's presence. Therefore, Ephrem says that grace never imposes itself by force *Carmina Nisibena* 16: 6. "Ironically, if compulsion is to be found anywhere, it can be said that it is God's own love for humanity that compels Him to take the initiative in providing the opportunities by which humanity can return to Him." T. Jansma, "Ephraem on Exodus II,5: Reflections on the Interplay of Human Freewill and Divine Providence," 17-19.

188. Brock, *The Luminous Eye*, 56. "Even though Your symbol may be small, (2nd line) yet it is a fountain of further mysteries." *Hymnen de Fide* 4: 10.

189. Brock, *The Luminous Eye*, 56. *Hymnen de Fide* 10: 3.

190. Brock, *The Luminous Eye*, 57.

191. McVey (ed.), *St. Ephrem the Syrian: Selected Prose Works*, 48. See the example cited from *Hymnen de Paradiso* 5: 2. Brock, *The Luminous Eye*, 55.

192. Brock, *The Luminous Eye*, 41. Brock illustrates this with an analogy. "Scripture could be described as a darkened plate of glass between humanity and divine reality (Ephrem's 'truth'). The outer meanings correspond to what can be seen on the surface of the glass: this is the object of enquiry for biblical scholarship. But on this surface are a whole number of pinpoints of varying size, where the glass is clear, thus giving the possibility of vision through and beyond the glass itself. These pinpoints correspond to Ephrem's *raze*, symbols and types. Their very presence on the glass is, in the first place, only visible to the inner eye which sees by the light of faith. But given that the inner eye does perceive them, then two rather different things will affect the vision of this eye: it may be obscured by sin or distorted by wrong belief (both very important points for Ephrem), and, secondly, any strength it has will depend on the strength of its faith. The greater the faith, the closer to the glass will the inner eye get, with a twofold result: in the first place it will see yet more pinpoints, that is *raze* or symbols, on the glass through which to look beyond to 'truth'; and secondly, the eye will get a much wider vision of

Murray also says the same when he notes the fulfilment of Old Testament persons in Jesus "is often called in Syriac *srara*, 'truth' or 'reality', the equivalent of ἀλήθεια. This level of fulfilment can also, of course, be itself related typologically to the ultimate, eschatological fulfilment."[193]

Faith is the starting point for one's search for 'truth'.[194] What is present in the types and symbols is the 'hidden power' or its 'meaning'. This hidden power, or meaning, lends an "inner objective significance of reality, which is different from that outer reality which the scientific observer would call objective. The presence of this 'hidden power' accords a deeper meaning and significance to whatever outward vehicle that symbol may be attached to, even though that vehicle (which may be a person or an object) will normally not be aware of the indwelling presence of this 'hidden power'."[195]

Types and symbols are "a dynamic and exciting way of looking at the world – and one that is profoundly ecological."[196] "Nothing in creation exists in isolation. The relationship of humanity to nature, and the attitude of mankind to the environment and his use of it, are matters of profound significance for Ephrem."[197]

2.2.2.2. Names and Metaphors

'Names' and 'metaphors' are another means that God allows to be used of Himself in Scripture in order to reveal Himself.[198] The Bible and Crea-

truth the closer it gets to the glass. This helps to explain why *raze* or symbols are multivalent; to say that a symbol can point to only one thing, has only one interpretation, is to misunderstand what these symbols are all about." About the inner eye of faith, see: *Hymnen de Paradiso* 5: 3-4. The analogy of Scripture as darkened glass in fact serves just as well to illustrate Ephrem's understanding of the role of symbols in nature. Brock, *The Luminous Eye*, 162-164.

193. Murray, "Symbolism in St. Ephrem's Theology (I)," 4.

194. Brock, *The Luminous Eye*, 161. For Ephrem faith is an important factor to understand "the symbolic potentiality of the whole created world." He develops the "common New Testament and patristic way of thinking of faith in his own way as an integral part of his theory of symbolism." Murray, "Symbolism in St. Ephrem's Theology (I)," 6. *Hymnen de Fide* 5: 18; 25: 5. See Edmund Beck, *Die Theologie des hl. Ephraem in seinen Hymnen über den Glauben*, Studia Anselmiana, 21 (Città del Vaticano: Libreria Edictrice Vaticana, 1949) 24ff.

195. Brock, *The Luminous Eye*, 55. See *Hymnen de Fide* 4: 9.

196. *Ibid.*, 56.

197. *Ibid.*, 164.

198. According to Robert Murray, "the polemic against Arianism is the context in which Ephrem develops most of his thought on the value of symbols and the analogical applicability of names and terms." Murray, "Symbolism in St. Ephrem's Theology (I)," 14. Murray even identifies that Ephrem "in his doctrine of 'names' anticipates the classical theory of analogy." *Ibid.*, 3.

tion present metaphors and images which the Creator has provided us to know God. The metaphors and images are 'mirrors' that helps one to see the glory of God beyond the symbols.[199]

Ephrem's theological method of articulating 'talk about God' by using the language between the apophatic and cataphatic poles, is clearly seen in his theology of names. On the one hand, we see "God's absolute transcendence, the incommunicability of his name to men and the inapplicability of human terms to him," however, on the other hand, we see "the loving condescension shown in God's 'clothing himself' alike in human names in order to communicate with us, and in a human body in order to heal us."[200] The dialectic between apophatic and cataphatic poles anticipates the "doctrine of 'analogy' in speaking of God,"[201] yet, Ephrem often speaks "of the inadequacy yet necessity of names and images when he contemplates natural symbols."[202]

The names that God accepts for Himself are two different sorts: the 'perfect and exact names,' which indicate something of his true Being, or 'borrowed names,' that is the metaphors borrowed from ordinary human experience.[203] The perfect names such as Being, Creator, Father, Son and Holy Spirit, are applicable at all times and are essential to faith.[204] They represent "the highest meeting point for humanity with God: they are

199. Bundy, "Language and Knowledge of God in Ephrem Syrus," 103. Edmund Beck, "Das Bild vom Spiegel bei Ephraem," *OCP* 19 (1953) 5-24.

200. Murray, "Symbolism in St. Ephrem's Theology (I)," 11. *Hymnen de Fide* 5: 6-7.

201. Murray, "St Ephrem' Dialogue of Reason and Love," 27.

202. Murray, "Symbolism in St. Ephrem's Theology (I)," 12. *Hymnen de Paradiso* 11: 5-8. "Syriac Christianity shows a uniquely luxuriant proliferation of names and epithets applied to Christ." This phenomenon seems to reflect a Mesopotamian religious mentality which is expressed already in Sumerian and Accadian liturgical prayers. Murray, "Symbolism in St. Ephrem's Theology (I)," 10. See Murray, *Symbols of Church and Kingdom,* 160. According to Sebastian Brock, Ephrem's theology of names anticipates the treatise on Divine Names in the dionysian corpus. Brock, *The Luminous Eye*, 60. Between Ephrem and the Cappadocian Fathers we also see a common interest in the 'names of God'. In his opinion, "For all these Fathers, as for the author of the dionysian corpus later, the divine names constitute one of the main modes of God's self-revelation to humanity. Gregory of Nyssa, like Ephrem, stresses that they are given purely out of God's condescension." Brock, *The Luminous Eye*, 146. Brock even goes on to say that "A little over a century later the unknown author of the Dionysian writings certainly will have drawn upon the Cappadoceans as well as upon the Neoplatonist philosopher Proclus when he wrote his famous treatise on the Divine Names. Could it be that this most hellenized of all Christian writers also owes something to the Semitic Ephrem, as far as his theology of names is concerned?" (*ibid.*, 147). Murray also notes, "Much of Ephrem's thought along these lines is remniscient of his contemporary Gregory of Nyssa." Murray, "Symbolism in St. Ephrem's Theology (I)," 13.

203. Brock, *The Luminous Eye*, 62.

204. *Ibid.*, 63. *Hymnen de Fide* 44: 3.

each a revelation of God's hiddenness, but to penetrate beyond that revelation is not possible or permitted, for what lies impenetrably beyond, in the divine hiddenness, is the *qnoma*, the person or self, of God."[205] Some of the perfect names that God shares with humanity such as Father, Son, King have different meanings in use. These terms "are eternally applicable to Him, whereas when applied to human beings this is only a temporal matter: no one is born already a father."[206] It is to be noted that these names "shared between Creator and created should not lead one to suppose that God and humanity have anything in common."[207] God's "borrowed names," however, are metaphors taken from the human condition. He even considers this "as an act of immense condescension on the part of God," and denotes God's coming "down to meet humanity on its own terms, in its own language."[208] Murray agrees that Ephrem's use of 'names,' which arise in daily human language, is the result of God's divine condescension, and validated by use in revelation.[209]

Brock emphasizes that "[a]t the roots of Ephrem's theology of names one can discern the idea of salvation history as following a pattern of exchange between God and humanity," a concept which is absolutely basic to Ephrem's thought.[210]

Ephrem uses imagery as another important way to understand God. Two sets of imagery are important among the Syrian Fathers: letter im-

205. Brock, *The Luminous Eye*, 63. *Memrê on Faith* 4: 29-40.

206. Brock, *The Luminous Eye*, 63-64.

207. *Ibid.*, 64. *Hymnen de Fide* 63: 9-11.

208. Brock, *The Luminous Eye*, 42. In Ephrem's words, 'He put on names'.

209. Murray, "Symbolism in St. Ephrem's Theology (I)," 2. See also Murray, *Symbols of Church and Kingdom*, 159-204, especially 166-170; McVey (ed.), *St. Ephrem the Syrian: Selected Prose Works*, 51. See I. Hausherr, "La philosophie du nom chez Ephrem," in idem, *Noms du Christ et voies d'oraison*, OCA, 157 (Rome: Pontificium Institutum Orientalium Studiorum, 1960) 64-72.

210. Brock, *The Luminous Eye*, 66. *Hymnen de Fide* 5: 7. Brock describes Ephrem's understanding of the course of salvation history "as a dramatic sequence consisting of four main scenes." (1) Before the Fall of Adam and Eve, when they are in Paradise. This is viewed as a mountain and they are clothed in "robes of glory," or "of light." This concept derives from Jewish speculation concerning the "garments of skin" in Gen 3:21. (2) At the Fall, Adam and Eve are stripped of their "robes of glory/light." (3) Adam/mankind is returned to divinity. The Divinity Himself "puts on Adam," when he "put on a body." Hence, the whole aim of the Incarnation is to "reclothe mankind in the robe of glory." (4) The baptism of Christ is the fountainhead and source of Christian Baptism, and the possibility for humanity to be born again in glory. Sebastian Brock, "Clothing Metaphors as a Means of Theological Expression in Syriac Tradition," *Typus, Symbol, Allegorie bei den östlichen Vätern und ihren Parallelen im Mittelalter*, ed. Margot Schmidt, Eichstätter Beiträge: Abteilung Philosophie und Theologie, 4 (Regensburg: Pustet, 1982) 11-40, pp. 11-12.

agery and the imagery of clothing. The clothing imagery is more consistently developed in Syriac tradition than in the Latin and Greek tradition.[211] In many places, Ephrem uses the idea of putting on clothes to picture God humbly clothing himself in our symbols and language.[212]

2.2.2.3. Incarnation

Finally the fullest self-revelation of God is seen in the Incarnation.[213] Ephrem even prays to Jesus to be a bridge to cross the ontological chasm.[214] Through the Incarnation God crosses the ontological chasm that separates Him from His Creation in order to reveal Himself. He does this out of His goodness and love for humanity.[215] "The greatest 'change' to God was ... His taking on human flesh (in Syriac, *lbeš basrâ*),"[216] and Ephrem argues that the Incarnation is "the miraculous and paradoxical self-abasement of God out of love for humankind."[217] He also takes note of the "change in the relationship between human beings and their Creator," through this divine condescension to humankind.[218] "In the incarnation the God who utterly transcends his creation has imprinted himself onto his creation like a seal."[219] McVey also notes "Ephrem's understanding of the ongoing process of the incarnation in sanctification, the full restoration in each human being of the lost *imago dei*."[220] It is the

211. Brock, "Clothing Metaphors as a Means of Theological Expression in Syriac Tradition," 11, 21. See note 3.

212. Murray, "Symbolism in St. Ephrem's Theology (I)," 5. 'Putting on clothes' was traditional in Syriac literature for speaking of the Incarnation. See Murray, *Symbols of Church and Kingdom*, 69ff. 310-12. (e.g. *Hymnen de Paradiso* 11: 6-7; *Hymnen de Fide* 5: 7; 11: 9) The Syriac expression literally means: "to put on or clothe oneself in flesh." See *Hymnen de Fide* 31: 4; 32: 8-13; *Hymnen contra Haereses* 30: 4; McVey (ed.), *St. Ephrem the Syrian: Selected Prose Works*, 52. Brock, "Clothing Metaphors as a Means of Theological Expression in Syriac Tradition," 11-40.

213. *Hymnen contra Haereses* 32: 9.

214. *Hymnen de Fide* 6: 17. Griffith, "A Spiritual Father for the Whole Church," 31-32.

215. McVey (ed.), *St. Ephrem the Syrian: Selected Prose Works*, 51.

216. *lbeš basrâ* means "to put on/clothe oneself in flesh." See *Hymnen de Fide* 31: 4, 32: 8-13; *Hymnen contra Haereses* 30: 4. See also Brock, "Clothing Metaphors as a Means of Theological Expression in Syriac Tradition," 11-40

217. This is the basic theological theme expressed in his *Hymns on the Nativity*. McVey, *Ephrem the Syrian: Hymns*, 30. *Hymnen de Nativitate* 13: 12-14.

218. McVey, *Ephrem the Syrian: Hymns*, 30. It is clearly stated in the *Hymnen de Nativitate* 1: 99: "the Deity imprinted Itself on humanity, so that humanity might also be cut into the seal of the Deity."

219. McVey, *Ephrem the Syrian: Hymns*, 34. *Hymnen de Nativitate* 1: 97-99; 2: 21; 3: 5.17.

220. McVey, *Ephrem the Syrian: Hymns*, 44.

result of the twofold mysteries of "God's condescending love for us" and the "access to divine love now open to human beings."[221]

It is "in his theology of Incarnation, that Ephrem demonstrates his greatest genius. He develops and refines a typology and symbolism to such a degree that together they become a unique vehicle for proclaiming this Good News. Symbols and types, from both nature and Scripture, now operate for Ephrem on two distinct planes: the horizontal, between the Old and New Testaments, and the vertical, between this world and Paradise."[222] These types and symbols find their fulfilment in Christ. Therefore, Ephrem calls Him, "the Lord of the Symbols."[223] Jesus Christ "is at once the apex of history and the metaphysical Mediator between the ineffable Creator and creation."[224] According to Brock, "it is at the Incarnation that God's hiddenness is most fully revealed to humanity, though even there the divinity retains its hiddenness."[225]

According to Brock "the relationship between symbols revealed in both the created world and in scripture, and their hidden reality in Christ" is paralleled to the relationship in the Eucharist between the unconsecrated bread and wine. Thus, "[t]he Bread, although it remains outwardly bread, has become, through the descent of the Holy Spirit, the Body of Christ; the Wine, though it remains wine outwardly, has become the blood of Christ. So Christ's symbols in the material world remain outwardly unchanged, but inwardly they have taken on, for the Christian, new and deeper meaning."[226] According to McVey, the Incarnation is "conceived not only as a singular historical event but also as an ongoing availability of God to each human being."[227] In this sense history also plays an important role in Ephrem's theology. "History and nature consti-

221. McVey, *Ephrem the Syrian: Hymns*, 44. These twofold mysteries are well depicted through Mary and John, and through them it is extended to us. *Hymnen de Virginitate* 25: 8.

222. McVey (ed.), *St. Ephrem the Syrian: Selected Prose Works*, 52-53.

223. *Ibid.*, 53. This title occurs in *Hymnen de Fide* 9: 11; *Commentary on the Diatessaron* 1: 1; *Hymnen de Virginitate* 6: 7, *De Azymis*, 3 among other places.

224. McVey, *Ephrem the Syrian: Hymns*, 43.

225. Brock, *The Luminous Eye*, 27-28. Brock gives two examples that of *Hymnen de Fide* 19: 7; 51: 2-3. The first one reads: "Who will not give thanks to the Hidden One, most hidden of all; Who came to open revelation, most open of all; For He who put on a body, and other bodies felt Him – though minds never grasped Him."

226. Brock, "World and Sacrament in the Writings of the Syrian Fathers," 692-693. See *Hymnen de Fide* 6: 4.

227. McVey, *Ephrem the Syrian: Hymns*, 43. McVey also notes that "the major theme of the nativity hymns is the wonder of the incarnation." McVey shows how "God's relationship to each human being" is well depicted through Jesus' encounter with the Samaritan woman. *Hymnen de Virginitate* 23: 3. McVey, *Ephrem the Syrian: Hymns*, 43.

tute the warp and woof of reality. ... Each moment of life is governed by the Lord of life and is an opportunity to see oneself and the community in relation to that Lord. So not only the events described in scripture but all historical events must have profound religious significance."[228] For example in *Hymns against Julian* and *Carmina Nisibena*, Ephrem "contemplates the political and military events of his time in the light of his ethical and theological tenets, looking for evidence of divine activity, rewards, punishments and edifying moral lessons."[229] "The political events provide a larger-than-life drama of the cosmic conflict between good and evil."[230] Ephrem tries to see God's presence in the daily life.[231]

Having observed Ephrem's sacramentology and worldview, we now look forward to see his understanding of the sacramentality of the world. In our discussions on sacraments and worldview, we came across the exhortation to acquire an attitude that demands us to look at things from a different angle.

3. The World as Sacrament

Having seen the sacramentology of the Syriac Orient, and its worldview we now will try to understand the necessary human response towards the sacramentality of Creation. We shall see this from two perspectives. In the first part, we shall see how Ephrem envisions the role of the human being in relation to Creation, based mainly on the exegetical tradition. Secondly, we shall see how human beings are partaking in the eschatological Kingdom through liturgical and sacramental celebrations.

3.1. Role of Human Being in Creation

In order to understand the role of human being in relation to Creation, we must first explore how the human person is understood in Ephrem. In particular, we must see how human beings who are endowed with authority and freedom are superior to other beings in creation. In continuation we shall also see their responsibilities as being God's image in this world.

228. McVey, *Ephrem the Syrian: Hymns*, 41.

229. *Ibid.*, 36.

230. *Ibid.*, 37. Ephrem illustrates this in *Hymns against Julian*. "Biblical examples of faithless sovereigns and the consequences of their erroneous ways." *Ibid*, 38.

231. *Hymnen de Virginitate* 31: 16.

3.1.1. Human Being: God's Image

In the aftermath of recent studies from 'ecological theology' that criticize the Christian presentation of Creation and human responsibility towards it, there have been various efforts to understand the meaning of Gen 1:26.28.[232] Reading of this passage based on the Syriac Bible, the *Peshitta*, can give better insight to it. "To have dominion over the animal world," in both verses, immediately follows reference to the creation of humanity in the "image of God." Therefore, one could clearly argue that the 'dominion' is a consequence of humanity's being created in God's image. As Kathleen McVey notes, the *Peshitta* here seems to follow the

232. Lynn White's criticism of the Jewish Christian religion for the present ecological crisis has become a turning point in the ecological discussions of the West. Lynn White, Jr., "The Historical Roots of Our Ecological Crisis," (originally published in *Science*, 1967) *Western Man and Environmental Ethics* (Reading, MA: Addison-Wesley, 1973) 18-30. Murray demonstrates how the theological presuppositions of the Reformation and the Evangelical tradition are important to interpreting it. Murray criticizes Karl Barth and his followers of the Reformation tradition for their failure "to incorporate a coherent doctrine of the created world and our relationship to it." Their focus was mainly on two poles: "God the saviour and man the saved, who receives grace only through the death of Christ and faith in the Gospel." For details see H. Paul Santmire, *The Travail of Nature: the Ambiguous Ecological Promise of Christian Theology* (Philadelphia, PA: Fortress, 1985) 143-155; W. Granberg-Michaelson, *A Worldly Spirituality* (San Francisco, CA: Harper & Row, 1984) 46-47. Though they accept that the world's creation by God and its goodness, creation is outside the essential drama of salvation by grace and faith. They criticise Catholicism for "drawing the world into the process of grace and salvation, both by valuing 'natural theology' and by developing a sacramental view of the world." However, evangelical theology underscores history as "the key perspective for understanding the Bible." For them, "the essential theme of the Bible is salvation, and its essential theatre is 'salvation-*history*'. In contrast to history stands the myth that expresses a vision of reality, which is of its nature non-historical. Its main concern is to express what is to be held true, either metaphysically (for example, notions of basic dualism or tension in the structure of all being), or in the endless recurrence (for example, the cycle of the seasons and the earth's fertility). Murray criticizes them for maintaining the basic structure of the Bible only in terms of the divine-human polarity. He contends that: "[I]f its fundamental theme is the working out of God's plan of salvation in human history, the many passages which speak less historically of the created order and our place in it may be regarded as less important." Rather, Murray proposes the "ideals of *order*." It speaks of the order of God's creation, displayed both in the whole cosmos and in nature on earth; peace and justice in the relationships of humankind, as between nations, parts of society and individuals, and again between humans and animals; right thinking (wisdom) and right worship." "Quite apart from historical narratives, the Bible teaches us that neither sin nor salvation are affairs merely between us humans and God; sin entails alienation from our nature which relates us to God's other creatures, while salvation entails our re-integration in a vaster order and harmony which embraces the whole cosmos." Robert Murray, "The Bible on God's World and Our Place In It," *The Month*, August/September (1988) 798-803, pp. 798-799.

Jewish *Targum*. "Dominion over the earth constituting the divine image was particularly characteristic of Jewish and Antiochene Christian tradition."[233] Hence, it is important to have a right understanding of the term 'image,' in order to interpret the meaning 'to have dominion'.

3.1.1.1. Image of God

Before entering into our discussion on the human being as the image of God in Ephrem, it seems important to comprehend how "image" is understood in the Antiochene tradition. The Antiochene Fathers generally accepted that "the *Logos* is the perfect image of the Father, but also the archetype in relation to which humankind bears the divine image in a dependent degree."[234] This could be one of the exceptions where the Antiochene Fathers do not use the natural sense of the meaning 'image,' but a prophetic vision similar to the Alexandrian *theoria*.[235] At the same time, it is crucial to note that there is a difference in the way that the Syriac Fathers interpreted this. The Alexandrians explained the creation of humankind in the image of God "as synonymous with 'likeness' to God alone." Furthermore, in their eagerness to explain how we are creatures "like" God, they explained that God "has created us with immortal souls," meaning that we are filled with spiritual qualities, which enable us to worship God.[236] Murray criticizes this approach, which was influenced

233. McVey (ed.), *St. Ephrem the Syrian: Selected Prose Works*, 94, no. 98.

234. Robert Murray, "The Image of God: Delegated and Responsible Authority," *Priests & People* 14/2 (2000) 49-54, p. 50.

235. Murray, "The Image of God," 50. *Theoria* is to be understood from the perspective of the Alexandrian school whose focus is on the divinity of Christ. On the other hand, the Antiochene school focused on the earthly life of Christ (*historia*). These methodological approaches had their impact in the liturgical rites of the respective traditions. As Bradley Nassif writes: "The hermeneutical theories of scriptural exegesis developed by the Alexandrian and Antiochene schools carried over to their methods of interpreting the church's liturgical rites. In the liturgical commentaries and the catechetical literature of Alexandria (e.g., by Origen, Gregory of Nyssa, and Pseudo-Dionysius), *theoria* described the spiritual illumination needed to allegorize the visible rites. The Antiochene commentators (e.g., Cyril of Jerusalem, Theodore of Mopsuestia, and John Chrysostom) tended to interpret the rites of baptism, eucharist, and the liturgy as literal portrayals of the mysteries of salvation. Their significance was often explained through a typological exegesis from the standpoint of salvation history (*oikonomia*)." Bradley Nassif, "Theoria," *Encyclopaedia of Early Christianity*, ed. Everett Ferguson (New York/London, Garland Publishing, INC. 1997) 1122-1123, p. 1123.

236. Murray, "The Image of God," 50. According to Murray this understanding of the Alexandrians was continued in the West. Western Christianity, in general, interpreted 'image' (Hebrew *selem*) in terms of 'likeness' (*dmut*) to God, as spiritual and intellectual qualities. In particular, he notes that in the Augustinian tradition, the 'image' defines human nature by spirituality and intellect, and viewed the rest of Creation as mere resources for human use by the power of their spiritual superiority. Murray, "The Image of God,"

by Platonism, for its inadequacy "to develop a strong theology of relationship to and care for other creatures."[237] The Syrians, however, although agreeing on 'man's analogical likeness to God, interpreted it differently on two bases: First, image, in Genesis 1:26, is an implicit metaphor from kingship. Second, the authority to rule explains the function of the image.[238]

It is also important to note how God is portrayed in the tradition to understand the creation of the "human being in the image of God." As we have already seen, names and metaphors are used in the Syrian tradition to picture the idea of God. Although we don't find any names or metaphors of God in the creation narrative, His act of Creation is qualified with qualities, such as wisdom, power and righteousness.[239] The ancient cultures of the Near East consider these three qualities as attributes of kingship, especially with the sacral or priestly functions. Based on this similarity, Murray argues that the image of God comes from the ancient concept of "kingship," where kings were attributed a "quasi-divine status."[240]

This is evident from the fact that in the Old Testament, royal images were ascribed to God. "YHWH was celebrated with royal acclamations and all the symbolism of kingship." It is more clearly expressed in the Psalms. "The Davidic kings claimed to be adopted sons of YHWH (Pss 2 and 110), while Psalm 89 celebrates, with close parallelism, first God in his supreme power and then the Davidic house to which YHWH promised eternal rule."[241] Thus, the meaning of the 'image of God' seems to be, in ancient thinking, concerned about the relation of kings to their patron deities. This is implicit behind the creation of the human race in Genesis 1–2. Although it was "edited at a time when the Jews no longer

51.

237. Murray, "The Image of God," 51.

238. *Ibid.*, 50.

239. "*Wisdom* in planning and naming his works, *power* in performing them, and '*righteousness*' (Hebrew *sedaqah*) in creating all things so that 'he saw that they were good'. Murray, "The Image of God," 51-52. See also, Robert Murray, *The Cosmic Covenant: Biblical Themes of Justice, Peace and the Integrity of Creation* (London: Sheed & Ward, 1992) 98.

240. Murray, "The Image of God," 52. In the Near East, in places like Sumer and Babylon, kings were regarded as 'living images' of the patron gods of their cities. For example "in Babylon the king was regarded as the living image (*salmu*, cognate with Hebrew *selem*, the word in Genesis 1:26) of the city god Marduk." *Ibid.*, 52; Idem., *The Cosmic Covenant*, 98.

241. Murray, "The Image of God," 52.

had kings; the old royal blessings and psalms were re-interpreted as looking forward to one to come, anointed *(mashiah,* 'messiah') by God."[242]

Although there are only implicit references to the metaphors of God's kingship, "it reflects the theory of sacral kingship," and means that God has "created a living image of himself on earth." This image, which is thoroughly democratised and included all humankind collectively, has "a *viceregal* role, to govern all other creatures with responsibility to God."[243] This means to say that human beings created in the image of God are not to be understood in terms of "likeness" rather they represent God in Creation. For this God has provided them with authority and free will. In this sense human beings are considered as God's viceroy in creation. Even though God has given humanity authority over other creatures, they are answerable to him because of their free will. This understanding of delegated authority with free will has become the basis of the Syrian tradition, particularly in the writings of Ephrem.[244]

3.1.1.2. Human Beings

The quasi-divine nature attributed to a king is applicable to all humankind. El-Khoury demonstrates how this idea is seen in the anthropological vision of the school of Antioch. For them, the human being is at the center of creation connecting the invisible, spiritual world with the material visible world. In order to realize this role, the human being "must be penetrated with the principle of divine life and, elevated through his union with the divine."[245] El-Khoury further elucidates this concept by using the theories of Theodore of Mopsuestia and Ephrem the Syrian.[246] But in order to understand the anthropology of Ephrem, it seems best to note the differences of approach between the Alexandrians and Antio-

242. Murray, "The Bible on God's World," 800-801; see also Id., "The Image of God," 52. Id., *The Cosmic Covenant*, 98.

243. Murray, "The Image of God," 52. Based on this, Murray criticises some of the recent efforts to attribute the metaphor of 'stewardship' to the human being, and argues to use the biblical metaphor "royal."

244. For details on Ephrem's understanding of human being created in the 'image of God' see Bou Mansour, *La Pensée symbolique de S. Éphrem le syrien*, 408-429.

245. N. El-Khoury, "Anthropological Concepts of the School of Antioch," *SP* 17 (1982) 1359-1365, p. 1359.

246. For Theodore of Mopsuestia, the human being is "a composite of an invisible, immortal soul, which is endowed with reason, and of a mortal, visible body." The body has two powers of mind (lo)goz)) and life. "Theodore of Mopsuestia espouses a dichotomized concept of man in which man is composed of body and soul and the soul exercises a vital as well as a spiritual function." We will not enter into the details of Theodore's anthropology here. N. El-Khoury, "Anthropological Concepts of the School of Antioch," 1359.

chenes. As noted earlier, following the *theoria*, the Alexandrians tended "towards mysticism, Monophysiticism and the emphasis on the doctrine of divine grace." Whereas, following *historia*, the Antiochenes emphasized the freedom of the free will. The Antiochenes were reluctant to adhere to strict theories of knowledge, but valued historical things and persons.[247]

Following a strict creationism, Ephrem begins his anthropology from the Creation narrative of the human being. Accordingly, he demonstrates two purposes for human creation. First, the human being is created for the glorification of God who placed him in his preeminent position (Lord of creation) for this purpose." Secondly, "man was to enter into the highest paradise, the House of God." Ephrem, from his Antiochene background, advocates a dichotomous view of the human being. He considered:

> [M]an as the only created being capable of reconciling that old dualistic pair, matter and spirit. In man they are blended in an indivisible unity; he participates in both but is not entirely subsumed in either. He is perhaps limited in some sense, but nevertheless provided with freedom; sinful, but capable of virtue and of enjoying divine favour. Burdened with partly conscious, and partly unconscious, drives and instincts of a sensual nature, he is also endowed with will, intelligence and reason.[248]

The human being is given a special position as "Lord of the Universe." This position "is exemplified not so much through his external, bodily form, as through the soul, which binds man to the transcendent; to this he is able to give exterior expression in the material sphere."[249] Hence, the human soul maintains a special status in comparison to others in Creation.[250] Similarly, in the *Hymn on Paradise*, he notes: "The soul is more praiseworthy than the body. The body is clothed with the beauty of

247. El-Khoury, "Anthropological Concepts of the School of Antioch," 1361. According to El-Khoury, "For the Antiochenes in general, and for Theodore of Mopsuestia in particular, man acquires merit in the sight of God by his struggle for perfection in this life which prepares him for resurrection to Eternal Life" (*ibid.*).

248. *Ibid.*, 1361. El-Khoury notes the omission of "[t]he traditional anthropological labels, such as 'animal rationale,' 'homo sapiens,' 'homo ludens,' 'homo faber'." Furthermore, El-Khoury sees the relevance of Ephrem's ideas in the context of the anthropological questions raised by natural sciences, genetics and evolution. The biblical idea of Creation is taken literally as it was the general intellectual atmosphere of that period of the flourishing of the Antiochene school. See also El-Khoury, *Die Interpretation der Welt bei Ephraem*, 97-144.

249. El-Khoury, "Anthropological Concepts of the School of Antioch," 1362.

250. *Hymnen de Ecclesia* 33: 2.

the soul."[251] This is even clearer when he speaks of the reuniting of the transfigured body with the soul after death.

> His bound feet will leap about in Paradise, his lame hands
> will gather the god (fruits), his blind eyes will contemplate
> him who illumines creation, his dumb mouth will be opened, his
> deaf ears will hear the trumpets and his ruined body will shine in glory.[252]

This is also clear from Ephrem's use of 'body'. He usually uses the Syriac word, *gûšmā*, for the human being. The former is used as 'a corporeal body,' having the role as the vessel of the soul. The latter is used in an anatomical sense, as the body not only of the human being, but of any entity.[253] Thus, his use of body (*gûšmā*) is specific to human beings alone. "It signifies the matter which was formed by the spirit, but it cannot be distinctly separated from the spirit, any more than the latter can dispense with the matter in which it is embodied, whereby it also communicates with the external world through the medium of senses."[254]

The Syriac word for soul (*nāfsā*) is also important here. *Nāfsā* "did not convey the metaphysical totality of man, but rather the bodily soul which gives life to matter and is completely united with the body." Furthermore, Ephrem "ascribes three qualities to the soul: reason, immortality and invisibility."[255] This enables him to speak of the union of body and soul in affectionate terms. For example, the soul is depicted as 'the bride of man' and the dwelling of the soul in the body is compared to someone who dwells within his own house.[256] Hence, the freedom given to humanity must be understood in this context.

In his Commentary on Genesis, Ephrem remarks that "God did not predetermine man for either mortality or immortality, but abandoned him

251. *Hymnen de Paradiso* 9: 20.

252. *Carmina Nisibena* 47: 4.

253. El-Khoury, "Anthropological Concepts of the School of Antioch," 1362. El-Khoury compares this vision of Ephrem, with the Pauline usage of σάρξ. It denotes: 1) material corporality (Gal 4:13), and 2) the flesh itself (Rom 2:28; Col 2:13). The Syriac word *pāgrā* corresponds to it. *Gūmā* corresponds with σῶμα, which in Pauline usage means exclusively the human body endowed with a soul (1 Thess 5:23; 1 Cor 5:3, 7:34).

254. El-Khoury, "Anthropological Concepts of the School of Antioch," 1362. Ephrem speaks of seven senses in the human being. See *Carmina Nisibena* 11: 20; *Hymnen de Ecclesia* 27: 10; *Prose Refutations* I, 122: 45-48. Ute Possekel denotes strong Stoic influence in the development of senses in the human being. Possekel, *Evidence of Greek Philosophical Concepts in the Writings of Ephrem the Syrian*, 187-188.

255. El-Khoury, "Anthropological Concepts of the School of Antioch," 1363.

256. *Hymnen de Ecclesia* 38: 8; see also *Hymnen de Fide* 18: 10; 19: 6; *Hymnen contra Haereses* 42: 8. El-Khoury, "Anthropological Concepts of the School of Antioch," 1363.

to his freedom and allowed him to act according to his own conclusions." El-Khoury considers this "problem about the immortality of man and his mortality that takes us on to the concept of free will and the relation of free will to the concept of man as being created in the image of God." Furthermore, El-Khoury argues that for Ephrem, the similarities of man to God as they are expressed in Gen 1:26f., consists mainly in his spiritual faculties. This freedom of will is "the capacity to make free decisions that constitutes the likeness to God, because through this capacity man has a way open to him which can take him beyond himself and can pull down the barriers that have been set for him."[257] This is also the reason for his fall.[258]

The right to one's own decision assumes personal freedom. It "presupposes the ability to possess knowledge. ... Knowledge, insight and comprehension are intellectual activities which complete each other and are based upon the ability to reflect." The spiritual principle of the body in Syriac is *rūhā*, and is independent of the body. For Ephrem, "knowledge, memory and spirit are inextricably bound up in the heart and soul."[259]

Ephrem's concern is not limited to soul alone as he affirms "the sublimity and dignity of the body." The emphasis on the human "drive to action" and "struggle to progress" is something particular to Ephrem. For him as well as for the Antiochene school, the greatness of man lies in his likeness to God, this likeness has set them up as Lord and ruler of all Creation. He is "characterised by a dynamic drive to self realisation and change. The true nature of man consists neither in the mere fact of his being nor in his own individual deeds and accomplishments, but rather in his capacity to change the world and form it into something new."[260]

3.1.1.3. Royal Authority

The Antiochene and Syrian tradition of presenting the human being's image as a king points to the delegated authority given to human beings. This is clear from the fact that the Syrian authors often "compared hu-

257. El-Khoury, "Anthropological Concepts of the School of Antioch," 1363. With regard to the 'likeness to God,' "the early Christians adopted the Platonic idea of a psyche which was guided by the nous." This was maintained until now. For Augustine, the similarity lies in '*memoria, intellectus et amor*'. The same is seen in Schleiermacher. "Contemporary exegesis finds the likeness to God in man's understanding, selfconsciousness, reason, freedom of will, i.e. in personality." *Ibid.*

258. El-Khoury, "Anthropological Concepts of the School of Antioch," 1363. *Hymnen de Fide* 31: 5.

259. *Ibid.*, 1364. *Hymnen de Fide* 57. Ephrem conceives spirit as the grains on the stalk of wheat. *Hymnen de Fide* 42: 10.

260. El-Khoury, "Anthropological Concepts of the School of Antioch," 1364.

manity as God's image in creation to the statue of a king."[261] Ephrem seems to recognize the delegated royal authority implicit in Gen 1:26-28, since he "teaches both that the image signifies authority (*shultana*) and also that it is held on conditions of freely willed obedience to God." This interpretation, which is rooted in the paradise story, "does hint at man's spiritual faculties, but not as the explanation of the image."[262] For Ephrem, authority and free will are essential aspects of God's image in humankind and it is clear in Ephrem when he says:

> *And God said, "Let us make man in our image."* According to what has been the rule until now, namely if it pleases God He will make it known to us, Moses explains in what way we are the image of God, when he said "*Let them have dominion over the fish of the sea, and over the birds, and over the cattle, and over the all earth.*" It is the dominion that Adam received over the earth and over all that is in it that constitutes the likeness of God who has dominion over the heavenly things and the earthly things.[263]

Murray in his translation of this passage avoids the term 'dominion' and use 'authority'. In his opinion, the word 'dominion' "connotes ownership, while the Syriac *shultana* implies an authority which in the human sphere is delegated, and that to an agent with free will." Furthermore, "the meaning of *shultana* covers authorisation, personal moral authority and responsible freedom of choice." *Shultana* implies 'authority' (Mk 1:22.27; 11:28), which is delegated to human beings. In reference to an agent, it is one's personal freedom to act (1 Cor 8–9).[264] According to Murray, this broader meaning of *shultana* is important to understand Ephrem's *Prose Refutations*. Ephrem in his *Letter to Hypatius*, notes: "If it is by *shultana* that Adam was the image of God, it is a most praiseworthy thing when a person, by knowledge of the truth and acting with truth, becomes the image of God, for that *shultana* consists in this also."[265]

261. Brock, "Humanity and the Natural World," 132. Ephrem applies the kingship metaphor in relation to the 'image' which was already present in Philo. *Prose Refutations* Eng. tr. pp. xiv and lxxxvi. Murray acknowledges that this kingship metaphor is not explicitly present in Ephrem. Robert Murray, "The Ephremic Tradition and the Theology of the Environment" http://www.acad.cua.edu/syrcom/Hugoye/Vol12No1/HV2NMurray.html.

262. Murray, "The Image of God," 51.

263. *Commentary on Genesis* 1: I, 29. Passages in italics are verses taken from Gen 1:26.

264. Murray, "The Image of God," 51. *Shultana* (authority) corresponds closely to the Greek *exousia*, used in the New Testament.

265. Robert Murray, "The Ephremic Tradition and the Theology of the Environment" Letter to Hypatius, Eng. tr. in Mitchell, *Prose Refutations* I, iii. See also Edmund Beck, "Ephraem Brief an Hypatios," *OrChr* 58 (1974) 76-120, 80-81. Mitchell first renders *shultana* by 'Freewill,' and the second time, by 'independence'. Beck uses both times the

Further, in the Fourth Discourse, Ephrem refers to Gen 1:26-28 in terms of authority, discussing those animals which do not serve humans but can overpower them. "[Adam] possessed this power (*shultana*) over them before he sinned, but they received this power (*shultana*) against him after he had sinned. Therefore God said, let us make man in our Image, that is in the Image of His authority (*shultana*), so that just as the authority of God rules over all so also the yoke of Adam's lordship (*maruta*) had been set over everything."[266]

Along this line, the metaphor of king and viceroy is seen also in the process of naming animals.[267] By naming the animals, Adam "defines their natures and establishes authority over them."[268] "In the thought of Ephrem, for something to have a name is to have a *qnōmā*, or substance, and that name designates just what that substance is."[269] The authority given by God excludes all tyranny and exploitation, as reflected in the biblical account of the naming of creatures (Gen 2:19-20). This act shows kingly wisdom and is the function of wisdom and royalty. Thus, Adam was also a king, and it belongs to a king to bestow titles upon each of his subjects. God made humanity worthy of this second place, by making him God's own viceroy and governor of all others.[270]

Nevertheless, Brock points to the theory's limitation. In his opinion, the statue of a king symbolises the 'king's authority,' but at the same time, he notes the lack of "a vital constituent element of this authority namely free will." Instead of this static view, he prefers a dynamic view that sees "humanity as God's agent or representative within creation."[271] Robert Murray underlines this more dynamic view through the image of viceroy. In general the "Antiochene and Syriac writers see the 'image' as

term '*Macht*' (Power/might). See no. 9.

266. Mitchell, *Prose Refutations* I, Syr p. 114; tr. lxxxvi.

267. Murray, "The Image of God," 51.

268. The naming scene, rich in symbolic potency, was enriched by the Isaian vision of peace and, later still, fused with the scene of Orpheus drawing other creatures by his music. The royal sense of the story was clear to the Jewish commentator Philo, *On the Creation of the World*, 148, Loeb Classics, *Philo*, vol. 1, 116-117. Murray, "The Image of God," 52; Id., *The Cosmic Covenant*, 100.

269. McVey (ed.), *St. Ephrem the Syrian: Selected Prose Works*, 74, no. 22. *Hymnen contra Haereses* 48: 2; *Sermons on Faith* 2; El-Khoury, *Die Interpretation der Welt bei Ephraem*, 45.

270. Murray, *The Cosmic Covenant*, 100. Murray further explores this metaphor as seen also in the writings of Diodore of Tarsus, Theodore of Mopsuestia, Theodoret of Cyrrhus, John Chrysostom, Narsai and Jacob of Serug. Murray, "The Image of God," 51-52.

271. This authority is not to be exercised unjustly as a tyrant, rather it is to be exercised in love.

a metaphor which pictures the human race as standing in position of God's viceroys, endowed by God with authority over other creatures, but also, because of our free will, answerable to him for how we treat them."[272]

3.1.1.4. Human Free Will

Free will is an important aspect in exercising the authority given to human beings. It is the condition of love for God and responsibility towards creation.[273] The human free will makes the human being different from other creatures. Thus, Ephrem notes: "man, owing to his Freewill, can be like them all [animals], while they cannot become like him. On this account they have a (fixed) Nature, while we have Freewill."[274] Ephrem is one among the Fathers who have laid the greatest emphasis on free will. At the same time, as Murray notes, "Ephrem's emphasis on human free will does not in fact deny the primacy or supremacy of grace."[275]

Although we have seen that free will is basic to Ephrem's anthropology, it is important to note that Ephrem has also emphasized humanity's free will over and again considering the polemical context in which he lived. In particular, it seems that the free will was emphasized in the context of Bardaisan's emphasis on the freedom of the human being to choose between good and evil.[276] Bardaisan "asserts that Christians are to determine their own ethic in freedom in accordance with the 'law of their Messiah'."[277] Like Ephrem, Bardaisan "asserted that evil did not have a personality of its own but evolved from the abuse of freedom, the misuse of natural objects and processes, or just misfortune."[278]

272. Murray, "The Ephremic Tradition and the Theology of the Environment" (no. 4).

273. *Commentary on Genesis* 1: 26; *Commentary on Genesis* 2: 29.

274. *Prose Refutations* 46: 4-16. T. Jansma, "Ephraem on Exodus II, 5: Reflections on the Interplay of Human Freewill and Divine Providence," 19.

275. Murray, "St Ephrem' Dialogue of Reason and Love," 30.

276. Bardaisan, *The Book of the Laws of the Countries: Dialogue on Fate of Bardaisan of Edessa*, tr., H. J. W. Drijvers (Assen: Van Gorcum, 1965) 10. Bundy, "Language and Knowledge of God in Ephrem Syrus," 95. As we have already noted Ephrem's *Hymnen contra Haereses* & *Prose Refutations* are responses to the controversies of his time. According to Jansma, Bardaisan's *Book of the Laws of Countries* (also known as *Dialogue on Fate*, although he prefers 'Dialogue on Freedom') speaks of the dignity and responsibility of Man. Still, Ephrem in his first discourse to Hypatius in *Prose Refutations* proposes free will against heretical teachings. Jansma, "Ephraem on Exodus II, 5: Reflections on the Interplay of Human Freewill and Divine Providence," 14.

277. Bardaisan, *The Book of the Laws of the Countries: Dialogue on Fate of Bardaisan of Edessa*, 61.

278. Bundy, "Language and Knowledge of God in Ephrem Syrus," 95-96.

Ephrem defended "freewill as the central concept of ethics," against the deterministic systems of his time.[279] And it was at this level that Ephrem condemned Bardaisan and his followers for their use of horoscopes and astrology.[280] In particular, Ephrem's reference is not towards the pagan worship of planets and astrology, but rather pagan worship, disguised in a Christian garment under the teachings of Marcion, Mani, Bardaisan and the Chaldaens.[281] Furthermore, Ephrem considers planetary worship and astrology as "a great danger to orthodox belief in God's omnipotence and human free will."[282] Similarly, he criticized the determinism in Manichaeism, since they upheld a lack of freedom of the will (determinism).[283]

For Ephrem, God created human beings from the beginning with free will.[284] Even though God could have created them in anyway, he desired to create them in this way.[285] As Jansma says "[t]he mystery of freewill appears to be that it is both one and many."[286] In his opinion, the opposite of freewill is nature.[287] God by creating the human being with a freewill forced them to struggle with his own nature.[288] The dismissal of the human being from Paradise is characterized as the misuse of freewill.[289] Nevertheless, humans will be rewarded again, depending on the correct use of their freewill.[290]

Freewill is given to all human beings in the same measure, even though it can be obscured in people who are enslaved to sin.[291] As we

279. Jansma, "Ephraem on Exodus II, 5: Reflections on the Interplay of Human Freewill and Divine Providence," 19.

280. *Hymnen contra Haereses* 51: 13.

281. Drijvers, *Cults and Beliefs at Edessa*, 157.

282. *Ibid.*

283. Bundy, "Language and Knowledge of God in Ephrem Syrus," 96.

284. *Hymnen de Paradiso* 12: 18; *Hymnen contra Haereses* 11.

285. *Hymnen de Fide* 31: 5.

286. Jansma, "Ephraem on Exodus II, 5: Reflections on the Interplay of Human Freewill and Divine Providence," 18. This means that although the will is one, it appears to be many. *Prose Refutations* 34: 14-27.

287. Jansma, "Ephraem on Exodus II, 5: Reflections on the Interplay of Human Freewill and Divine Providence," 18. See *Prose Refutations* 44: 17-44: 1.

288. Jansma, "Ephraem on Exodus II, 5: Reflections on the Interplay of Human Freewill and Divine Providence," 18. *Prose Refutations* 45: 4-9. Jansma also calls attention to the diversity of freewill among different people. Jansma, "Ephraem on Exodus II, 5: Reflections on the Interplay of Human Freewill and Divine Providence," 19. *Prose Refutations* 45: 23-46, 3.

289. Brock, *The Luminous Eye*, 34.

290. *Hymnen contra Haereses* 11: 4.

291. Brock, *The Luminous Eye*, 35-36. He explains this using a medical analogy. For example, a person who is sick may not be able to taste the sweetness or bitterness of a

have already seen, God's revelation as it is manifested in different ways points to an objective reality. This objective reality always remains stable, but the human response to it varies, depending on how we react to the types and symbols we encounter.

Freewill depends much on man's ability to contemplate on the mysteries. The contemplation of the "mysteries of God reflected in the images provided in Scripture and the creation and his free will to live out the implications of that contemplation which distinguishes him from the other animals and which brings into actuality the image of God in mankind."[292] One "can affirm our free will and can gather evidence for its actuality" through the analysis of different cultural traditions, experience, Scriptures, the teachings of the Church and from the need of salvation. "However, the exact manner in which free will operates cannot be known." It is "a pedagogical technique of the creator."[293]

The use and misuse of freewill, which is the responsibility of each individual human person, is important in determining the human attitude towards and use of the natural world. "For Ephrem the right response is essentially one of wonder and gratitude, whereas the wrong response will be made wherever greed and arrogance are present." Responsibility arises from the awareness of the hidden power inherent in nature itself.[294] In the same vein, with regard to Ephrem's idea of authority Brock notes a conditional and a reciprocal element in it. "Rightly exercised, it will instill a love which results in harmony between ruler and ruled; wrongly exercised it instills hatred and sows disharmony."[295]

The experience of harmony in society and in creation depends much on the exercise of human justice. Hence, the exercise of injustice can disturb the harmony. Again, exercise of justice depends upon the use and misuse of freewill. The harmony that is lost by the misuse of the freewill can be recovered only "through right choices and through the right use of creation."[296] Ephrem presents Noah's generation as the best example of the use and abuse of freewill.[297] Since our response to God's revelation

food, but a healthy person can. So also a wicked man fails to understand the freewill present in him. He acts according to his nature. The spiritual person, however, can act according to his freewill. *Hymnen de Fide* 2: 18-23.

292. Bundy, "Language and Knowledge of God in Ephrem Syrus," 103.

293. *Ibid.*, 98.

294. Brock, *The Luminous Eye*, 164-165. Id., "Humanity and the Natural World in the Syriac Tradition," 138-139.

295. Brock, "Humanity and the Natural World," 135.

296. Brock, *The Luminous Eye*, 166-167.

297. *Hymnen de Fide* 3: 9.

depends on our free will,[298] the right exercise of freewill is important to determining our Christian faith.

3.1.2. Ethical Responsibility

The authority and freewill that have been given to humanity demand ethical responsibility. Although this word is not explicitly used in the Creation narrative, it is implicit. The very freedom charged with authority entails a relationship of responsibility as the source of authority. The more understanding and freedom one has, the more he becomes responsible. This is what is observed in the story of Adam's Fall.

3.1.2.1. Fall

Before the Fall, all creatures and all the elements existed together in harmony in the cosmic, moral and social realms. Ephrem explicates this through Adam's relation to Creation in the naming story, after Adam's entry into Paradise.

> *He brought them [all creatures] to Adam*, so that God might make known the wisdom of Adam and the harmony that existed between the animals and Adam before he transgressed the commandment. The animals came to Adam as to a loving shepherd. Without fear they passed before him in orderly fashion, by kinds and by species. They were neither afraid of him nor were they afraid of each other. A species of predatory animals would pass by with a species of animal that is preyed upon following safely right behind.[299]

The same is reflected in the writings of Narsai, Jacob and Isaac of Nineveh.[300] It is the consequence "of the right exercise of human authority."[301]

The misuse of freewill leads to the destruction of the cosmic harmony, and disorder. Ephrem expresses this already in his treatise on Paradise and the Fall.[302] After disobedience came disorder. The Fall imposed the loss of the "paradisiacal harmony between humanity and the animal world, characterised by a relationship of love inspired by the correct use of the divine gift of authority."[303] Ephrem compares the situation of Adam to the "thorns and thistles" with which he had to contend in Gen

298. *Hymnen de Fide* 13: 5.

299. *Commentary on Genesis* II, 9: 3.

300. Murray, "The Image of God," 54.

301. Brock, "Humanity and the Natural World," 133.

302. *Hymnen contra Haereses* 28: 9. The same theme is expressed in *Commentary on Genesis* 2: 31. See also his biblical narrative of *Commentary on Genesis* 3: 18. Brock, "Humanity...," 139. Id., *The Luminous Eye*, 165.

303. Brock, "Humanity and the Natural World," 133.

3:18; after symbolize the effects of the abuse of freewill.[304] Ephrem could never have dreamed at how far the abuse of freewill would lead to exploit Creation, rather than to live in harmony with other creatures. They seem to see the same sense as the fault: irresponsible abuse of freedom.

Human injustice has a deeper impact on the relation to Creation.[305] According to Brock, "Sin in the form of the misuse of our divinely given free will and authority, thus leads to disharmony both in human society and in creation as a whole. Nevertheless the potential for recovery is always present, provided that we realize this and seek to put this potential into practice."[306]

3.1.2.2. Restoration

From the Fall onwards, one sees the failed efforts to restore the lost harmony. Ephrem, in his Genesis Commentary, pictures a scene of temporary restoration of harmony granted by God to Noah.[307] Similarly the theme of restoration is also presented through the image of the entry into the Promised Land.[308]

The effort to recover the original perfection is in progress in the salvific mission of Jesus. Commenting on Jesus' death Ephrem says, "the voice of creation cried to proclaim Him innocent."[309] Christ repaired the disorder brought about by the abuse of freedom symbolized in the biblical story of Adam; He is presented as the second Adam, the antitype of the First.[310]

A sixth-century homily, transmitted under the name of Ephrem, speaks of Jesus who kept company with the animals, which knelt and worshipped him.[311] Brock argues that "Paradoxically, the far-flung consequences of human injustice may themselves provide the possibility for

304. *Hymnen contra Haereses* 28: 9. Brock, *The Luminous Eye*, 165.

305. For example it is shown through the example of Jezebel. *Hymnen de Virginitate* 7: 3.

306. Brock, "Humanity and the Natural World," 139.

307. *Commentary on Genesis* 2: 59-60.

308. Brock, "World and Sacrament in the Writings of the Syrian Fathers," 688. The escape from bondage in Egypt, as further reflected in Ephrem is seen as the escape of the Christian in Baptism from the domains of both Satan and Death. *De Azymis*, 3.

309. *Commentary on the Diatessaron* 21: 5.

310. This is principally a Pauline theme; but it is possible that Mark hints at it when he says that Jesus in the desert "was with the wild beasts" (Mk 1:13). Most modern exegetes prefer another explanation, but for those of a more poetic inclination, the idea of this scene as the antitype of Adam's naming the animals has a strong attraction. Murray, *The Cosmic Covenant*, 127-128.

311. *Memrê for Holy Week* I: 93-94.

restoration."[312] "Man was to respond to the revelation in Christ and confirmed by nature, and, by responsible exercise of his free will, to renew himself and his context."[313]

3.1.2.3. Harmony

In order to understand ethical responsibility for the Creation, it is still not enough to look at the authority and freewill that was given to human beings. It is important to emphasize the interconnectedness of all in Creation. In this sense Ephrem's use of "the image of human society as a body" is worth noting.[314] Ephrem extends Paul's allegory of the body in 1 Cor 12 and Rom 12 to the whole human race and even to the animals.[315] According to Brock, "Genesis 1:26 is primarily concerned with the relationship of humanity to the animal world. But frequently the Fathers see this as also applicable to our relationship to the whole of creation."[316] It is the interconnectedness of Creation that makes solidarity with Creation important. Similarly, Ephrem emphasizes the interdependence of human beings and our need to care for the animal world. It is for this reason that he says that interdependence binds us with love for everything.[317]

Often, especially in the West, many Church Fathers, when commenting on the 'image of God,' were dominated by an anthropocentrism that was too dependent on Stoicism. Ephrem's account of the necessity of interrelationships offers a far better basis for a true environmental theology. Elsewhere, Murray notes that the Syrian Fathers' reading of Genesis offers a valuable ecological teaching "in comparison with traditions dominated by Alexandrian exegesis, Platonist spirituality and Stoic-influenced anthropocentrism."[318] Although Murray sees a similar view in Maximus the Confessor in the East and in Francis of Assisi in the West, he criticizes the overemphasis on 'duty' in the West. He states that "If humankind has been seen as in some sense the *syndesmos* of creation, this view has been too much influenced by an anthropocentrism which owed more to Stoicism than to biblical vision, and was taken further by scholastics."[319]

312. Brock, *The Luminous Eye*, 166. He cites examples from *Hymnen de Virginitate* 30: 10; *Hymnen contra Haereses* 10: 9.

313. Bundy, "Language and Knowledge of God in Ephrem Syrus," 97.

314. Brock, *The Luminous Eye*, 167.

315. Murray, "The Image of God," 52.

316. Brock, "Humanity and the Natural World," 135.

317. Brock, *The Luminous Eye*, 167.

318. Murray, "The Image of God," 54.

319. *Ibid.*, 53. He also underscores the fact that the ascetics of the West, even though

According to Brock, the idea "of the interconnectedness between everything" and the abuse of nature, through the misuse of a freewill that adversely affects Creation, points to the connection between physical and spiritual ecospheres.[320] In the same vein, Murray notes: "Ephrem's account of interrelationships hints at a better basis for a true 'ecotheology'."[321]

In Ephrem, the sense of the renewal of Creation, which Christ has inaugurated through His resurrection, is celebrated in the Paschal month of Nisan, and points to the the calming of nature.[322] Such a vision of reconciliation and restored harmony cannot be left to merely imaginative enjoyment of its beauty. Ephrem's prose passage quoted earlier, in which he extends the Pauline body image for interrelations within the Church to human relations with other creatures, expresses a challenge to put the vision into practice.[323]

The image of "human society as a body" points to Ephrem's vision of the interconnection of creation at three levels: "within humanity as a whole; within creation as a whole (thus including between humanity and the environment); and between the material world and the spiritual world." Furthermore, based on this interconnectedness of everything and every individual, Brock argues that "every individual has both a responsibility and a potential role to play in the process of recovery from the disharmony caused by human misuse of free will."[324] Brock also argues that the ultimate recovery of the lost harmony will take place only in the eschatological Paradise. At the same time, he notes its occasional anticipation on earth by the saints.[325] This fulfillment in eschatological Paradise makes the sacramental life important in Ephrem.

3.2. Celebration of Christian Life

Similar to the Greek Fathers, the Syrian Fathers uphold the worldview that maintains the sequence: Creation, Fall and Redemption. Central to their worldview is the perfection of the original Creation, the Fall through the misuse of human freewill, and finally restoration through the work of Christ. The restoration will reinstate the human being into the state of

they experienced good relationships with animals, "hardly anywhere was a theology of our relationship and duties to our fellow creatures in God's world developed." *Ibid.*, 54.

320. Brock, *The Luminous Eye*, 167.

321. Murray, "The Image of God," 53.

322. *Hymnen de Resurrectione* 5: 4.

323. Murray, *The Cosmic Covenant*, 144-48, 146.

324. Brock, "Humanity and the Natural World," 140.

325. Brock, *The Luminous Eye*, 165. Compare *Hymnen contra Haereses* 21: 6; *Commentary on Genesis* 2: 9; *Prose Refutations* I, lxxxv-lxxxvi.

primordial paradise that was originally given to Adam. This redemptive experience is at the core of Syriac liturgical and sacramental celebrations, anticipating the Christian participation in the *eschaton*. The primary example of this is seen in the sacraments of Baptism and Eucharist. Therefore, at this juncture, we shall see the celebratory dimension of the sacramentality of the world from three perspectives: first from the spacetime reality in Ephrem, and following upon this, its realization in the sacraments of Baptism and Eucharist.

3.2.1. Spacetime

Spacetime is an important symbol where Creator meets Creation. It transcends the limits of space and time in this world and looks forward to the realities of the other world. This is expressed in Christian liturgy in various ways.[326] With respect to this other dimension of reality, Ephrem seems to be aware of the distinction between 'horizontal' time and 'vertical' time. Horizontal, or linear, time is a consecutive string of events that one could speak of a "before" or "after." On the contrary, vertical, or sacred, time has no "before" or "after." All events are of equal significance and converge together in sacred time.[327] In other words, one could say that historic time continues in the liturgical, or sacred, time.[328] Thus, for example, "a liturgical feast and the particular salvific event that it commemorates, though far separate in historical time, can, in sacred time, come together."[329] These dimensions seem to be important to understand the spacetime reality of Christian celebration. Christological, ecclesial and pneumatological dimensions have an important role in this understanding of spacetime.

3.2.1.1. Christological Dimensions of Spacetime

The Syriac liturgy and sacraments participate in the spacetime of Christ. Furthermore, Christ stands central in the baptismal and the eucharistic celebrations. This is clear from the fact that Ephrem develops his soteriology by using the typology that centers on the paschal lamb, from the

326. In particular the spacetime reality is expressed through the liturgical and sacramental celebrations. The physical reality of the Church also expresses the same. In this sense, Church architecture always took into account this spacetime dimension by building the churches facing East and also by giving them different interconnections. Although the Church architecture is an important aspect that expresses the cosmic dimension of the sacraments, we limit our study to the liturgical meaning of spacetime reality.

327. Sebastian Brock, "St Ephrem on Christ as Light in Mary and in the Jordan: *Hymni de Ecclesia* 36," *ECR* 7 (1975) 137-144, p. 141.

328. Yousif, "St Ephrem on Symbols in Nature," 58.

329. Brock, "The Poet as Theologian," 245-246.

Exodus-event and explains the Paschal mystery of Jesus through the Passover context.[330] The passover lamb of the Old Testament is only seen in relation to Christ and the salvation gained through Him.

In Ephrem, "the realization of the paschal lamb in Christ has been fulfilled in three stages namely at the Last Supper, at Calvary and in the Eucharistic Sacrifice of the Church."[331] Although it is realized in three stages Ephrem's typological usage seems to suggest that the Paschal meal is central. First, he relates the Paschal meal of the Old Testament to the Paschal meal of Jesus and, from there, to the crucifixion and, then, to the Eucharistic celebration.[332] This means that the Upper Room celebration "includes the three aspects of paschal mystery, namely the paschal meal, the paschal sacrifice on Calvary, and the celebration of the eucharist." Moreover, this celebration witnesses both "the process of the fulfillment of the plan of salvation" and the "passage into the new time in the person of Christ." In this sense, the liberation brought by the Paschal Lamb is not only liberation from the bondage of Satan, but also it converts death to life. In Jesus' celebration of the Paschal Lamb, he brings to perfection the lambs of the Old Testament and institutes the sacraments of Eucharist and Baptism.[333]

For Ephrem, the presentation of Jesus as the new Paschal Lamb is the key to the understanding of the suffering of Jesus.[334] Faith in the Trinity grows through the power of the Cross.[335] Ephrem also speaks of the inspiring role of Christ's Cross in our life.[336] The Cross is "the symbol of the suffering of the paschal lamb, which symbolizes also the victory over Death, Sheol and Satan."[337] This is because the action of the Cross at

330. Joseph Naduvilezham, "Paschal Lamb in Ephrem of Nisibis," *The Harp* 5/1-3 (1992) 53-66, pp. 53, 57. Ephrem prefigures the image of lamb even before Exodus. For him, the "lamb of Abel [Gen 4: 4] is the forerunner of the lamb of Abraham (Gen 22:13), of the passover lamb of the exodus night in Egypt and of the Lamb of God (Jn 1:29)." In the case of Abel, he became first a victim (Gen 4:8). Thus, he is both an offerer and an offering. Hence, Jesus, the good shephered becomes an offering on the Cross. Naduvilezham, "Paschal Lamb in Ephrem of Nisibis," 57. Abel himself wished to be the lamb in the place of the lamb he offered. Ephrem writes: "Abel yearned for Him that He came during his time so that he might see the Lamb of God instead of the lamb that he offered." *Hymnen de Nativitate* 1: 42.

331. Naduvilezham, "Paschal Lamb in Ephrem of Nisibis," 53.

332. Kollamparambil, *From Symbol to Truth*, 108. See also Yousif, *L'Eucharistie chez s. Éphrem*, 75-85.

333. Kollamparambil, *From Symbol to Truth*, 121.

334. *Ibid.*, 108. See also Pierre Yousif, "Le symbolisme de la croix dans la nature chez saint Ephrem de Nisibe," *OCA* 205 (1978) 207-227. Brock, *Luminous Eye*, 41-43.

335. *Hymnen de Fide* 18: 2.

336. *Hymnen de Fide* 18: 9-10.

337. Kollamparambil, *From Symbol to Truth*, 121. The victory over Death, Sheol and

Golgotha is not static, but is supposed to continue in Christian life. The historic Cross of Christ remains as the source of power for Christian life and it is continued through the Eucharist.[338]

3.2.1.2. Church

The Church is the image of the Kingdom of Heaven, transcending linear spacetime reality. In the Eucharistic liturgy, both temporal and eternal beings participate. This liturgical celebration is the occasion to enter into the new spacetime, which sometimes Ephrem refers to as the bridal chamber.[339] Maniyattu demonstrates two parallels in Ephrem referring to the entry into the eschatological bridal chamber: Adam's entry into the inner Tabernacle and Israel's entry into the Promised Land.[340] As we shall see, the Eucharist is the real entry into the eschatological Paradise.

John 19:34 is one of the focal points of Early Syriac exegesis. It is a vantage point from where Ephrem looks back "to the paradise narrative of Genesis, and forward to the new Paradise, the sacramental life of the Church."[341] Elsewhere he notes that John 19:34 "is a meeting point between past and future, looking back to the genesis narrative of the Fall and the Exodus narrative (the rock in the Wilderness) and forward to the sacramental life of the church."[342] Three 'types' in this verse: the side, the lance as well as the blood and water that issued forth are important. The side looks back to Adam's rib, from where Eve was created (Gen 2:21), and the lance looks back to the sword of the Cherub, who guards humankind from re-entering into the paradise (Gen 3:24); the blood and water, however, look forward to the Church and sacraments, Baptism and Eucharist.[343] The piercing of the side of Christ is depicted as the re-entry of humankind into Paradise.[344]

Satan is a favorite theme of Ephrem.

338. Yousif, "St Ephrem on Symbols in Nature," 58.

339. Maniyattu, *Heaven on Earth*, 60. The bridal chamber (*gnona* in Syriac) "may refer to the Kingdom in its eschatological dimensions, or it may refer to the Kingdom as realized, or as realizable, here on earth by individuals." When it refers to the eschatological Kingdom, then, it is illustrated through events in historical time and eschatological time. For example, in the imagery of a marriage, "the betrothal is seen as taking place in the historical time ..., while the marriage feast and the mystery of consummation of the marriage in the bridal chamber belong to the eschaton." Brock, *The Luminous Eye*, 116.

340. Maniyattu, *Heaven on Earth*, 61.

341. Sebastian Brock, "The Mysteries Hidden in the Side of Christ," *Sobornost* 7/6 (1978) 462-472, p. 462.

342. Brock, *The Luminous Eye*, 80.

343. Brock, "The Mysteries," 462; Id., *The Luminous Eye*, 80.

344. Sebastian Brock, "'The Wedding Feast of Blood on Golgotha': an Unusual Aspect of John 19:34 in Syriac Tradition," *The Harp* 6/2 (1993) 121-134, p. 121; Id., "The Mysteries," 462. *Nisibene Hymns* 39: 7. See also Robert Murray, "The Lance which Re-

In the fifth-sixth century poets in the Syriac tradition introduced a new imagery to this passage: namely the bride.[345] The image of the bride follows two paths of interpretation. First, the side of Second Adam gives birth to the Bride, the sacraments. Second, the water and blood represent not Baptism and Eucharist, but are rather the betrothal gift from Bridegroom to the Bride.[346] The second meaning indicates that the Bride, the Church, was already existing. This should be understood in the light of Ephrem's imagery of the Bride of Christ.[347] It is presented in two contexts. First, in the Baptism of Christ in Jn 3:29, John the Baptist reveals the Bridegroom to the Bride.[348] Second, Ephrem portrays Israel's (Bride) rejection of her betrothed to the entry of Christ in Jerusalem. Due to Israel's rejection, she is replaced with the Church of the Gentiles (the new bride).[349] The blood from Christ's side, which is Eucharist, is his gift to the Bride. Ephrem also equates the wine served at the wedding feast in Cana with the Eucharist.[350]

3.2.1.3. Pneumatological Dimension of Eschatology

The Syrian Fathers in general emphasize the pneumatological dimension of eschatology, as the continuation of the "Christ event in the Spirit."[351] Adam lost his promised glory to remain in the eschatological Paradise through the misuse of his freewill.[352] As already noted, when he would have used his freewill rightly, he would have been guaranteed the crowning of the eschatological glory.[353] Nevertheless, in human beings' effort to enter the eschaton, God promises to protect them with His Spirit.

opened Paradise: A Mysterious Reading in the Early Syriac Fathers," *OCP* 39 (1973) 224-234, p. 224.

345. Brock, "'The Wedding Feast of Blood on Golgotha'," 121.

346. *Ibid.*, 122-123.

347. For different images of Ephrem in relation to Bride see Brock, *Luminous Eye*, 116-130.

348. *Hymnen contra Haereses* 24: 6. Brock, "'The Wedding Feast of Blood on Golgotha'," 123.

349. *Hymnen de Resurrectione* 3. For Ephrem this is the second time Israel rejects the Bridegroom. The first stage of rejection occurs with the royal Bridegroom (God) at Sinai. The second is the rejection of the King's Son (Jesus) at his entry into Jerusalem. *Hymnen de Crucifixione* 1: 2. Brock, "'The Wedding Feast of Blood on Golgotha'," 123.

350. *Hymnen de Virginitate* 16: 2. Brock, "'The Wedding Feast of Blood on Golgotha'," 124.

351. George Karukaparampil, "Experience of Pneumatological Eschatology in Ephrem," *The Harp* 8/9 (1995) 161-165, p. 161.

352. See *Hymnen de Paradiso* 3: 12. He lost his original purity and had to leave the Paradise. *Hymnen de Paradiso* 4: 6. Karukaparampil, "Experience of Pneumatological Eschatology in Ephrem," 162.

353. Karukaparampil, "Experience of Pneumatological Eschatology in Ephrem," 162.

Here, the spacetime reality of the Church resembles the primordial Paradise where Adam was created; however, the experience of the eschatological Paradise is only possible in the life of the Spirit. The Holy Spirit is the architect of the restoration of fallen Creation.[354] The Holy Spirit comes to our aid in exercising the free will. Therefore, Ephrem notes:

> [H]ow essential for the individual to respond to the prompting of the Holy Spirit, by means of the analogy of the effect of light on the eye: Mary is the model of someone who allows the light to enter her eye, and so she is able to see clearly, and at the same time to radiate that light (which is, of course, on one level identical with Christ). Her opposite is Eve, who allows her eye to be darkened, so becoming spiritually blind herself, and at the same time casting darkness on all ground.[355]

"The Spirit is the author of the new creation."[356] "In effect, the communion is a personal pentecost and an anticipated experience of the full communion with the glory of God in the eschatological paradise."[357] "Each sacrament is a theophany, a joined action of Spirit and Christ, in which the Spirit continues his re-creative activity as in the incarnation (*EC Syr.* 1: 25)."[358]

As we indicated, the spacetime reality, which is manifested in the liturgical celebrations, is expressed especially through the Eucharistic and Baptismal liturgy.[359]

3.2.2. Baptism

For Ephrem in particular and the Syriac Fathers in general, Baptism is central to a proper Christian understanding of the World as sacrament. It is understood as the gateway for Christians to restore the original nature of humanity in Creation that will be completed only in the *eschaton*. The first manifestation of spacetime reality is expressed through Christ's baptism in the Jordan. His baptism "together with the Nativity and Passion

Hymnen contra Haereses 11: 4.

354. *Commentary on the Diatessaron* 1: 25.

355. Brock, "The Poet as a Theologian," 248. He depicts Eve and Mary as the left and right eyes of the world. See *Hymnen de Ecclesia* 37: 5-7.

356. Karukaparampil, "Experience of Pneumatological Eschatology in Ephrem," 164. *Hymnen de Virginitate* 37: 29; *Hymnen de Fide* 4: 70; 24.

357. Karukaparampil, "Experience of Pneumatological Eschatology in Ephrem," 164. *Paschahymnen* 17: 2.

358. Karukaparampil, "Experience of Pneumatological Eschatology in Ephrem," 163.

359. Brock, "The Poet as Theologian," 246. See also Id., "St Ephrem on Christ as Light in Mary and in the Jordan: *Hymni de Ecclesia* 36," 142.

and Resurrection, form a single salvific unit, a single moment as it were in sacred time, which can be localized as a whole at any of these points in historical time – Nativity, Baptism, Passion or Resurrection."[360]

3.2.2.1. Baptism: New Creation and Re-entry into Paradise

Ephrem conceives Baptism as the re-entry for each individual Christian into Paradise. It effects "the transformation, by means of the Holy Spirit, of fallen creation into its pristine paradisiacal state."[361] It is important to note that re-entry here does not mean re-entry into the Paradise of the beginning, but into the eschatological paradise. Nevertheless, "the Christian is not simply 'born anew' in the 'spiritual womb' of the baptismal water, but this rebirth is put into relationship with the original creation of the world."[362] Entry into the eschatological paradise means that the full reality of re-entry into paradise "will only be experienced at the resurrection."[363]

This new possibility is expressed through the image of the "robe of glory." The image of the robe of glory/praise is that which clothed Adam and Eve before the Fall. This robe is the symbol of their royal and priestly roles. Adam and Eve were robed in glory in paradise, before the Fall. But with the Fall they were driven out from paradise and were stripped out from the glory. In his *Hymn on the Epiphany* Ephrem similarly characterizes Baptism. "In baptism, Adam found again that glory that was among the trees of Eden."[364] Mitchell considers it as the "undoing of the harm that was then done." In his opinion, instead of clothing

360. Brock, "The Poet as Theologian," 246.

361. Brock, "World and Sacrament," 687. For Ephrem's references to baptism see Id., *The Holy Spirit in the Syrian Baptismal Tradition*, The Syrian Churches Series, 9 (Kottayam: Anita Printers, 1975) 28-29. For a general study on baptism in the writings of Ephrem see Edmund Beck, "Le baptême chez S. Ephrem," *L'Orient Syrien* 2 (1956) 111-136; Georges Saber, *La théologie baptismale de Saint Ephrem: Essai de théologie historique*, Bibliothèque de l'Université Saint-Esprit, 8 (Kaslik: Université Saint-Esprit, 1974); Leonel L. Mitchell, "Four Fathers on Baptism," *Studies on Syrian Baptismal Rites*, ed. Jacob Vellian, The Syrian Churches Series, 6 (Kottayam: CMS Press, 1973) 37-56, pp. 43-47. Mitchell's study is mainly based on Ephrem's *Hymns on the Epiphany*, which Beck avoids doubting its genuineness.

362. Brock, "World and Sacrament," 687. According to Brock, there are two conceptual models of baptism in the New Testament: "rebirth in the Gospel of John, and death and resurrection in the Epistles of Paul." The idea of "re-birth" rooted in the Johanine tradition was taken up in the earliest Syriac tradition. *Syriac Dialogue*, ed. Marte & Wilflinger, 88.

363. Sebastian Brock, "The Priesthood of the Baptised: Some Syriac Perspectives," *Sobornost* 9/2 (1987) 14-22, 18.

364. *Hymnen De Nativitate* 12: 1.

Adam and Eve with leaves of the trees, God clothes the baptized "with glory in the water."[365]

It is also important to note that in Syriac tradition the image of the 'robe of glory/praise' is used to "describe the entire course of salvation history."[366] Ephrem sums up various episodes in the drama of salvation:

> All these changes did the Merciful one make, stripping off (glory) and putting on (a body); for He had devised a way to reclothe Adam in that glory which Adam had stripped off. He was wrapped with swaddling clothes, corresponding to Adam's leaves, He put on clothes instead of Adam's skins; He was baptized for Adam's sin, he was embalmed for Adam's death, he rose and raised up Adam in his glory. Blessed is He who descended, put Adam on and ascended.[367]

The stripping of the robe of glory at the fall and putting it on again at baptism is just not a cyclical movement but rather it has a linear quality. Because "the final stage of mankind is seen as far more glorious than that in the primordial paradise, for God will finally grant to mankind the divinity which Adam and Eve had previously tried to snatch, in disobedience to the divine command."[368]

One of the most significant images used to express the Christian's reentry into Paradise at Baptism is the image of Baptism as a 'new creation'. Here the Church itself becomes a symbol of Paradise. The baptized are reborn as 'sons of God,' and have the potential to join the angelic beings and praise God.[369] Ephrem sees the praise of God as an essential element of a Christian life. In other words, praise is the true and proper expression of life. According to Brock, "This newly gained freedom to praise was frequently expressed in 'mythic' terms of the 'robe of glory' or 'robe of praise'."[370]

The baptismal anointing symbolizes the restoration of the *imago dei*.[371] In this sense the Syriac writers often use an Adam/Christ typology. Here, Christ is pictured as one who restores Adam (humanity) to the state before the fall.[372] As Konat notes, "Through baptism the Adamic

365. Mitchell, "Four Fathers on Baptism," 46.

366. Brock, "The Priesthood of the Baptised: Some Syriac Perspectives," 18.

367. *Hymnen De Nativitate* 23: 13.

368. Brock, "Clothing Metaphors as a Means of Theological Expression in Syriac Tradition," 12.

369. The term 'sons of God' in the Old Testament, in fact, often refers to the angelic beings. Brock, "World and Sacrament," 689. See, Id., "Early Syrian Asceticism," *Numen* 20 (1973) 6ff.

370. Brock, "World and Sacrament," 689.

371. *Hymnen de Virginitate* 5: 8. 5-6; 7: 5-7; 7: 7. 1-2.

372. Brock, "The Priesthood of the Baptised," 16. In Ephrem's words: "Through the

nature of man is restored. The nature of the first Adam dies and it is transformed to the nature of the second Adam – Christ."[373] This Adam/Christ typology is very important to the Syriac writers. For them:

> Adam and Eve in paradise were in an intermediary state. Obedience to God's command would have brought them immortality and made them not subject to corruption; disobedience, however, would (and did) bring them mortality and subjection to corruption. Baptism, on this understanding, puts us back potentially into this pre-Fall state where we too have the same choice: listening to God leads to divine life, and disobedience or failure to results in death.[374]

The whole aim of the Incarnation is to ensure the return of humanity to Paradise. Incarnation is the very source of Christian making a person worthy of adoption as a child of God.[375] Therefore, the Syriac fathers connect Christian Baptism with Jesus' own Baptism and solidified, in the Syrian sacramental tradition of individual Baptism to the Baptism of Jesus in the Jordan.[376]

In *Hymns on Virginity*, Ephrem notes: "In those who are signed in baptism, which conceives them in its breast; In place of the form of the first Adam, which has been corrupted; Baptism forms a new image and begets them with a triple birth; In the worshipful name of the Trinity; Father and Son and Holy Spirit."[377] Furthermore, The Holy Spirit who consecrates the baptismal water is the same Holy Spirit who hovered over the waters of the primordial deep at Creation (Gen 1–2).[378] Baptism enables all Christians to receive the Holy Spirit as Christ received it.[379] Ephrem contrasts this reception of the Spirit with the anointing of David. With David, it was the Spirit that dwelled in him that made him sing. The Christian anointing, however, is done in the name of the Father, the Son, and the Holy Spirit, meaning that through Baptism there is an indwelling

Second Adam who entered Paradise, everyone has entered it; for through the first Adam who left it, everyone left it." *De Azymis*, 17: 10.

373. Johns Abraham Konat, "The Sacrament of Initiation (Baptism) in the West Syrian Tradition," *Syriac Dialogue*, ed. Marte & Wilflinger, 78-89, p. 79.

374. Brock, "The Priesthood of the Baptised," 16.

375. Konat, "The Sacrament of Initiation," 78.

376. Brock, "The Priesthood of the Baptised," 18. See also Konat, "The Sacrament of Initiation," 79, 81.

377. *Hymnen de Virginitate* 7: 5.

378. Brock, "World and Sacrament," 688. See Id., "The Epiklesis in the Antiochene Baptismal Ordines," *OCA* 197 (1974) 208. For the importance of the term 'hovered' in Syriac sacramental theology see Murray, "A Hymn of St Ephrem to Christ on the Incarnation," 148-149.

379. Konat, "The Sacrament of Initiation," 79.

of the Trinity.[380] Baptism signals the indwelling of the Trinity into human life, in as much as it is an entry of the human being into a relationship with the Trinity at Baptism.[381]

The early Syrian Church perceived Christ's presence in the Jordan as something that sanctifies all baptismal water. The consecration of the water at each baptism was understood as a re-enactment of this event.[382] It is also rooted in the event of Creation. The brooding of the Spirit of the Lord over the water (Gen 1:2) gives the impression that Creation emerged from water. Similarly, Baptism understood as the new Creation also emerges from water. Furthermore, the use of water is linked to the water that flowed from the pierced side of Christ.[383] Joseph Chalassery notes that in Ephrem "the Holy Spirit, who is bestowed upon the baptismal candidate through the *Rušma*, leads him to the twin sources of his life: the waters of the Jordan hallowed and made effective by the baptism of Christ and the water flowed from the pierced side of the crucified Christ."[384]

This restoration is also expressed through another image of the entry of Israel into the Promised Land.[385] "As Israel enters the Promised Land through the crossing of the River Jordan, the candidate for baptism, by passing through the baptismal font, the figurative Jordan, enters the land of life and becomes the inheritor with Abraham."[386] Thus, the Syrian Fathers view the crossing of the Red Sea and of the river Jordan as types of Baptism. These two types have two distinctive connotations. The former one pictures the Christian's life on earth corresponding to the Israelites in the wilderness, who are fed with manna that resembles the Eucharist. The latter, on the other hand, pictures the Christian who enters the Promised Land and partakes of the 'milk and honey'. This seeming contradiction, in the opinion of Brock, reflects "the mysterious conjunction of the temporal with the eschatological that takes place in the liturgy." "The baptized Christian is thus in the paradoxical position of having already en-

380. *Hymnen de Epiphania* 3: 14.

381. Peter Yousif, "St Ephrem on Symbols in Nature: Faith, the Trinity and the Cross (Hymnen de Fide No. 18)," *ECR* 10 (1978) 52-60, p. 55. *Hymnen de Fide* 18: 3-4.

382. Brock, "St Ephrem on Christ," 140-141.

383. Konat, "The Sacrament of Initiation," 81. See also Brock, "Baptismal Themes in the Writings of Jacob of Serugh," 329-330.

384. Joseph Chalassery, "Sacraments of Initiation in the Syro-Malabar Church," *Syriac Dialogue*, ed. Marte & Wilflinger, 90-106, p. 92.

385. Brock, "World and Sacrament," 688. For example the escape from bondage in Egypt represents the escape of the Christian in baptism from the domains of both Satan and Death. *De Azymis*, 3.

386. E. J. Duncan, "Baptism in the Demonstrations of Aphraates the Persian Sage," *SCA* 8 (1945) 57.

tered Paradise by means of baptism, and yet, because he lives among people in many of whom Christ's work has not yet come to fruition, Paradise is not fully experienced." It means to say that "the Christian is already in paradise, but in so far as the created world, through man's misuse of it, falls short of its true potential, the Christian, by his own awareness of what that potential is, so far has only a 'pledge' of what is to come."[387]

It is in this context that one comes to understand the communion service attached to the baptismal liturgy. Holy Communion is the living bread and living fruit which delivers from his death and renders life. It is like the *medicine of life* which removes the curse with which Adam was bound.[388]

3.2.2.2. Priesthood of the Baptised

Through Baptism all Christians, both priests and laity, enter into the common priesthood of Christ. Unlike the relation between the royal priesthood and Baptism present in Latin and Greek writers, this connection is rarely mentioned in the Syrian baptismal tradition. But it is frequently seen in the catechetical tradition. It is also important to note that in cases where "royal priesthood is referred to in actual baptismal rites," it is most often associated with anointing.[389] The priesthood of all believers is to be understood as a priestly role given to all baptised Christians. It is the real and actual meaning of baptism. Therefore, it is not an office conferred as in ordained priesthood.[390]

As stated, the Syrian tradition connects anointing with the triad of king, prophet and priest. For example, when referring to anointing Aphrahat states: "Christians are perfected as priests, kings and priests."[391] The Old Testament anointing and the baptismal anointing are based on the anointing of Christ at His Baptism.[392] Thus, Ephrem notes that "The Spirit who rested on him at his baptism testified that he was the shepherd [that is king, following Old Testament usage], and that he had received the roles of prophet and priest through John."[393] As we have

387. Brock, "World and Sacrament," 688.

388. *Hymnen de Virginitate* 31: 14.

389. Brock, "The Priesthood of the Baptised," 15.

390. *Ibid.*, 21.

391. Brock also notes that "The reference to prophets does not occur in 1 Peter, [which is the central biblical verse which speaks of the priesthood of all the baptized] but the triad of king, priest and prophet goes back to ancient Israelite practice, where not only kings and priests were anointed, but also prophets (see 1 Kings 19:16)." "The Priesthood of the Baptised," 16.

392. *Ibid.*

393. *Commentary on the Diatessaron* 4: 3. Brock, "The Priesthood of the Baptised,"

already seen, since the baptismal robe of glory is connected to the royal and priestly robes, Brock argues that "baptism is the entry into a priestly role for all Christians."[394]

The basic function of a priest is to make offerings to the divine and a precondition for this offering is the 'holiness' of the priest. In order to exercise this aspect of priesthood, the individual and communal aspect of priesthood is important. With respect to individual holiness the Syrian fathers generally stress on the need for an inner heart and purity of heart.[395] The priesthood of all Christians only starts to function when the individual Christian grows in holiness.[396] In this sense, many fathers compare this process of growth with the Eucharist. It is in the Eucharist that one exercises the communal aspect of priesthood. First of all, one needs to underscore that it is the Christian community that makes the offering, not the individual ordained priest. The mediatory role of the ordained priest is to help the Christian community make this offering possible. From this we can see that the baptised Christians exercise their priestly role in two ways: first, by making the offering along with the priest and, secondly, consuming the offering, which was confined only to the priests in the Old Testament.[397]

From this, we can infer another positive aspect of the common priesthood of the baptised, that is, its missionary imperative. It involves in the "proclamation of God's wonderful works – a proclamation directed outwards from the Church towards the unbaptised world at large."[398]

3.2.2.3. Denial and Acceptance of the World

The renunciation of this world in Baptismal liturgy is very important in the sacramental understanding of the world. God has created two worlds: the earthly world you live in and the other world. The first denotes the world that represents the fallen aspects of our human nature. Negatively it means, "a way of life that is concerned only with the body, and a mentality which is concerned only with the flesh." This is the world that we reject in Baptism. We however accept the other world that is really our 'ancestral home'. It "is the 'new world' of the resurrection life, which can

16. In Jewish tradition, also Adam in Paradise was understood both as a king and priest.

394. Brock, "The Priesthood of the Baptised," 18.

395. "The Priesthood of the Baptised," 18-19. The inner heart does not mean "the physical heart, but the heart in the biblical sense, as the centre of being (intellectual as well as emotional) of the entire human person" (p. 18). See also Sebastian Brock, "The Prayer of the Heart in Syriac Tradition," *Sobornost* 4/2 (1982) 131-142.

396. Brock, "The Priesthood of the Baptised," 21.

397. *Ibid.*, 19-20.

398. *Ibid.*, 21.

occasionally be anticipated in this world by the saints who make real the potential for a life of holiness which all are given at baptism." As we noted earlier it is not "a return to the primordial paradise of the pre-fall state, but to the eschatological paradise, the attainment of which would have been the initial intention of God when he created Adam and Eve."[399]

3.2.3. Eucharist

Christ is the new spacetime of the eucharistic celebration. All symbols concerning the spacetime of the Eucharist are fulfilled in Christ. It is the bridge that helps one to enter into the eschatological paradise, and being a passage from this world to the other world, it includes the features of both the earthly world and the eschatological world.[400]

3.2.3.1. The Eucharistic Body

The Eucharist is pictured as food to be used in our passage to the eschaton. It is for this reason that the Eucharist is called "living bread," "bread of life," "medicine of life," etc.[401] These expressions have Christological overtones and are extensively used in the writings of Ephrem. For him, the eucharistic body of Christ is in "dynamic continuity with the actual body of the historical Jesus."[402] He "juxtaposes images of the actual body of the historical Jesus with allusions to the eucharistic body of Christ."[403] Ephrem calls Jesus' body the "Treasury of Healing" against the denigrating tendency towards Jesus body by Marcionites and Manichaeans.[404] Against Marcionites' criticism of the body as evil, Ephrem asks: "how could Christ have despised the body yet *put on* the Bread?"[405] As Amar notes, Ephrem pictures the Eucharist by using different images. Thus in the *Hymns on Nativity* we read:

> Blessed is the Shepherd who became a lamb for our atonement.
> Blessed is the Vine that became a chalice for our salvation.
> And blessed is the Farmer who became the Wheat that was planted,

399. Brock, "Humanity and the Natural World," 136-138.

400. Maniyattu, *Heaven on Earth*, 61.

401. *Ibid.*, 62. Jesus as medicine of life is an important theme in Ephrem. See Brock, *The Luminous Eye*, 99-103.

402. Joseph P. Amar, "Perspectives on the Eucharist In Ephrem the Syrian," *Worship* 61: 5 (1987) 441-454, 444.

403. *Ibid.*, 446.

404. *Ibid.*, 447.

405. *Hymnen contra Haereses* 47: 2. Brock, *The Luminous Eye*, 108. For the value of Body in Ephrem see *Ibid.*, 36-38.

and the Sheaf that was harvested.[406]

Furthermore, the baptismal rebirth is continually re-presented in the Eucharist. In this sense Brock notes that "Ephrem brings the Eucharist into specific relationship with these baptismal themes of 'entry into Paradise' and 'new creation'."[407]

For Ephrem, Christ himself is the 'first sheaf' (Lev 23:11) of the earth, offered to the Father.[408] It is the elements from Creation – the bread and wine – that are transformed into the saving Body and Blood of Christ.[409] The material things, like bread and wine that are used in the Eucharist are important not only because they are a symbol of the sacrament, but because of their importance for nourishment of the body.[410] Since "the earth is meant to be fertile and bring forth vegetation," Ephrem argues that "man is primarily meant to bear fruit of praise for his Creator." He compares those who fail in this regard to a "barren piece of earth."[411]

3.2.3.2. Transformation of Individuals

Brock further underscores the transformation that has to take place in the life of the individual. In his opinion, the Great Intercession that follows the Epiclesis directs attention to the invocation of the Holy Spirit on the offerings that is extended to all the needs of the world. Thus, the Holy Spirit has the power, not only to transform the eucharistic gifts, but also "to transform everyone and every thing and every situation."[412] This idea is also important in the communion service, because it is not only a communion on the horizontal level, but also a communion on the vertical level. In other words, the celebration of the communion is extended to the whole cosmos.[413]

3.2.3.3. Praise and Thanksgiving

The Eucharist sacrifice is described as a 'sacrifice of praise'. Ephrem often points out that the created world is continually urging man on to the

406. *Hymnen de Nativitate* 3: 15. Amar, "Perspectives on the Eucharist," 445.

407. Brock, "World and Sacrament," 688-689. See *De Azymis*, 17.9f.; *Hymnen de Fide* 10: 9.17; F. Graffin, "L'Eucharistie chez saint Ephrem," *ParOr* 4 (1973) 93-121.

408. *Hymnen de Nativitate* 4: 32.

409. Brock, "World and Sacrament," 693.

410. *Hymnen de Virginitate* 16: 2.4.5; 31: 13-14.

411. See *Hymns on Nisibis* L: 1.

412. Brock, "World and Sacrament," 693.

413. Pauly Maniyattu, "Celebration of the Cosmos in the East Syrian Liturgy," *Christian Orient* 22 (2001) 76-90, 88-89.

praise of the Creator.[414] "Praise of God is also seen essentially a gift from God," and expresses Creation's essential relation to the Creator.[415] The theme of wonder, a theme which is key to Ephrem's understanding of the world as sacrament, is often seen in the Eucharist. Ephrem is constantly amazed, not only at the wonder of the Incarnation and the Eucharist, but also at the wonder of the created world."[416] "Ephrem's wonder at the created world is in fact intimately related to his sense of wonder at the whole economy of the Incarnation."[417]

3.2.3.4. Role of the Spirit

Ephrem also argues about the need of human's co-operation "for the Spirit to work through the created world." According to Brock this "co-operation between the created world and the spirit" is depicted in a hymn on the baptismal oil (*meshha*), which itself is a symbol of Christ (*meshiha*).[418] "The fire that descends from heaven is a symbol of the consecratory role of the Holy Spirit, whose descent is invited by the priest at the epiclesis."[419]

As with the Eastern Christian tradition, the Syrian tradition also sees a parallelism between "the coming upon the Holy Spirit upon the Eucharistic offerings and the coming upon the Holy Spirit upon Mary. The effect in Mary's case was physical conception and birthgiving. The effect on Christian who receives communion was likewise sometimes seen as spiritual conception and birthgiving of Christ."[420]

For Ephrem "Everything in creation is clothed by the Holy Spirit with new meaning."[421] Since the baptised Christians are illumined by the Holy Spirit, the depth of the symbolic meaning of things in the World and in the Scripture will be greater. The baptized are enabled to understand the meanings of Scripture, with the help of the Spirit. Ephrem compares this to "the traveling rock that accompanied the Israelites in the wilderness."[422]

414. Brock, "World and Sacrament," 691. See *Hymnen de Virginitate* 33: 7-8.

415. Brock, "World and Sacrament," 690. See for example: *Hymnen de Fide* 14: 1-5.

416. Brock, "World and Sacrament," 694-695.

417. See *Hymnen de Virginitate* 5: 6.

418. See *Hymnen de Virginitate* 7:1-3.11-12.

419. Sebastian P. Brock, "Fire from Heaven: from Abel's Sacrifice to the Eucharist. A Theme in Syriac Christianity," *SP* 25 (1993) 229-243, p. 229.

420. Brock, "The Priesthood of the Baptised," 20-21.

421. Brock, "World and Sacrament," 691. Thus for example, Ephrem compares the new flower buds to "a symbol of resurrection." *De Azymis*, 11; *Hymnen de Crucifixione* 7: 1-2.

422. Brock, "World and Sacrament," 691. *Hymnen de Paradiso* 5: 1. For him rock is like letters of the Scripture. The flowing water is like the Spirit that inspires.

4. Conclusion

This chapter was aimed at delineating the sacramentality of the world from the perspective of the Syrian tradition. Unlike the Greek or Latin Christian traditions, which are rooted in the Greco-Roman culture, the Syrian tradition stems from the Semitic roots of the region of Mesopotamia. Influenced by the Semitic thinking of his time, Ephrem developed an epistemology that denied the rationalistic approach of the Greeks and Latins in pursuit of God. His approach is neither apophatic, nor cataphatic, but on the contrary, is a middle way between these paradoxes. His very epistemology itself is termed 'sacramental' and is an intuitive way of understanding the Transcendent who is immanent in the world. This very approach gives us further clues to reading and understanding Ephrem's view of the world and the human being.

We have also discussed at length the idea of *rozo/rāzā* in order to better understand the meaning of sacrament from the Syrian perspective. In our study we have underscored the two distinctive meanings of the term *rozo/rāzā*: its liturgical/sacramental meaning as well as the exegetical meaning. In its liturgical use, we looked into its close relation to the Hebrew word *sôd*. The Semitic background of its Greek equivalent, *mysterion*, also points to the possibility of widening the understanding of sacraments. It is this broader understanding of sacraments that enabled the Syrian Churches to experience the sacraments more in terms of sacramentality than "rites," thus allowing different liturgical celebrations into the ambit of sacraments. We have also delineated how their theology of sacraments is central to theology.

In the second part we demonstrated how Ephrem rejected the gnostic worldview of Marcion, Bardaisan and Mani. Here we tried to underscore how he responded to the critical positions of heretics, who tried to devise different eternal principles other than those of the Orthodox Judeo-Christian tradition. Against such tendencies, he insisted that God is the Absolute and reveals Himself in various ways to his people. We emphasized the non-dualistic nature of the human being. Moreover, he highlights the importance of the inner aspects of human nature and its free will that makes the human being distinct from other beings in Creation. For Ephrem, the human being is endowed with a free will and remains the Lord of Creation.

We have also gone further to see Ephrem's anthropology in view of understanding the uniqueness of the human being in relation to Creation. Human beings who were created in the image of God have the responsibility to represent God in Creation. Using the imagery of 'King,' Ephrem underscores human responsibility in keeping a harmonious relation to

Creation. We also draw attention to the importance of the notion of 'free will' in this regard. The right to exercise one's free will offers the possibility to enter into the eschaton as such. The human being is exhorted to exercise his or her free will in a responsible way, by maintaining the harmony of Creation. Furthermore, we noted the possibility of eschatological participation through the liturgical and sacramental celebrations of the Church. In this sense, one begins to see a more balanced view towards the sacramentality of Creation that points towards the necessity of ethical engagement as well as the importance of celebration.

From this perspective, it is quite natural to question the relevance of the fourth century author, Ephrem, at the beginning of the third Christian millennium. This is all the more relevant when we discuss him from a theological perspective. The polemic or socio-historic context of the fourth century has a different tone of conversation than today. Still its relevance remains. Perhaps in our presentation, we have used Ephrem more as a mystic than as a theologian. As a mystic, intuitively, he went deeper into the inner realities of life. Although aware and concerned about the living situations of his time, he also mediated on the God-world-human relations. This study was mainly intended to bring out the effect of such an approach and to see its relevance today. It is not running away from the realities that we grapple with today, but an effort to look deeper into the realities and to see the core of the role of the Christian in society.

GENERAL CONCLUSION

This dissertation aimed at discovering a new paradigm in sacramentology relevant to the multi-religious context of the contemporary society. In this effort, it finds the emerging paradigm "world as sacrament" as serving this purpose best. However, this is not an entirely new concept. Hence our effort was to rediscover the possibilities it offers to contemporary sacramentology. We have underscored two aspects of this paradigm. First, it affirms God's sacramental presence in the world. Second, it accentuates the importance of human role in relation to God and world. Thus, this study emphasizes God, World, Human relationship. Although there exist a consensus in theological world towards the sacramentality of the world and human response to it, one could find different shades of arguments behind such a consensus. Hence, the particular focus of this study was to review the major theological trends concerning God-world-human relationship. However, the review of major trends is limited to the writings of Leonardo Boff, Alexander Schmemann and Saint Ephrem. They are selected as they represent three distinct Christian cultural traditions: Latin, Greek and Syrian.

Résumé

As indicated, in reviewing the transitions in sacramentology this study emphasized the influence of cultural shifts on liturgy and theology. It has also stressed the centrality of liturgical and sacramental celebrations in Christian life. Liturgy and sacraments being central to Christian life, there were always efforts to make liturgical and sacramental celebrations relevant to the changing contexts. Although there effected manifold changes in the liturgical and sacramental life of the Church through the centuries, one could categorize the major shifts in this regard into the narrowing of the early Christian understanding of sacraments into seven culminated at Trent and its further broadening into sacramentality beginning with enlightenment. We demonstrated this change of emphasis by reviewing the study of sacraments from three perspectives: the early understanding till its reductions in the medieval period, the renewal efforts beginning with the liturgical movement and its further developments in the post-Vatican period.

This study demonstrated sacraments in its relation to liturgy, theology, symbol and salvation history. The "reduction" of the earlier understanding of sacraments affected all these realms. The renewal movements started at various contexts and various places called for a return to the early tradition. This call for renewal helped to get rid of the juridical understanding of sacraments and thus paved the way for the rediscovery of "sacramentality." Sacraments studied in the larger frame of liturgy, theology, symbol and above all as part of God's salvific plan enabled theologians to recognize the sacramentality of Christ and the Church.

One of the important turning points in the study of sacraments was the widespread recognition received for the theology of Christ and Church as sacraments. Both of these concepts contributed in extending the sacramental meaning beyond the liturgical and sacramental celebration. Jesus, the primordial sacrament of God to human being is the *Ursakrament*. Jesus as the culmination of God's revelation to humankind is the sacrament of the encounter between God and human being. This new emphasis laid on the sacramentality of Christ was a call to go beyond the ritual understanding of sacraments and it underscored *life in Christ*. This new understanding had wider implications. For example, Jesus as the sacrament of encounter between divine and human was used to explain God's intervention in the unjust systems of contemporary society. Moreover, the universal salvific will manifested in Jesus and extended to all humanity and to the whole world offered the potentiality to go beyond the limits of Christianity.

The Church is the continuation of Jesus' mystery. From a Christological perspective the Church is the *Grundsakrament* continuing Jesus' presence in the world. It has also a pneumatological perspective in the sense that the Church is the gathering of the new people of God through the Spirit. It helped going beyond the ritual and juridical understanding of sacraments. The Church as sacrament, on the one hand affirmed liturgy and sacraments as the events of the Church and on the other hand recognised the sacramental presence of the Church for the world. The Church as sacrament is not confined to the members of the Church, but extended to all humanity and even to the whole cosmos.

The Christ and Church understood as sacraments deepened the understanding of sacramentality. As it affirms *life in Christ* and *life in the Church*, it opened the horizons to and for the world. This understanding of the sacramentality of Christ and Church, although indicates its opening to the whole world has its limitation of an exclusive character. The emphasis on Christ and Church as sacrament is the result of a worldview, which is theocentric and anthropocentric. This often undermined the importance of cosmos. In order to cross over this impasse this study tried to unravel the sacramentality of Creation as a new paradigm in contemporary sacramentology. There are various attempts that underscored the sacramentality of Creation from various contexts and from various perspectives. But in responding to the sacramentality of Creation one could observe divergence in the emphasis. For example, various responses include emphasis on ethical commitment to the society, the act of praise and worship, harmony with nature etc.

For a deeper understanding of the sacramentality of Creation, this study further examined the writings of Leonardo Boff and Alexander Schmemann. These two authors represent two different traditions. While Boff represents the western theology of Latin tradition, Schmemann represents eastern theology of Greek tradition. Moreover, they represent two theological trends as well, namely liberation theology and liturgical theology. Both of them argue for the anticipation of the Kingdom of God already in this world. At the same time, they differ regarding the way it is realized. The liberation theologians emphasize the need for constant engagement with the realities of the world. However, for liturgical theologians, liturgy provides the mode of such an experience. Hence, we tried to see how the sacramentality of the world is appropriated by Boff, who keeps social engagement at the center, and Schmemann, who keeps liturgical life at the center. While for Boff "the poor" was the *locus theologicus*, for Schmemann, liturgy was the *locus theologicus*. This very difference in their presuppositions made their emphasis also different.

Boff, as an heir of Latin theology, makes his evaluation of the theme from the perspective of the Latin West. He integrated the Franciscan tradition he received from the religious congregation he joined and the academic excellence he received from the European universities to find answer to the troubled unjust systems in Latin America. His theology is the fruit of all these.

In the case of sacramentology, Boff speaks of 'sacramental thinking.' The sacramental thinking enables one to perceive God in the world. For him, it is an effort to understand the transparent presence of God who is to be sought between the transcendent and the immanent. Experience plays a crucial role in his understanding of sacraments. The experience, for Boff, is not merely subjective but objective. One's self-experience and the experience drawn from contextual realities are helpful tools to enter into the realization of God's presence.

Boff underscored history, Christ and the Church as sacraments. The exodus experience of the Israelites and other similar experiences in the Old Testament are interpreted as signs of God's intervention in history. God who has manifested Himself in Creation is continued in history through the elected people of God. Jesus is seen as its culmination. The cosmic dimension of Christology is very important to Boff. Jesus is anticipated in Creation and also in the historical persons of the Old

Testament. The historical Incarnation in Jesus is the encounter of divine and human. It is this encounter that makes Jesus the sacrament of God's encounter with human being. Boff's emphasis on the humanity of Jesus and on Jesus' option for the poor is the foundation for his call to the liberation of all the people of the earth. His understanding of cosmic Christology even recognize God's presence in other religions.

Boff perceives the continuing mission of Christ in the Church. The Church witnesses the risen Christ in the world. This implies the anticipation of the Kingdom of God in the concrete situations of life. In this sense he proposes a model for the Church from the perspective of the poor. He also finds no difficulty in perceiving God's presence in other communities. The goodness seen in other people is the criterion for membership to the Church. He criticizes the attitude that limits the sacramentality of the Church to "Roman Catholic Church" alone. He is of the view that the salvation is extended to all humankind. The Church also contains the union of divine and human in an analogous way. Since it contains the human dimension, the Church is always in need of purification. For this, he suggested the pneumatological dimension of ecclesiology.

With respect to his worldview, Boff clearly explained the transition from a theocentric worldview to anthropocentric one and finally to the new cosmology, where cosmos is at the center. Although he criticizes theocentrism and anthropocentrism of the earlier worldviews, his cosmos centered worldview did not negate them. He demonstrates the presence of God in the world from the perspective of theology, science, culture etc. In this sense the mystery encountered by scientists, various evolution theories, as well the energy fields observed in the nature resemble God, Cosmic Christ and the Holy Spirit of our Christian faith. He also tries to demonstrate similar views in other religions and in other cultures.

Boff in his cosmocentric worldview presents human being as an ethical and sacramental being. In his understanding human being is not superior to any other Creation. The moral principles that guide human beings assign them certain responsibility in their relation to Creation. He proposed a mystical approach towards this. For Boff, a mystical approach to Creation with one's deep ethical responsibility to it is of paramount importance. The mystical approach here is not detachment from the world, but is the result of a deep commitment to the world. In this sense, he emphasizes social ecology, which insists upon an ethical responsibility to everything in Creation. He also highlights the necessity of a mental ecology, with its emphasis on an integral approach. This integral approach clearly affirms the sacramentality of the world and the sacramentality of human being.

Alexander Schmemann is an eastern Orthodox theologian who was in constant dialogue with the western theologians. His open yet critical approach was not only limited to the West, but also extended to the East. In his critical approach, he always referred back to the early Christians, whose faith is rooted in eschatology. The *antinomy* of Christian eschatology of being in this world yet not of this world guided Schmemann in all his theological enterprise. His theology was always an effort to keep the balance between sacred and profane dichotomy.

This eschatological belief of the early Christianity guided Schmemann in explaining sacramental symbolism and the Christian worldview. Critically observed, the deviations in sacramentology both in the East and in the West are the result of the alienation from the eschatological symbolism of the early Christian faith. For him, sacramental symbol is a space between this world and the other world. It is a passage from this world to the other world. The liturgical experience is nothing but the experience of being in this world, yet not of this world.

The eschatological belief of the early Church shaped the Christian worldview. Here also the changes in the worldview, both in the East and in the West, are the result of the deviation from the eschatological belief. His critical stand on the rational, juridical approach in theologizing is seen in his worldview. The crucial point in his exploration is his efforts to counter the negative attitude that is shown to eschatology. His critical position towards the futuristic interpretation of eschatology and the tendency towards running away from the realities of the world is of particular importance. He named his attitude to the world 'sacramental.' His worldview too is nothing but the experience of being in this world, yet not of this world.

The eschatological sacramental symbolism and the eschatological worldview are detrimental to Schmemann in explaining the role of human being in Creation. According to him, human beings are created as priests and placed at the center of Creation. Creation manifests God's goodness. This goodness, which is still revealing is taken up by human beings and offered back to God. Therefore, in his anthropology, human beings stand at the center with a priestly role. This priestly role is exercised not primarily in a cultic sense. Conversely it is a life in communion with God. This communion underscores a life in Christ. Therefore, life in communion with Jesus or 'sacramental living' is the main characteristic of the priestly role of human being. This sacramental living or life in communion with God also demands a sacramental view of Creation.

This priestly character of human beings is seen at the center of Christian *leitourgia*. Therefore, keeping the liturgical tradition of eastern Orthodoxy intact, Schmemann emphasized the expression of human being's priestly role through Christian *leitourgia*. For him, the Church is nothing but the experience derived from the liturgy. In other words, liturgical experience is the ecclesial experience. Therefore, Christian *leitourgia* primarily expresses the ecclesial character of Christian faith. Moreover, Christian *leitourgia* has cosmic and eschatological dimensions. In this sense, the tension of elevating this world to the other world, and the other world descending to this world, is held together. Here again we come across the antinomical character of Christian faith.

What is emphasized is not merely a renewed insistence upon the importance of liturgical and sacramental celebrations in Christian life. Moreover, he tried to show the "sacramental character in the whole of life." This sacramental character of human living helps one to bridge the gap between the sacred and the profane keeping the eschatological tension of being concerned about the world and yet detached from it. This open but critical attitude to the world is the result of a life in faith. Although a vision of this kind could be negatively interpreted as "mystical" in nature, Schmemann has tried to show that it is a positive view of the world, that seeks to transcend the limits of time and space.

Finally, we delineated the sacramentality of world from the Syrian tradition. Unlike the Greek or Latin Christian traditions, rooted in the Greco-Roman cultural domain, the Syrian tradition stems from the Semitic roots of the region of Mesopotamia. Influenced by the Semitic thinking of his time, Ephrem developed an epistemology that is different from the rational approach of the Greeks and Latins in the pursuit of God. His approach is neither apophatic nor cataphatic, on the contrary, it is a middle way between these paradoxes. His very epistemology itself is termed 'sacramental.' It is an intuitive way of understanding the Transcendent who is immanent. This very approach gives clues to understand Ephrem's view of the world and human being.

For Ephrem, the Scripture and Cosmos are the *locus theologicus*. The importance given to Cosmos along with Scripture is something unique in Ephrem. He often employed symbols from nature to explain God's revelation to human beings. His epistemology of explaining Christian faith between cataphatic and apophatic poles impelled him to draw a line between paradoxes in life. This is reflected in his literary style as well as in the explanation of divine mysteries.

The theology of *raza* is of particular importance to understand the meaning of sacrament from the Syrian perspective. The two distinctive meanings of the term *raza*, namely the liturgical and sacramental meaning and the exegetical meaning, deserve particular mention. In its liturgical use we observed its closeness to the Hebrew *sôd*. The Semitic background of its Greek equivalent *mysterion* also denotes the possibilities of widening the understanding of sacraments. This broader understanding that enabled the Syrian Churches to understand sacraments more in terms of sacramentality. We have also delineated how the theology of sacraments becomes central to theology in Syrian tradition.

Ephrem defended the Christian worldview against the gnostic woldviews of Marcion, Bardaisan and Mani of his time. He criticizes these heretics who tried to find different eternal principles. For him, God is 'the absolute' and reveals Himself in various ways to his people. Ephrem also underscored the non-dualistic nature of human being against the heretic dualism. According to him, the inner aspects of human nature and the free will makes human being distinct from other beings in Creation. For him, the human being endowed with free will, remains the "Lord of all Creation."

Ephrem's anthropology presents the uniqueness of human being in its relation to the Creation. Human beings created in the image of God represent God in Creation. Using the imagery of 'King,' Ephrem underscored human responsibility in keeping a harmonious relation to Creation. We also draw attention to the importance of the notion of 'free will' in this regard. A right exercise of the free will offers the possibility to enter into the eschaton. This view impels human being to exercise the free will in a responsible way to keep harmony of the Creation. Furthermore, we noted the eschatological participation through the liturgical and sacramental celebrations of the Church.

It is quite natural to question the relevance of a fourth century author Ephrem at the dawn of Third Millennium. This is all the more relevant when we discuss him from a theological perspective. Theology as a science deals with the grammar of language and therefore the polemic or socio- historic context of fourth century has a different conversation than that of today. But Ephrem as a mystic intuitively went deeper into the inner realities of life. Although aware and concerned about the living situations of his time and a participant of the conversations of his time, he meditated more on the God-world-human relations.

Synthesis

In short, the proposed paradigm 'world as sacrament' emphasizes the importance of world in Christian theology. We have noted the presence of a sacramental view of the world in all Christian traditions. Although the way the sacramentality of the world perceived in these traditions differs, the cosmic and eschatological dimensions are present in all these worldviews.

Boff's theology from the perspective of the poor criticizes the oppression against human being and nature and argues for social and ecological justice. The mystical strand seen in Boff stems from his integral view of Creation encompassing human beings and nature forming a web of relationships. His sacramental thinking and the notion of transparence by which he sees the transcendent God in the immanent world constrain him to commitment and to respect the Creation as a whole. His identification of the Kingdom of God with the liberation all the more accentuates his view of human being as a "sacramental" and "ethical" being.

Schmemann from his part looks at theology from the perspective of liturgy. For him too the realities of the World points to its Creator. He emphasizes the priestly responsibility of human being in their relation to Creation. Although he accepts the definition of human being as *homo sapiens* and *homo faber*, he says first of all human being is ***homo adorans***. This definition of human being as priest enables him to receive the world from God and to offer it back to God. This is the result of a transformation taking place in him, which in eastern theology is called *deification*, *divinization*, or *theosis*. It is life in communion with God. Thus, the liturgical celebrations become passage from this world to the other world. At the horizontal level it is an ascension to God and to his eschaton, but from the vertical level it is going to the Church and returning to the world with the renewed spirit in Jesus. Although the horizontal dimension seems emphasized, Schmemann tried his best to emphasize both equally.

The Syrian understanding in general and Ephrem's view in particular sees theology through the prism of Bible and nature. The exegetical tradition mainly based on the Antiochene tradition looks into the typology in the Bible and nature. All these point to the mystery of God revealing His sacramental presence. Human being is presented in the image of a King. At the same time the image of a King does not negate the priestly role. As Aphrahat states: "Christians are perfected as priests, kings and priests." Thus the image of human being as King emphasizes both the ethical responsibility to Creation and the priestly responsibility of thanking God.

Implications

The world as sacrament as a rediscovered paradigm has wider implications in contemporary sacramentology. First of all, it offers broader possibilities in the multi-religious context of contemporary society.

Christian liturgical and sacramental celebration often emphasized the relation between God and human being. The liturgical and sacramental celebrations are the movements of sacramental encounter between divine and human. This dualism between the divine and human realm distinguishes the realities between heavenly and earthly, between supernatural and natural grace. A dualistic approach of this kind is inherent in all the theocentric and anthropocentric worldviews prevalent often in Christian tradition. Such a dualistic worldview further distinguishes between sacred and profane. Thus, the world is often looked down as profane. The world understood as sacrament places it in proper relation with God and Human being. In other words, the sacramentality of the world positively appreciates the goodness of Creation. A positive appraisal of the world suggests to appreciate and thank God for His gifts. It also emphasizes our responsibility to respect other members in the Creation.

The broader understanding of sacramentality has already deepened the Christian understanding of Sacraments. Thus the sacramentality of Christ and the sacramentality of the Church emphasized the *life in Christ* and the *life in the Church*. Moreover, the Christological and ecclesial dimensions of sacraments remind us of a Christian mission in the world. However, the sacramentality of the world is the completion of the sacramentality of Christ and the sacramentality of the Church. This does not rule out the relevance of the particular sacramental celebrations of the Church. Conversely the sacramentality of the world is broadened from the conventional understanding of liturgical and sacramental gestures that confer grace to a graceful living. In other words, the world as sacrament emphasizes the sacramental living, a mystical response of praising God and ethical responsibility to Creation, can be an effective tool in the multi-religious context of contemporary society.

The sacramental view of the World is significant in the midst of the widespread ecological crisis. It also serves as a genuine answer to the accusation of Jewish-Christian responsibility in the exploitation of nature raised from some corners of early ecologists. The sacramentality of the world can effectively serve as a mediating principle between various Christian denominations, between various religions and moreover between various ideologies.

BIBLIOGRAPHY

This bibliography consists of three main divisions of cited works: (1) the books (2) the articles, and (3) the Patristics. Books and articles are listed in alphabetical order. Books and articles of the same author are listed in chronological order.

Abbreviations

CBQ	Catholic Biblical Quarterly
CQR	Church Quarterly Review
CSCO	Corpus Scriptorum Christianorum Orientalium
ECR	Eastern Churches Review
EO	Ecclesia Orans
ER	Ecumenical Review
ET	Expository Times
ETL	Ephemerides theologicae Lovanienses
FrS	Franciscan Studies
GOTR	Greek Orthodox Theological Review
ITS	Indian Theological Studies
JES	Journal of Ecumenical Studies
JTS	Journal of Theological Studies
LJ	Liturgisches Jahrbuch
LM	Le Muséon
LS	Louvain Studies
LTK	Lexikon für Theologie und Kirche
OCA	Orientalia Christiana Analecta
OCP	Orientalia Christiana Periodica
OrChr	Oriens Christianus
ParOr	Parole de l'Orient
PBR	The Patristic and Byzantine Review
PG	Patrologiae Cursus Completus, Series Graeca
PL	Patrologiae Cursus Completus, Series Latina
QL	Questions Liturgiques/Studies in Liturgy
SCA	Studies in Christian Antiquity
Scot. Jour.	Scottish Journal of Theology
SL	Studia Liturgica
SP	Studia Patristica
SVSQ	Saint Vladimir's Seminary Quarterly

SVTQ	Saint Vladimir's Theological Quarterly
TI	Theological Investigations
TS	Theological Studies
ZKG	Zeitschrift für Kirchengeschichte
ZKT	Zeitschrift für Katholische Theologie
ZTK	Zeitschrift für Theologie und Kirche

Books

Androutsos, Chrestos, *The Validity of English Ordinations from an Orthodox Catholic Point of View* (London: Richards, 1909).

Bardaisan, *The Book of the Laws of the Countries: Dialogue on Fate of Bardaisan of Edessa*, trans. H. J. W. Drijvers (Assen: Van Gorcum, 1965).

Barth, Markus, *Ephesians, Introduction, Translation and Commentary on Chapters 1–3* (New York: Doubleday & Company Inc., 1974).

Beati Lanfrancus, *De Corpore et Sanguine Domini*, PL, 150, 410 D, J. P. Migne (Paris: Migne, 1854) 407-412.

Beck, Edmund, *Die Theologie des hl. Ephraem in seinen Hymnen über den Glauben*, Studia Anselmiana, 21 (Città del Vaticano: Libreria Edictrice Vaticana, 1949).

Beirnaert, Louis, *Expérience Chrétienne et Psychologie* (Paris: Éditions de L'EPI, 1964).

Boeve, Lieven & Leijssen, Lambert (eds.), *Contemporary Sacramental Contours of a God Incarnate* (Leuven: Peeters, 2001).

— & Leijssen, Lambert (eds.), *Sacramental Presence in a Postmodern Context* (Leuven: Peeters, 2001).

— & Ries, John C. (eds.), *The Presence of Transcendence: Thinking Sacrament in a Postmodern Age* (Leuven: Peeters, 2001).

Boff, Leonardo & Boff, Clodovis, *Introducing Liberation Theology* (Maryknoll, NY: Orbis, 1987).

—, *Die Kirche als Sakrament im Horizont der Welterfahrung: Versuch einer Legitimation und einer struktur-funktionalistischen Grundlegung der Kirche im Anschluß an das II. Vatikanische Konzil* (Paderborn: Bonifacius, 1972).

—, *Jesus Christ Liberator: A Critical Christology for Our Time* (Maryknoll, NY: Orbis, 1978).

—, *Way of Cross – Way of Justice* (Maryknoll, NY: Orbis, 1980).

—, *God's Witness in the Heart of the World* (Chicago, IL: Claret Center for Resources in Spirituality, 1981).

—, *Saint Francis: A Model for Human Liberation* (New York: Crossroad, 1982).

—, *The Lord's Prayer: A Prayer of Integral Liberation* (Maryknoll, NY: Orbis, 1983).

—, *Church: Charism and Power: Liberation Theology and the Institutional Church*, trans. John W. Diercksmeier (New York: Crossroad, 1985).

—, *Ecclesiogenesis: The Base Communities Reinvent the Church*, trans. Robert R. Barr (Maryknoll, NY: Orbis, 1986).

—, *Passion of Christ, Passion of the World: The Facts, Their Interpretation, and Their Meaning Yesterday and Today* (Maryknoll, NY: Orbis, 1987).
—, *Sacraments of Life, Life of the Sacraments: Story Theology*, trans. John Drury (Beltsville, MD: Pastoral Press, 1987).
—, *Trinity and Society* (London: Burns & Oates, 1988).
—, *Holy Trinity: Perfect Community* (Maryknoll, NY: Orbis, 1988).
—, *Faith on the Edge, Religion and Marginalized Existence*, trans. Robert R. Barr (Maryknoll, NY: Orbis, 1989).
—, *Liberating Grace*, trans. John Drury (Maryknoll, NY: Orbis, 1990).
—, *The Path to Hope: Fragments from a Theologian's Journey*, trans. Phillip Berryman (Maryknoll, NY: Orbis, 1993).
—, *Ecology and Liberation: A New Paradigm*, trans. John Cumming (Maryknoll, NY: Orbis, 1995).
—, *Cry of the Earth, Cry of the Poor*, trans. Philip Berryman (Maryknoll, NY: Orbis, 1997).
Bornert, René, *Les Commentaires byzantins de la divine liturgie, du VIIe au XVe siècle* (Paris: Institut Français d'Études Byzantines, 1966).
Brim, Joseph, *Dictionarium Syriaco-Latinum* (Soc. Jesu Beryti Phoneniciorum, 1911).
Brock, Sebastian, *The Holy Spirit in the Syrian Baptismal Tradition*, The Syrian Churches Series, 9 (Kottayam: Anita Printers, 1975).
—, *The Syriac Fathers on Prayer and the Spiritual Life* (Kalamazoo: Cistercian Publications, 1987).
—, *The Luminous Eye: The Spiritual World Vision of Saint Ephrem the Syrian* (Kalamazoo: Cistercian Publications, 1992).
Brown, Francis, Driver, S. R. & Briggs, Charles A., *A Hebrew and English Lexicon of the Old Testament: With an Appendix Containing the Biblical Aramaic*, trans. Edward Robinson (Oxford: Oxford University Press, [1]1901, 1959).
Capéran, L., *Le problème du salut des infidèles* (Paris: Beauchesne, 1912).
Carol, Juniper B, *Why Jesus Christ? Thomistic, Scotistic and Conciliatory Perspectives* (Manassas, VA: Trinity Communications, 1986).
Casel, Odo, *Das christliche Kultmysterium* (Regensburg: Pustet, 1960).
—, *The Mystery of Christian Worship and Other Writings*, ed. Burkhard Neunheuser (Westminster, MD: Newman, 1962).
Cayré, Fulbert, *Précis de patrologie et d'histoire de la théologie* (Paris: Desclée, [2]1931).
Chauvet, Louis-Marie, *Symbol and Sacrament: A Sacramental Reinterpretation of Christian Existence*, trans. Patrick Madigan & Madeleine Beaumont (Collegeville, MN: Liturgical Press, 1995).
Chupungco, Anscar J., *Liturgical Inculturation: Sacramentals, Religiosity, and Catechesis* (Collegeville, MN: Liturgical Press, 1992).
—, *Cultural Adaptation of the Liturgy* (New York: Paulist, 1982).
—, *Liturgies of the Future: The Process and Methods of Inculturation* (Mahwah, NJ: Paulist, 1989).
Congar, Yves, *La Parole et le Souffle* (Paris: Desclée, 1984).
Cox, Harvey, *The Silencing of Leonardo Boff: The Vatican and the Future of World Christianity* (Oak Park: Meyer/Stone, 1988).

d'Eypernon, Taymans, *The Blessed Trinity and the Sacraments* (Dublin: Clonmore & Reynolds Ltd., 1961).

Dalmais, Irénée-Henri, *Introduction to the Liturgy*, trans. Roger Capel (Baltimore, MD: Helicon, 1961).

Dixon, David Carey, *A Critical Analysis of Liberationist Christology in the Writings of Gustavo Gutierrez, Leonardo Boff, and John Sobrino* (Fort Worth, TX, Southwestern Baptist Theological Seminary: A Dissertation presented to the Faculty of the School of Theology, 1988).

Drijvers, H. J. W., *Bardaisan of Edessa* (Assen: Van Gorcum & Comp. N. V., 1966).

—, *Cults and Beliefs at Edessa* (Leiden: Brill, 1980).

—, *East of Antioch: Studies in Early Christianity* (London: Variorum, 1984).

Dyovouniotis, K.I., *Ta mysteria tes Anatolikes Orthodokson Ekklesias eks apopseos dogmatikes* (Athens, 1913), trans. J. A. Douglas: *The Relations of the Anglican Churches with the Eastern-Orthodox* (London: Faith Press, 1921).

El-Khoury, Nabil, *Die Interpretation der Welt bei Ephraem: Beitrag zur Geistesgeschichte*, Tübinger theologische Studien, 6 (Mainz: Grünewald, 1976).

Evdokimov, Paul, *Les âges de la vie spirituelle* (Paris, Desclée de Brouwer, 1964).

Fagerberg, David W., *What is Liturgical Theology? A Study in Methodology* (Collegeville, MN: Liturgical Press, 1992).

Finkenzeller, Josef, *Die Lehre von den Sakramenten im allgemeinen. Von der Schrift bis zur Scholastik*, Handbuch der Dogmengeschichte, 4/1a (Freiburg: Herder, 1980)

Fittkau, Gerard, *Der Begriff des Mysteriums bei Johannes Chrysostomus* (Bonn: Hanstein, 1953).

Florensky, Pavel, *The Pillar and Ground of the Truth: An Essay in Orthodox Theodicy in Twelve Letters*, trans. Boris Jakim (Princeton, NJ: Princeton University Press, 1997).

Florovsky, Georges, *The Ways of Russian Theology (Part I)*, gen. ed. Richard S. Haugh (Belmont, MA: Nordland Publishing Co., 1979).

Gibellini, Rosino, *The Liberation Theology Debate* (Maryknoll, NY: Orbis, 1987).

Granberg-Michaelson, W., *A Worldly Spirituality* (San Francisco, CA: Harper & Row, 1984).

Griffith, Sidney H., *"Faith Adoring the Mystery": Reading the Bible with St. Ephraem the Syrian* (Milwaukee, WI: Marquette University Press, 1997).

Hartmann, Stephanie, *Trinitätslehre als Sozialkritik? Das Verhältnis von Gotteslehre und Sozialkritik in den trinitätstheologischen Entwürfen von Jürgen Moltmann und Leonardo Boff* (Frankfurt/M: Lang, 1997).

Hayes, Zachary, *The Hidden Centre: Spirituality and Speculative Christology in Saint Bonaventure* (New York: Paulist, 1981).

Hidal, Sten, *Interpretatio syriaca: die Kommentare des Heiligen Ephräm des Syrers zu Genesis und Exodus mit besondere Berücksichtigung ihrer Auslegungsgeschichtlichen Stellung*, Coniectanea Biblica. OT Series, 6 (Lund: Gleerup, 1974).

Hilkert, Mary Catherine, *Naming Grace: Preaching and the Sacramental Imagination* (New York: Continuum, 1997).

Irwin, Kevin W., *Liturgical Theology: A Primer*, American Essays in Liturgy (Collegeville, MN: Liturgical Press, 1990).

—, *Context and Text: Method in Liturgical Theology* (Collegeville, MN: Liturgical Press, 1994).

Kavanagh, Aidan, *On Liturgical Theology* (New York: Pueblo, 1984).

Kelly, Geffrey B. (ed.), *Karl Rahner: Theologian of the Graced Search for Meaning* (Edinburgh: T&T Clark, 1993).

Koehler, Ludwig, Baumgartner, Walter & Stamm, Johann Jakob, *The Hebrew and Aramaic Lexicon of the Old Testament*, trans. & ed. under the supervision of M. E. J. Richardson (Leiden/New York/Köln: Brill, 1995).

—, *Hebrew Man* (Nashville, TN: Abingdon, 1956).

Kollamparambil, Antony George, *From Symbol to Truth: A Syriac Understanding of the Paschal Mystery* (Roma: CLV – Edizoni Liturgiche, 2000).

Kronholm, Tryggve, *Motifs from Genesis 1–11 in the Genuine Hymns of Ephrem the Syrian, with Particular Reference to the Influence of Jewish Exegetical Tradition*, Coniectanea Biblica. OT Series, 11 (Lund: Gleerup, 1978).

LaCugna, Catherine Mowry, *God for Us: The Trinity and Christian Life* (San Francisco, CA: Harper, 1991).

Ladrière, Jean, *Language and Belief* (Dublin: Gill & Macmillan, 1972).

Lamberts, Jozef (ed.), *Liturgy and Inculturation: Introduction*, Textes et études liturgiques / Studies in Liturgy, 14 (Louvain: Peeters, 1996).

— (ed.), *Popular Religion, Liturgy and Evangelization*, Textes et études liturgiques / Studies in Liturgy, 15 (Leuven: Peeters, 1998).

Lathrop, Gordon W., *Holy Things: A Liturgical Theology* (Minneapolis, MN: Fortress, 1993).

Leeuw, G. van der, *Sakramentstheologie* (G. F. Callenbach, 1949).

Lies, Lothar, *Sakramententheologie: Eine personale Sicht* (Graz: Styria, 1990).

Lieu, Samuel N.C., *Manichaeism in the Later Roman Empire and Medieval China: A Historical Survey* (Manchester: Manchester University Press, 1988).

Lukken, Gerard, *Per visibilia ad invisibilia: Anthropological, Theological, and Semiotic Studies on the Liturgy and Sacraments*, Liturgia Condenda, 2, ed. Louis van Tongeren & Charles Caspers (Kampen: Kok Pharos, 1994).

Maniyattu, Pauly, *Heaven on Earth: The Theology of Liturgical Spacetime in the East Syrian Qurbana* (Rome: Mar Thoma Yogam, 1995).

Mansour, P. Tanios Bou, *La Pensée symbolique de S. Éphrem le syrien* (Kaslik: Bibliothèque de l'Université Saint-Esprit XVI, 1988).

Mantzaridis, Georgios I., *The Deification of Man* (Crestwood, NY: St. Vladimir's Seminary Press, 1984).

Marte, Johann & Wilflinger, Gerhard (eds.), *Syriac Dialogue: Fourth Non-Official Consultation on Dialogue within the Syriac Tradition* (Vienna: Pro Oriente, 2001).

Martos, Joseph, *Doors to the Sacred: A Historical Introduction to Sacraments in the Catholic Church* (London: SCM, 1981, expanded edition 1992).

Masure, Canon Eugène, *The Sacrifice of the Mystical Body* (London: Burns & Oates, 1954).

May, Rollo, *Symbolism in Religion and Literature* (New York: Braziller, 1960).

McCullough, W. Stewart, *A Short History of Syriac Christianity to the Rise of Islam* (Chico, CA: Scholars, 1982).

McElrath, Damian (ed.), *Franciscan Christology* (Assisi: Tipografia Portiuncola, 1980).

McMahon, L. M., "Towards a Theology of the Liturgy: Dom Odo Casel and the 'Mysterientheorie'," *SL* 3 (1964) 129-154

McVey, Kathleen, *Ephrem the Syrian: Hymns* (New York/Mahwah, NJ: Paulist, 1989).

— (ed.), *St. Ephrem the Syrian: Selected Prose Works*, trans. Edward G. Mathews, Jr. & Joseph P. Amar (Washington, DC: Catholic University of America Press, 1994).

Meyendorff, John, *Byzantine Theology. Historical Trends and Doctrinal Themes* (New York: Fordham University Press, ^{2}1983).

Murray, Robert, *Symbols of Church and Kingdom: A Study in Early Syriac Tradition* (Cambridge: Cambridge University Press, 1975).

—, *The Cosmic Covenant: Biblical Themes of Justice, Peace and the Integrity of Creation* (London: Sheed & Ward 1992).

Nichols, Aidan, *Theology in the Russian Diaspora: Church, Fathers, Eucharist in Nikolai Afanas'ev (1893-1966)* (Cambridge: Cambridge University Press, 1989).

Nyberg, Henrik Samuel, *A Manual of Pahlavi* (Wiesbaden: Harassowitz, 1964-74).

Osborne, Kenan B., *Sacramental Theology. A General Introduction* (Mahwah, NJ: Paulist, 1988).

—, *Christian Sacraments in a Postmodern World: A Theology for the Third Millennium* (New York/Mahwah, NJ: Paulist, 1999).

Pathikulangara, Varghese, *Resurrection, Life and Renewal* (Bangalore: Dharmaram Publications, 1982).

Payne, Richard L., *Sacramentality in the Writings of Leonardo Boff: Its Franciscan Roots, Its Elaboration, and Its Role in the Process of Liberation.* A Thesis submitted for the licentiate degree (M.A.) in Religious Studies at K.U. Leuven (Leuven: K.U. Leuven, 1993).

Poovannikunnel, Jose, *The Concept of "Mystery" (rāzā) in the Syro-Malabar Qurbana: A Study on the Biblical and Theological Dimensions of the Liturgical Theology of the Eucharistic Celebration* (Kottayam: OIRSI, 1989) .

Poovathanikunnel, Thomas, *The Sacraments: The Mystery Revealed* (Kottayam: OIRSI, 1998).

Power, David N., *Unsearchable Riches: The Symbolic Nature of Liturgy* (New York: Pueblo, 1984).

—, *Worship: Culture and Theology* (Washington, DC: Pastoral Press, 1990).

—, *The Eucharistic Mystery: Revitalizing the Tradition* (New York: Crossroad, 1992).

Prestige, George L., *God in Patristic Thought* (London: SPCK, 1952).

Rahner, Karl, *The Church and the Sacraments* (London: Burns & Oates, 1957).

—, *The Trinity*, trans. J. Donceel (New York: Seabury, 1974).

Robinson, H. Wheeler, *Inspiration and Revelation in the Old Testament* (Oxford: Clarendon, 1946).

Roo, William A. Van, *The Christian Sacrament*, Analecta Gregoriana, 262 (Rome: Pontificia Università Gregoriana, 1992).

Russell, Paul S., *St. Ephraem the Syrian and St. Gregory the Theologian Confront the Arians* (Kottayam: Saint Ephrem Ecumenical Research Centre, 1994).

Rynne, Xavier, *Pope John Paul's Extraordinary Synod* (Wilmington, DE: Michael Glazier, 1986).

Saber, Georges, *La théologie baptismale de Saint Ephrem: Essai de théologie historique*, Bibliothèque de l'Université Saint-Esprit, 8 (Kaslik: Université Saint-Esprit, 1974).
Santmire, H. Paul, *The Travail of Nature: The Ambiguous Ecological Promise of Christian Theology* (Philadelphia, PA: Fortress, 1985).
Schillebeeckx, Edward, *De Sacramentele Heilseconomie: Theologische bezinning op S. Thomas' Sacramentenleer in het licht van de traditie en van de hedendaagse sacramentsproblematiek* (Antwerp/Bilthoven: 't Groeit/H. Nelissen, 1952).
—, *Christ, the Sacrament of Encounter with God* (New York: Sheed and Ward, 1963).
Schilson, Arno, *Theologie als Sakramententheologie: Die Mysterien-theologie Odo Casels* (Mainz: Matthias-Grünewald-Verlag, 1982).
Schmaus, Michael, *The Church as Sacrament* (London: Sheed and Ward, 1975).
Schmemann, Alexander, *The Historical Road of Eastern Orthodoxy*, trans. Lydia W. Kesich (New York: Rinehart & Winston, Inc. 1963).
—, *Sacraments and Orthodoxy* (New York: Herder and Herder, 1965).
—, *The World as Sacrament* (London, Darton: Longman & Todd, 1966).
—, *Introduction to Liturgical Theology*, trans. Asheleigh E. Moorhouse (London: Faith Press, 1966).
—, *For the Life of the World* (Crestwood, NY: St. Vladimir's Seminary Press, 1973).
—, *Of Water and the Spirit: A Liturgical Study of Baptism* (London: SPCK, 1976).
—, *Ultimate Questions: An Anthology of Modern Russian Religious Thought* (New York: St. Vladimir's Seminary Press, 1977).
—, *Church, World, Mission: Reflections on Orthodoxy in the West* (Crestwood, NY: St. Vladimir's Seminary Press, 1979).
—, *The Eucharist: Sacrament of the Kingdom*, trans. Paul Kachur (Crestwood, NY: St. Vladimir's Seminary Press, 1988).
—, *Celebration of Faith.* Vol. I: *I Believe* (Crestwood, NY: St. Vladimir's Seminary Press, 1991).
—, *Celebration of Faith.* Vol. II: *The Church Year* (Crestwood, NY: St. Vladimir's Seminary Press, 1994).
—, *Celebration of Faith.* Vol. III: *The Virgin Mary*, trans. John A. Jillions (Crestwood, NY: St. Vladimir's Seminary Press, 1995).
—, *The Journals of Father Alexander Schmemann 1973-1983*, trans. Juliana Schmemann (Crestwood, NY: St. Vladimir's Seminary Press, 2000).
—, *Great Lent: Journey to Pascha* (Crestwood, NY: St. Vladimir's Seminary Press, 2001).
Schneider, Theodore, *Zeichen der Nähe Gottes: Grundriss der Sakramententheologie* (Mainz: Matthias Grünewald, 1979).
Semmelroth, Otto, *Die Kirche als Ursakrament* (Frankfurt: Knecht, 1953).
Senn, Frank C., *Christian Liturgy: Catholic and Evangelical* (Minneapolis, MN: Fortress, 1997).
Smith, R. Payne (ed.), *Thesaurus Syriacus.* Vol. 2 (Oxford: Clarendon, 1901).
Sobrino, John, *Jesus the Liberator*, trans. Paul Barns & Francis McDonagh (Maryknoll, NY: Orbis, 1993).
Tsirpanlis, Constantine N., *Introduction to Eastern Patristic Thought and Orthodox Theology* (Collegeville, MN: Liturgical Press, 1991).

Turner, J. David, *An Introduction to Liberation Theology* (Lanham, MD/New York/London: University Press of America, 1994).

Ute Possekel, *Evidence of Greek Philosophical Concepts in the Writings of Ephrem the Syrian*, CSCO, 580 (Louvain: Peeters, 1999).

Vaillancourt, Raymond, *Toward a Renewal of Sacramental Theology*, trans. Matthew O' Connell (Collegeville, MN: Liturgical Press, 1979).

Vonier, Anscar, *A Key to the Doctrine of the Eucharist* (London: Burns & Oates, 1952).

Vorgrimler, Herbert, *Sacramental Theology*, trans. Linda M. Maloney (Collegeville, MN: Liturgical Press, 1992).

Vries, Wilhelm de, *Sakramententheologie bei den syrischen Monophysiten*, OCA, 125 (Rome: Pontificium Institutum Orientalium Studiorum, 1940).

Vries, Wilhelm de, *Sakramententheologie bei den syrischen Nestorianern*, OCA, 133 (Rome: Pontificium Institutum Orientalium Studiorum, 1947).

Wackernagel, Jakob & Debrunner, A., *Altindische Grammatik* (Göttingen: Vandenhoeck & Ruprecht, 1954).

Wainwright, Geoffrey, *Doxology: The Praise of God in Worship, Doctrine and Life* (New York: Oxford University Press, 1980).

Ware, Timothy, *The Orthodox Church* (Harmondsworth: Penguin Books, 1978).

Worgul, George S., *From Magic to Metaphor. A Validation of the Christian Sacraments* (New York/Ramsey, NJ: Paulist, 1980).

Yousif, Pierre, *L'Eucharistie chez s. Éphrem de Nisibe* (Rome: Pontificium institutum orientale, 1984).

Zimmermann, Joyce Ann, *Liturgy as Language of Faith: A Liturgical Methodology in the Mode of Paul Ricœur's Textual Hermeneutics* (New York: University Press of America, 1988).

Articles

Aland, B., "Marcion: Versuch einer neuen Interpretation," *ZTK* 70 (1973) 420-447.

Amaladoss, Michael, "Semiotics and Sacraments," *ITS* 16-17 (1979) 32-54.

Amar, Joseph P., "Perspectives on the Eucharist In Ephrem the Syrian," *Worship* 61 (1987) 441-454.

—, "Byzantine Ascetic Monachism and Greek Bias in the Vita Tradition of Ephrem the Syrian," *OCP* 58 (1992) 123-156.

Appleyard, J.A., "How Does a Sacrament Cause by Signifying?," *Science et Esprit* 23 (1971) 167-200.

Balthasar, Hans Urs von, "Le mystère d'Origène," *Recherches de science religieuse* 26 (1937) 38-64.

Barnes, Michel René, "Augustine in Contemporary Trinitarian Theology," *TS* 56 (1995) 237-250.

—, "Oeconomia," *Encyclopaedia of Early Christianity*, ed. Everett Ferguson (New York/London: Garland Publishing, 1997) 825-826.

Bartholomäus, W., "Communications in the Church: Aspects of a Theological Theme," *Concilium* 111 (1978) 95-110.

Beck, Edmund, "Das Bild vom Spiegel bei Ephraem," *OCP* 19 (1953) 5-24.

—, "Le baptême chez S. Ephrem," *L'Orient Syrien* 2 (1956) 111-136.

—, "Symbolum-Mysterium bei Aphraat und Ephräm," *OrChr* 41-42 (1957-1958) 19-40.

—, "Ephraem Brief an Hypatios," *OrChr* 58 (1974) 76-120.

—, "Ephräms Rede gegen eine philosophische Schrift des Bardaisan," *OrChr* 60 (1976) 24-68.

—, "Bardaisan und Seine Schule bei Ephräm," *LM* 91 (1978) 271-333.

—, "Die Hyle bei Markion nach Ephräm," *OCP* 44 (1978) 5-30.

—, "Zwei ephrämische Bilde," *Christianus* 71 (1987) 1-9.

Beinert, Wolfgang, "Die Sakramentalität der Kirche im theologischen Gespräch," *Theologische Berichte* 9 (1980) 13-66.

Berger, Teresa, "Liturgy - a Forgotten Subject-matter of Theology?," *SL* 17 (1987) 10-18.

Bernard, Leslie W., "The Origins and Emergence of the Church in Edessa during the First Two Centuries A.D.," *Vigiliae Christianae* 22 (1968) 161-175.

Bishops, Synod of, "The Final Report," *Origins* 15 (Dec. 19, 1985).

Bobrinskoy, Boris, "Introduction," in Nicholas Cabasilas, *The Life in Christ*, trans. Carmino J. de Catanzaro (Crestwood, NY: St. Vladimir's Seminary Press, 1974) 17-42.

Boeve, Lieven, "Postmodern Sacramento-Theology: Retelling the Christian Story," *ETL* 74 (1998) 326-343.

—, "Thinking Sacramental Presence in a Postmodern Context: A Playground for Theological Renewal," *Sacramental Presence in a Postmodern Context*, ed. Lieven Boeve & Lambert Leijssen (Leuven: Peeters, 2001) 3-35.

Boff, Leonardo & Elizondo, Virgil, "Ecology and Poverty: Cry of the Earth, Cry of the Poor" (Editorial), *Concilium* (1995), n. 5, ix-xii.

—, "Salvation in Jesus Christ and the Process of Liberation," *Concilium* 10/6 (1974) 78-91.

—, "Is the Distinction between 'Ecclesia Docens' and 'Ecclesia Discens' Justified?," *Concilium* 148 (1981) 47-51.

—, "Images of Jesus in Brazilian Liberal Christianity," *Faces of Jesus: Latin American christologies*, ed. José Miguez Bonino (Maryknoll, NY: Orbis, 1984) 9-29.

—, "Integral Liberation and Partial Liberations," *Salvation and Liberation: In Search of a Balance between Faith and Politics*, ed. Leonardo Boff & Clodovis Boff (Maryknoll, NY: Orbis, 1984) 46-47.

—, "Salvation in Liberation: The Theological Meaning of Socio-historical Liberation," *Salvation and Liberation: In Search of a Balance between Faith and Politics*, Leonardo & Clodovis Boff (Maryknoll, NY: Orbis, 1984) 1-13.

—, "Trinitarian Community and Social Liberation," *Cross Currents* 38 (1988) 289-308.

—, "The Originality of the Theology of Liberation," *The Future of Liberation Theology: Essays in Honor of Gustavo Gutierrez*, ed. Marc Ellis & Otto Maduro (Maryknoll, NY: Orbis, 1989) 38-48.

—, "Social Ecology: Poverty and Misery," *Ecotheology: Voices from South and North*, ed. David G. Hallman (Geneva: World Council of Churches, 1994) 235-263.

—, "Liberation Theology and Ecology: Alternative, Confrontation or Complementarity?" *Concilium* (1995), n. 5, 67-77.

Bornkamm, Günther, "μυστήριον, μυέω" *Theological Dictionary of the New Testament*, ed. Gerhard Kittel, trans. & ed. Geoffrey W. Bromiley, vol. IV (Grand Rapids, MI: Eerdmans, 1967) 802-828.

Botha, P.J., "Original Sin and Sexism: St. Ephrem's Attitude towards Eve," *SP* 33 (1997) 483-489.

Botte, Bernard, "On Liturgical Theology," *SVSQ* 12 (1968) 170-173.

Brock, Sebastian, "Early Syrian Asceticism," *Numen* 20 (1973) 1-19.

—, "The Epiklesis in the Antiochene Baptismal Ordines," *OCA* 197 (1974) 184-208.

—, "World and Sacrament in the Writings of the Syrian Fathers," *Sobornost* 6/10 (1974) 685-696.

—, "St Ephrem on Christ as Light in Mary and in the Jordan: *Hymni de Ecclesia* 36," *ECR* 7 (1975) 137-144.

—, "The Poet as Theologian," *Sobornost* 7/4 (1977) 243-250.

—, "The Mysteries Hidden in the Side of Christ," *Sobornost* 7/6 (1978) 462-472.

—, "Baptismal Themes in the Writings of Jacob of Serugh," *OCA* 205 (1978) 325-347.

—, "Jewish Traditions in Syriac Sources," *Journal of Jewish Studies* 30 (1979) 212-232.

—, "An Introduction to Syriac Studies," *Horizons in Semitic Studies*, ed. John H. Eaton, Semitics Study Aids, 8 (Birmingham: University of Birmingham, 1980) 1-33.

—, "Clothing Metaphors as a Means of Theological Expression in Syriac Tradition," *Typus, Symbol, Allegorie bei den östlichen Vätern und ihren Parallelen im Mittelalter*, ed. Margot Schmidt, Eichstätter Beiträge: Abteilung Philosophie und Theologie, 4 (Regensburg: Pustet, 1982) 11-40.

—, "The Prayer of the Heart in Syriac Tradition," *Sobornost* 4/2 (1982) 131-142.

—, "The Priesthood of the Baptised: Some Syriac Perspectives," *Sobornost* 9/2 (1987) 14-22.

—, "Humanity and the Natural World in the Syriac Tradition," *Sobornost* 12/2 (1990) 131-142.

—, "'The Wedding Feast of Blood on Golgotha': an Unusual Aspect of John 19/34 in Syriac Tradition," *The Harp* 6/2 (1993) 121-134.

—, "Fire frome Heaven: from Abel's Sacrifice to the Eucharist. A Theme in Syriac Christianity," *SP* 25 (1993) 229-243.

Brown, Raymond E., "The Pre-Christian Semitic Concept of 'Mystery'," *CBQ* 20 (1958) 417-443.

—, "The Semitic Background of the New Testament Mysterion," *Biblica* 39 (1958) 426-448; 40 (1958) 70-87.

Brown, Robert McAfee, "Leonardo Boff: Theologian for All Christians," *Christian Century* (July 2-9, 1986) 615.

Bundy, David D., "Ephrem's Critique of Mani: The Limits of Knowledge and the Nature of Language," *Gnosticisme et monde hellénistique: Actes du Colloque de Louvain-la-Neuve (11-14 mars 1980)*, ed. J. Ries, et al., Publications de l'Institut Orientaliste de Louvain, 27 (Louvain-la-Neuve: Institut Orientaliste de Louvain, 1982) 289-298.

—, "Language and Knowledge of God in Ephrem Syrus," *PBR* 5 (1986) 91-103.

—, "Marcion and the Marcionites in Early Syriac Apologetics," *LM* 101 (1988) 21-32.

—, "Ephrem's Exegesis of Isaiah," *SP* 18/4 (1990) 234-239.

Butler, Michael E., "Neo-Arianism: Its Antecedents and Tenets," *SVTQ* 36 (1994) 355-371.

Cappuyns, Maieul, "Liturgie et théologie," *Le vrai visage de la liturgie*, Cours et conférences des semaines liturgiques (Louvain: Abbaye de Mont César, 1938) 175-209.

Catella, Alceste, "Theology of the Liturgy," *Handbook for Liturgical Studies.* Volume II, *Fundamental Liturgy*, ed. Anscar J. Chupungco (Collegeville, MN: Liturgical Press, 1998) 3-28.

Celano, Thomas, "The First Life of St Francis," *Saint Francis of Assisi: Writings and Early Biographies: English Omnibus of the Sources for the Life of St Francis*, ed. Marion A. Habig (Chicago, IL: Franciscan Herald Press, 1979).

Chalassery, Joseph, "Sacraments of Initiation in the Syro-Malabar Church," *Syriac Dialogue: Fourth Non-Official Consultation on Dialogue within the Syriac Tradition*, ed. Johann Marte & Gerhard Wilflinger (Vienna: Pro Oriente, 2001) 90-106.

Chauvet, Louis-Marie, "Liturgy and the Body" (Editorial), *Concilium* (1995), n. 3, vii-x.

Chryssavgis, John, "The World as Sacrament: Insights into an Orthodox Worldview," *Pacifica* 10 (1997) 1-24.

Cocksworth, Christopher, "The Trinity Today: Opportunities and Challenges for Liturgical Study," *SL* 27 (1997) 61-78.

Collins, Mary, "Liturgical Methodology and the Cultural Evolution of Worship in the United States," *Worship* 49 (1975) 85-102.

—, "Critical Questions for Liturgical Theology," *Worship* 53 (1979) 302-317.

Congar, Yves, "Propos en vue d'une théologie de l'Économie dans la tradition latine," *Irénikon* 45 (1972) 155-206.

Conn, Marie, "The Sacramental Theology of Leonardo Boff," *Worship* 64 (1990) 523-532.

Coppens, Joseph, "'Mystery' in the Theology of Saint Paul and Its Parallels at Qumran," *Paul and Qumran: Studies in New Testament*, ed. J. Murphy O'Connor (London: Geoffrey Chapman, 1968) 132-158.

Crutcher, Timothy James, "Personally Speaking: Reflections on Relational Thinking for the Ecumenical Sacramentological Dialogue," *Contemporary Sacramental Contours of a God Incarnate*, ed. Lieven Boeve & Lambert Leijssen (Leuven: Peeters, 2001) 154-165.

Dalmais, Irénée-Henri, "Raza et Sacrament," *Rituels: Mélanges offerts au Père Gy o.p.*, ed. Paul de Clerck & Eric Palazzo (Paris: Institute Catholique de Paris, 1990) 173-182.

De Mey, Peter, "Church as Sacrament: A Conciliar Concept and Its Reception in Contemporary Theology," *The Presence of Transcendence: Thinking Sacrament in a Postmodern Age*, ed. Lieven Boeve & John C. Ries (Leuven: Peeters, 2001) 181-196.

Depoortere, Kristiaan, "From Sacramentality to Sacraments and Vice-versa," *Contemporary Sacramental Contours of a God Incarnate*, ed. Lieven Boeve & Lambert Leijssen (Leuven: Peeters, 2001) 51-62.

De Schrijver, Georges, "Experiencing the Sacramental Character of Existence: Transition from Premodernity to Modernity, Postmodernity, and the Rediscovery of Cosmos," *QL* 75 (1994) 12-27.

Desbonnets, Théophile, "The Franciscan Reading of the Scriptures," *Concilium* 149 (1981) 37-45.

Downey, Michael, "Widening Contexts of Sacramental Worship," *Pastoral Science* 13 (1994) 139-156.

Drijvers, H.J.W., "Marcionism in Syria: Principles, Problems, Polemics," *The Second Century* 8 (1987-88) 167.

Driscoll, Jeremy, "Liturgy and Fundamental Theology. Frameworks for a Dialogue," *EO* 11 (1994) 69-99.

—, "The Eucharist and Fundamental Theology," *EO* 13 (1996) 407-437.

—, "Anamnesis, Epiclesis and Fundamental Theology," *EO* 15 (1998) 211-238.

Duffy, Regis A., "The Sacramental Economy: (Paragraphs 1066-1209)," *Commentary on the Catechism of the Catholic Church*, ed. Michael J. Walsh (London: Geoffrey Chapman, 1994) 225-241.

Dulles, Avery, "A Half Century of Ecclesiology," *TS* 50 (1989) 419-442.

Duncan, E. J., "Baptism in the Demonstrations of Aphraates the Persian Sage," *SCA* 8 (1945) 57.

Dupuy, Bernard, "Un témoin de l'Orthodoxie Contemporaine: le Père Alexandre Schmemann (1921-1983)," *Istina* 30 (1985) 117-130.

Dyovouniotis, K.I., "The Principle of Economy," *CQR* 116 (1933) 93-101.

Ehlers, B., "Bardesanes – ein Syrische Gnostiker," *ZKG* 81 (1970) 334-351.

El-Khoury, Nabil, "Anthropological Concepts of the School of Antioch," *SP* 17 (1982) 1359-1365.

—, "Hermeneutics in the Works of Ephraim the Syrian," *OCA* 229 (1987) 93-99.

Empereur, James L., "Models for a Liturgical Theology," *The Sacraments: Readings in Contemporary Sacramental Theology*, ed. Michael J. Taylor (New York: Alba House, 1981) 53-70.

Erickson, John H., "Sacramental 'Economy' in Recent Roman Catholic Thought," *The Jurist* 48 (1988) 653-667.

—, "The Reception of Non-Orthodox into the Orthodox Church," *SVTQ* 41 (1997) 1-17.

Evdokimov, Paul, "Nature," *Scot. Jour.* 18 (1965) 1-22.

Eynde, Damian Van den, "The Theory of the Composition of the Sacraments in Early Scholasticism," *FrS* 11/1 (1951) 1-20; *FrS* 11/2 (1951) 117-144.

—, "Stephen Langton and Hugh of St. Cher on the Causality of Sacraments," *FrS* 11/3-4 (1951) 141-155.

Fisch, Thomas, "Introduction: Schmemann's Theological Contribution to the Liturgical Renewal of the Churches," *Liturgy and Tradition: Theological Reflections of Alexander Schmemann*, ed. Thomas Fisch (Crestwood, NY: St. Vladimir's Seminary Press, 1990) 1-10.

FitzGerald, Thomas, "The Holy Eucharist as Theophany," *GOTR* 28 (1983) 27-38.

Florovsky, George, "The Limits of the Church," *CQR* 117 (1933-1934) 117-131.

—, "The Elements of Liturgy," *The Orthodox Church in the Ecumenical Movement. Documents and Statements 1902-1975*, ed. Constantin G. Patelos (Geneva: World Council of Churches, 1978) 172-182.

Fox, M., "Is the 'Cosmic Christ' a Term That Is Anti-Ecumenical?," *The Coming of the Cosmic Christ* (San Francisco, CA: Harper and Row, 1988) 241-244.

Fransen, Piet F., "Sacraments as Celebrations," *Irish Theological Quarterly* 43 (1976) 151-170.

Funk, Virgil C., "The Liturgical Movement (1830-1969)," *The New Dictionary of Sacramental Worship*, ed. Peter E. Fink (Collegeville, MN: Liturgical Press, 1990) 695-715.

Galadza, Peter, "Restoring the Icon: Reflections on the Reform of Byzantine Worship," *Worship* 65 (1991) 238-255.

Gerson, D., "Die Commentarien des Ephraem Syrus im Verhältnis zur jüdischen Exegese: ein Beitrag zur Geschichte der Exegese," *Monatsschrift für Geschichte und Wissenschaft des Judentums* 17 (1868) 15-33, 64-72, 98-109, 141-149.

Gillan, Garth, "Expression, Discourse and Symbol," *Worship* 41 (1967) 16-31.

—, "Symbol: Word for the Other," *Worship* 41 (1967) 275-283.

Graffin, F., "L'Eucharistie chez saint Ephrem," *ParOr* 4 (1973) 93-121.

Griffith, Sidney H, "A Spiritual Father for the Whole Church: St Ephrem the Syrian," *Sobornost* 20/2 (1998) 21-40.

—, "Images of Ephraem: the Syrian Holy Man and his Church," *Traditio* 45 (1989-90) 7-33.

Grigorieff, Dimitry, "The Historical Background of Orthodoxy in America" *SVSQ* 5/1-2 (1961) 3-54.

Grisbrooke, W. Jardine, "Liturgical Theology and Liturgical Reform: Some Questions," *SVTQ* 13 (1969) 212-217.

—, "An Orthodox Approach to Liturgical Theology: The Work of Alexander Schmemann," *SL* 23 (1993) 140-157.

Groot, Jan, "The Church as Sacrament of the World," *Concilium* 4/1 (1968) 27-34.

Guillaumont, A., "Genèse 1, 1-2 selon les commentateurs syriaques," *In principio: Interprétations des premiers versets de la Genèse*, Études augustiniennes, série antiquité, 51 (Paris: Études augustiniennes, 1973) 115-132.

Gunton, Colin E., "Relation and Relativity: The Trinity and the Created World," *Trinitarian Theology Today: Essays on Divine Being and Act*, ed. Christoph Schwöbel (Edinburgh: T & T Clark, 1995) 92-112.

Guttierez, Gustavo, "Statement by Gustavo Guttierez," *Theology in the Americas*, ed. Sergio Torres & John Eagleson (Maryknoll, NY: Orbis, 1976) 309-313.

Hausherr, I., "La philosophie du nom chez Ephrem," in idem, *Noms du Christ et voies d'oraison*, OCA, 157 (Rome: Pontificium Institutum Orientalium Studiorum, 1960) 64-72.

Hoffmann, K., "Altiranisch," *Iranistik Linguistik*, Handbuch der Orientalistik, I. Abt., IV. Bd., I. Absch. (Leiden: Brill, 1958).

Hopko, Thomas, "Two 'Nos' and One 'Yes'," *SVTQ* 28 (1984) 45-48.

Houssiau, Albert, "The Rediscovery of the Liturgy by Sacramental Theology (1950-1980)," *SL* 15 (1982-83) 158-177.

—, "La liturgie, lieu privilégié de la théologie sacramentaire," *QL* 54 (1973) 7-12.

Hussey, M. Edmund, "Nicholas Afanassiev's Eucharistic Ecclesiology: A Roman Catholic Viewpoint," *JES* 12 (1975) 235-252.

Ibrahim, Mar Gregorios Yohanna, "Introduction to the Sacraments: An Oriental Orthodox Perspective," *Syriac Dialogue: Fourth Non-Official Consultation on Dialogue within the Syriac Tradition*, ed. Johann Marte & Gerhard Wilflinger (Vienna: Pro Oriente, 2001) 107-117.

Irwin, Kevin W., "Recent Sacramental Theology: A Review Discussion," *The Thomist* 47 (1983) 592-608.

—, "Liturgical Theology," *The New Dictionary of Sacramental Worship*, ed. Peter E. Fink (Collegeville, MN: Liturgical Press, 1990) 721-733.

—, "Sacramentality and the Theology of Creation: A Recovered Paradigm for Sacramental Theology," *LS* 23 (1998) 159-179.

—, "The Sacramentality of Creation and the Role of Creation in Liturgy and Sacraments," *Preserving the Creation: Environmental Theology and Ethics*, ed. Kevin W. Irwin & Edmund D. Pellegrino (Washington, DC: Georgetown University Press, 1994) 67-111.

—, "Liturgical Actio: Sacramentality, Eschatology and Ecology," *Contemporary Sacramental Contours of a God Incarnate*, ed. Lieven Boeve & Lambert Leijssen (Leuven: Peeters, 2001) 111-123.

Jansma, T., "Narsai and Ephraem," *ParOr* I (1970) 49-68.

—, "Ephraems Beschreibung des ersten Tages der Schöpfung," *OCP* 37 (1971) 300-305.

—, "Ephraem on Exodus II,5: Reflections on the Interplay of Human Freewill and Divine Providence," *OCP* 34 (1973) 5-28.

John, Donald St, "The Symbolic Spirituality of St Francis," *FrS* 39 (1979) 192-205.

Joncas, Jan Michael, "Joyce Ann Zimmermann's 'Text Hermeneutics' Approach to Liturgical Studies: A Review and Some Methodological Reflections," *QL* 74 (1993) 208-220.

Kadavil, Mathai, "A Journey form East to West: Alexander Schmemann's Contribution to Orthodoxy in the West," *Exchange* 28 (1999) 224-246.

—, "Sacramental-Liturgical Theology: A Critical Appraisal of Alexander Schmemann's Sacramentology of 'Eschatological Symbolism'," *QL* 82 (2001) 112-127.

—, "De Sacramentologie van Alexander Schmemann: Een kritische beschouwing," *Het Christelijk Oosten* 52 (2000) 5-27.

Karukaparampil, George, "Experience of Pneumatological Eschatology in Ephrem," *The Harp* 8/9 (1995) 161-165, 161.

Karukaparampil, Joy, "The Spiritual World View of St Ephrem compared to Vēdānta," *OCA* 256 (1998) 243-248.

Kelleher, Margaret Mary, "Liturgy as a Source for Sacramental Theology," *QL* 72 (1991) 25-42.

Kennedy, Eugene C., "The Contribution of Religious Ritual to Psychological Balance," *Concilium* 7/2 (1971) 53-58.

Khalifé-Hachem, Elie, "Maronite Sacramental Theology," *Syriac Dialogue: Fourth Non-Official Consultation on Dialogue within the Syriac Tradition*, ed. Johann Marte & Gerhard Wilflinger (Vienna: Pro Oriente, 2001) 53-61.

Khodr, Georges, "Christianity in a Pluralistic World - the Economy of the Holy Spirit," *The Ecumenical Movement: An Anthology of Key Texts and Voices* (Geneva: World Council of Churches, 1997) 401-406.

Kilmartin, Edward, "A Modern Approach to the Word of God and Sacraments of Christ: Perspectives and Principles," *The Sacraments: God's Love and Mercy Actualized*, ed. Francis A. Eigo (Philadelphia, PA: Villanova University Press, 1979) 59-110.

Konat, Johns Abraham, "The Sacrament of Initiation (Baptism) in the West Syrian Tradition," *Syriac Dialogue: Fourth Non-Official Consultation on Dialogue within the Syriac Tradition*, ed. Johann Marte & Gerhard Wilflinger (Vienna: Pro Oriente, 2001) 78-89.

Koonammackal, Thomas, "Changing Views on Ephrem," *Christian Orient* 14 (1993) 113-130.

—, "Ephrem's Imagery of Chasm," *OCA* 256 (1998) 175-183.

Kruse, H., "Die 'mythologischen Irrtümer' Bar-Daisāns," *OrChr* 71 (1987) 24-52.

LaCugna, Catherine Mowry, "Problems with a Trinitarian Reformulation," *LS* 10 (1985) 324-340.

—, "Re-conceiving the Trinity as the Mystery of Salvation," *Scot. Jour.* 38 (1985) 1-23.

Ladrière, Jean, "The Language of Worship: The Performative of Liturgical Language," *Concilium* 9/2 (1973) 50-62.

Lamberts, Jozef, "Active Participation as the Gateway towards an Ecclesial Liturgy," *Omnes Circumadstantes*, ed. C. Caspers & M. Schneiders (Kampen: Kok, 1990) 234-261.

—, "Contemporary Feeling and Liturgy," trans. John Bowden, *Concilium* (1995), n. 3 130-136.

Lane, Thomas, "The Sacramentals Revisited," *The Furrow* 33 (1982) 272-281.

Leijssen, Lambert, "Introduction: Liturgy and Language," *Liturgy and Language: A Tribute to Silveer De Smet*, ed. Lambert Leijssen, Te xtes et études liturgiques / Studies in Liturgy, 12 (Leuven: Abdij Keizersberg/Faculteit der Godgeleerdheid, 1992) 5-14.

—, "Rahner's Contribution to the Renewal of Sacramentology," *Philosophy and Theology* 9 (1995) 201-222.

—, "The Sacramental Economy of Salvation in the Catechism of the Church," *QL* 77 (1996) 229-239.

Leloir, Louis, "Symbolisme et parallélisme chez Saint Ephrem," *À la rencontre de Dieu: mémorial Albert Gelin*, Bibliothèque de la faculté catholique de théologie de Lyon, 8 (Le Puy: Mappus, 1961) 363-374.

Levesque, Paul J., "A Symbolical Sacramental Methodology: An Application of the Thought of Louis Dupré," *QL* 76 (1995) 161-181.

Lies, Lothar, "Trinitätsvergessenheit gegenwärtiger Sakramententheologie?" *ZKT* 105 (1983) 290-314; 415-429.

Limouris, Gennadios, "The Sanctifying Grace of the Holy Spirit," *ER* 42 (1990) 288-297.

Lukács, László, "Communication – Symbols – Sacraments," *Contemporary Sacramental Contours of a God Incarnate*, ed. Lieven Boeve & Lambert Leijssen (Leuven: Peeters, 2001) 137-153.

Lukken, Gerard, "La liturgie comme lieu théologique irremplaçable," *QL* 56 (1975) 97-112.

—, "Plaidoyer pour une approche intégrale de la liturgie comme lieu théologique: un défi à toute la théologie," *QL* 68 (1987) 242-255.

—, "Semiotics and the Study of Liturgy," *SL* 17 (1987) 108-117.

—, "Die Architektonischen Dimensionen des Rituals," *LJ* 39 (1989) 19-36.

—, "Liturgy and Language: An Approach from Semiotics," *Liturgy and Language: A Tribute to Silveer De Smet*, ed. Lambert Leijssen, Textes et études liturgiques / Studies in Liturgy, 12 (Leuven: Abdij Keizersberg/Faculteit der Godgeleerdheid, 1992) 36-52.

—, "Semiotics of the Ritual: Signification in Rituals as a Specific Mediation of Meaning," & "Zur theologischen Rezeption der Semiotik von Greimas: Widerstände und Mißverständnisse," *Per visibilia ad invisibilia: Anthropological, Theological, and Semiotic Studies on the Liturgy and Sacraments*, Liturgia Condenda, 2, ed. Louis van Tongeren & Charles Caspers (Kampen: Kok Pharos, 1994) 269-298.

—, "Church and Liturgy as Dynamic Sacrament of the Spirit," *Per visibilia ad invisibilia: Anthropological, Theological, and Semiotic Studies on the Liturgy and Sacraments*, Liturgia Condenda, 2, ed. Louis van Tongeren & Charles Caspers (Kampen: Kok Pharos, 1994) 140-157.

MacQuarrie, J., "Creation and Environment," *ET* 83 (1971-72) 4-9.

Mahon, L. M. Mc, "Towards a Theology of the Liturgy: Dom Odo Casel and the 'Mysterientheorie'," *SL* 3 (1964) 129-154.

Maniyattu, Pauly, "Celebration of the Cosmos in the East Syrian Liturgy," *Christian Orient* 22 (2001) 76-90.

Marsh, H.G., "The Use of *mysterion* in the Writings of Clement of Alexandria with Special Reference to his Sacramental Doctrine," *JTS* 37 (1936) 64-80.

Mathews, Edward G., Jr., "The Vita Tradition of Ephraem the Syrian, the Deacon of Edessa," *Diakonia* 22 (1988-89) 15-42.

—, "St. Ephrem, Madrase on Faith, 81-85 Hymns on the Pearl, I-V," *SVTQ* 38 (1994) 45-72.

McDonnell, Killian, "Ways of Validating Ministry," *JES* 7 (1970) 208-265.

Mertens, Herman-Emiel, "Nature and Grace in Twentieth-Century Catholic Theology," *LS* 16 (1991) 224-262.

Meyendorff, John, "Creation in the History of Orthodox Theology," *SVTQ* 27 (1983) 27-37.

—, "A Life Worth Living," *SVTQ* 28 (1984) 3-10.

Meyendorff, Paul, "Liturgy and Spirituality. I. Eastern Liturgical Theology," *Christian Spirituality*, ed. Bernard McGinn & John Meyendorff, World Spirituality, 16 (New York: Crossroad Publishing Company, 1985) 350-363.

—, "The Liturgical Path of Orthodoxy in America," *SVTQ* 40 (1996) 43-64.

Miller, Vincent J., "An Abyss at the Heart of Mediation: Louis-Marie Chauvet's Fundamental Theology of Sacramentality," *Horizons* 24 (1997) 230-247.

Mitchell, Leonel L., "Four Fathers on Baptism," *Studies on Syrian Baptismal Rites*, ed. Jacob Vellian, The Syrian Churches Series, 6 (Kottayam: CMS Press, 1973) 37-56.

Mollat, Michael, "The Poverty of Francis: A Christian and Social Option," *Concilium* 149 (1981) 23-29.

Murray, Robert, "A Hymn of St Ephrem to Christ on the Incarnation, the Holy Spirit, and the Sacraments," *ECR* 3 (1970) 142-150.

—, "The Lance which Re-Opened Paradise: A Mysterious Reading in the Early Syriac Fathers," *OCP* 39 (1973) 224-234.

—, "Symbolism in St. Ephrem's Theology (I)," *ParOr* 6-7 (1975-76) 1-20.

—, "Der Dichter als Exeget: der hl. Ephräm und die heutige Exegese," *ZKT* 100 (1978) 484-494.

—, "St Ephrem' Dialogue of Reason and Love," *Sobornost* 2/2 (1980) 26-40.

—, "The Ephremic Tradition and the Theology of the Environment" http://www.acad.cua.edu/syrcom/Hugoye/Vol12No1/HV2NMurray.html (1999).

—, "The Bible on God's World and Our Place In It," *The Month*, August/September (1988) 798-803.

—, "The Image of God: Delegated and Responsible Authority," *Priests & People* 14/2 (2000) 49-54.

Naduvilezham, Joseph, "Paschal Lamb in Ephrem of Nisibis," *The Harp* 5/1-3 (1992) 53-66.

Nassif, Bradley, "Theoria," *Encyclopaedia of Early Christianity*, ed. Everett Ferguson (New York/London: Garland Publishing, INC, 1997) 1122-1123.

Neunheuser, Burkhard, "Masters in Israel: V. Odo Casel," *The Clergy Review* 55 (1970) 194-212.

—, "Mystery Theology," *Sacramentum Mundi*, ed. Karl Rahner, Gen. Ed. Adolf Darlap (New York: Herder and Herder, 1970) 385-387.

—, "Odo Casel in Retrospect and Prospect," *Worship* 50 (1976) 489-504.

—, "The Mystery Presence: Dom Odo Casel and the Latest Research," *The Downside Review* 76 (1958) 266-273.

Nichols, Robert L., "Translator's Note," *The Ways of Russian Theology* (Part I), gen. ed. Richard S. Haugh (Belmont, MA: Nordland Publishing Co., 1979) xi-xv.

Noujaim, G., "Anthropologie et économie de salut chez S. Ephrem: autour des notions de ghalyatâ, kasyatâ et kasyâ," *ParOr* 9 (1979-80) 313-315.

O'Connell, Matthew, "New Perspectives in Sacramental Theology," *Worship* (1965) 196-206.

O'Donnell, John, "The Trinity as Divine Community: A Critical Reflection upon Recent Theological Developments," *Gregorianum* 69 (1988) 5-34.

Osborne, Kenan, "Jesus as Human Expression of the Divine Presence: Toward a New Incarnation of the Sacraments." *The Sacraments: God's Love and Mercy Actualized*, ed. Francis A. Eigo (Philadelphia, PA: Villanova University Press, 1979) 29-58.

—, "Methodology and Christian Sacraments," *The Sacraments: Readings in Contemporary Sacramental Theology*, ed. Michael Taylor (New York: Alba House, 1981) 39-52.

Otto, Michel, "οἰκονομία," *Theological Dictionary of the New Testament*, vol. V, trans. Geoffrey W. Bromiley, ed. Gerhard Friedrich (Grand Rapids, MI: Eerdmans, 1968) 119-159.

Padinjarekuttu, Isaac, "Sacrament in Catholic History," *The World as Sacrament: Interdisciplinary Bridge-building of the Sacred and the Secular*, ed. Francis X. D'Sa, Isaac Padinjarekuttu & Jacob Parappally (Pune: Jnana-Deepa Vidyapeeth, 1998) 17-37.

Papaioannou, George, "Efforts toward Orthodox Unity in America: A Historical Appraisal," *Orthodox Theology and Diakonia*, ed. Demetrios J. Constantelos (Brookline, MA: Hellenic College Press, 1981) 273-304.

Perl, Eric Justin David, "Symbol, Sacrament, and Hierarchy in Saint Dionysios the Areopagite," *GOTR* 39 (1994) 311-356

Philip, Metropolitan, "I have fought the good fight," *SVTQ* 28/1 (1984) 37-39.

Plekon, Michael, "The Church, the Eucharist and the Kingdom: Towards an Assessment of Alexander Schmemann's Theological Legacy," *SVTQ* 40 (1996) 119-143.

Post, Paul, "De synthese in de huidige liturgiewetenschap: Proeve van positionering van *De weg van de liturgie*," *Jaarboek voor liturgie-onderzoek* 14 (1998) 141-172.

Power, David N., "Theological Trends: Symbolism in Worship: A Survey, I, II, III, IV," *The Way* 13 (1973) 310-313; 14 (1974) 57-66; 15 (1975) 56-64; 137-46.

—, "Cult to Culture: The Liturgical Foundation of Theology," *Worship* 54 (1980) 482-495.

—, "People at Liturgy," *Worship: Culture and Theology* (Washington, DC: Pastoral Press, 1990) 273-283.

—, "Sacrament: An Economy of Gift," *LS* 23 (1998) 143-158.

—, et al., "Sacramental Theology: A Review of Literature," *TS* 55 (1994) 657-705.

Puthanangady, Paul, "Inculturation of the Liturgy in India Since Vatican II," *Concilium* 162 (1983) 71-77.

Rahner, Karl, "Sakramente, alttestamentliche," *LTK* 9 (1964) 239-240.

—, "Sakramententheologie," *LTK* 9 (1964) 240-243.

—, "Der dreifaltige Gott als transzendenter Urgrund der Heilsgeschichte" *Mysterium Salutis: Grundriss heilsgeschichtlicher Dogmatik*, vol. 2, ed. Johannes Feiner & Magnus Löhrer (Einsiedeln: Benziger, 1967) 317-397.

—, "Membership of the Church according to the Teaching of Pius XII's Encyclical 'Mystici Corporis Christi'," *TI* 2 (Baltimore, MD: Helicon, 1969) 253-269.

—, "Remarks on the Dogmatic Treatise 'de Trinitate'," *TI* 4 trans. Kevin Smyth (London: Darton, Longman & Todd, 1974) 77-102.

—, "The Mystery of the Trinity," *TI* 16, trans. David Morland (London: Darton, Longman & Todd, 1979) 255-259.

Reumann, John, "The 'Righteousness of God' and the 'Economy of God': Two Great Doctrinal Themes Historically Compared," *Aksum Thyateria: A Festschrift for Archbishop Methodios of Thyateira and Great Britain*, ed. George Dion. Dragas (London: Thyateira House, 1985) 615-637.

Robinson, H. Wheeler, "The Council of Yahweh," *JTS* 45 (1944) 151-157.

Roll, Susan, "Language and Justice in the Liturgy," *Liturgy and Language: A Tribute to Silveer De Smet*, ed. Lambert Leijssen, Textes et études liturgiques / Studies in Liturgy, 12 (Leuven: Abdij Keizersberg/Faculteit der Godgeleerdheid, 1992) 66-81.

Russell, Paul S., "Ephraem the Syrian on the Utility of Language and the Place of Silence," *Journal of Early Christian Studies* 8/1 (2000) 21-37.

Ryk, Marta, "The Holy Spirit's Role in the Deification of Man according to Contemporary Orthodox Theology," *Diakonia* 10 (1975) 24-39.

—, "The Holy Spirit's Role in the Deification of Man according to Contemporary Orthodox Theology II," *Diakonia* 10 (1975) 109-131.

Sabourin, L., "The Parable of Kingdom," *Biblical Theological Bulletin* 4 (1976) 126.

Sandanam, John Peter, "Do This in Remembrance of Me: A Social Dimension of the Eucharist with Special Reference to the Indian Christian Communities," *QL* 82 (2001) 225-246.

Sanon, Anselme, "Cultural Rooting of the Liturgy in Africa Since Vatican II," *Concilium* 162 (1983) 61-70.

Schilson, Arno, "Erneuerung der Sakramententheologie im 20. Jahrhundert," *LJ* 37 (1987) 18-41.

Schmemann, Alexander, "Trying the Spirits," *SVSQ* 1/1 (1957) 3-4.

—, "St. Mark of Ephesus and the Theological Conflicts in Byzantium," *SVSQ* 1/1 (1957) 11-24.

—, "The Unity of Orthodoxy," *SVSQ* 1 (1957) 2-3.

—, "Liturgical Theology: Its Task and Method," *SVSQ* 1 (1957) 16-27.

—, "The Western Rite," *SVSQ* 2 (1958) 37-38.

—, "The Orthodox Church, the World Council and Rome," *SVSQ* 3 (1958) 40.

—, "Fast and Liturgy: Notes in Liturgical Theology," *SVSQ* 3 (1959) 2-9.

—, "Rome, the Ecumenical Council and the Orthodox Church (I) Possibilities and Impossibilities," *SVSQ* 3/2 (1959) 2-5.

—, "Rome, the Ecumenical Council and the Orthodox Church (II) Possibilities and Impossibilities," *SVSQ* 3/3 (1959) 45-46

—, "The Church is Hierarchical," *SVSQ* 3/4 (1959) 36-41.

—, "The Idea of Primacy in Orthodox Ecclesiology," *SVSQ* 4/2-3 (1960) 49-75.

—, "Episcopatus Unus Est: On the Standing Conference of Canonical Orthodox Bishops in the Americas," *SVSQ* 4/4 (1960) 26-29.

—, "The Liturgical Revival and the Orthodox Church," *Liturgy and Tradition: Theological Reflections of Alexander Schmemann*, ed. Thomas Fisch (Crestwood, NY: St. Vladimir's Seminary Press, 1990) 101-114. Originally published in *The Eucharist and Liturgical Renewal*, ed. Massey Hamilton Shepherd (New York: Oxford University Press, 1960).

—, "Theology and Eucharist," *SVSQ* 5 (1961) 10-23.

—, "The Missionary Imperative," *Church, World, Mission*, ed. Alexander Schmemann (Crestwood, NY: St. Vladimir's Seminary Press, 1979) 209-216. Originally published in *The Theology of Christian Mission*, ed. Gerald H. Anderson (New York: McGraw Hill, 1961) 250-257.

—, "Towards a Theology of Councils," *SVSQ* 6 (1962) 170-184.

—, "Theology and Liturgical Tradition," *Liturgy and Tradition: Theological Reflections of Alexander Schmemann,* ed. Thomas Fisch (Crestwood, NY: St. Vladimir's Seminary Press, 1990) 11-20. Originally published in *Worship in Scripture and Tradition*, ed. Massey Hamilton Shepherd Jr. (New York: Oxford University Press, 1963) 165-178.

—, "Problems of Orthodoxy in America: The Canonical Problem," *SVSQ* 8/4 (1964) 67-85.

—, "Problems of Orthodoxy in America: The Liturgical Problem," *SVSQ* 8/4 (1964) 164-185.

—, "Problems of Orthodoxy in America: The Spiritual Problem," *SVSQ* 9 (1965) 171-193.

—, "The World as Sacrament," *Church, World, Mission*, ed. Alexander Schmemann (Crestwood, NY: St. Vladimir's Seminary Press, 1979) 217-227. Originally published in *The Cosmic Piety: Modern Man and the Meaning of the Universe*, ed. Christopher Derrick (New York: P. J. Kennedy and Sons, 1965) 119-130.

—, "Roll of Honour," *SVSQ* 10/1-2 (1966) 7-8.

—, "The Task of Orthodox Theology in America Today," *SVSQ* 10/4 (1966) 180-188.

—, "Ecclesiological Notes," *SVSQ* 11 (1967) 35-39.

—, "A Brief Response," *SVSQ* 12 (1968) 173-174.

—, "Thoughts for the Jubilee," *SVTQ* 13/1-2 (1969) 95-102.

—, "Debate on Liturgy: Liturgical Theology, Theology of Liturgy, and Liturgical Reform," *SVTQ* 13 (1969) 217-224.

—, "Sacrament and Symbol," *For the Life of the World* (Crestwood, NY: St. Vladimir's Seminary Press, [2]1973) 135-151. Originally published in *Evangelium und Sacrament* (Strasburg: Oecumenica, 1970) 94-107.

—, "The 'Orthodox World', Past and Present," *Church, World, Mission* (Crestwood, NY: St. Vladimir's Seminary Press, 1979) 25-66. Originally published in *Christian Action and Openness to the World*, ed. Joseph Papin (Philadelphia, PA: Villanova University Press, Vol. 2 & 3, 1970) 65-96.

—, "Father Alexander Schmemann Replies to the "Sorrowful Epistle,"" *Diakonia* 5 (1970) 89-94.

—, "Theology or Ideology?," *Technology and Social Justice*, ed. Ronald H. Preston (London: SCM, 1971) 226-236.

—, "Liturgy and Theology," *Liturgy and Tradition: Theological Reflections of Alexander Schmemann*, ed. Thomas Fisch (Crestwood, NY: St. Vladimir's Seminary Press, 1990) 49-68. Originally published in *GOTR* 17 (1972) 86-100.

—, "Worship in a Secular Age," *SVTQ* 16 (1972) 3-16.

—, "Russian Theology: 1920-1972. An Introductory Survey," *SVTQ* 16 (1972) 172-194.

—, "The East and the West May Yet Meet," *Against the World for the World: The Hartford Appeal and the Future of American Religion*, ed. Peter L. Berger & Richard John (New York: Neuhaus Seabury Press, 1976) 229-231.

—, "The Problem of the Church's Presence in the World in Orthodox Consciousness," *SVTQ* 21 (1977) 3-17.

—, "Sacrifice and Worship," *Liturgy and Tradition: Theological Reflections of Alexander Schmemann*, ed. Thomas Fisch (Crestwood, NY: St. Vladimir's Seminary Press, 1990) 129-135. Originally published in *Parabola* 3 (1978) 60-65.

—, "The Underlying Question," *Church, World, Mission: Reflections on Orthodoxy in the West*, ed. Alexander Schmemann (Crestwood, NY: St. Vladimir's Seminary Press, 1979) 7-24.

—, "Some Reflections Upon 'A Case Study'," *SVTQ* 24 (1980) 266-269.

—, "Symbols and Symbolism in the Byzantine Liturgy: Liturgical Symbols and their Theological Interpretation," *Liturgy and Tradition: Theological Reflections of Alexander Schmemann,* ed. Thomas Fisch (Crestwood, NY: St. Vladimir's Seminary Press, 1990) 115-128. Originally published in *Orthodox Theology and Diakonia. Festschrift Iakovos,* ed. D. Constantelos (Brookline, MA: Hellenic College Press, 1981) 91-102.

—, "Liturgical Theology: Remarks on Method," *Liturgy and Tradition: Theological Reflections of Alexander Schmemann,* ed. Thomas Fisch (Crestwood, NY: St. Vladimir's Seminary Press, 1990) 137-144. Originally published in *La liturgie: son sens, son esprit, sa méthode.* Conférences Saint-Serge, XXVIII Semaine d'Études Liturgiques, Paris, June 30 through July 3, 1981, Bibliotheca Ephemerides Liturgica. Subsidia, 27 (Roma : Edizioni liturgiche, 1982) 297-303.

—, "Liturgy and Eschatology," *Sobornost* 7/1 (1985) 6-14.

—, "Orthodoxy," *The Study of Spirituality,* ed. Cheslyn Jones, Geoffrey Wainwright & Edward Yarnold (London: SPCK, 1986) 519-524.

—, "Review of *The Service of the Laity in the Church* (in Russian) by Nicholas Afanassief," *SVSQ* 1/1 (1957) 41-44.

—, "Review of Eastern Christiandom – A Study of the Origin and Development of the Eastern Orthodox Church, by Nicholas Zernov," *SVSQ* 7/2 (1963) 96-97.

Schmidt, Herman, "Lex orandi, lex credendi in recentioribus documentis pontificiis," *Periodica* 40 (1951) 5-28.

Schmied, A., "Perspektiven und Akzente heutiger Sakramententheologie," *Wissenschaft und Weisheit* 44 (1981) 20-22.

Schwöbel, Christoph, "Christology and Trinitarian Thought," *Trinitarian Theology Today: Essays on Divine Being and Act*, ed. Christoph Schwöbel (Edinburgh: T & T Clark, 1995) 113-146.

—, "Introduction: The Renaissance of Trinitarian Theology: Reasons, Problems and Tasks," *Trinitarian Theology Today: Essays on Divine Being and Act*, ed. Christoph Schwöbel (Edinburgh: T & T Clark, 1995) 1-30.

Scorer, Peter, "Alexander Schmemann (1921-83)," *Sobornost* 6/2 (1984) 64-68.

Sed, N., "Les hymnes sur le Paradis de Saint Ephrem et les traditions juives," *LM* 81 (1968) 455-501.

Semmelroth, Otto, "Natursakramente," *LTK* 7 (1962) 829-830.

Senior, Donald, "God's Creative Word at Work in our Midst," *The Sacraments: God's Love and Mercy Actualized* (Philadelphia, PA: Villanova University Press, 1979) 1-28.

Shaw, Lewis, "John Meyendorff and the Heritage of the Russian Theological Tradition," *New Perspectives on Historical Theology*, ed. Bradley Nassif (Grand Rapids, MI: Eerdmans, 1996) 10-42.

Sherrard, Philip, "The Sacrament," *The Orthodox Ethos: Essays in Honour of the Centenary of the Greek Orthodox Archdiocese of North and South America*, ed. A. J. Philippou (Oxford: Holy Well Press, 1964) 133-139.

Skublics, Ernest, "Communion Ecclesiology and the World: The Church as *Sacramentum Mundi*," *One in Christ* 34 (1998) 125-135.

Slesinski, Robert, "The Theological Legacy of Alexander Schmemann," *Diakonia* 29 (1984-1985) 87-95.

Sœba, M., "dOs *sôd* secret," *Theological Lexicon of the Old Testament*, ed. Ernst Jenni & Claus Westermann, trans. Mark E. Biddle, Vol. 2 (Peabody, MA: Hendrickson, 1997) 793-795.

Sony, B., "Hymne sur la création de l'homme de l'hexaméron de Jacques de Saroug," *ParOr* 11 (1983) 167-99.

Soro, Mar Bawai, "Understanding Church of the East Sacramental Theology: The Theodorian Perspective," *Syriac Dialogue: Fourth Non-Official Consultation on Dialogue within the Syriac Tradition*, ed. Johann Marte & Gerhard Wilflinger (Vienna: Pro Oriente, 2001) 22-43.

Staniloae, Dumitru, "The Economy of Salvation and Ecclesiastical 'Economy'," *Diakonia* 5 (1970) 218-231.

Stuhlman, Byron, "The Theme of Creation in the Liturgical Theology of Alexander Schmemann," *Creation and Liturgy: Studies in Honor of H. Boone Porter*, ed. Ralph McMichael, Jr., *La Maison Dieu* (1995) 113-127.

Telgedi, S., "Essai sur la phonétique des emprunts Iraniens en Araméen talmudique," *Journal Asiatique* 226 (1935) 177-265.

Thomson, Francis J., "Economy: An Examination of the Various Theories of Economy Held within the Orthodox Church, with Special Reference to the Economical Recognition of the Validity of Non-Orthodoxy Sacraments," *JTS* 16 (1965) 368-420.

Valenziano, Crispino, "Liturgy and Symbolism," *Handbook for Liturgical Studies* Volume II, *Fundamental Liturgy*, ed. Anscar J. Chupungco (Collegeville, MN: Liturgical Press, 1998) 29-44.

—, "Liturgy and Anthropology: The Meaning of the Question and the Method for Answering It," *Handbook for Liturgical Studies.* Vol. II: *Fundamental Liturgy*, ed. Anscar J. Chupungco (Collegeville, MN: Liturgical Press, 1998) 189-226.

Varghese, Baby, "Some Aspects of West Syrian Liturgical Theology," *SL* 31 (2001) 171-178.

Vassiliadis, Petros, "Eucharistic and Therapeutic Spirituality," *GOTR* 42 (1997) 1-23.

Verghese, Paul, "Relation between Baptism, 'Confirmation' and the Eucharist in the Syrian Orthodox Church," *SL* 4 (1965) 81-93.

Vergote, Anton, "Regard du Psychologue sur le Symbolisme Liturgique," *La Maison Dieu* 91 (1967) 129-151.

—, "The Vertical and Horizontal Dimensions in Symbolic Language about God," *Lumen Vitae* 25 (1970) 185-208.

—, "Symbolic Gestures and Actions in the Liturgy," *Concilium* 7/2 (1971) 40-52.

Waal, Victor de, "Review of *The World as Sacrament*, by Alexander Schmemann," *Sobornost* 5/5 (1967) 374-375.

Walsh, Liam G., "Liturgy in the Theology of St. Thomas," *The Thomist* 38 (1974) 557-583.

White, Lynn, Jr., "The Historical Roots of Our Ecological Crisis," (originally published in *Science*, 1967) *Western Man and Environmental Ethics* (Reading, MA: Addison-Wesley, 1973) 18-30.

Williams, Rowan, "Eastern Orthodox Theology," *The Modern Theologians: An Introduction to Christian Theology in the Twentieth Century*, ed. David F. Ford (Oxford: Basil Blackwell, 1995) 152-170.

Wolterstorff, Nicholas, "Liturgy, Justice, and Tears," *Worship* 62 (1988) 386-403.

Yousif, Peter, "St Ephrem on Symbols in Nature: Faith, the Trinity and the Cross (Hymns on Faith, No. 18)," *ECR* 10 (1978) 52-60.

Yousif, Pierre, "Le symbolisme de la croix dans la nature chez saint Ephrem de Nisibe," *OCA* 205 (1978) 207-227.

—, "Exegetical Principles of St Ephraem of Nisibis," *SP* 18 (1990) 296-302.

—, "The Sacrament of Marriage in the Tradition of the Church of the East (Assyrian, Chaldean, Malabar)," in a paper presented at the fifth Syriac Consultation (Vienna: Pro Oriente, February 26 – March 1, 2002) 1-12.

Zirkel, Patricia McCormik, "The Ninth-Century Eucharistic Context for the Beginnings of Eucharistic Doctrine in the West," *Worship* 68 (1994) 2-23.

Zizioulas, John D., "The Early Christian Community," *Christian Spirituality*, ed. Bernard McGinn & John Meyendorff, World Spirituality, 16 (New York: Crossroad, 1985) 23-43.

—, "The Mystery of the Church in Orthodox Tradition," *One in Christ* 24 (1988) 294-303.

Patristics

Works by Ephrem

Beck, Edmund, *Des heiligen Ephraem des Syrers Carmina Nisibena*. CSCO.S 92-93, 102-103 (Louvain: Peeters, 1961-1963).

—, *Des heiligen Ephraem des Syrers Hymnen contra Haereses*. CSCO.S 76-77, 169-170 (Louvain: Peeters, 1957).

—, *Des heiligen Ephraem des Syrers Hymnen Contra Julianum*. CSCO.S 78-79, 174-175 (Louvain: Peeters, 1957).

—, *Des heiligen Ephraem des Syrers Hymnen de Fide*. CSCO.S 73-74, 154-155 (Louvain: Peeters, 1955.)

—, *Des heiligen Ephraem des Syrers Hymnen de Ieiunio*. CSCO.S 106-107, 246-247 (Louvain: Peeters, 1964).

—, *Des heiligen Ephraem des Syrers Hymnen de Paradiso*. CSCO.S 78-79, 174-175 (Louvain: Peeters, 1957).

—, *Des heiligen Ephraem des Syrers Hymnen de Ecclesia*. CSCO.S 84-85, 198-199 (Louvain: Peeters, 1960).

—, *Des heiligen Ephraem des Syrers Hymnen de Epiphania*. CSCO.S 82-83, 186-187 (Louvain: Peeters, 1959).

—, *Des heiligen Ephraem des Syrers Hymnen de Nativitate*. CSCO.S 82-83, 186-187 (Louvain: Peeters, 1959).

—, *Des heiligen Ephraem des Syrers Hymnen de Virginitate*. CSCO.S 94-95, 223-224 (Louvain: Peeters, 1962).

—, *Des heiligen Ephraem des Syrers Paschahymnen (de Azymis, de Crucifixione, de Resurrectione)*. CSCO.S 108-109, 248-249 (Louvain: Peeters, 1960).

—, *Des heiligen Ephraem des Syrers Memre on Hymnen de Fide* CSCO.S 88-89, 212-213 (Louvain: Peeters, 1979).

Leloir, Louis, *Commentary on the Diatessaron*, CSCO 137, 145 (Louvain: Peeters, 1953, 1954). ET McCarthy, *Saint Ephrem's Commentary on Tatian's Diatessaron* (Oxford: Oxford University Press, 1993).

Mitchell, C. W., Beven, A.A. & F. C. Burkitt (ed.), *S. Ephrem's Prose Refutations of Mani, Marcion, and Bardaisan.* Vol. I *The Discourses Addressed to Hypatius* (London: Williams and Norgate, 1912); Vol. II, *The Discourse called "Of Domnus" and Six Other Writings* (London: Williams and Norgate, 1921).

Commentary on Genesis. Ed. with German translation R.M. Tonneau. *In Genesim et in Exodum Commentarii.* CSCO.S 71-72, 152-153 (Louvain: Peeters, 1955). English translation E. G. Mathews & J. P. Amar. *St. Ephrem the Syrian, Selected Prose Works* (Washington, DC: Catholic University of America Press, 1994).

Other Patristic Sources

Augustine, *Epistola*, *PL* 33, 55.1.2, Migne, J. P. (Paris: Migne, 1845) 204-205.

Augustine, *Johannis Evangelium*, *PL* 35, 80,3, Migne, J. P. (Paris: Migne, 1840).

Chrysostom, John, *Epistolam Secundam ad Timotheum Commentarius*, II: 4, *PG* 62, Migne, J. P. (Paris: Migne, 1860) 612.

Chrysostom, John, *Ad Homiliam in Natalem Christi Diem*, *PG* 56, Migne, J. P. (Paris: Migne, Paris, 1859) 385-396.

Concillium in Trullo, canon 82 in *Sacrorum conciliorum nova et amplissima collectio*, ed. Giovanni D. Mansi, vol. 11, 977-980.

Cyprian, *Epistolae* 73, *PL* 4, 413, Migne, J. P. (Paris: Migne, 1844) 412.

Dionysius Areopagite, *De Ecclesiastica Hierarchia*, III, 3/1-2, *PG* 3, 428 AC, Migne, J. P. (Paris: Migne, 1857) 429.

Gregory of Nyssa, *Quod non Sint Tres Dei*, *PG* 45, 126. D, Migne, J. P. (Paris: Migne, 1858) 115-135.

Irenaeus, *Adversus Haereses*, IV 18:5, *PG* 7, Migne, J. P. (Paris: Migne, 1857) 1024-1029.

Isaac of Niniveh, *On Ascetical Life*, trans. Mary Hansbury (Crestwood, NY: St. Vladimir's Seminary Press, 1989).

Isidore, *Etymologiae*, *PL* 82, 255cd, Migne, J. P. (Paris: Migne, 1850) 252-260.

Jacob of Serug, *Homiliae selectae Mar Jacobi Sarugensis*, ed. P. Bedjan (Leipzig, 1907), Hom. "On the Creation of the World, Day 6," in vol. 3, 108, 7-14.

Nicholas Cabasilas, *De Vita in Christo*, Book II, *PG* 150, Migne, J. P. (Paris: Migne, 1865) 548-568.

Symeon of Thessalonika, *De Sacramentis*, 78, *PG* 155, Migne, J. P. (Paris: Migne, 1886).

Theodore of Mopsuestia, *Commentary on the Lord's Prayer and on the Sacraments of Baptism and the Eucharist*, ed. Alphonse Mingana, Woodbrooke Studies, 6 (Cambridge: Heffer, 1933).

Theodoret Cyrensis, *Quaestiones in Genesim*, *PG* 80, Migne, J. P. (Paris: Migne, Paris, 1860) 104-112 .